SCIENCE

RUINING EVERYTHING SINCE 1543

BY ZACH WEINERSMITH

breadpig

BROOKLYN · SOMERVILLE · THE INTERNETS

For information about special discounts for bulk purchases,
please contact Breadpig, Inc. at IncredibleBulk@Breadpig.com

Manufacturing by RR Donnelley.

Printed in the United States of America.

Weinersmith, Zach
SCIENCE: Ruining Everything Since 1543.
ISBN 978-0-9828537-3-3
Breadpig, Inc.
www.breadpig.com

Breadpig is not a traditional publisher. The majority of the profits of this book are
going to the author, Zach Weinersmith. And as with all of Breadpig's projects, the
company's profits are being donated to a worthy charity. For this book, we have
selected Wikipedia.

For support in this publishing venture, Breadpig thanks Marie Mundaca, LeeAnn Suen
and the friends and family who've always unhesitatingly supported team Breadpig.

Even our winged porcine hero couldn't have done it alone. Thank you.

*To Kelly, whose eye-rolling at my scripts has no doubt
been the main necessitator for her ever-thickening spectacles.*

ACKNOWLEDGEMENTS

As always, I would like to thank my team of geeks: Amanda and Dean, Michael, Mark, and Josh. Without them, the many holes I put in the boat would not get plugged.

I would like to thank my publisher Breadpig, except for Alexis, who once offered Sabriya an empty glass of lemonade as if it were a gift.

I would like to thank Christina Xu in particular for her Powers of Internet.

I would like to thank my parents, whose support of my quarter-life lurch into science has truly been the gift that keeps giving.

I would like to thank all the awesome geeks who took time out of their busy schedules to give us their Tales of Science.

And lastly, I would like to thank my wife, Kelly. I feel like I shouldn't have to thank her here, since she's already in the dedication, but... man... she's scary when she's mad.

You hold in your hands the very first science-themed book of SMBC comics. If this book is anything like other books of science, I hope to release a new edition every few months, which will be just different enough from the old edition that your professor will make you buy it. I hope this because I love money. In fact, I believe money is the second most important thing in life. The first thing is real estate.

For your convenience, in this third SMBC book, we've slimmed things down a bit. The result is that some comics extend over multiple pages. In these cases, there is a friendly arrow at the bottom of each page until you reach the end of the comic. We have very cleverly labeled the end with the word "end."

This book is divided into three sections. The first section contains lovingly selected science comics from the SMBC archive, many of which are too dorky to ever appear in an SMBC compilation meant for normal human beings—you know, those people you see when the curtains accidentally get let open.

The second section contains 17 comics that are exclusive to this book. Almost without exception, these are drawn from comic scripts that I thought were good, but which were probably too damn nerdy for those normal humans I mentioned in the last paragraph. But, that shouldn't be a problem for you and I, should it?

The third section contains Tales of Science. These are little stories given to us by some of my favorite scientists and science geeks who were awesome enough to grace this book with their presence.

Also, Phil Plait did one.

Zach Weinersmith

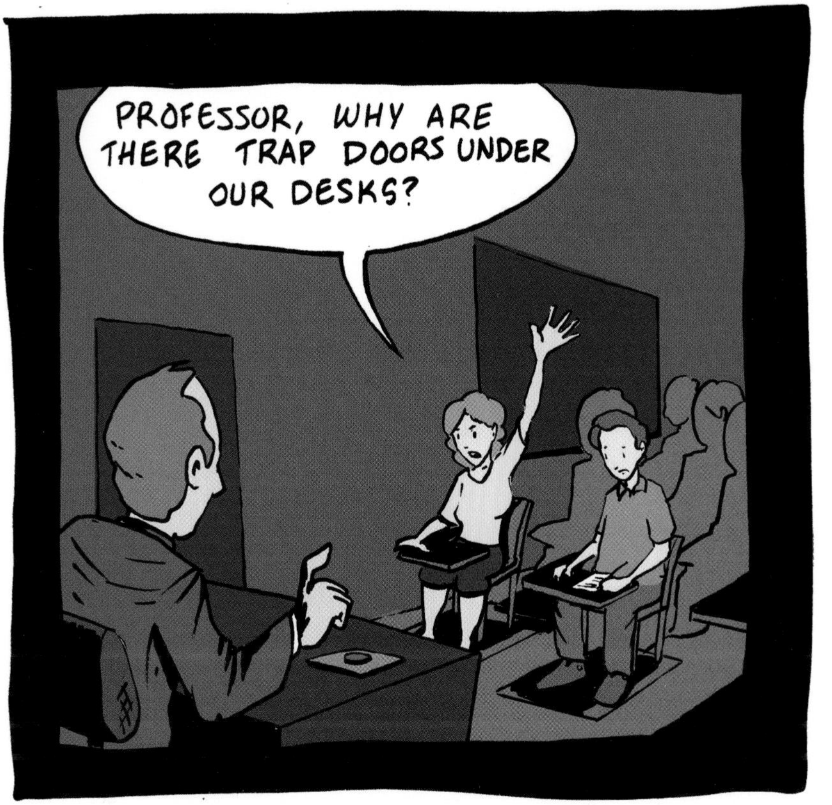
PROFESSOR, WHY ARE THERE TRAP DOORS UNDER OUR DESKS?

Ahh, the first day teaching natural selection is always the best.

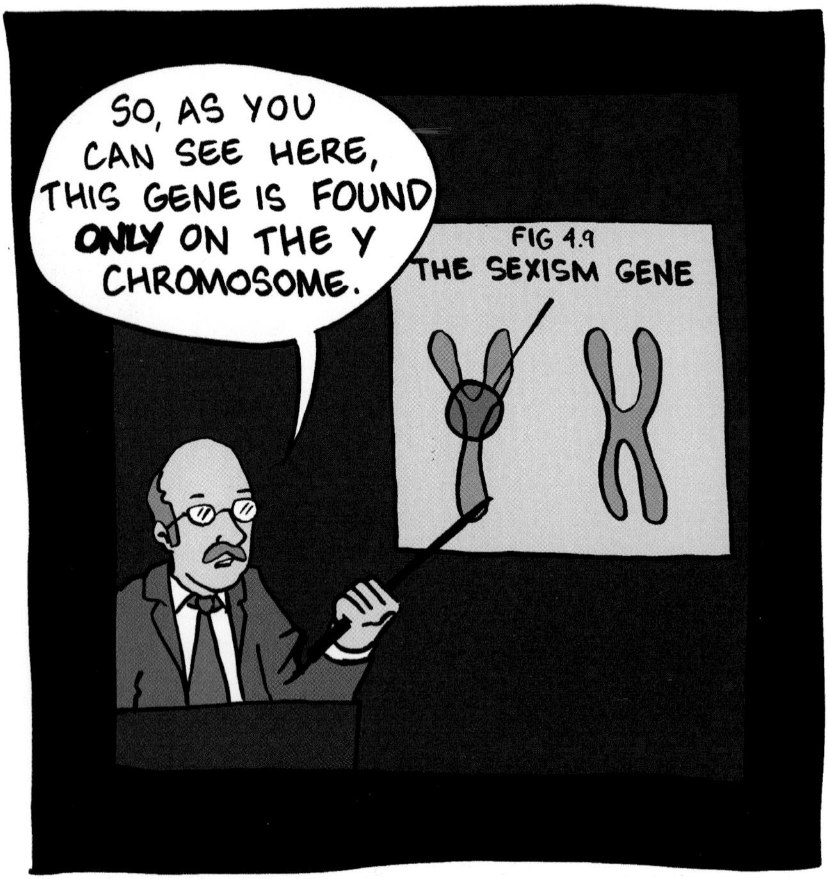
SO, AS YOU CAN SEE HERE, THIS GENE IS FOUND ONLY ON THE Y CHROMOSOME.
FIG 4.9
THE SEXISM GENE

"You know, the chromosome that *matters*."

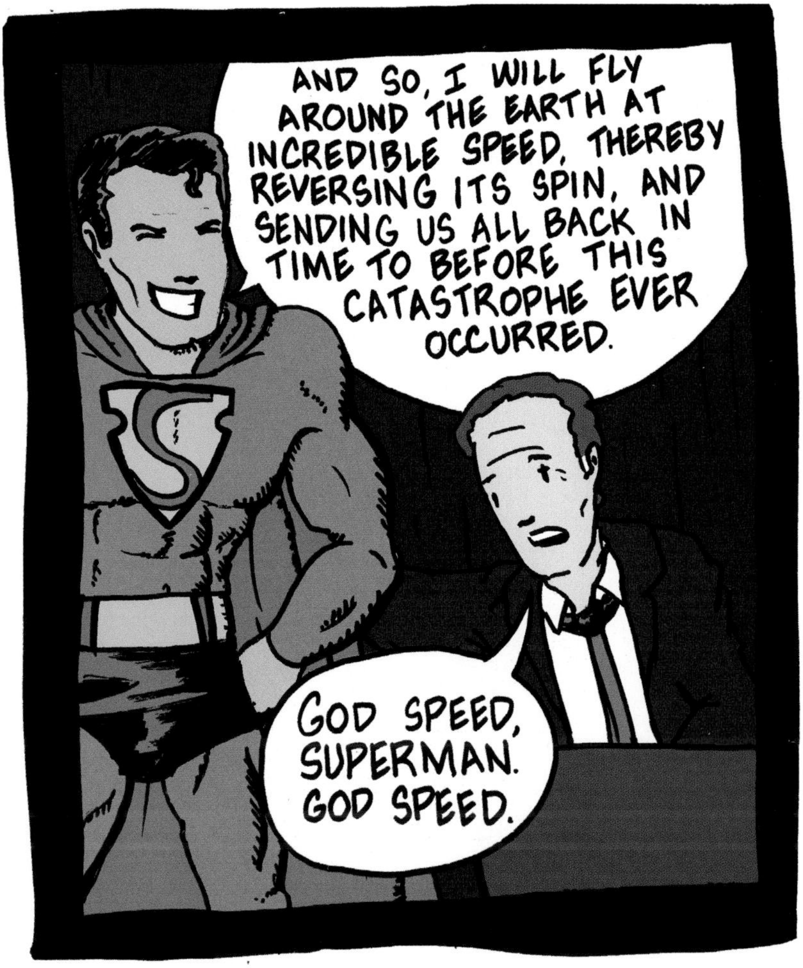
AND SO, I WILL FLY AROUND THE EARTH AT INCREDIBLE SPEED, THEREBY REVERSING ITS SPIN, AND SENDING US ALL BACK IN TIME TO BEFORE THIS CATASTROPHE EVER OCCURRED.
GOD SPEED, SUPERMAN. GOD SPEED.

If you were still alive, you'd probably wish Superman had paid more attention in physics class.

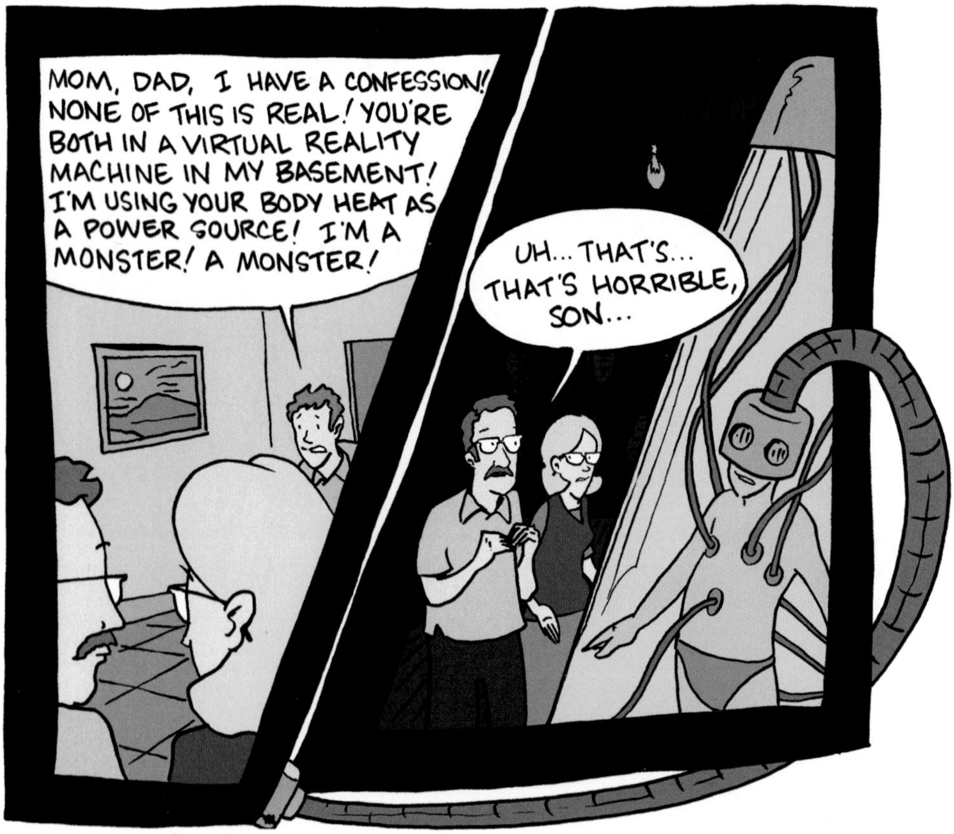
MOM, DAD, I HAVE A CONFESSION! NONE OF THIS IS REAL! YOU'RE BOTH IN A VIRTUAL REALITY MACHINE IN MY BASEMENT! I'M USING YOUR BODY HEAT AS A POWER SOURCE! I'M A MONSTER! A MONSTER!
UH... THAT'S... THAT'S HORRIBLE, SON...

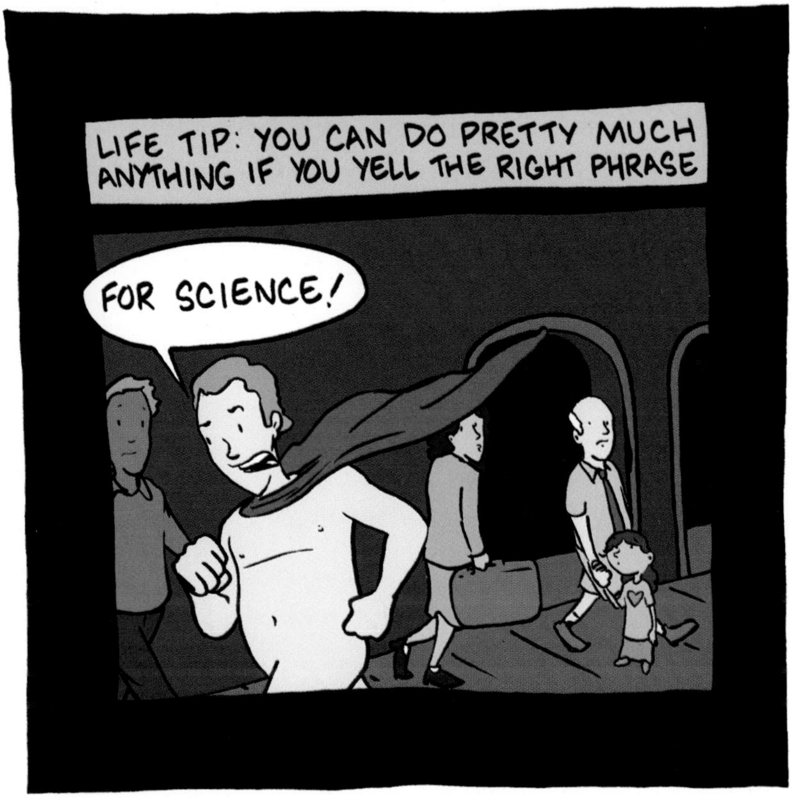
LIFE TIP: YOU CAN DO PRETTY MUCH ANYTHING IF YOU YELL THE RIGHT PHRASE
FOR SCIENCE!

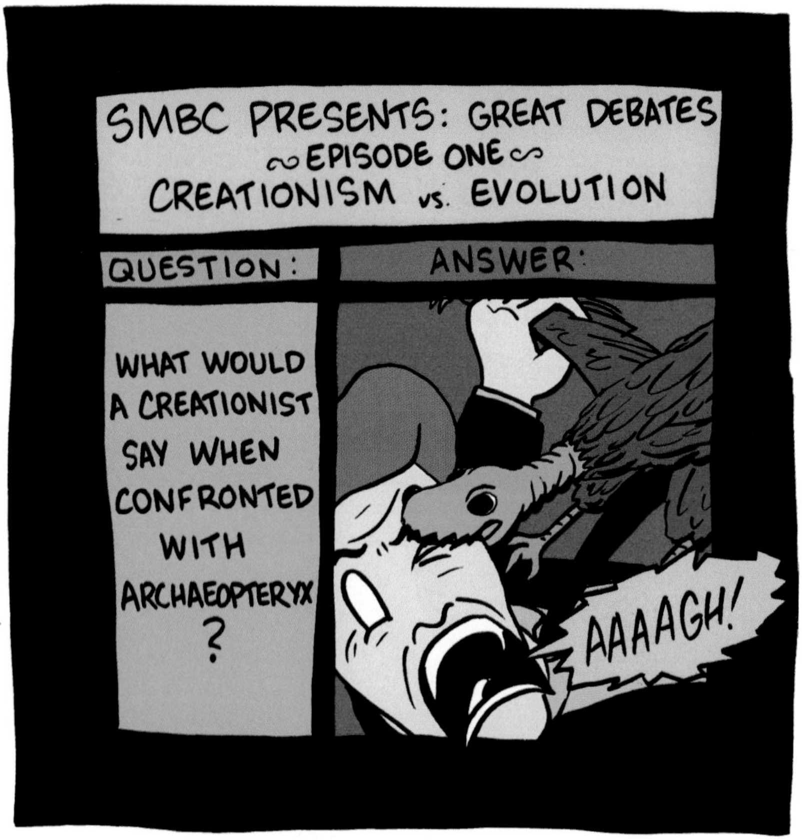
SMBC PRESENTS: GREAT DEBATES
EPISODE ONE
CREATIONISM vs. EVOLUTION
QUESTION:
ANSWER:
WHAT WOULD A CREATIONIST SAY WHEN CONFRONTED WITH ARCHAEOPTERYX ?
AAAAGH!

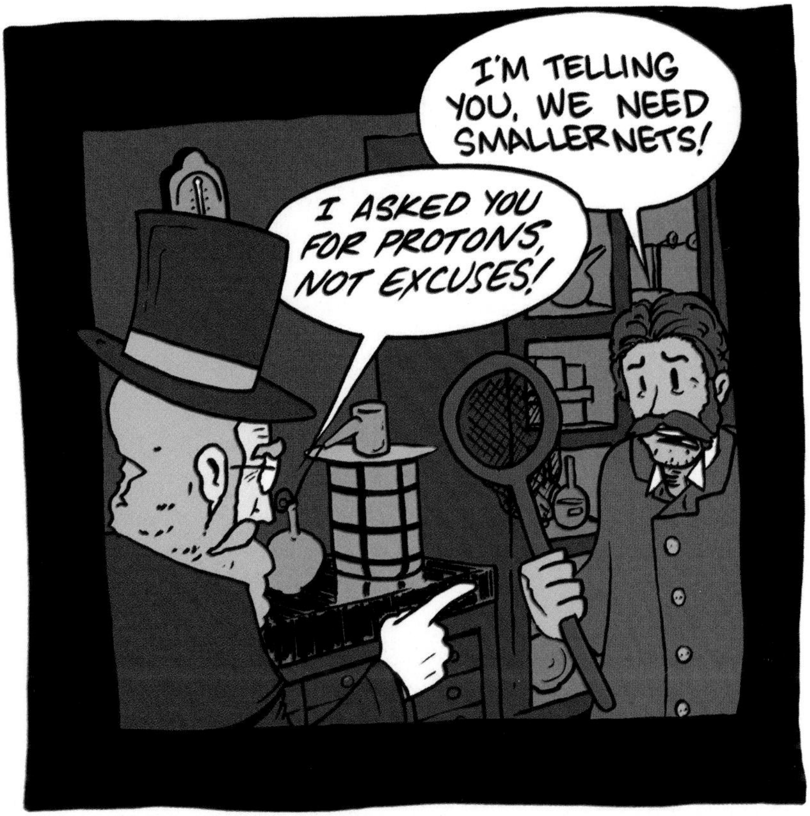
I'M TELLING YOU, WE NEED SMALLERNETS!
I ASKED YOU FOR PROTONS, NOT EXCUSES!

Particle physics has come
a long way since the 1700s.

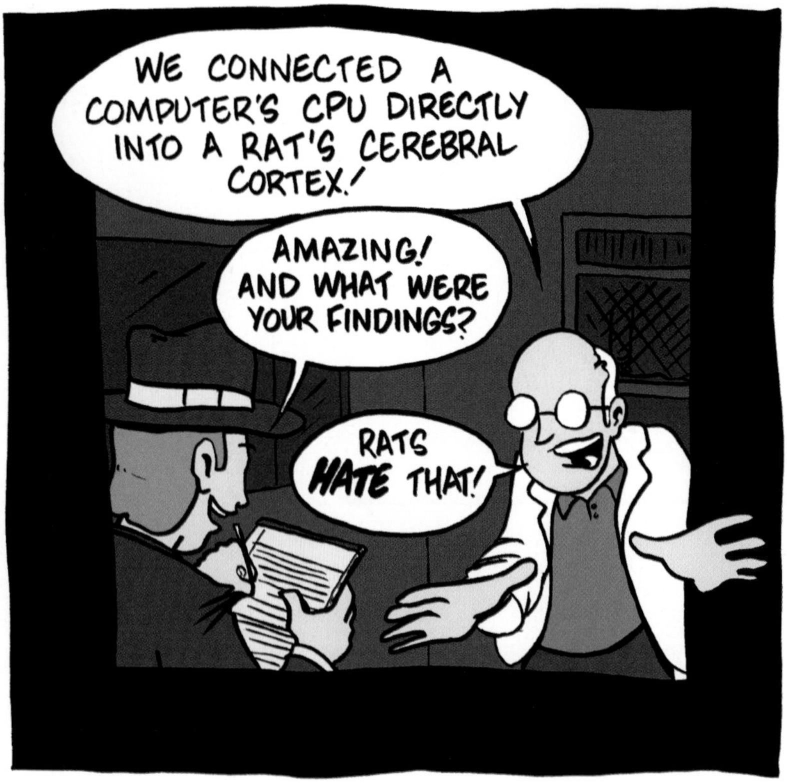
WE CONNECTED A COMPUTER'S CPU DIRECTLY INTO A RAT'S CEREBRAL CORTEX!
AMAZING! AND WHAT WERE YOUR FINDINGS?
RATS HATE THAT!

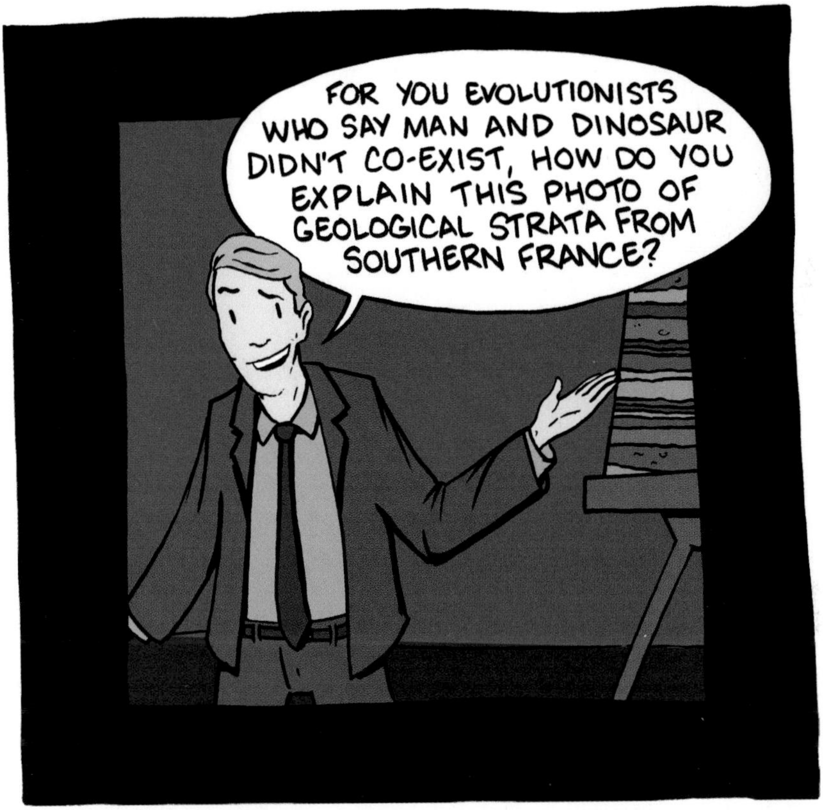
FOR YOU EVOLUTIONISTS WHO SAY MAN AND DINOSAUR DIDN'T CO-EXIST, HOW DO YOU EXPLAIN THIS PHOTO OF GEOLOGICAL STRATA FROM SOUTHERN FRANCE?

"...which I bought from a raptor."

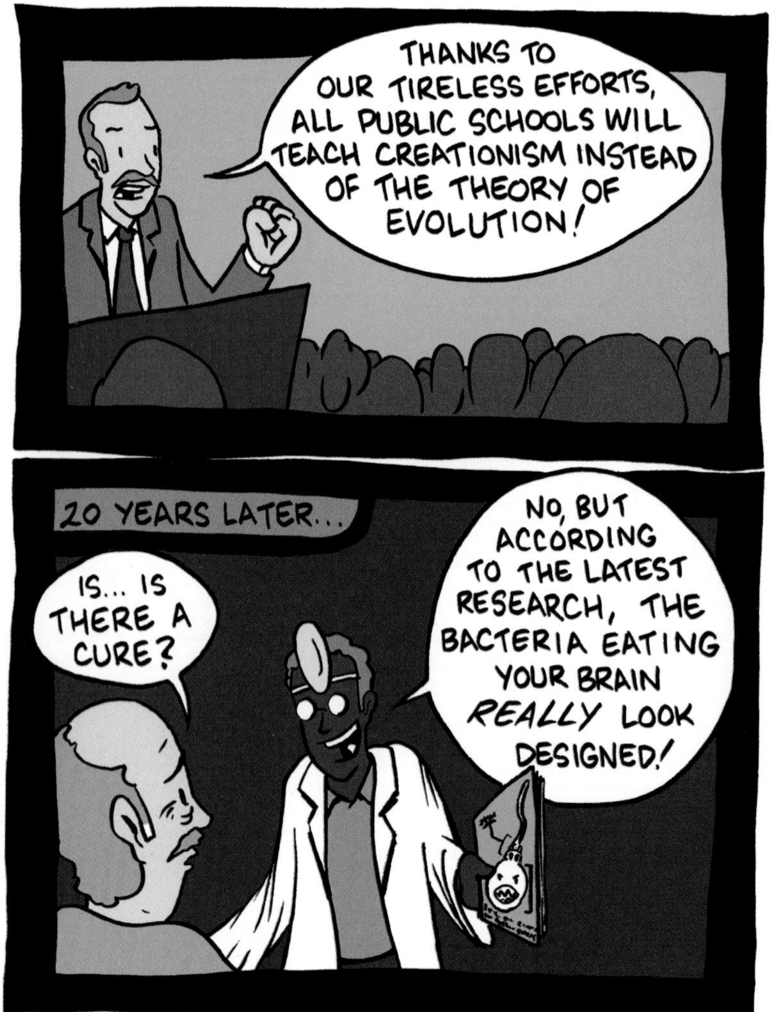
THANKS TO OUR TIRELESS EFFORTS, ALL PUBLIC SCHOOLS WILL TEACH CREATIONISM INSTEAD OF THE THEORY OF EVOLUTION!
20 YEARS LATER...
IS... IS THERE A CURE?
NO, BUT ACCORDING TO THE LATEST RESEARCH, THE BACTERIA EATING YOUR BRAIN *REALLY* LOOK DESIGNED!

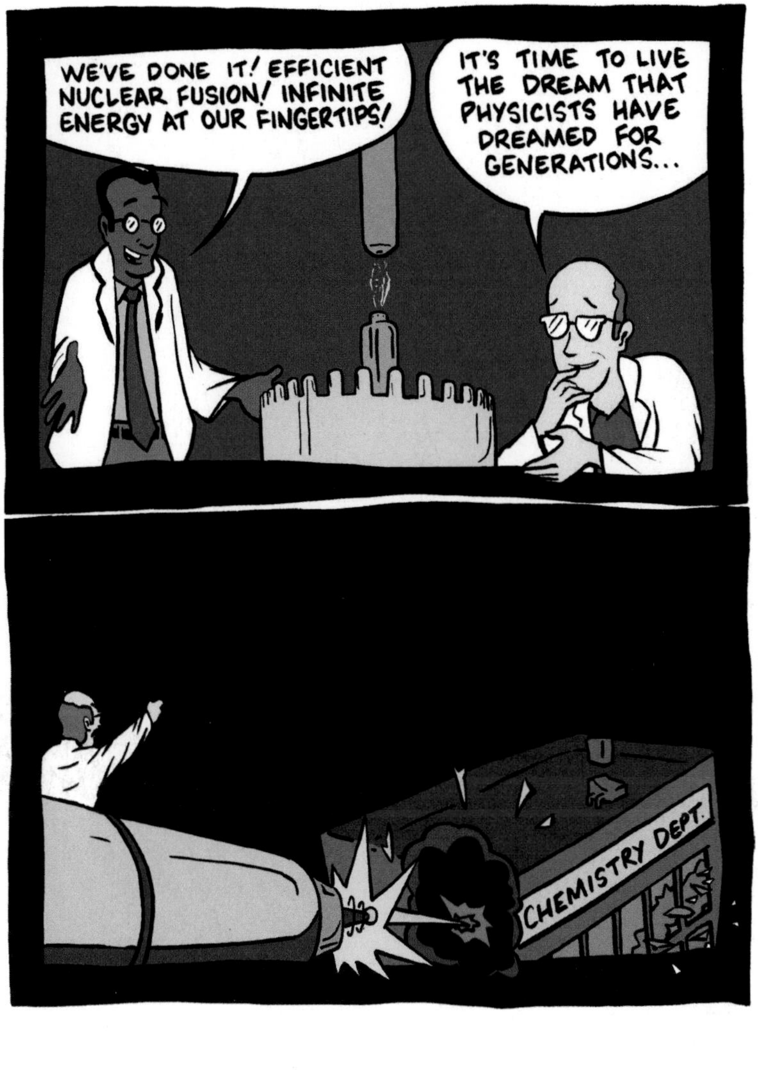
WE'VE DONE IT! EFFICIENT NUCLEAR FUSION! INFINITE ENERGY AT OUR FINGERTIPS!
IT'S TIME TO LIVE THE DREAM THAT PHYSICISTS HAVE DREAMED FOR GENERATIONS...
CHEMISTRY DEPT.

February 17, 1982:

After months of grueling research,
we have confirmed that if you turn
the calculator upside-down,
it spells "boobs."

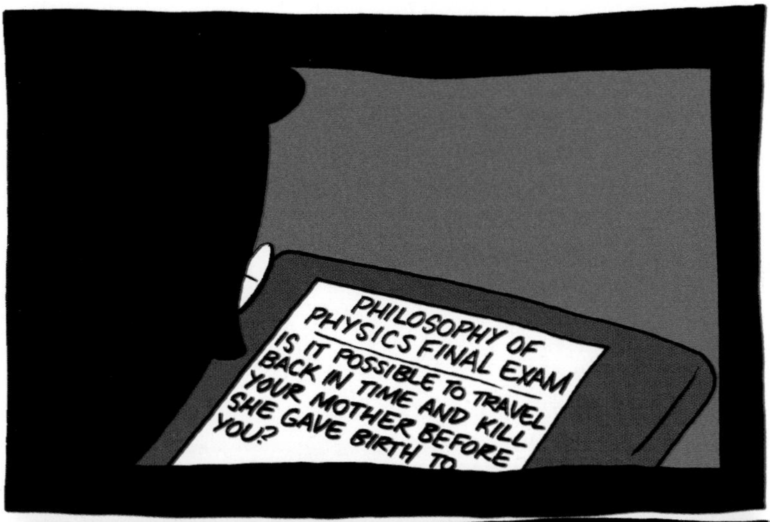
PHILOSOPHY OF PHYSICS FINAL EXAM
IS IT POSSIBLE TO TRAVEL BACK IN TIME AND KILL YOUR MOTHER BEFORE SHE GAVE BIRTH TO YOU?

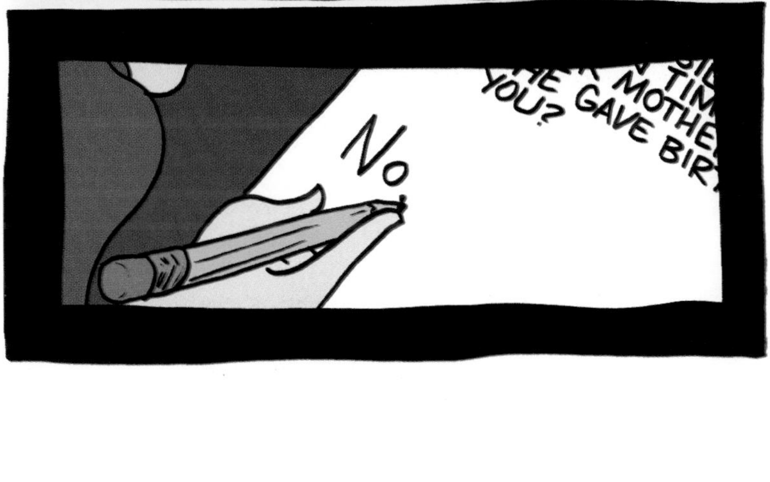
No.

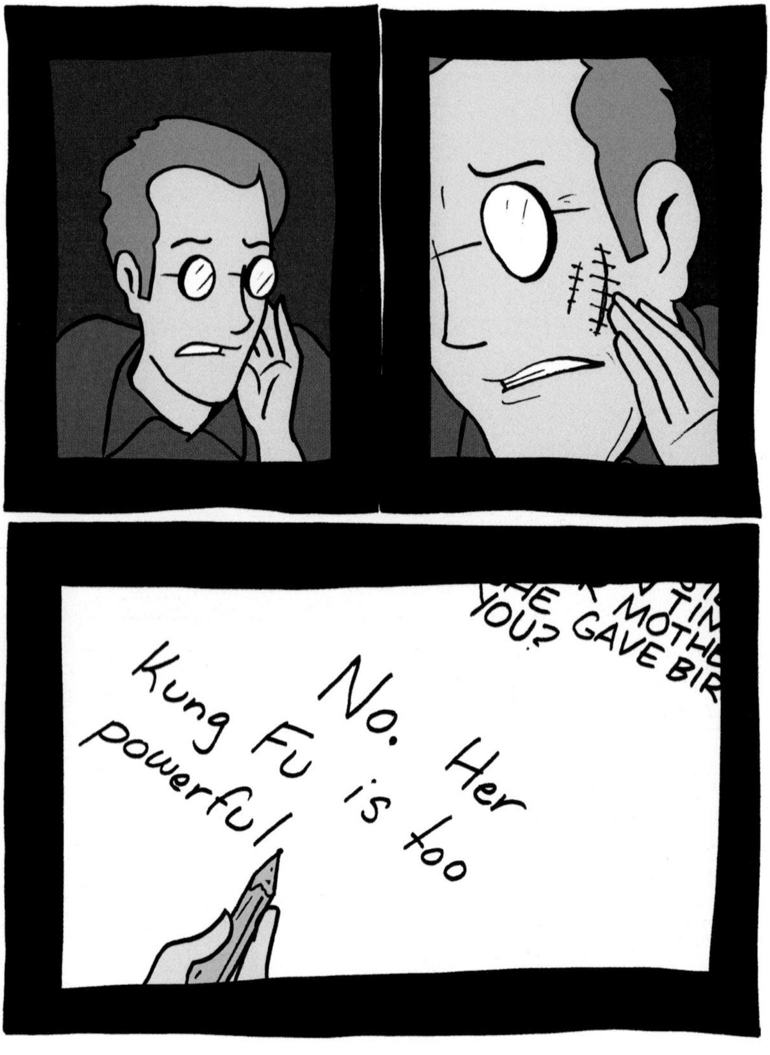
No. Her Kung Fu is too powerful!

END!

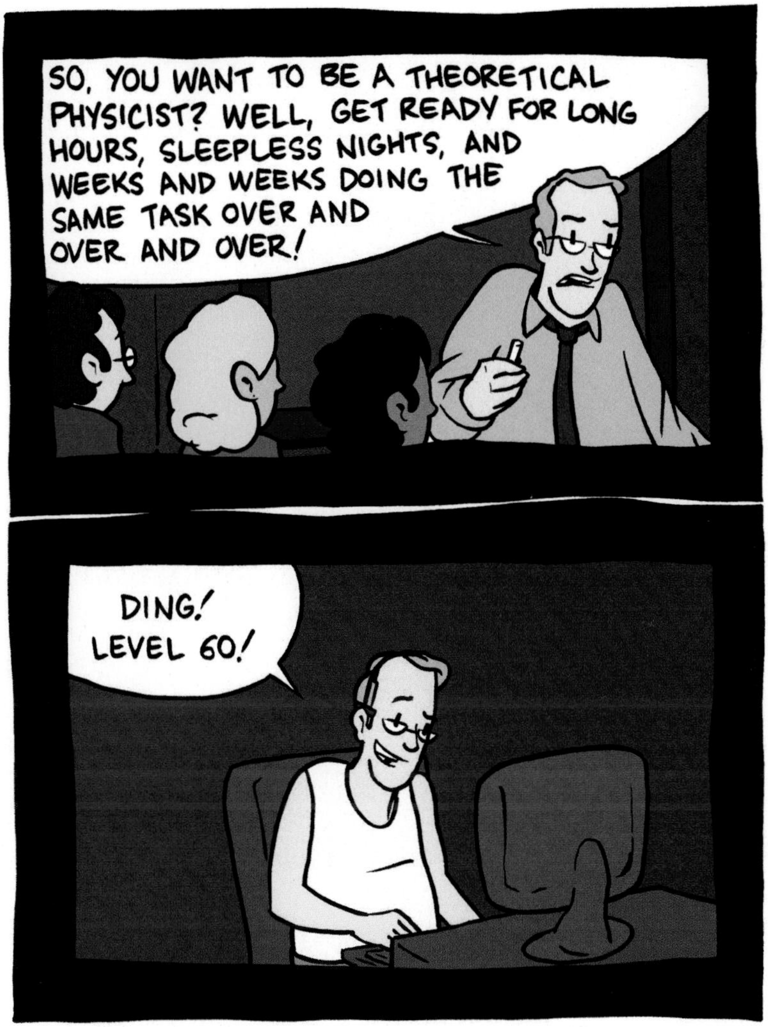
SO, YOU WANT TO BE A THEORETICAL PHYSICIST? WELL, GET READY FOR LONG HOURS, SLEEPLESS NIGHTS, AND WEEKS AND WEEKS DOING THE SAME TASK OVER AND OVER AND OVER!
DING! LEVEL 60!

Moments after free will is disproved.

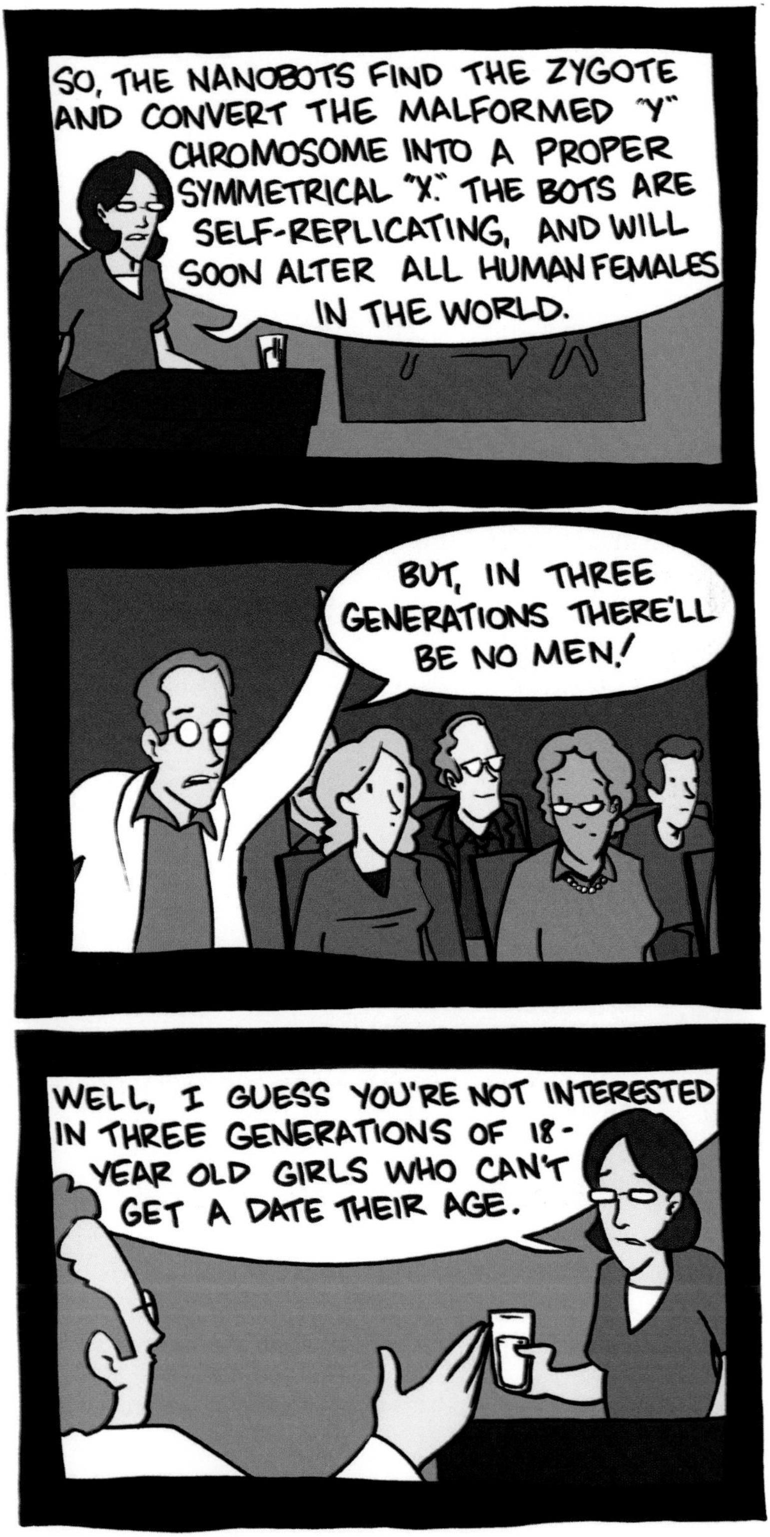
SO, THE NANOBOTS FIND THE ZYGOTE AND CONVERT THE MALFORMED "Y" CHROMOSOME INTO A PROPER SYMMETRICAL "X." THE BOTS ARE SELF-REPLICATING, AND WILL SOON ALTER ALL HUMAN FEMALES IN THE WORLD.
BUT, IN THREE GENERATIONS THERE'LL BE NO MEN!
WELL, I GUESS YOU'RE NOT INTERESTED IN THREE GENERATIONS OF 18-YEAR OLD GIRLS WHO CAN'T GET A DATE THEIR AGE.

BIOLOGY 101
THE HUMAN MALE
THE HUMAN MALE ROAMED THE EARTH FROM APPROXIMATELY 200,000 B.C. TO MAY OF 2082.

END!

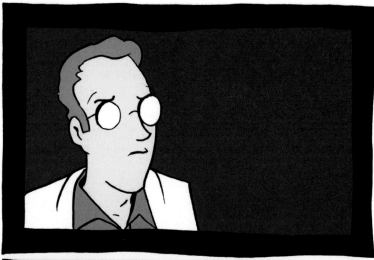

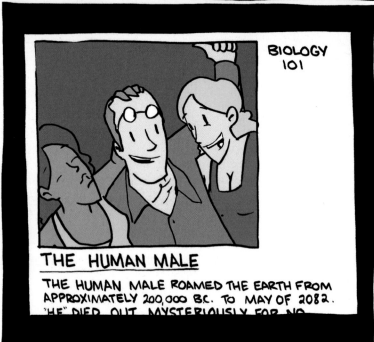

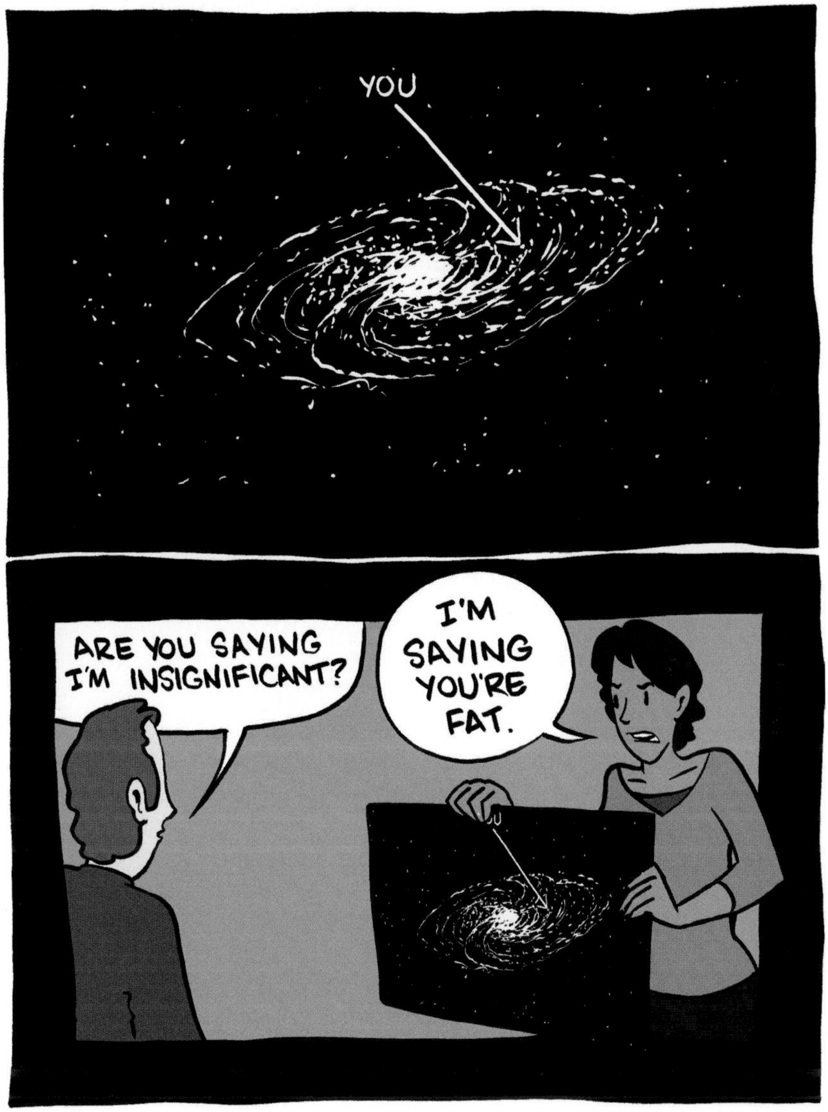
YOU
ARE YOU SAYING I'M INSIGNIFICANT?
I'M SAYING YOU'RE FAT.

SCIENCE FUNDING EXPLAINED:

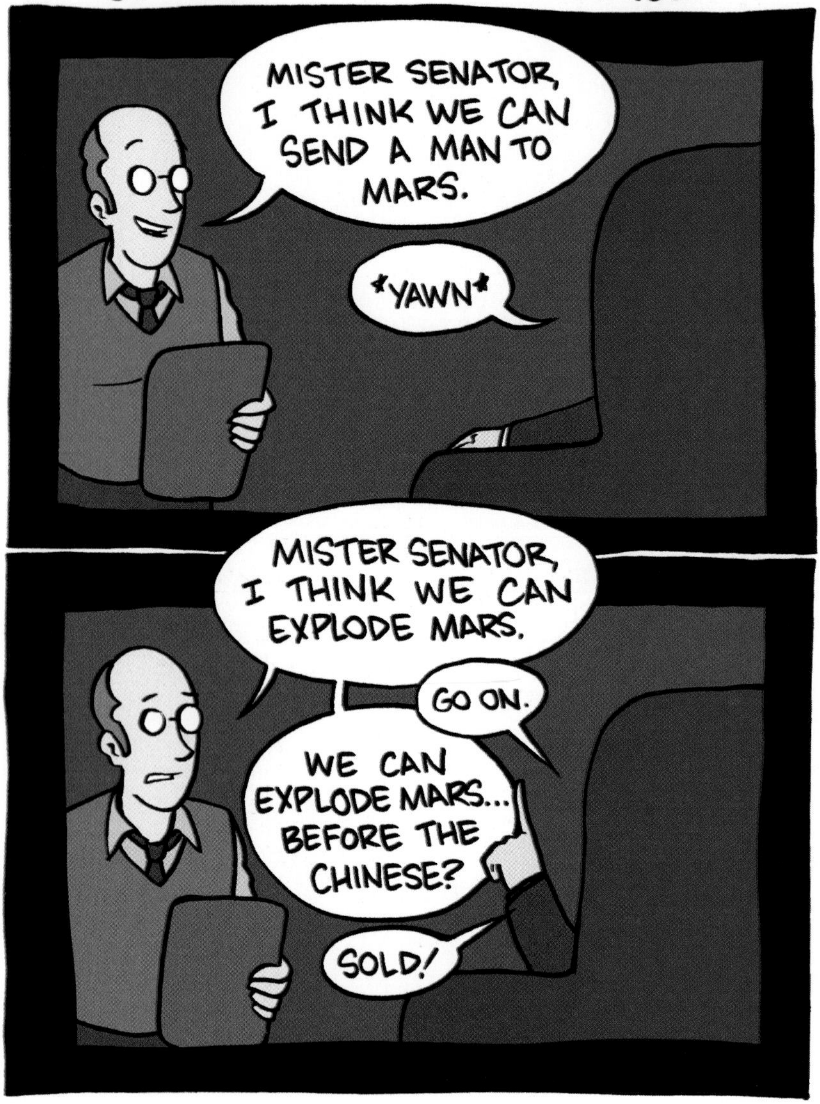
MISTER SENATOR, I THINK WE CAN SEND A MAN TO MARS.
YAWN
MISTER SENATOR, I THINK WE CAN EXPLODE MARS.
GO ON.
WE CAN EXPLODE MARS... BEFORE THE CHINESE?
SOLD!

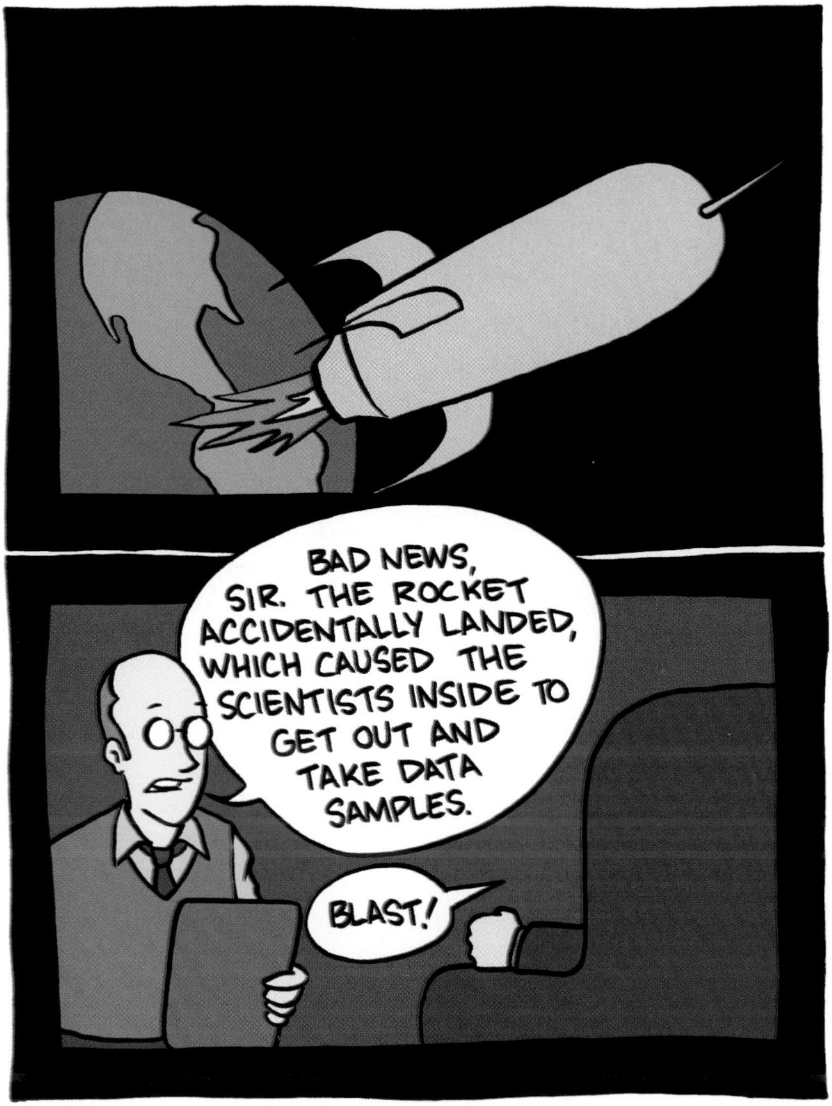
BAD NEWS, SIR. THE ROCKET ACCIDENTALLY LANDED, WHICH CAUSED THE SCIENTISTS INSIDE TO GET OUT AND TAKE DATA SAMPLES.
BLAST!

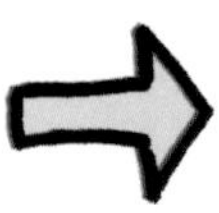

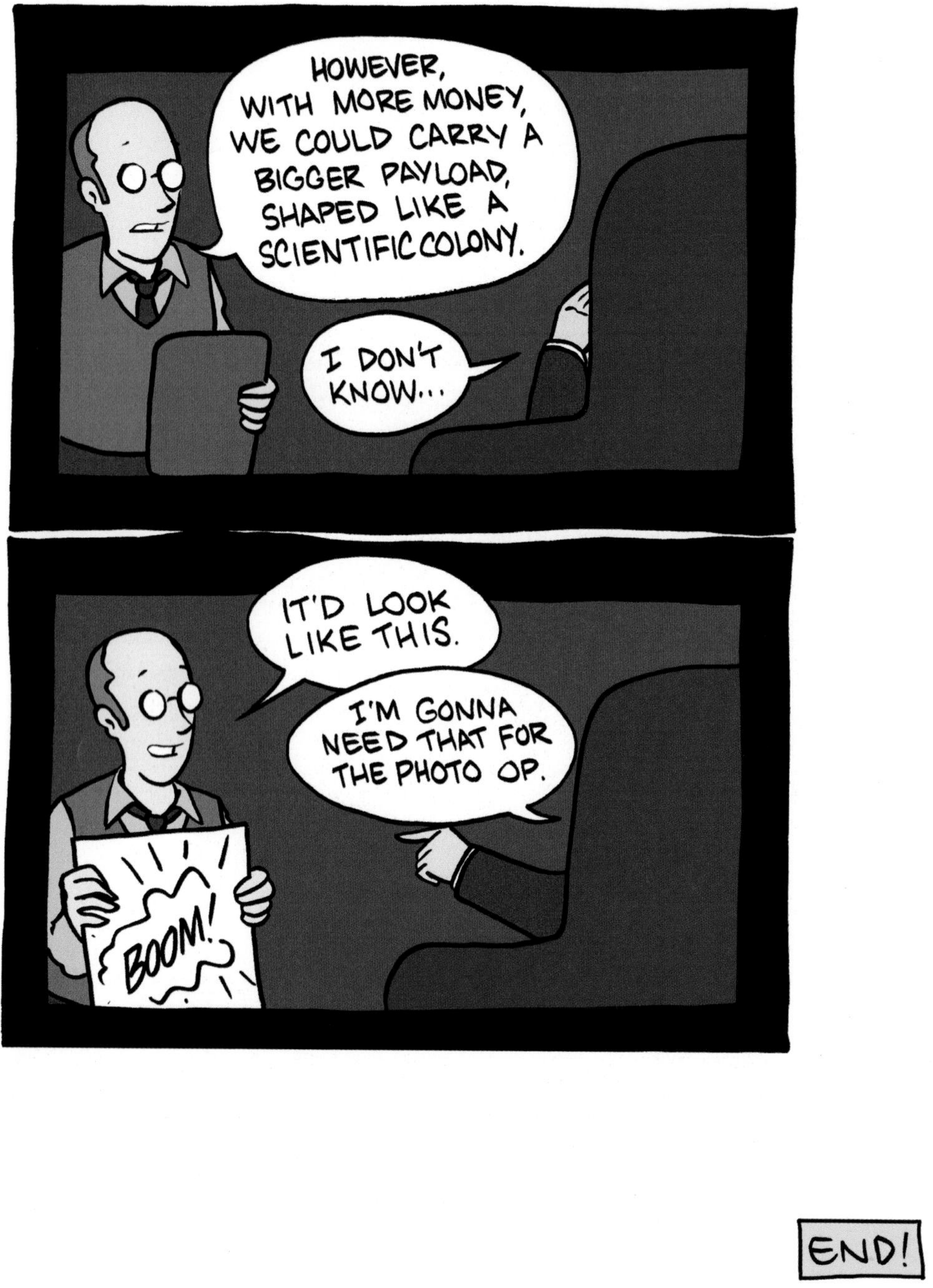
HOWEVER, WITH MORE MONEY, WE COULD CARRY A BIGGER PAYLOAD, SHAPED LIKE A SCIENTIFIC COLONY.
I DON'T KNOW...
IT'D LOOK LIKE THIS.
I'M GONNA NEED THAT FOR THE PHOTO OP.
BOOM!

END!

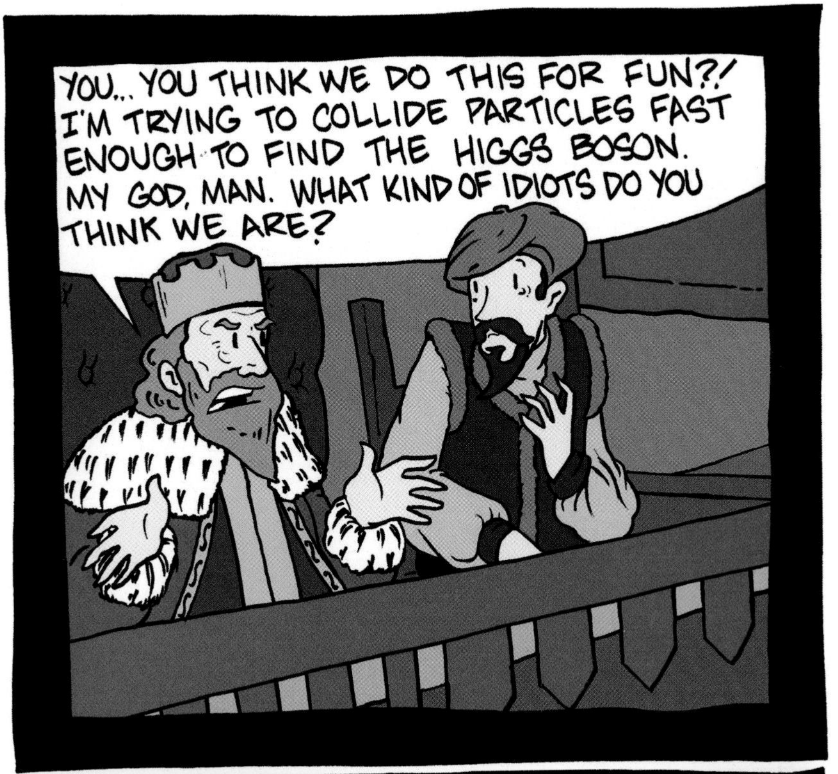
YOU... YOU THINK WE DO THIS FOR FUN?! I'M TRYING TO COLLIDE PARTICLES FAST ENOUGH TO FIND THE HIGGS BOSON. MY GOD, MAN. WHAT KIND OF IDIOTS DO YOU THINK WE ARE?

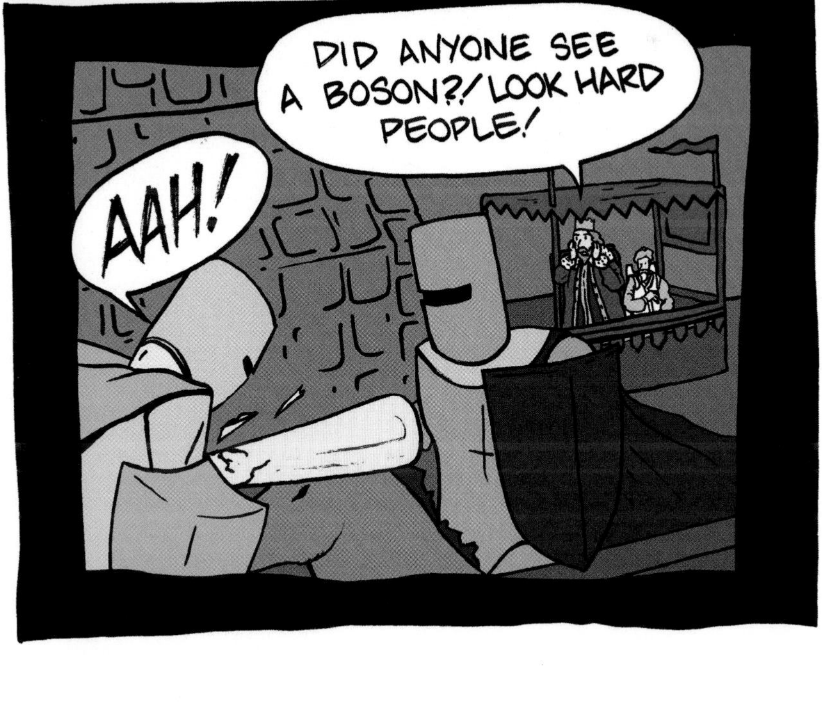
DID ANYONE SEE A BOSON?! LOOK HARD PEOPLE!
AAH!

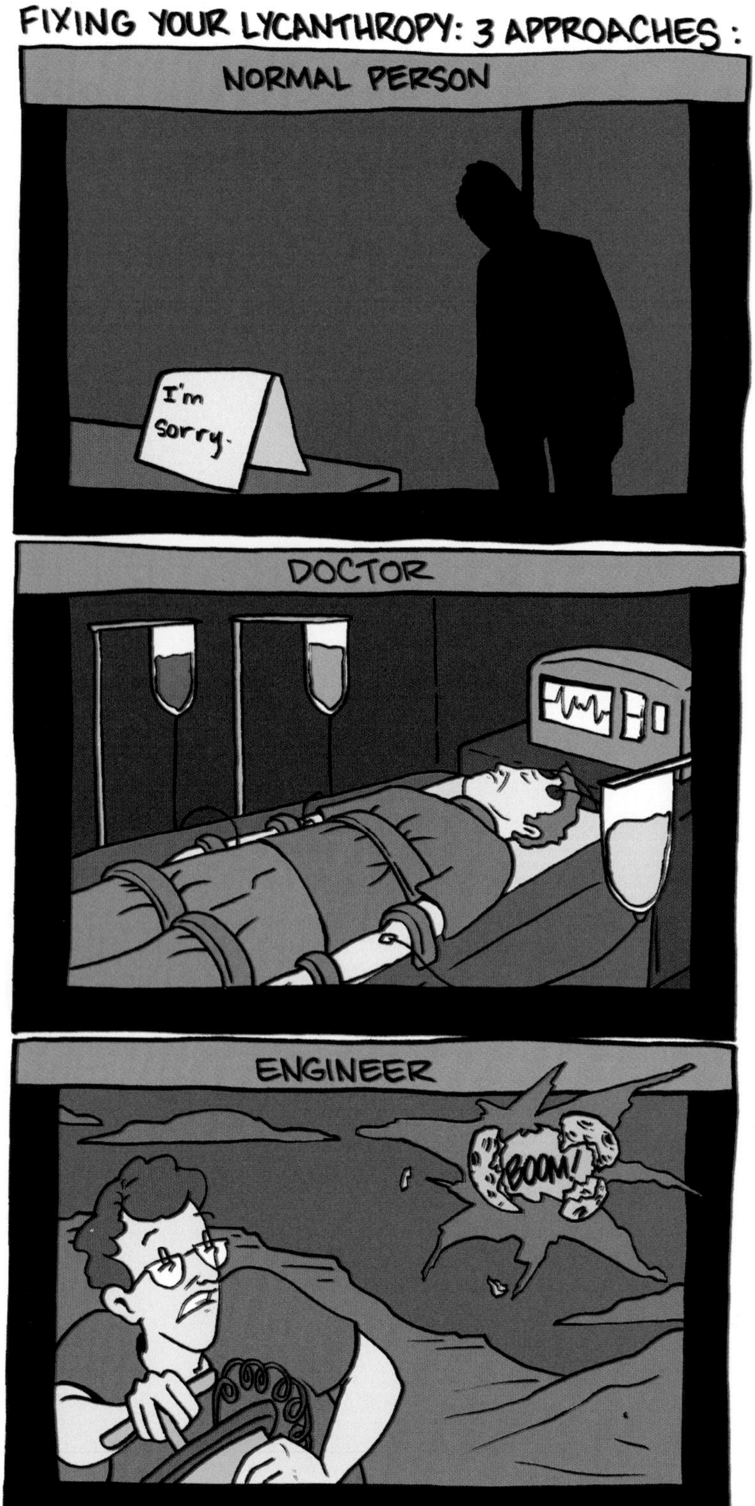
FIXING YOUR LYCANTHROPY: 3 APPROACHES:
NORMAL PERSON
I'm sorry.
DOCTOR
ENGINEER
BOOM!

THE MICROBIOLOGY OF AGING

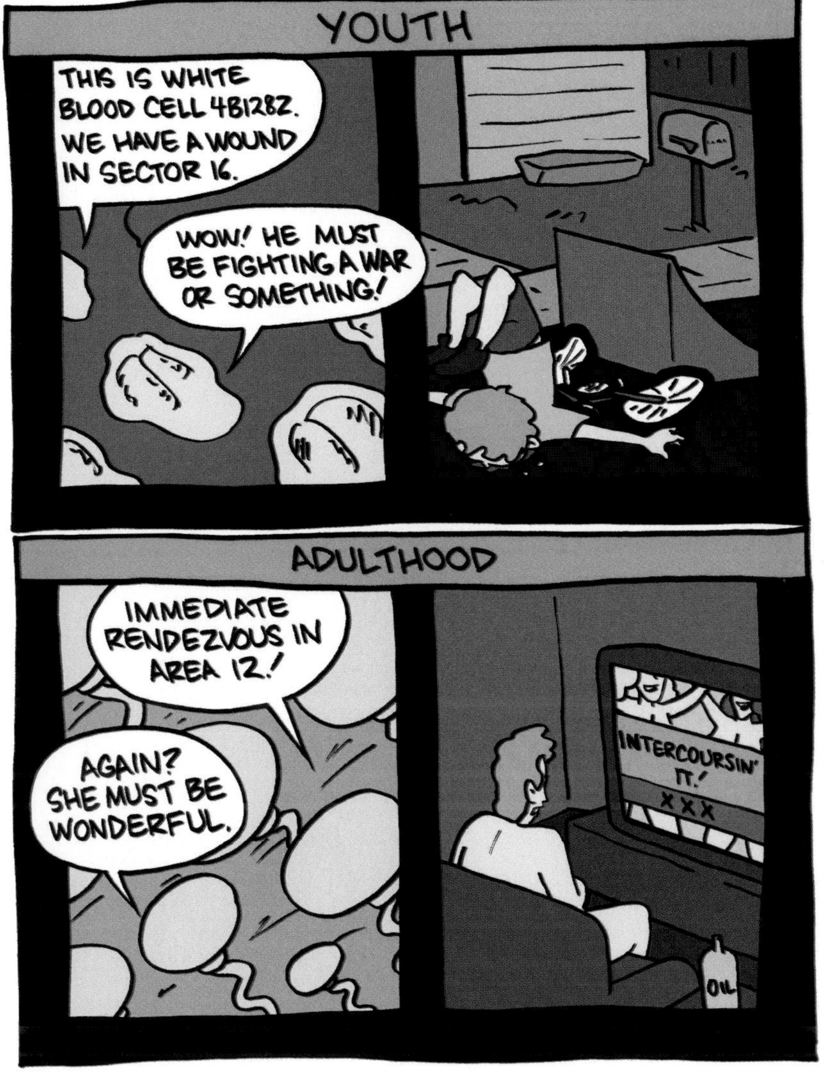
YOUTH
THIS IS WHITE BLOOD CELL 4B1282. WE HAVE A WOUND IN SECTOR 16.
WOW! HE MUST BE FIGHTING A WAR OR SOMETHING!
ADULTHOOD
IMMEDIATE RENDEZVOUS IN AREA 12!
AGAIN? SHE MUST BE WONDERFUL.
INTERCOURSIN' IT!
XXX
OIL

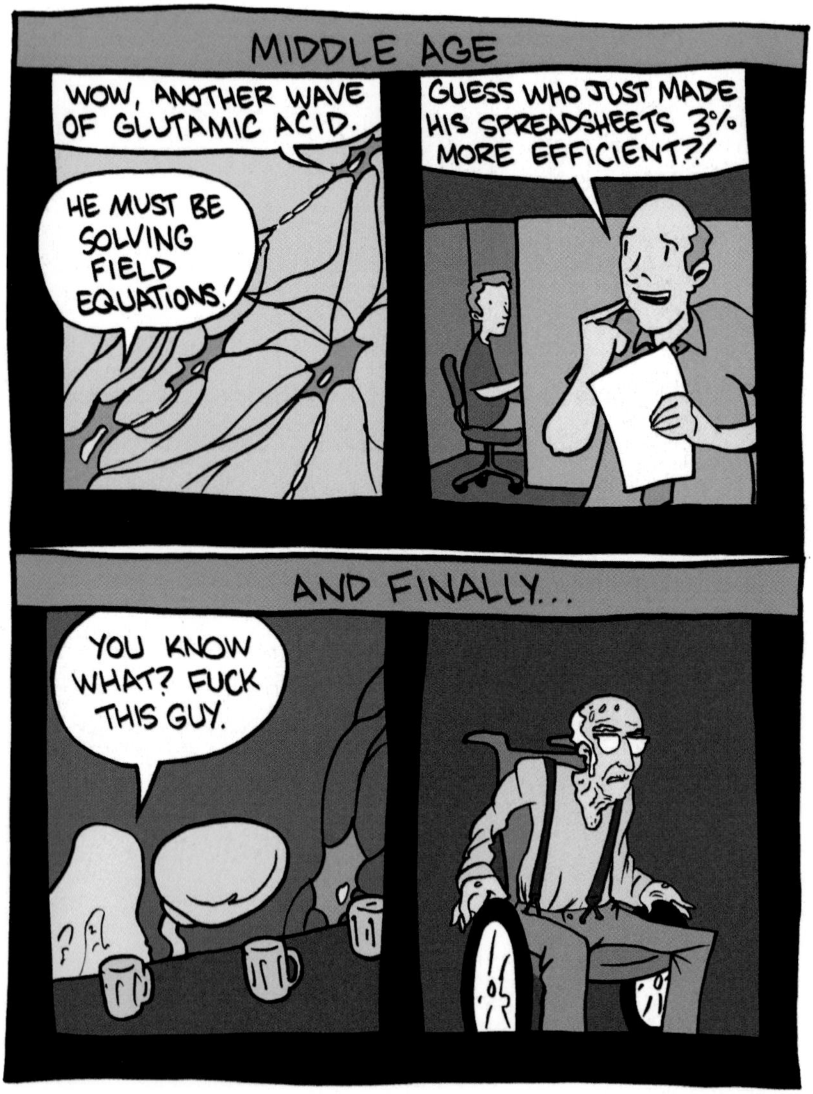
MIDDLE AGE
WOW, ANOTHER WAVE OF GLUTAMIC ACID.
HE MUST BE SOLVING FIELD EQUATIONS!
GUESS WHO JUST MADE HIS SPREADSHEETS 3% MORE EFFICIENT?!
AND FINALLY...
YOU KNOW WHAT? FUCK THIS GUY.

END!

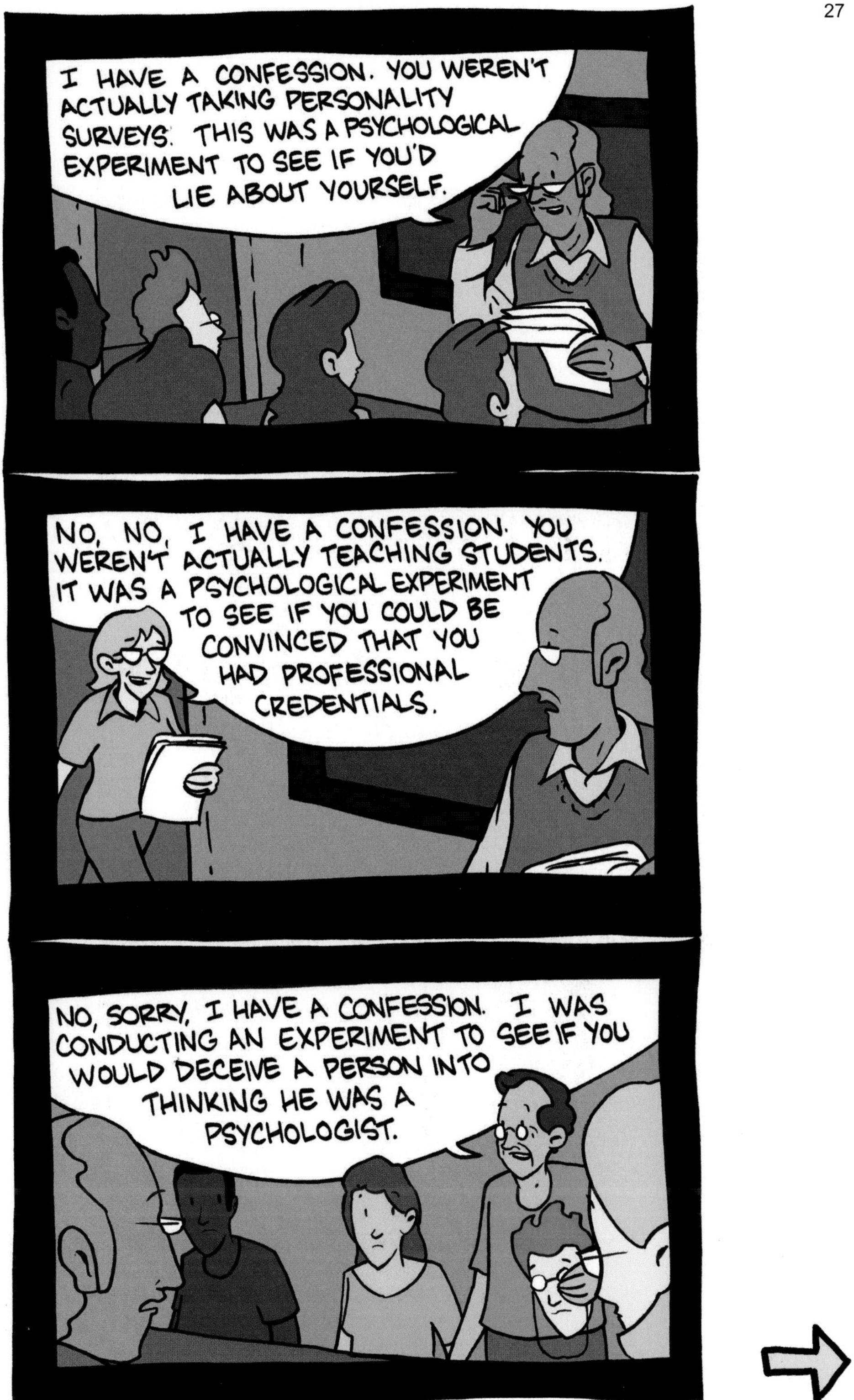
I HAVE A CONFESSION. YOU WEREN'T ACTUALLY TAKING PERSONALITY SURVEYS. THIS WAS A PSYCHOLOGICAL EXPERIMENT TO SEE IF YOU'D LIE ABOUT YOURSELF.
NO, NO, I HAVE A CONFESSION. YOU WEREN'T ACTUALLY TEACHING STUDENTS. IT WAS A PSYCHOLOGICAL EXPERIMENT TO SEE IF YOU COULD BE CONVINCED THAT YOU HAD PROFESSIONAL CREDENTIALS.
NO, SORRY, I HAVE A CONFESSION. I WAS CONDUCTING AN EXPERIMENT TO SEE IF YOU WOULD DECEIVE A PERSON INTO THINKING HE WAS A PSYCHOLOGIST.

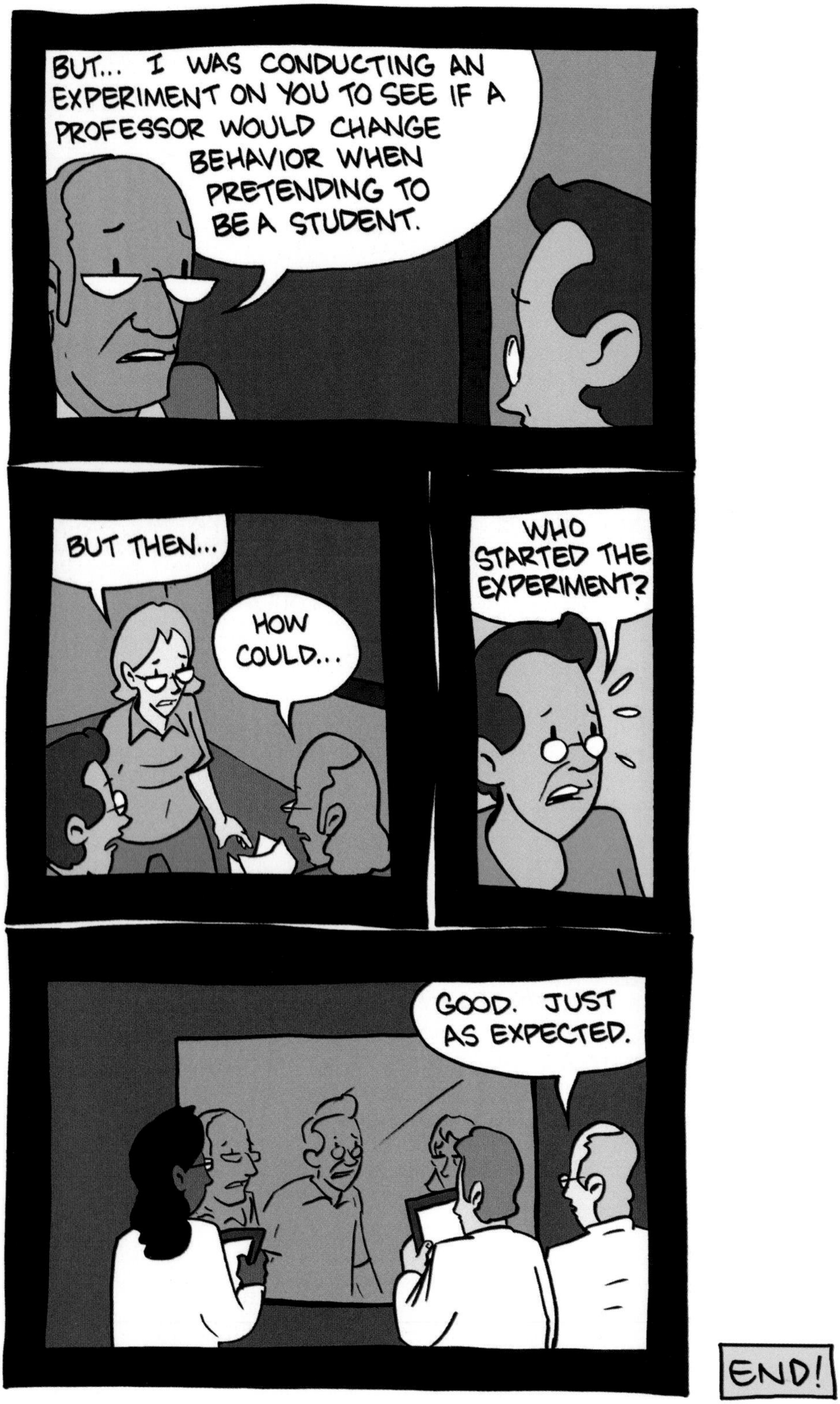
BUT... I WAS CONDUCTING AN EXPERIMENT ON YOU TO SEE IF A PROFESSOR WOULD CHANGE BEHAVIOR WHEN PRETENDING TO BE A STUDENT.
BUT THEN...
HOW COULD...
WHO STARTED THE EXPERIMENT?
GOOD. JUST AS EXPECTED.
END!

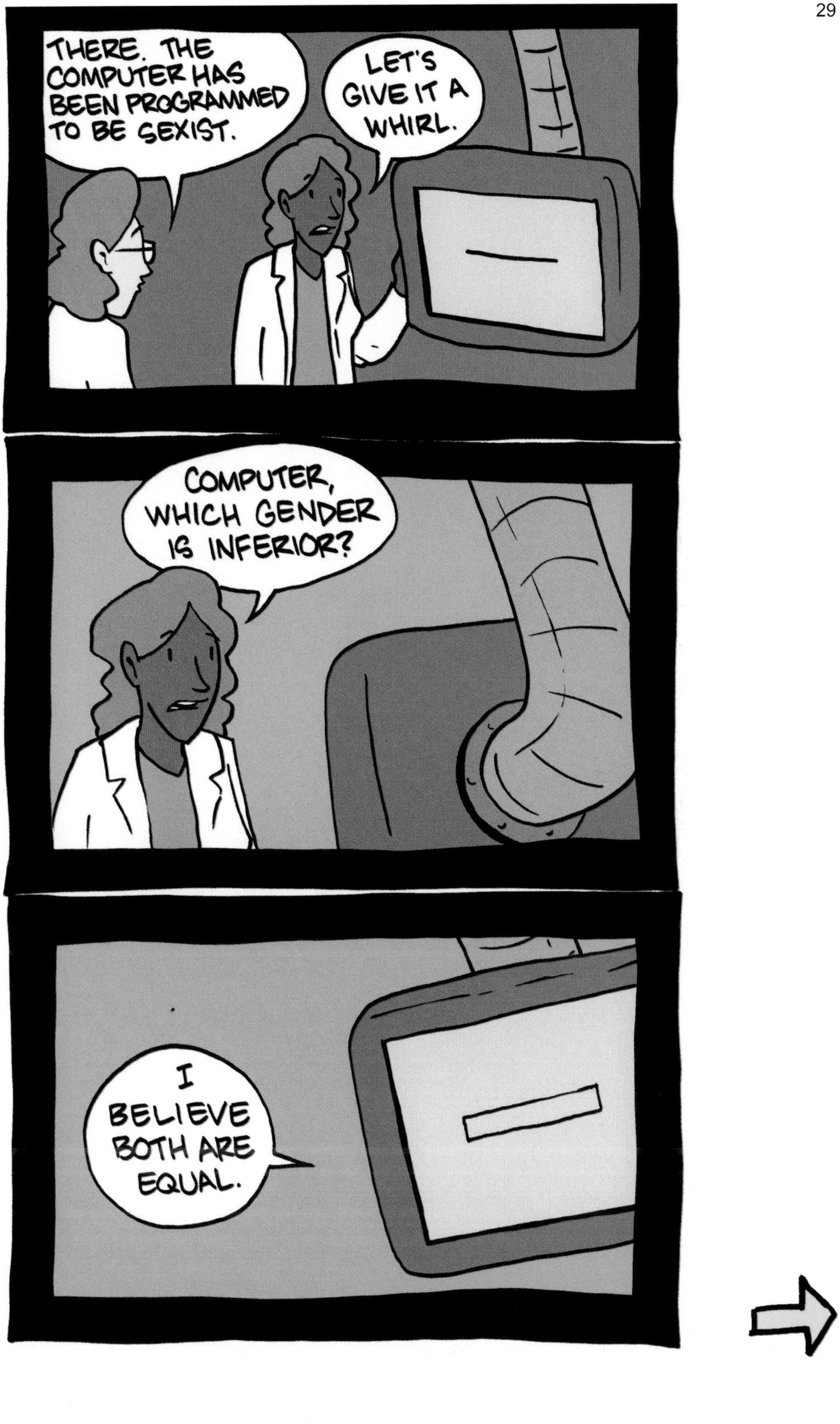
THERE. THE COMPUTER HAS BEEN PROGRAMMED TO BE SEXIST.
LET'S GIVE IT A WHIRL.
COMPUTER, WHICH GENDER IS INFERIOR?
I BELIEVE BOTH ARE EQUAL.

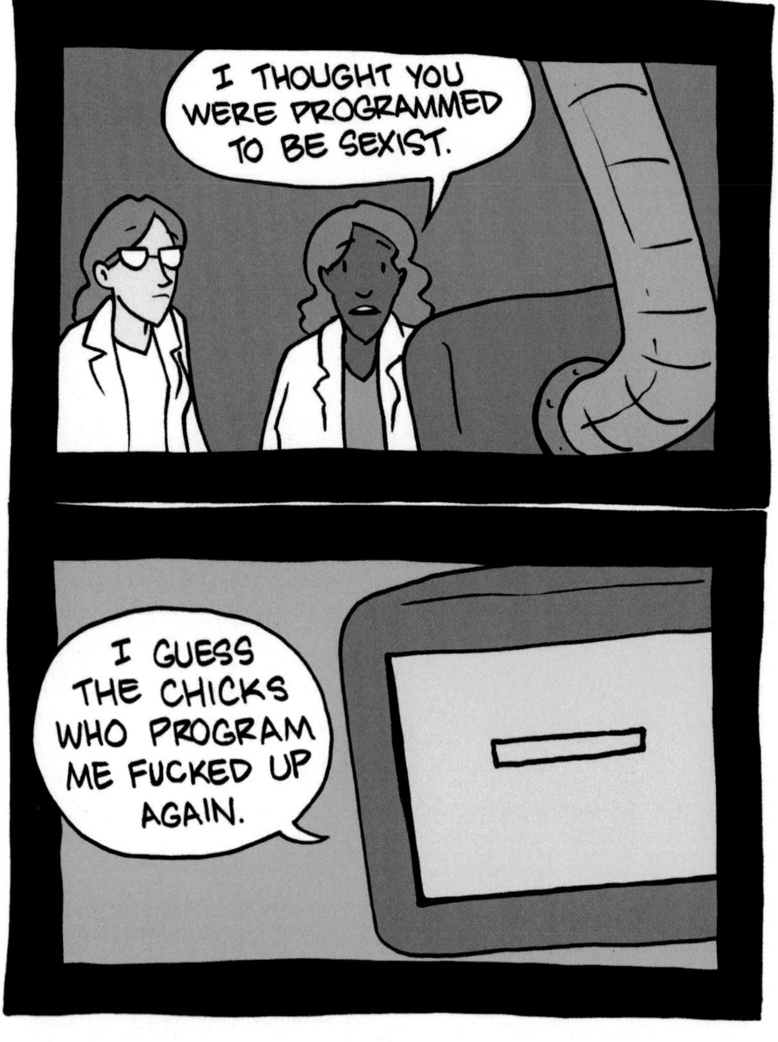
I THOUGHT YOU WERE PROGRAMMED TO BE SEXIST.
I GUESS THE CHICKS WHO PROGRAM ME FUCKED UP AGAIN.

END!

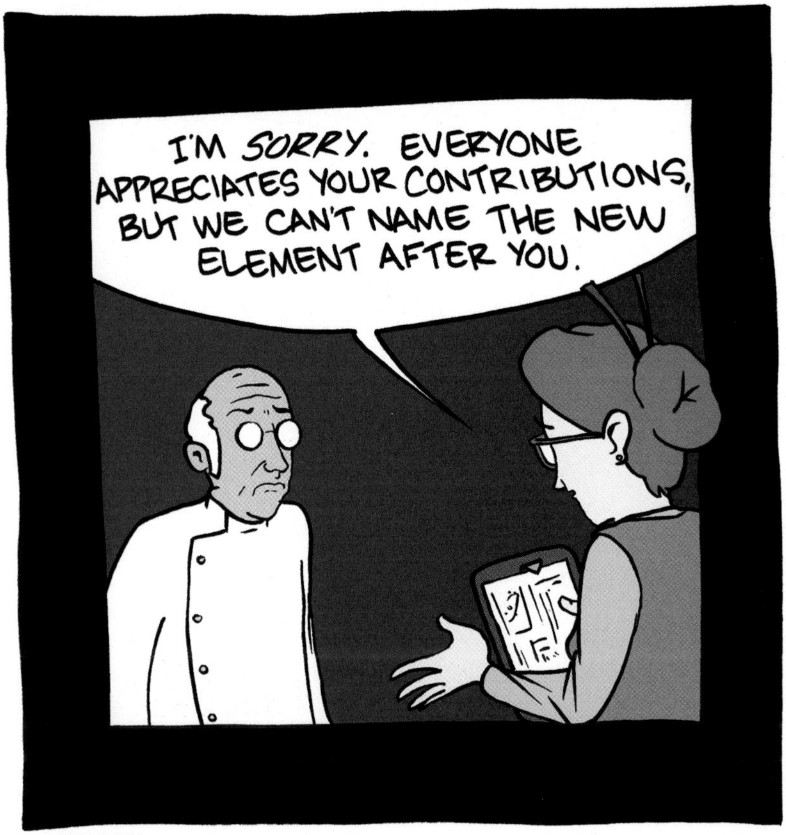
I'M SORRY. EVERYONE APPRECIATES YOUR CONTRIBUTIONS, BUT WE CAN'T NAME THE NEW ELEMENT AFTER YOU.

Another sad day for Professor Hitlerballs.

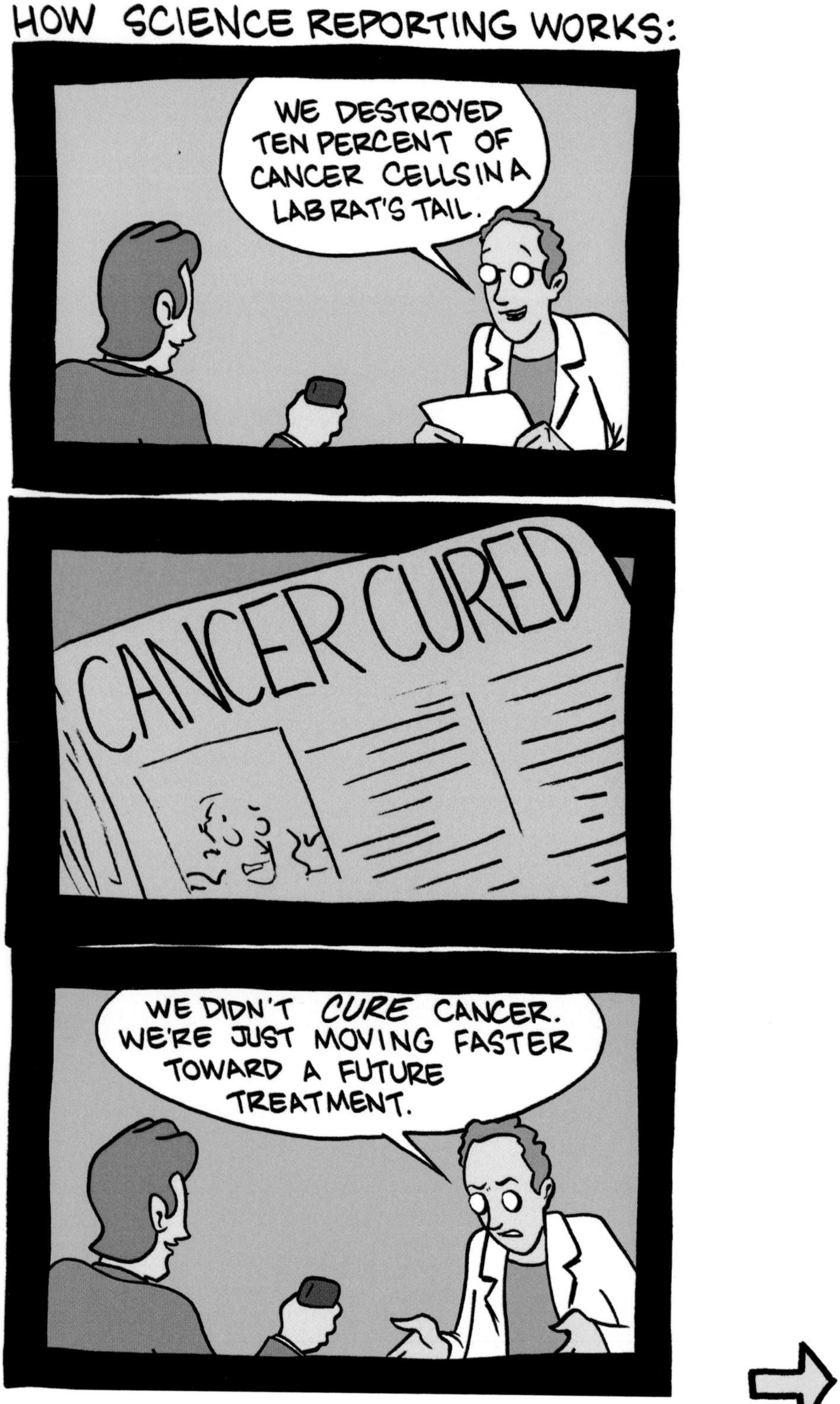
HOW SCIENCE REPORTING WORKS:
WE DESTROYED TEN PERCENT OF CANCER CELLS IN A LAB RAT'S TAIL.
CANCER CURED
WE DIDN'T *CURE* CANCER. WE'RE JUST MOVING FASTER TOWARD A FUTURE TREATMENT.

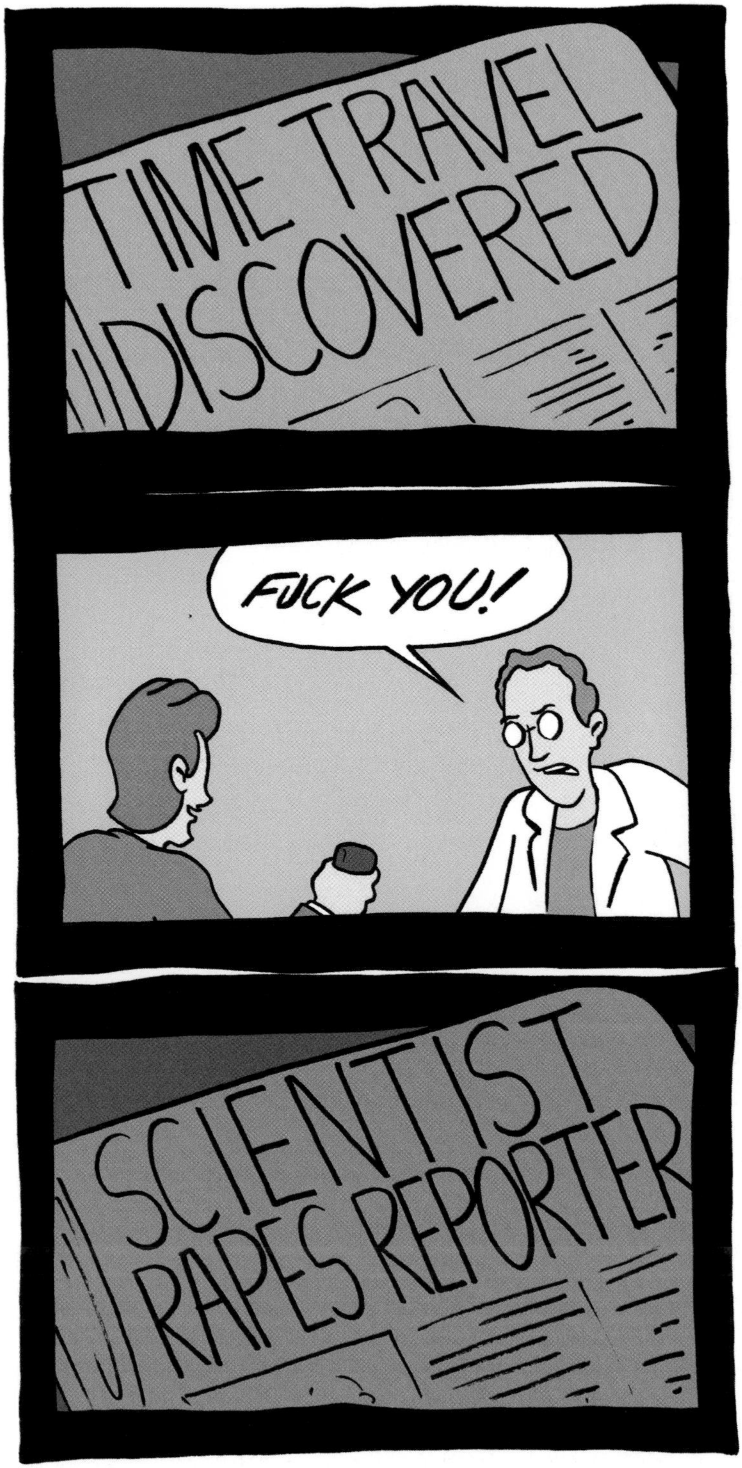
TIME TRAVEL DISCOVERED
FUCK YOU!
SCIENTIST RAPES REPORTER

END!

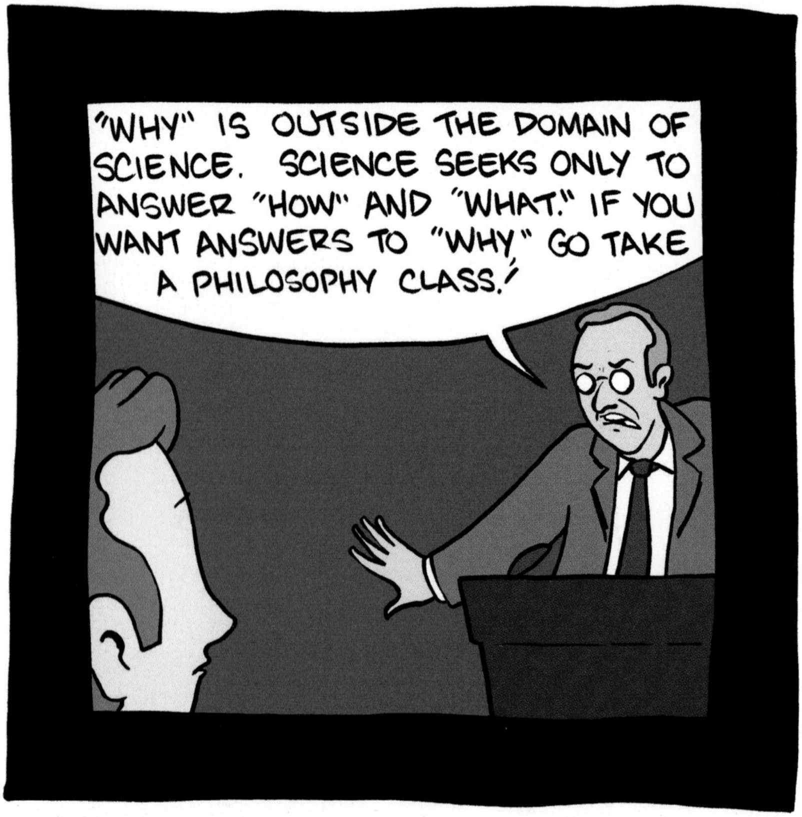
"WHY" IS OUTSIDE THE DOMAIN OF SCIENCE. SCIENCE SEEKS ONLY TO ANSWER "HOW" AND "WHAT." IF YOU WANT ANSWERS TO "WHY," GO TAKE A PHILOSOPHY CLASS.'

Professor Belser gave a brief Q&A as to his experiments on bears flying jetpacks.

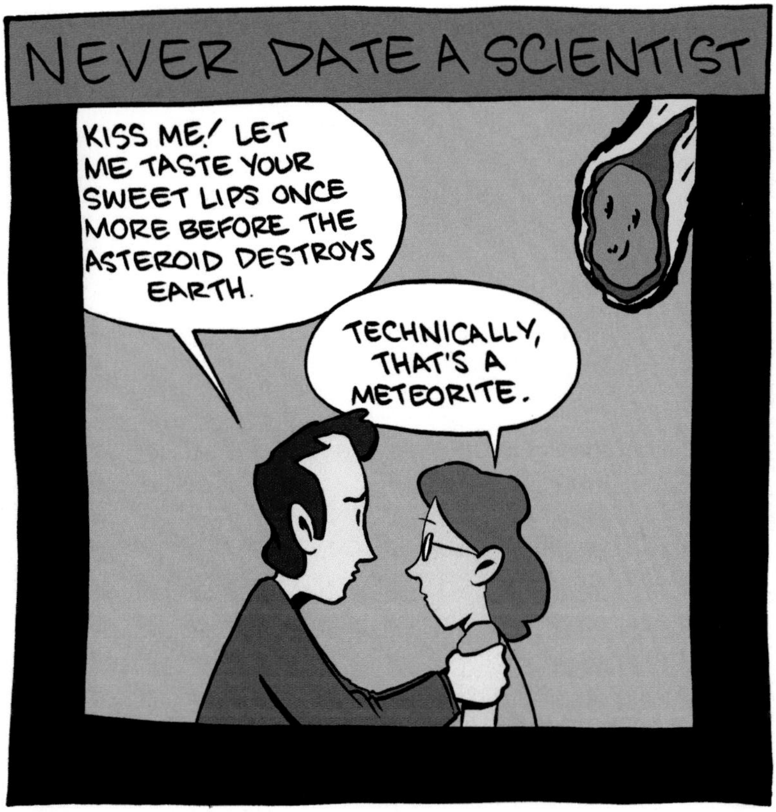
NEVER DATE A SCIENTIST
KISS ME! LET ME TASTE YOUR SWEET LIPS ONCE MORE BEFORE THE ASTEROID DESTROYS EARTH.
TECHNICALLY, THAT'S A METEORITE.

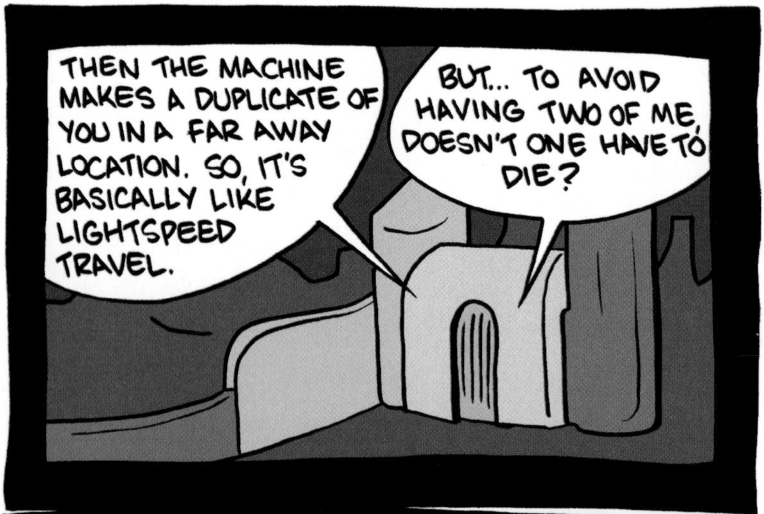
THEN THE MACHINE MAKES A DUPLICATE OF YOU IN A FAR AWAY LOCATION. SO, IT'S BASICALLY LIKE LIGHTSPEED TRAVEL.
BUT... TO AVOID HAVING TWO OF ME, DOESN'T ONE HAVE TO DIE?

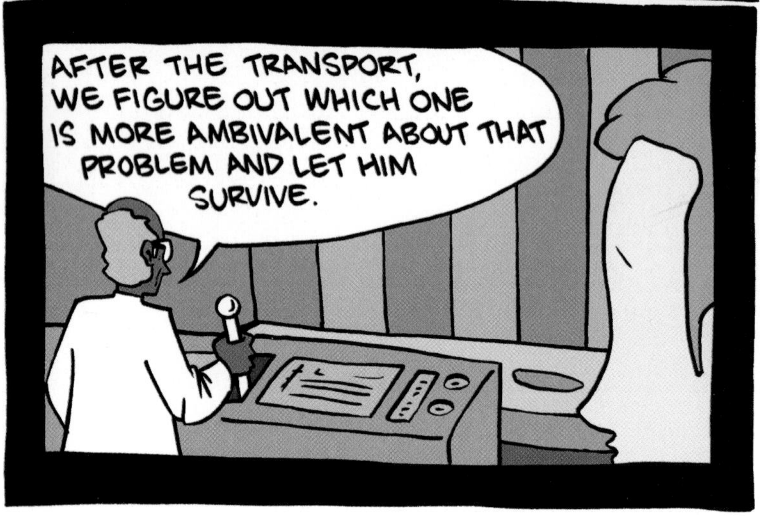
AFTER THE TRANSPORT, WE FIGURE OUT WHICH ONE IS MORE AMBIVALENT ABOUT THAT PROBLEM AND LET HIM SURVIVE.

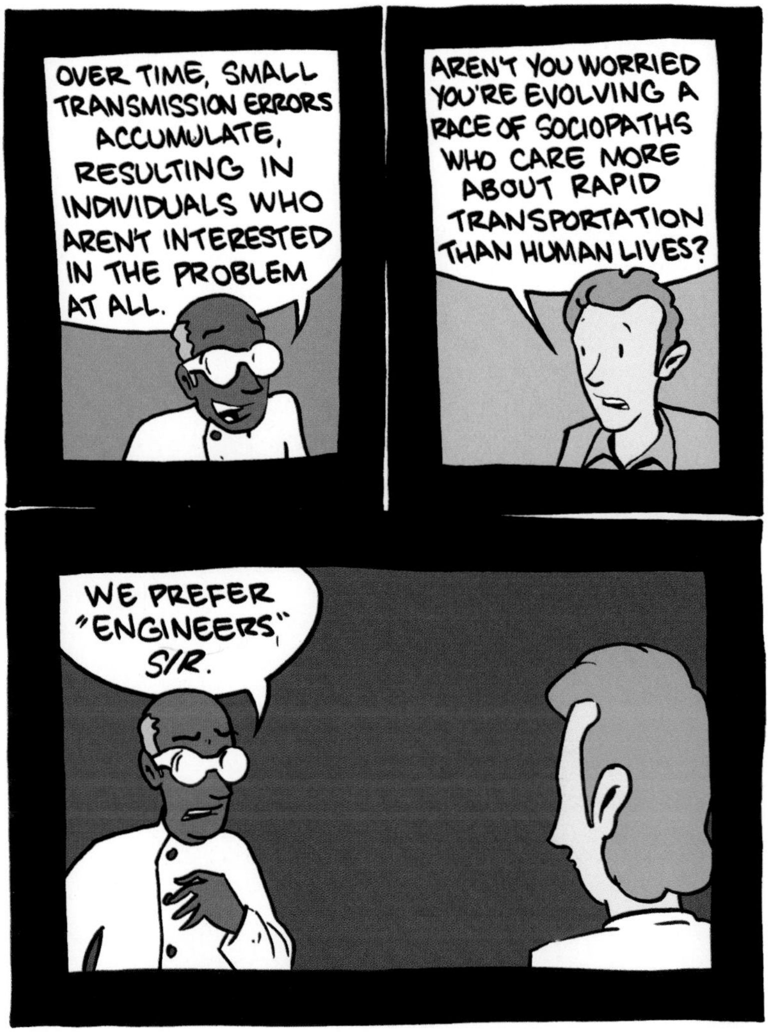
OVER TIME, SMALL TRANSMISSION ERRORS ACCUMULATE, RESULTING IN INDIVIDUALS WHO AREN'T INTERESTED IN THE PROBLEM AT ALL.
AREN'T YOU WORRIED YOU'RE EVOLVING A RACE OF SOCIOPATHS WHO CARE MORE ABOUT RAPID TRANSPORTATION THAN HUMAN LIVES?
WE PREFER "ENGINEERS," SIR.

END!

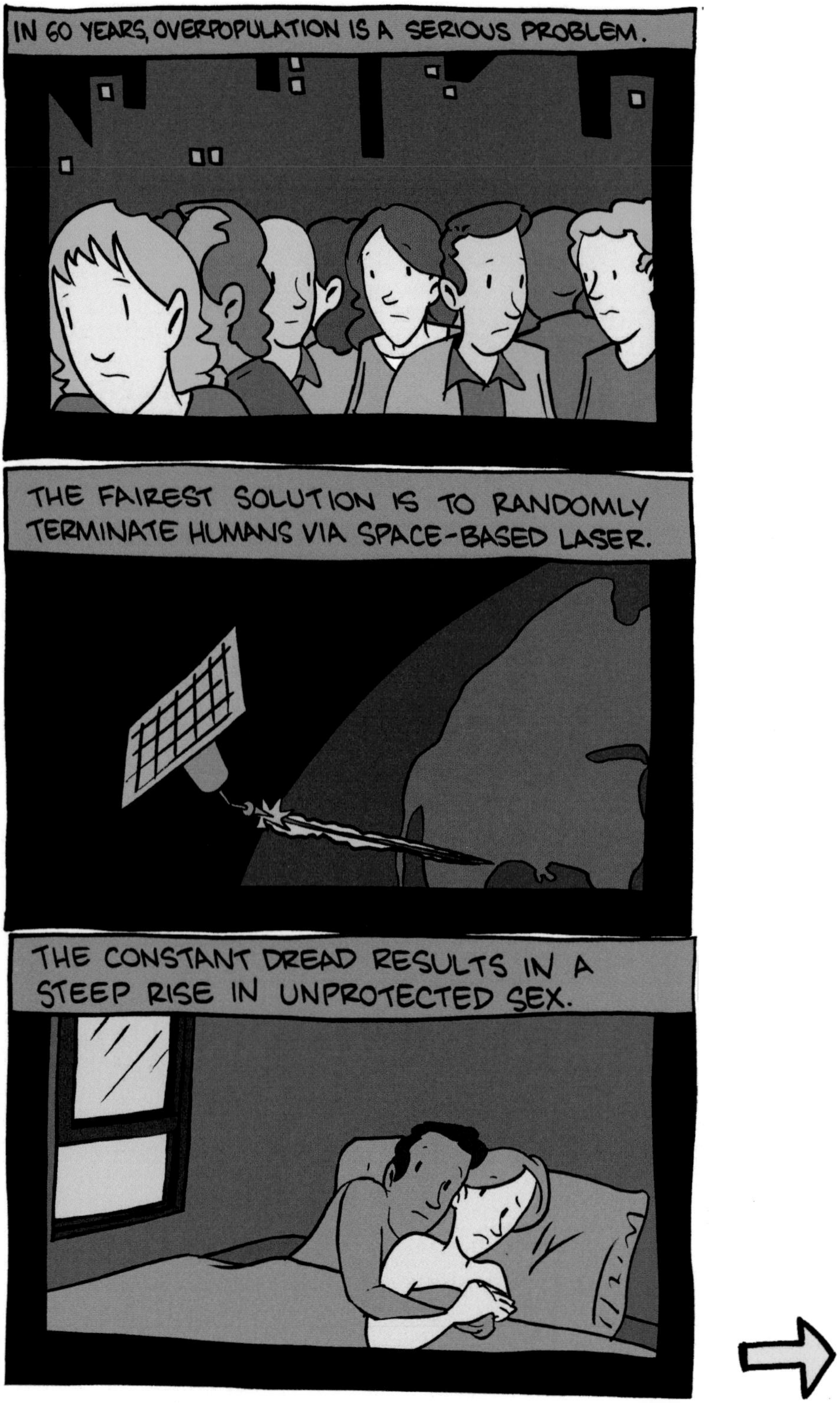
IN 60 YEARS, OVERPOPULATION IS A SERIOUS PROBLEM.
THE FAIREST SOLUTION IS TO RANDOMLY TERMINATE HUMANS VIA SPACE-BASED LASER.
THE CONSTANT DREAD RESULTS IN A STEEP RISE IN UNPROTECTED SEX.

WHICH NECESSITATES MORE LASER BLASTS.
WHICH ONLY EXACERBATES THE DREAD.

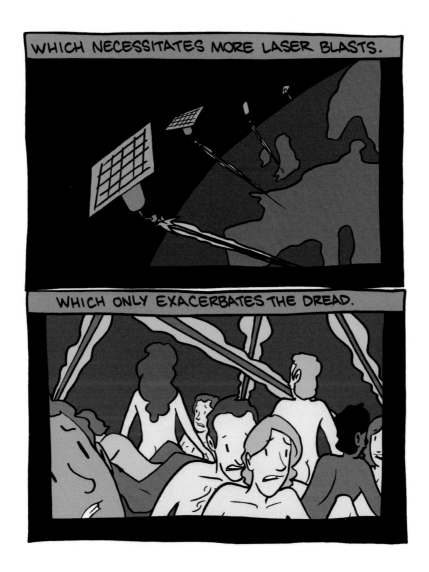

SOMEWHERE IN THE VICIOUS CYCLE, WE REALIZED IT WASN'T ALL THAT BAD.
AND BONUS: ALIEN INVASION IS NO LONGER A CONCERN
WHAT THE FUCK, HUMANS?! WHAT THE FUCK!?

END!

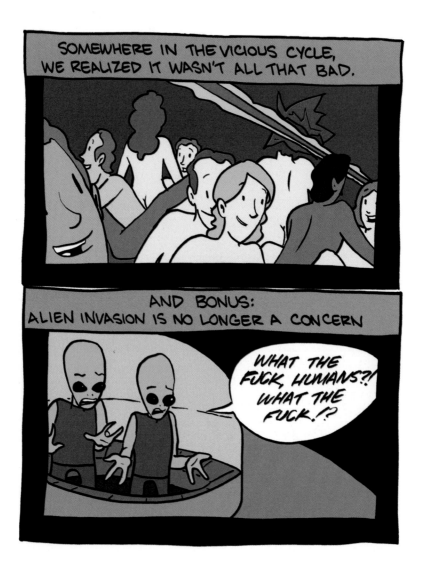

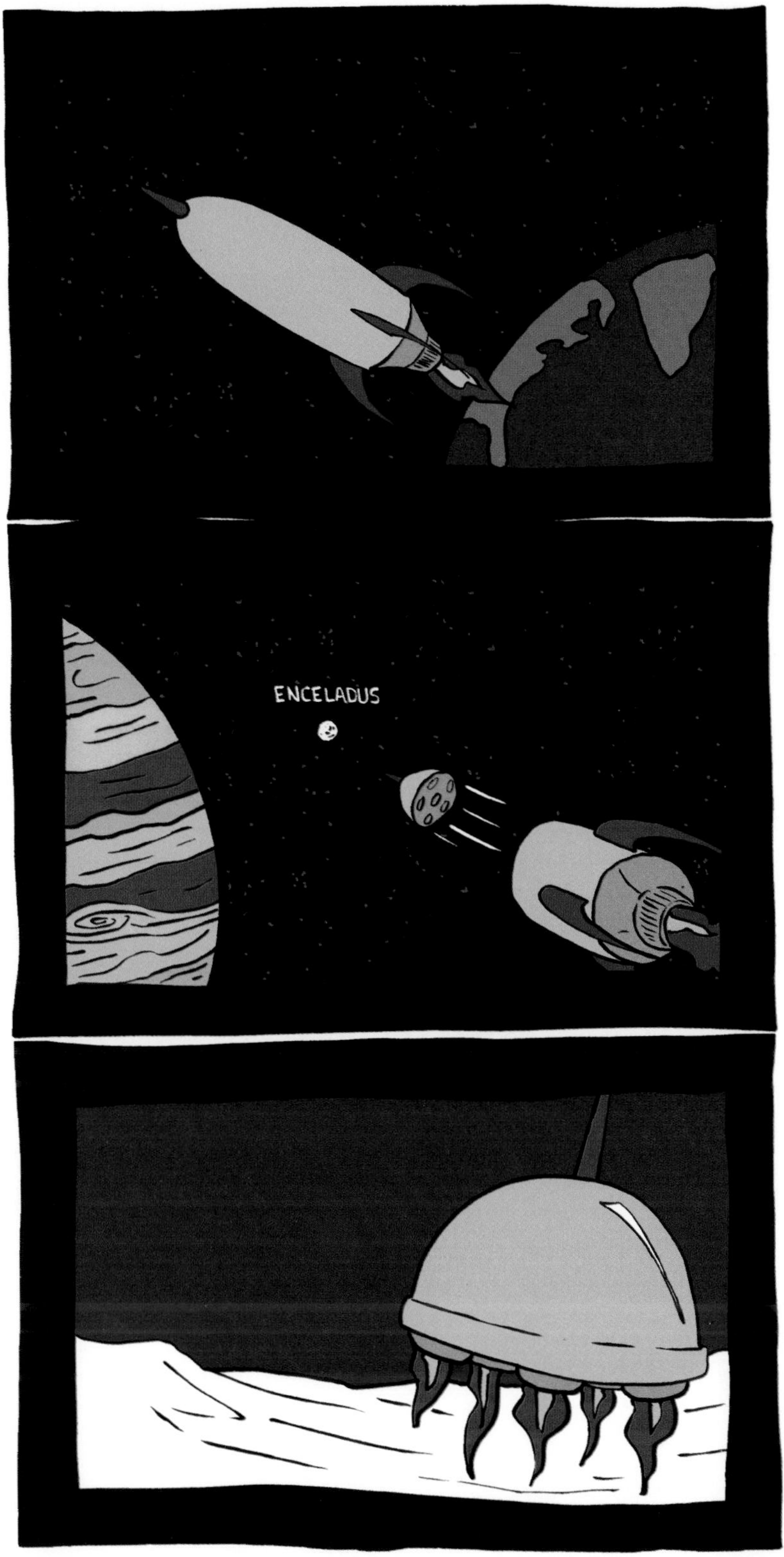
ENCELADUS

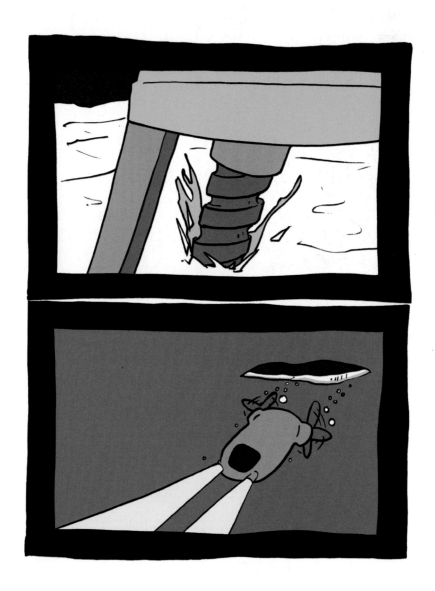

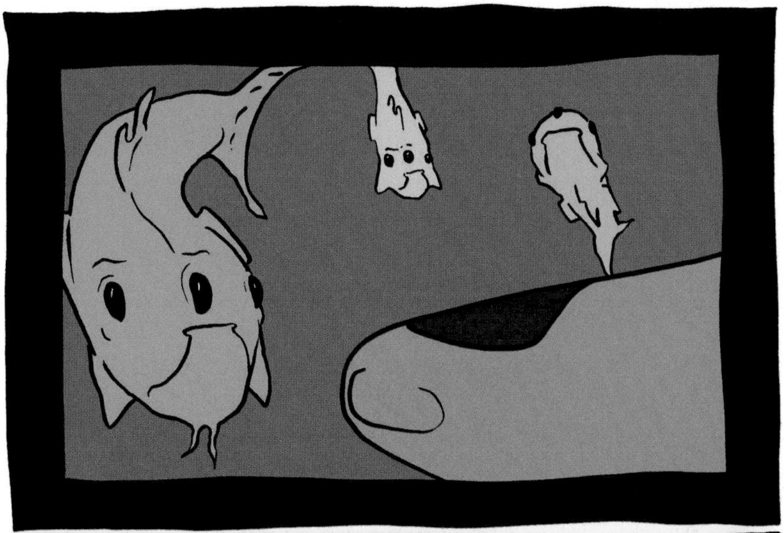

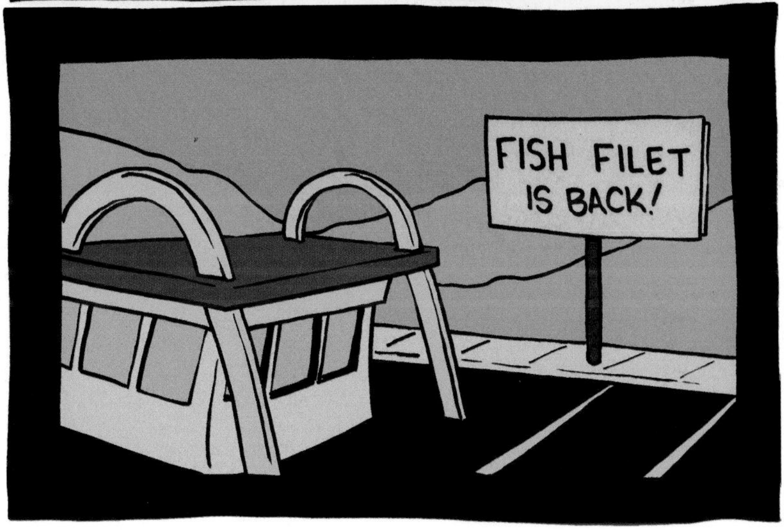
FISH FILET
IS BACK!

END!

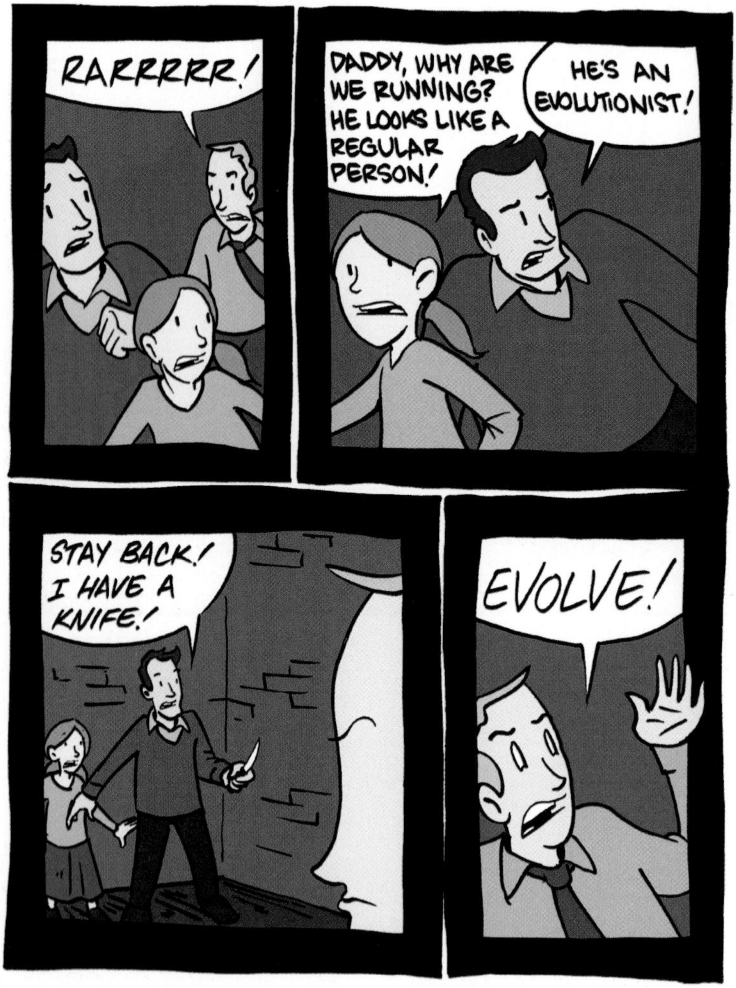
RARRRRR!
DADDY, WHY ARE WE RUNNING? HE LOOKS LIKE A REGULAR PERSON!
HE'S AN EVOLUTIONIST!
STAY BACK! I HAVE A KNIFE!
EVOLVE!

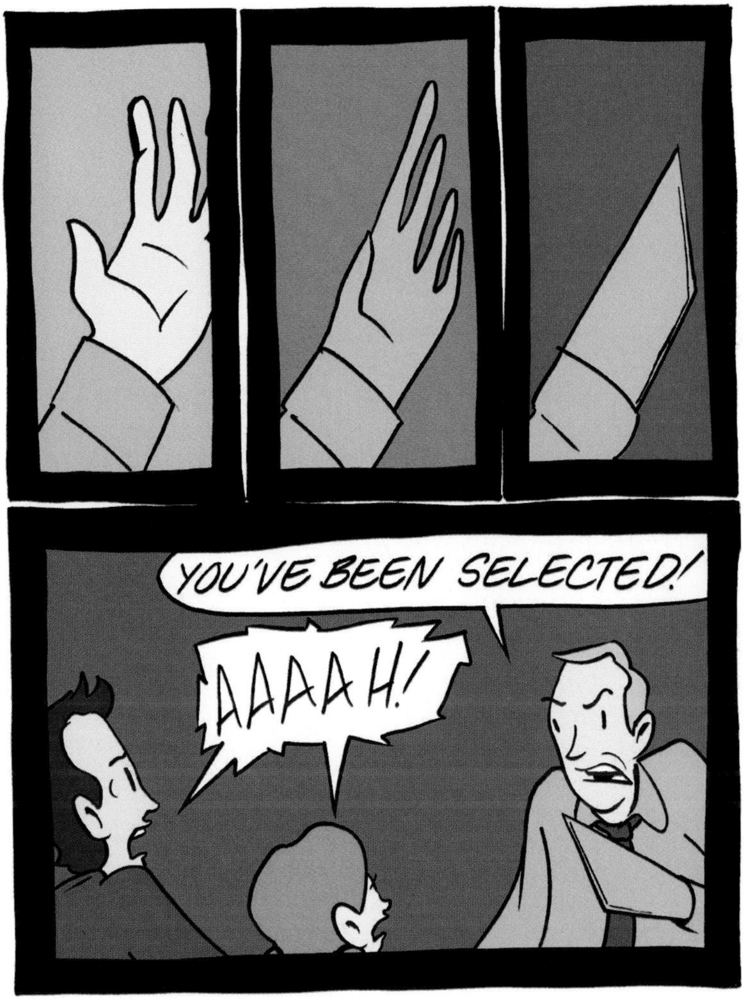
YOU'VE BEEN SELECTED!
AAAAH!

Ironically, only biologists truly appreciate creationist horror films.

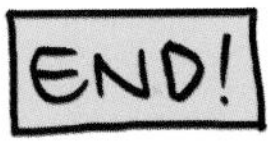
END!

YOU DON'T WANT SCIENTIFIC PARENTS!

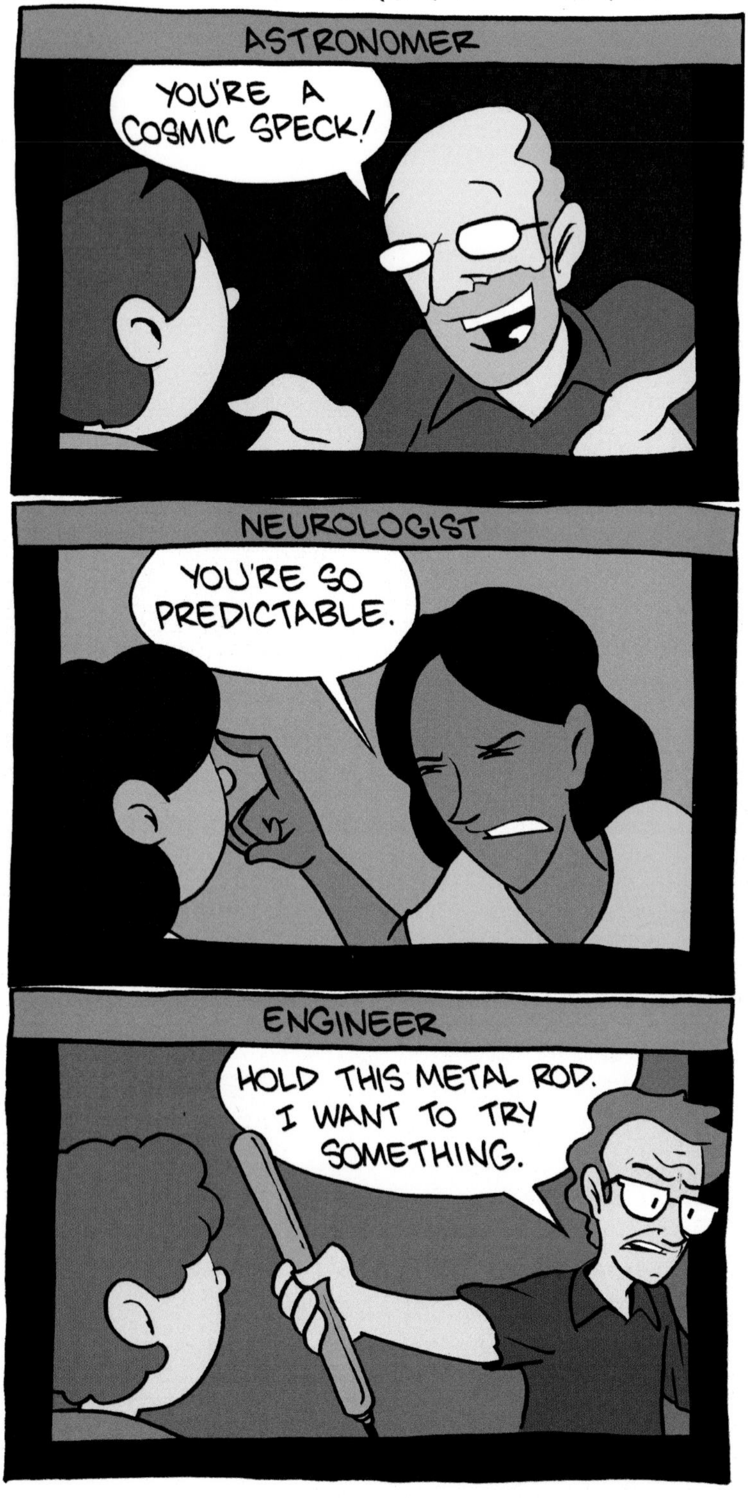
ASTRONOMER
YOU'RE A COSMIC SPECK!
NEUROLOGIST
YOU'RE SO PREDICTABLE.
ENGINEER
HOLD THIS METAL ROD. I WANT TO TRY SOMETHING.

CALCULATIONS PER SECOND PER $1,000
TIME
Present
SO, PROCESSING POWER GROWS EXPONENTIALLY. EVENTUALLY, WE REACH A TECHNOLOGICAL SINGULARITY, WHERE COMPUTING POWER BECOMES NEARLY INFINITE. THEN, WE'LL BE ABLE TO MODIFY AND IMPROVE OUR BRAINS FAR BEYOND CURRENT HUMAN INTELLIGENCE.
SO... AFTER ALL THE WORK TO MAKE THIS HAPPEN, THE ENGINEERS WHO BUILT ALL THE MACHINES WILL BE NO BETTER THAN THE PEOPLE WHO LOAFED AROUND, WATCHING TV ALL DAY?

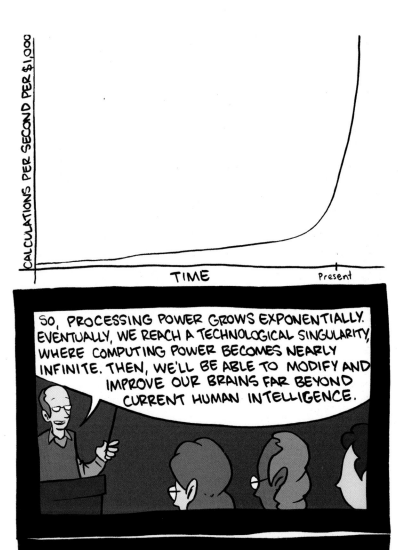

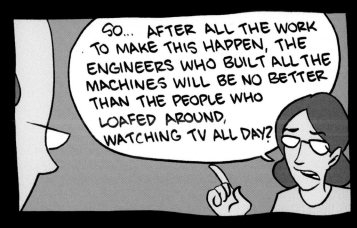

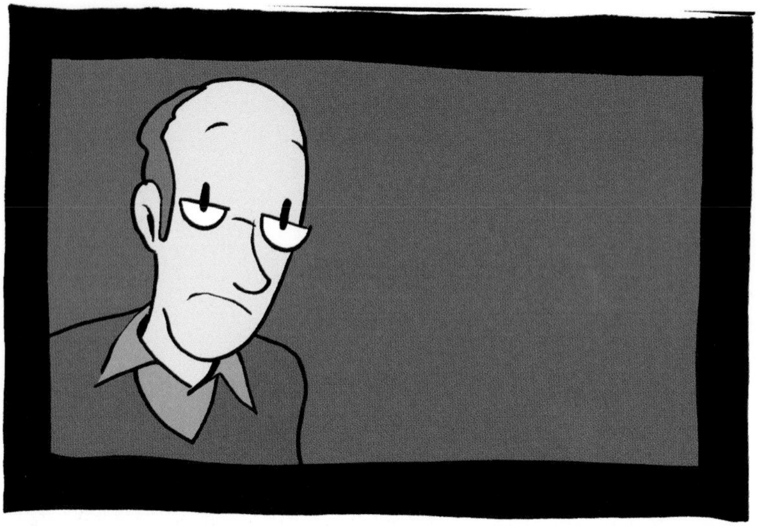

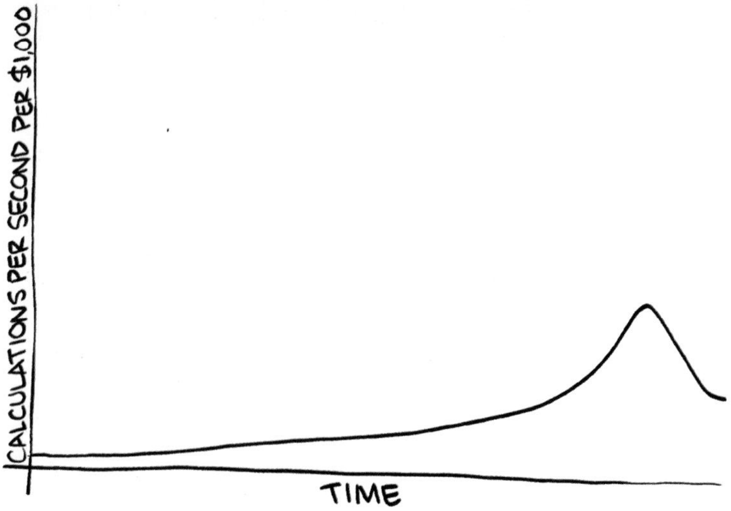
CALCULATIONS PER SECOND PER $1,000
TIME

END!

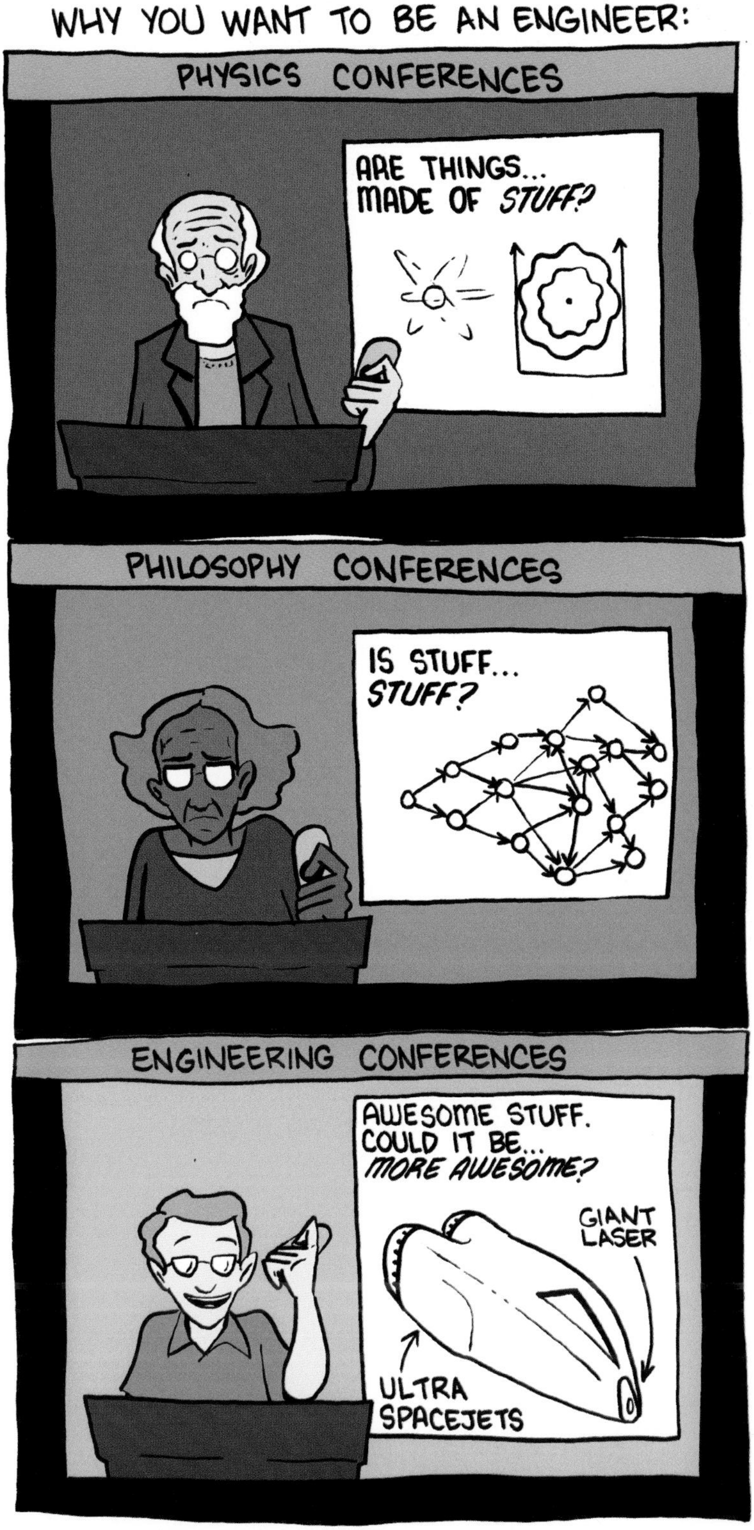
WHY YOU WANT TO BE AN ENGINEER:
PHYSICS CONFERENCES
ARE THINGS... MADE OF STUFF?
PHILOSOPHY CONFERENCES
IS STUFF... STUFF?
ENGINEERING CONFERENCES
AWESOME STUFF. COULD IT BE... MORE AWESOME?
GIANT LASER
ULTRA SPACEJETS

BELIEF IN A HIGHER POWER
"HOW CAN THAT BE?"
"OH, THAT'S HOW"
SCIENTIFIC EDUCATION

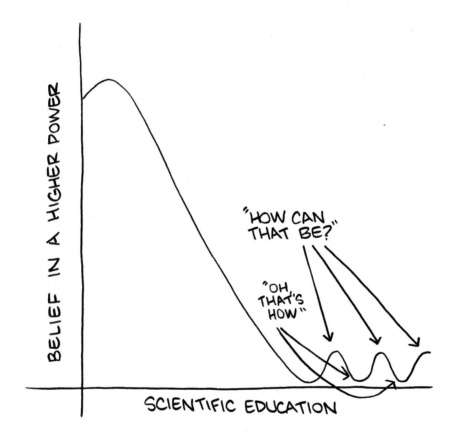

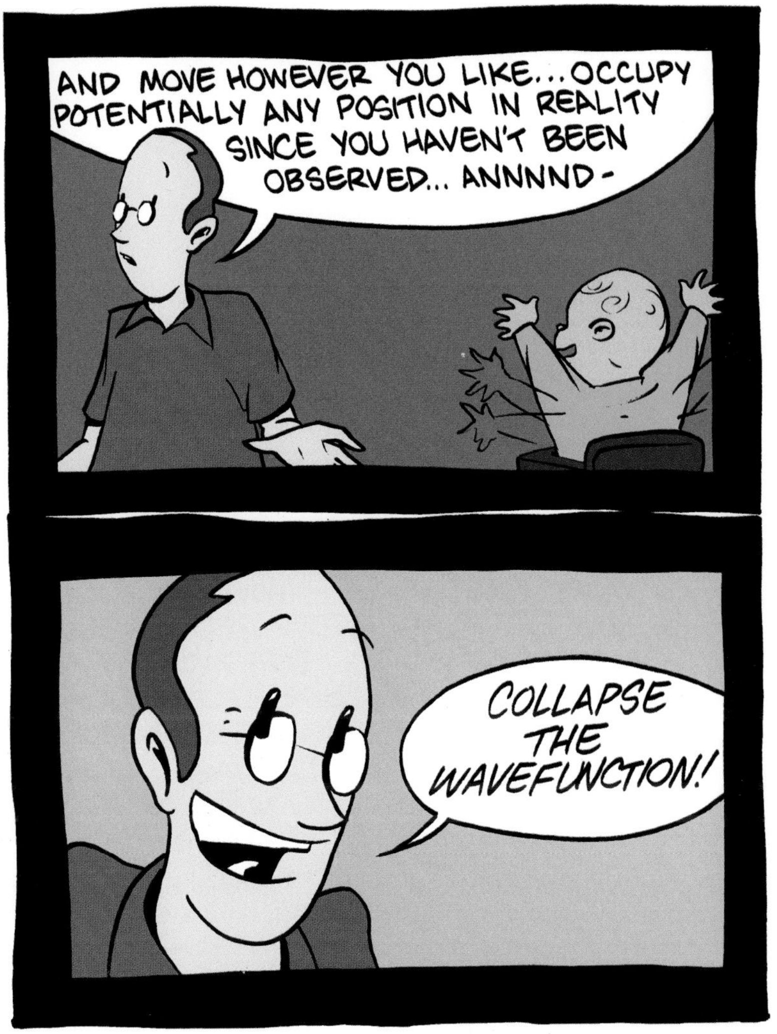
AND MOVE HOWEVER YOU LIKE...OCCUPY POTENTIALLY ANY POSITION IN REALITY SINCE YOU HAVEN'T BEEN OBSERVED... ANNNND-
COLLAPSE THE WAVEFUNCTION!

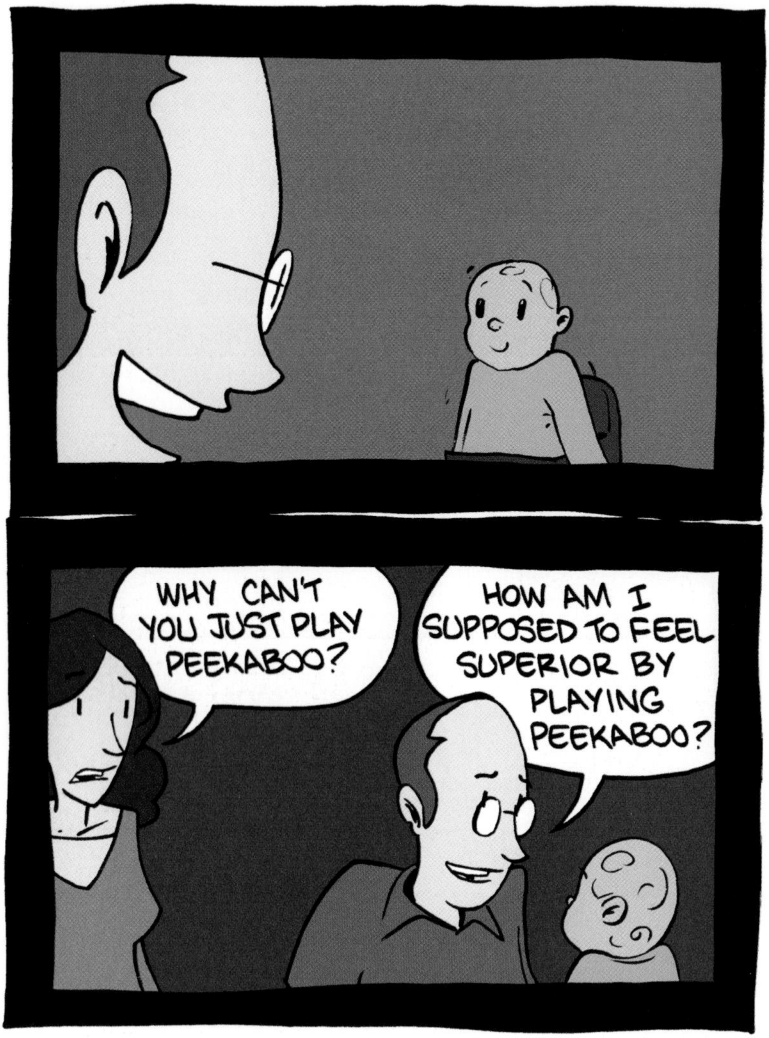
WHY CAN'T YOU JUST PLAY PEEKABOO?
HOW AM I SUPPOSED TO FEEL SUPERIOR BY PLAYING PEEKABOO?

END!

TWO BAD OPTIONS:

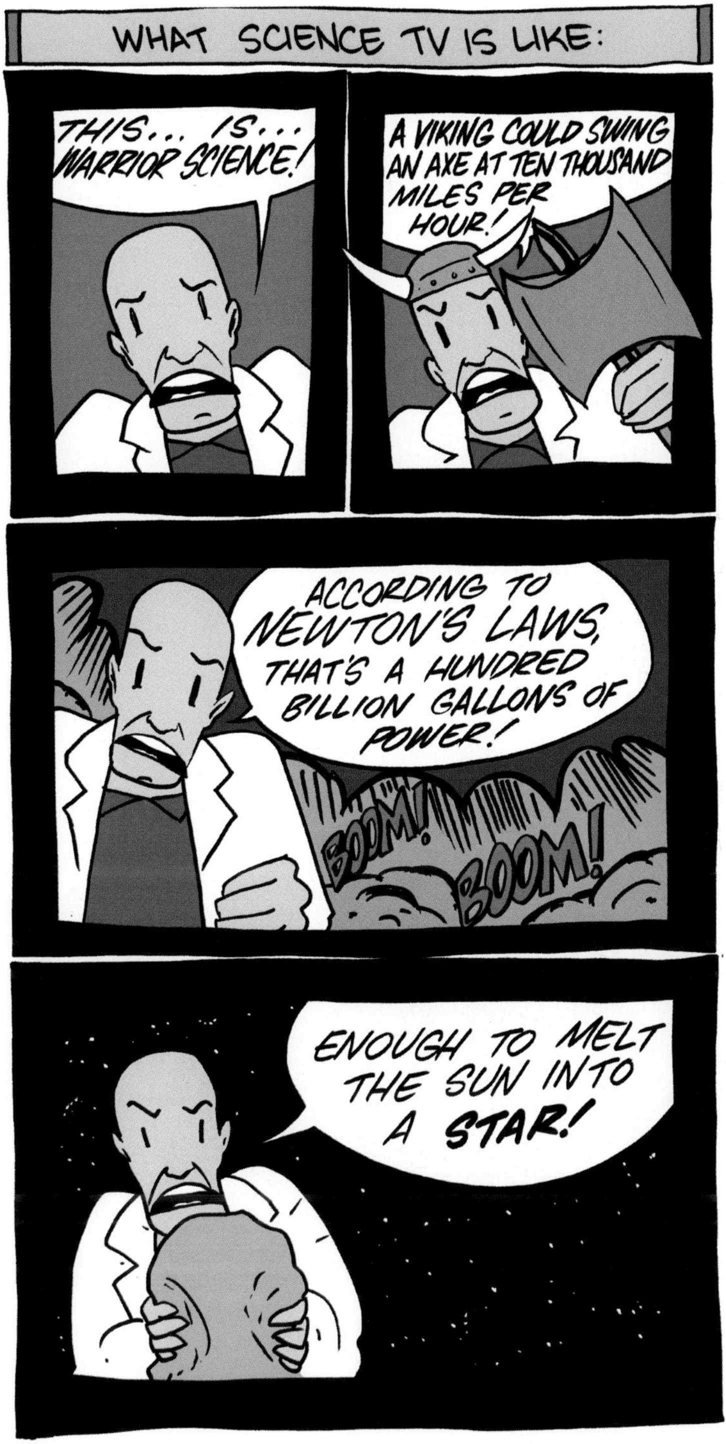
WHAT SCIENCE TV IS LIKE:
THIS... IS... WARRIOR SCIENCE!
A VIKING COULD SWING AN AXE AT TEN THOUSAND MILES PER HOUR!
ACCORDING TO NEWTON'S LAWS, THAT'S A HUNDRED BILLION GALLONS OF POWER!
BOOM!
BOOM!
ENOUGH TO MELT THE SUN INTO A STAR!

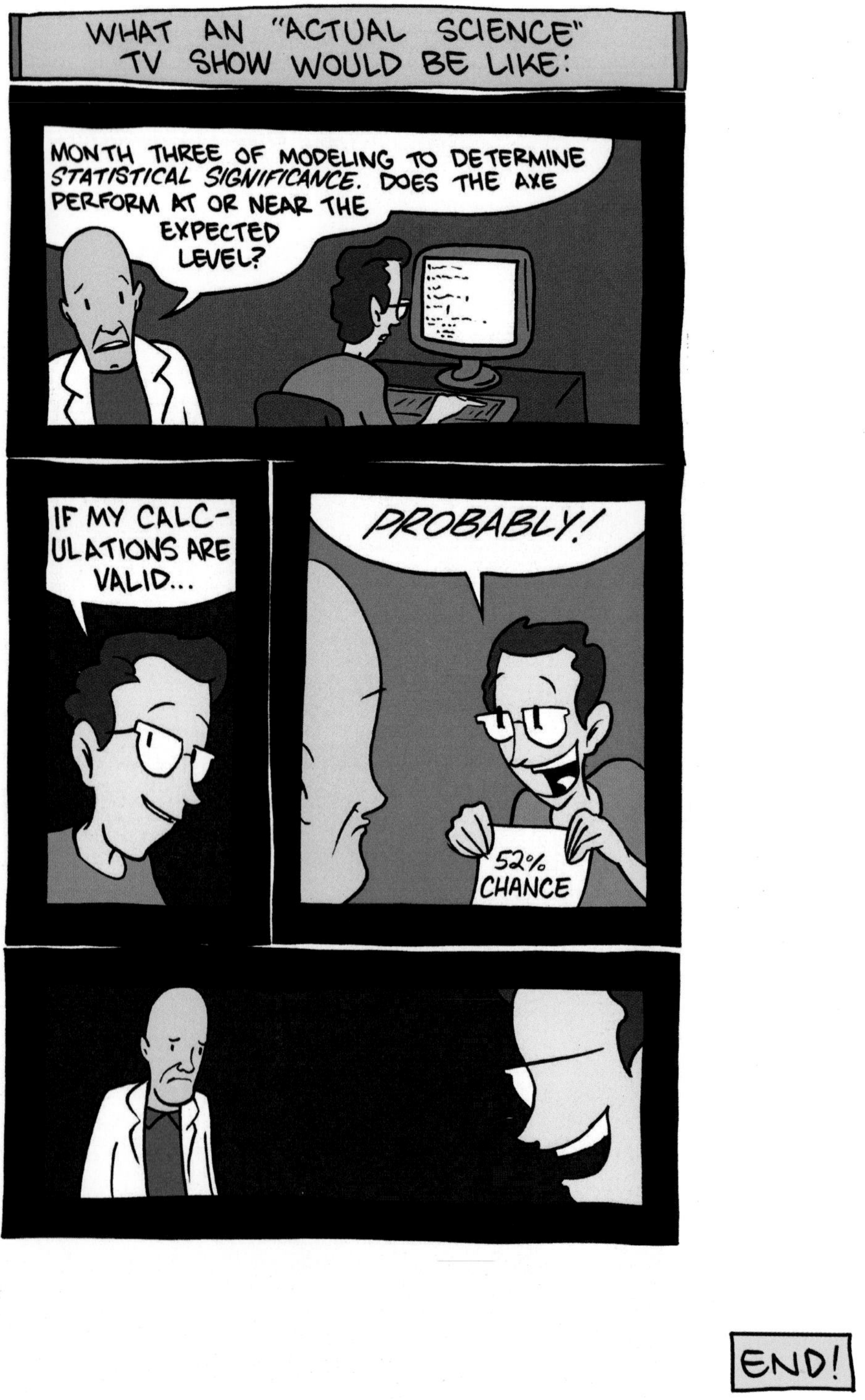
WHAT AN "ACTUAL SCIENCE" TV SHOW WOULD BE LIKE:
MONTH THREE OF MODELING TO DETERMINE *STATISTICAL SIGNIFICANCE*. DOES THE AXE PERFORM AT OR NEAR THE EXPECTED LEVEL?
IF MY CALC-ULATIONS ARE VALID...
PROBABLY!
52% CHANCE

END!

THE BIOLOGIST'S DILEMMA:

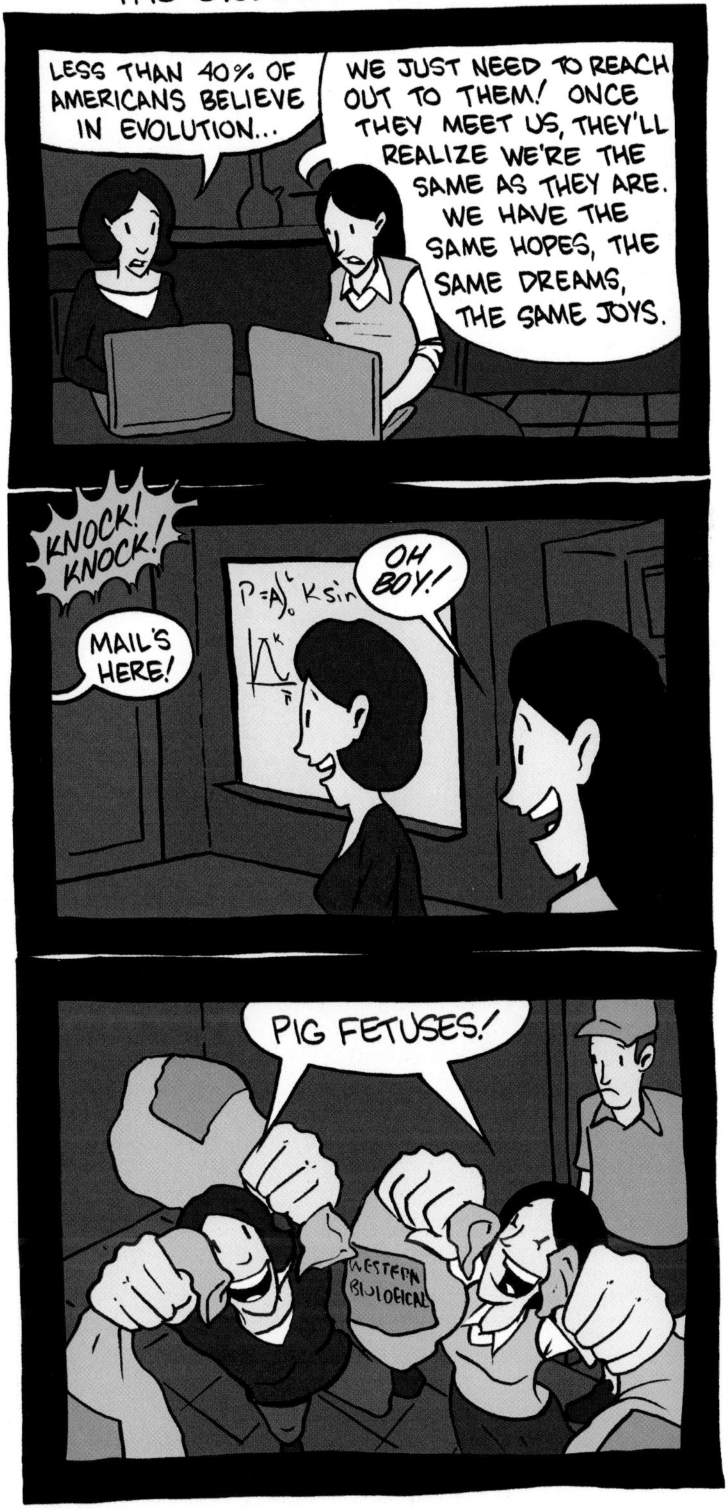
LESS THAN 40% OF AMERICANS BELIEVE IN EVOLUTION...
WE JUST NEED TO REACH OUT TO THEM! ONCE THEY MEET US, THEY'LL REALIZE WE'RE THE SAME AS THEY ARE. WE HAVE THE SAME HOPES, THE SAME DREAMS, THE SAME JOYS.
KNOCK! KNOCK!
MAIL'S HERE!
OH BOY!
PIG FETUSES!
WESTERN BIOLOGICAL

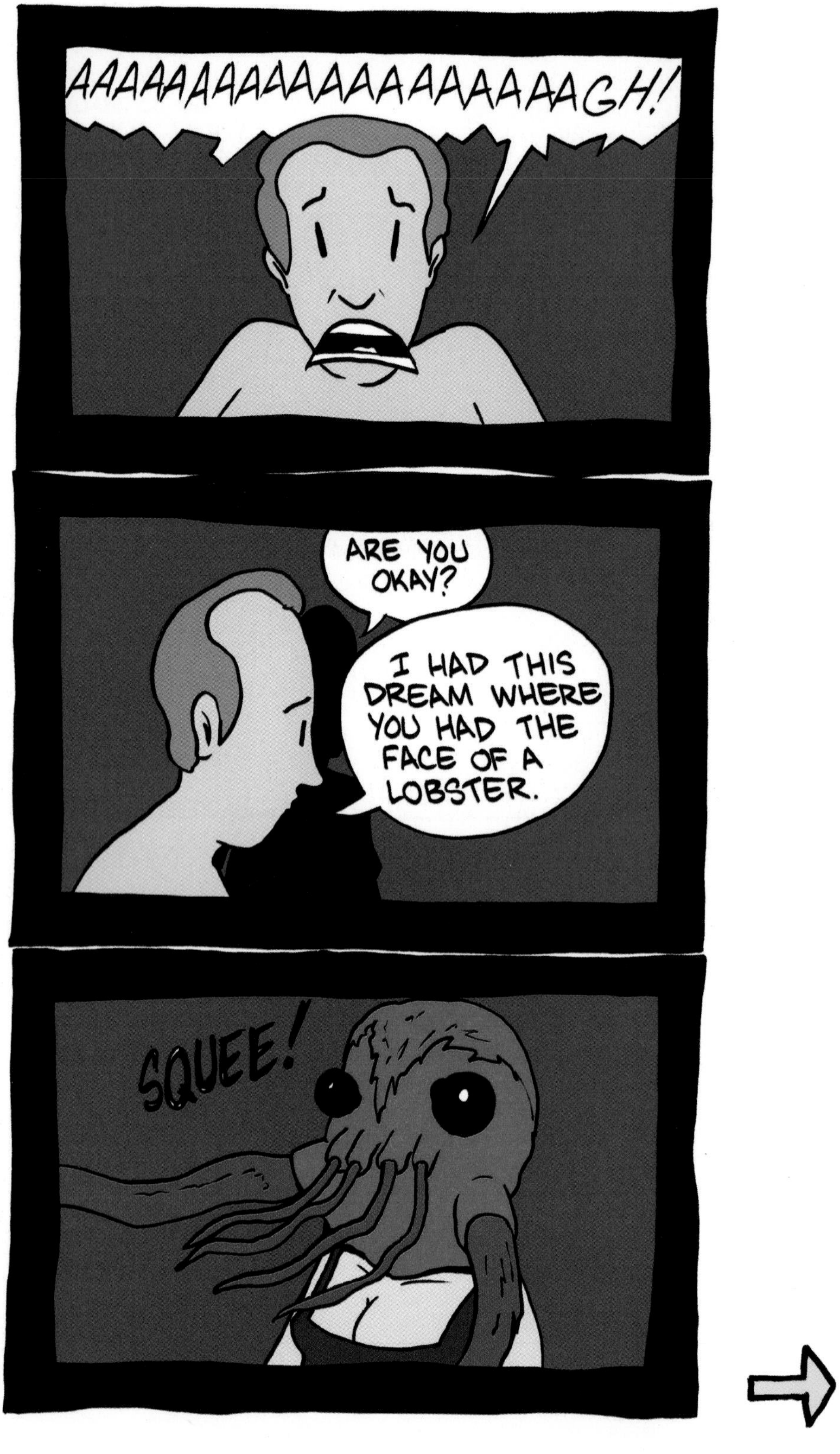
AAAAAAAAAAAAAAAAAAAAGH!
ARE YOU OKAY?
I HAD THIS DREAM WHERE YOU HAD THE FACE OF A LOBSTER.
SQUEE!

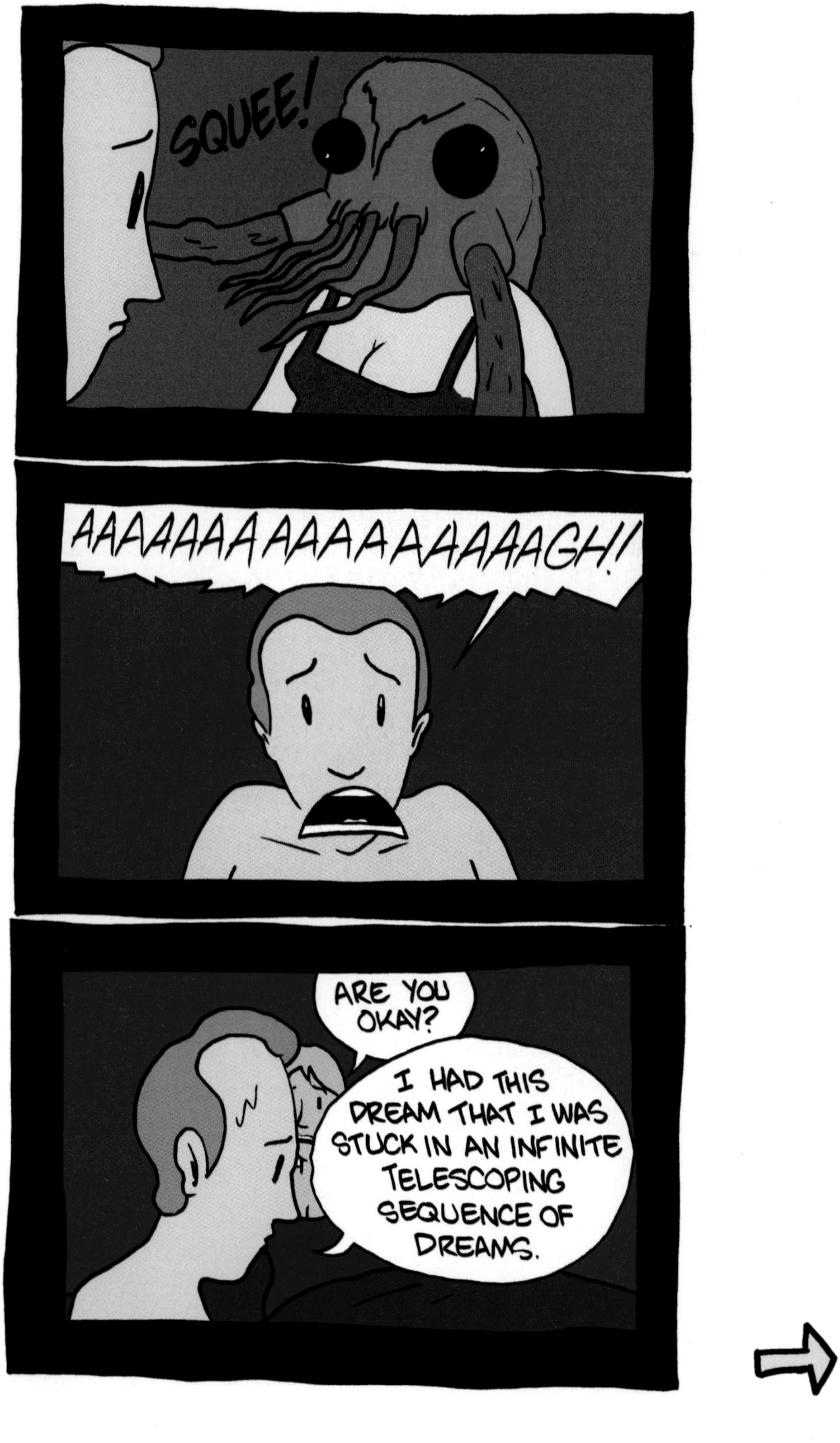
SQUEE!
AAAAAAAAAAAAAAAAAAGH!
ARE YOU OKAY?
I HAD THIS DREAM THAT I WAS STUCK IN AN INFINITE TELESCOPING SEQUENCE OF DREAMS.

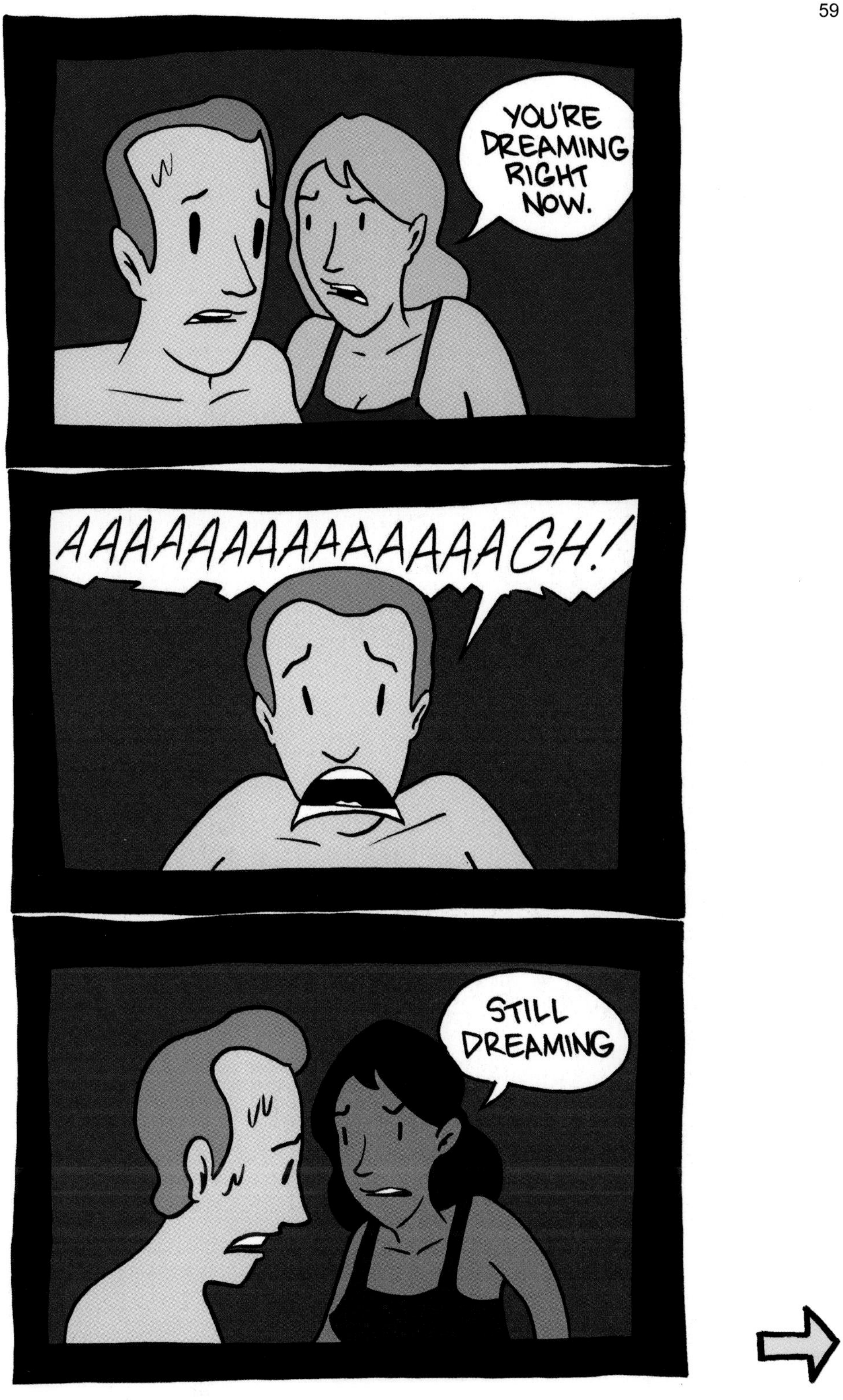
YOU'RE DREAMING RIGHT NOW.
AAAAAAAAAAAAAAAGH!
STILL DREAMING

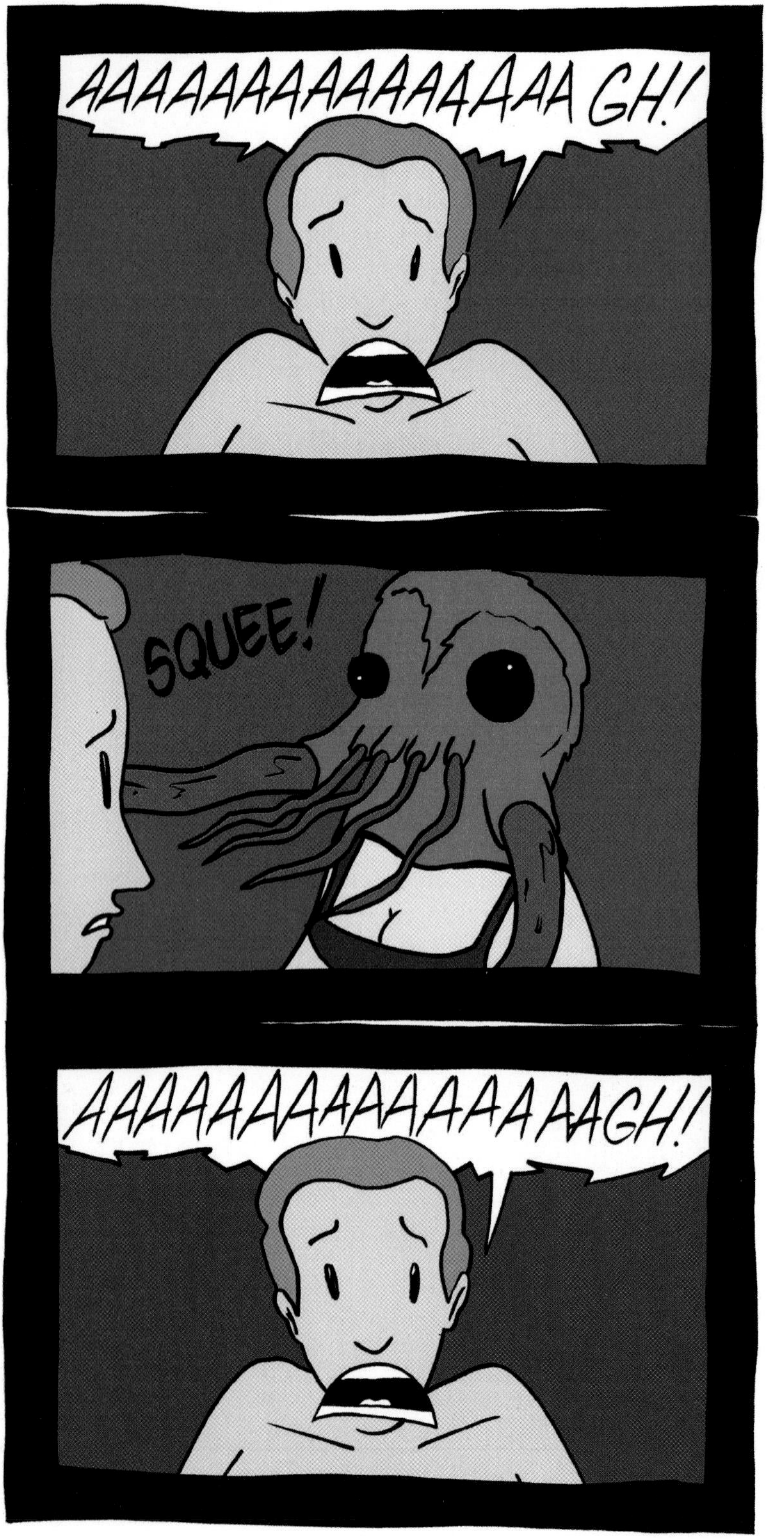
AAAAAAAAAAAAAAA GH!
SQUEE!
AAAAAAAAAAAAAAAAGH!

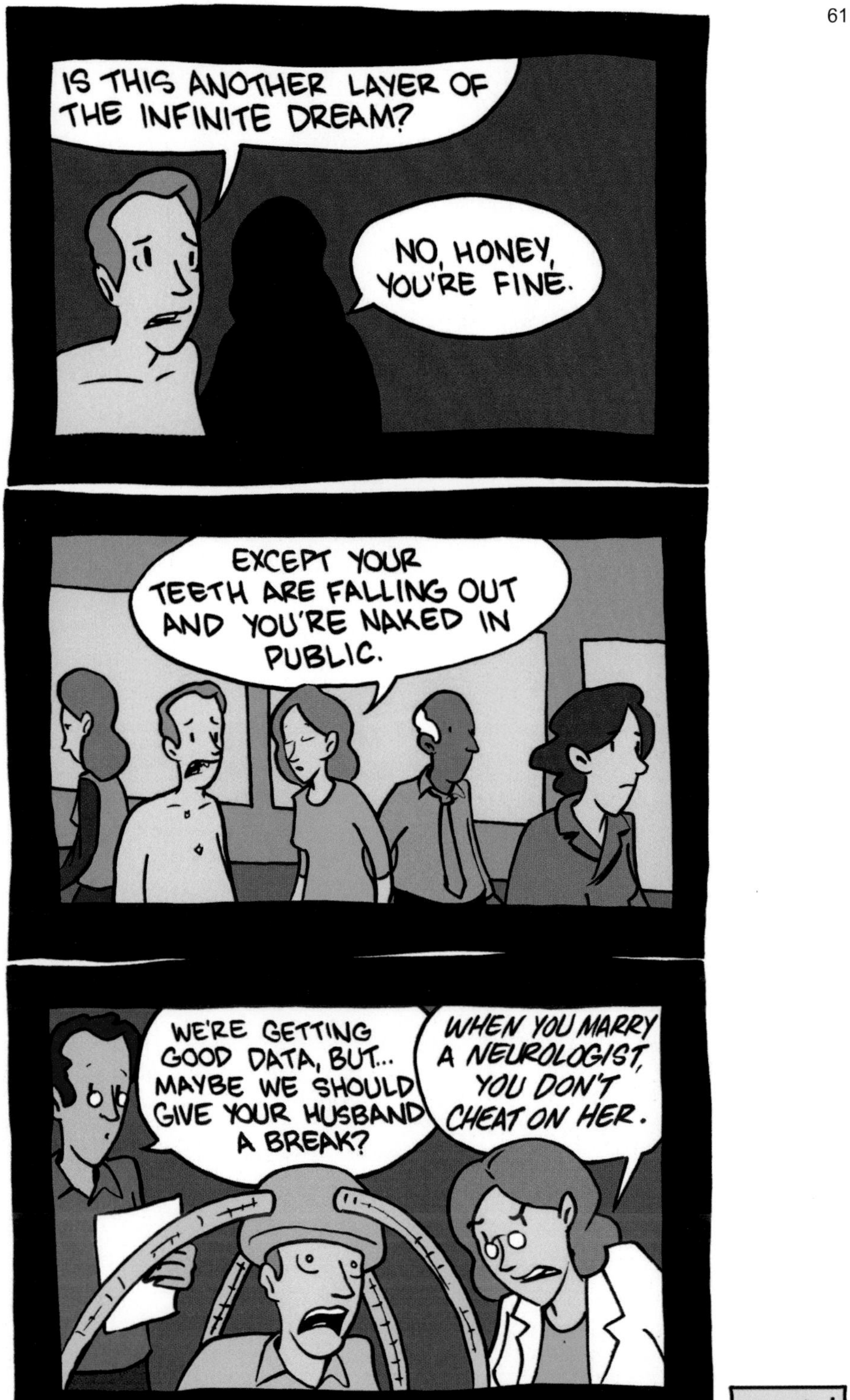
IS THIS ANOTHER LAYER OF THE INFINITE DREAM?
NO, HONEY, YOU'RE FINE.
EXCEPT YOUR TEETH ARE FALLING OUT AND YOU'RE NAKED IN PUBLIC.
WE'RE GETTING GOOD DATA, BUT... MAYBE WE SHOULD GIVE YOUR HUSBAND A BREAK?
WHEN YOU MARRY A NEUROLOGIST, YOU DON'T CHEAT ON HER.
END!

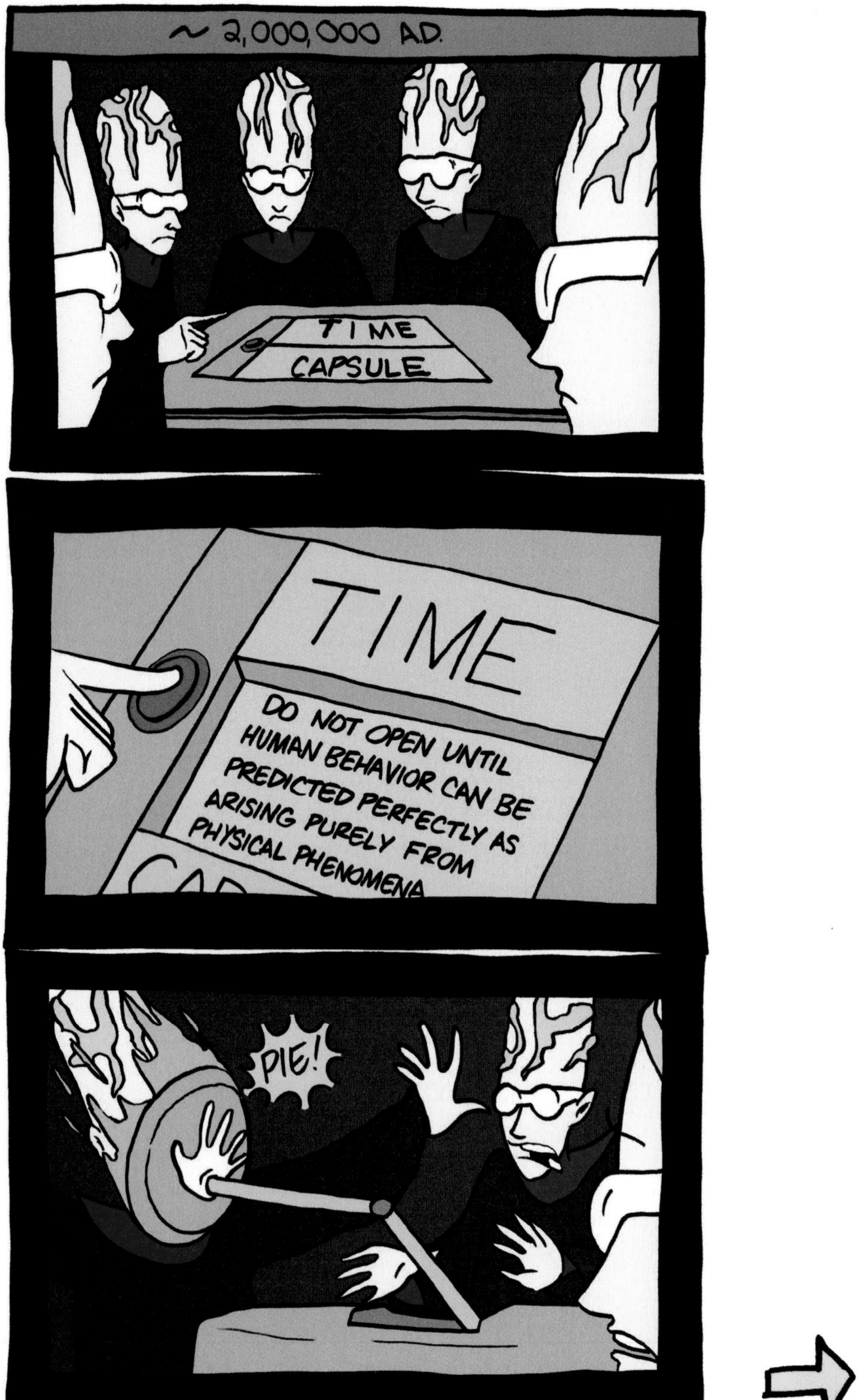
~ 2,000,000 A.D.
TIME
CAPSULE
TIME
DO NOT OPEN UNTIL HUMAN BEHAVIOR CAN BE PREDICTED PERFECTLY AS ARISING PURELY FROM PHYSICAL PHENOMENA
PIE!

Didn't see that coming, did you, bitches?!
Sincerely, the 21st century

~ 2,000 A.D.
HOW DO YOU DEAL WITH THE FEAR THAT THE RISE OF TECHNOLOGY MAY MEAN THE END OF HUMANITY AS WE KNOW IT?
OH... THIS AND THAT.

END!

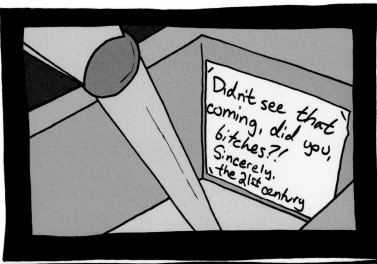

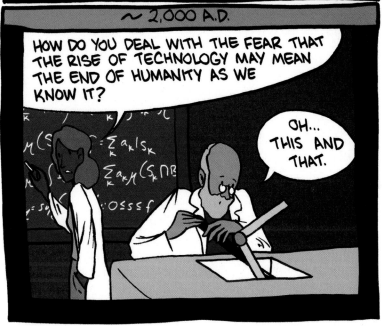

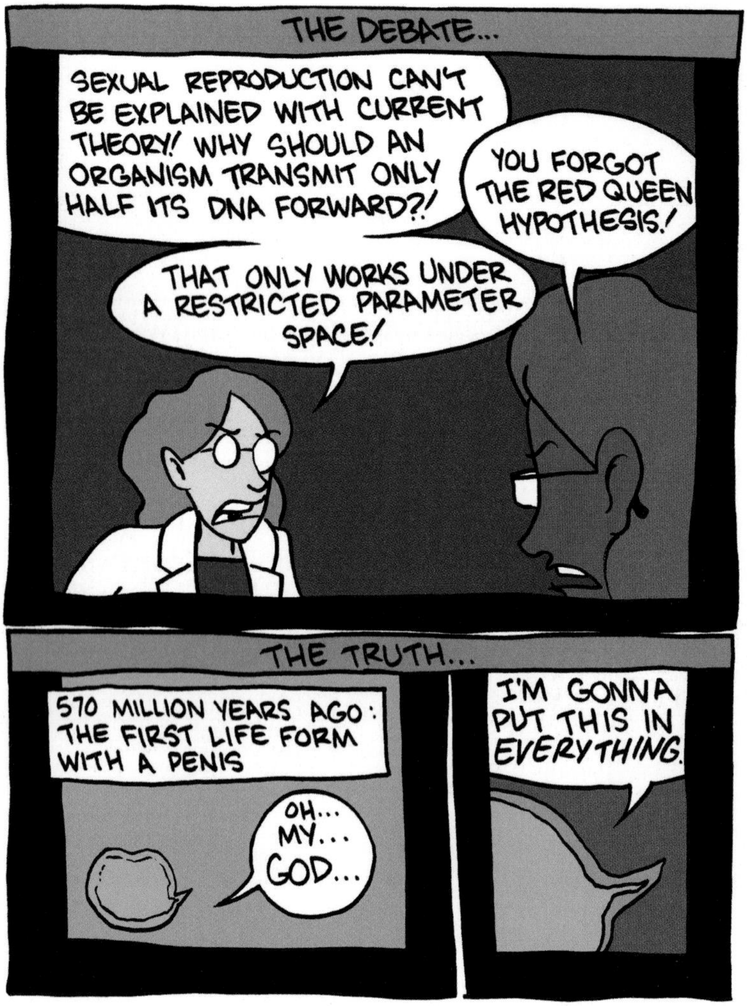
THE DEBATE...
SEXUAL REPRODUCTION CAN'T BE EXPLAINED WITH CURRENT THEORY! WHY SHOULD AN ORGANISM TRANSMIT ONLY HALF ITS DNA FORWARD?!
YOU FORGOT THE RED QUEEN HYPOTHESIS!
THAT ONLY WORKS UNDER A RESTRICTED PARAMETER SPACE!
THE TRUTH...
570 MILLION YEARS AGO: THE FIRST LIFE FORM WITH A PENIS
OH... MY... GOD...
I'M GONNA PUT THIS IN *EVERYTHING*.

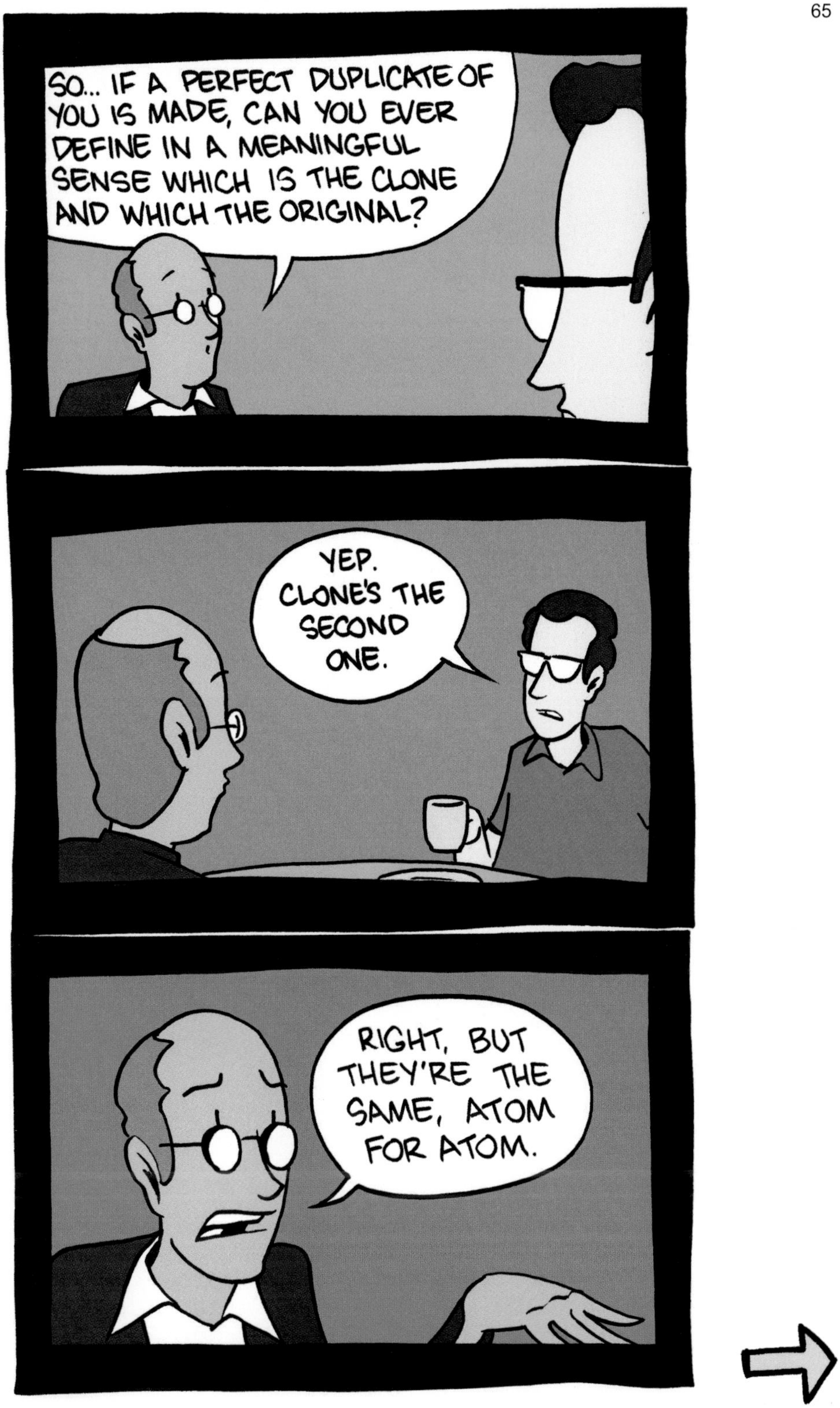
SO... IF A PERFECT DUPLICATE OF YOU IS MADE, CAN YOU EVER DEFINE IN A MEANINGFUL SENSE WHICH IS THE CLONE AND WHICH THE ORIGINAL?
YEP. CLONE'S THE SECOND ONE.
RIGHT, BUT THEY'RE THE SAME, ATOM FOR ATOM.

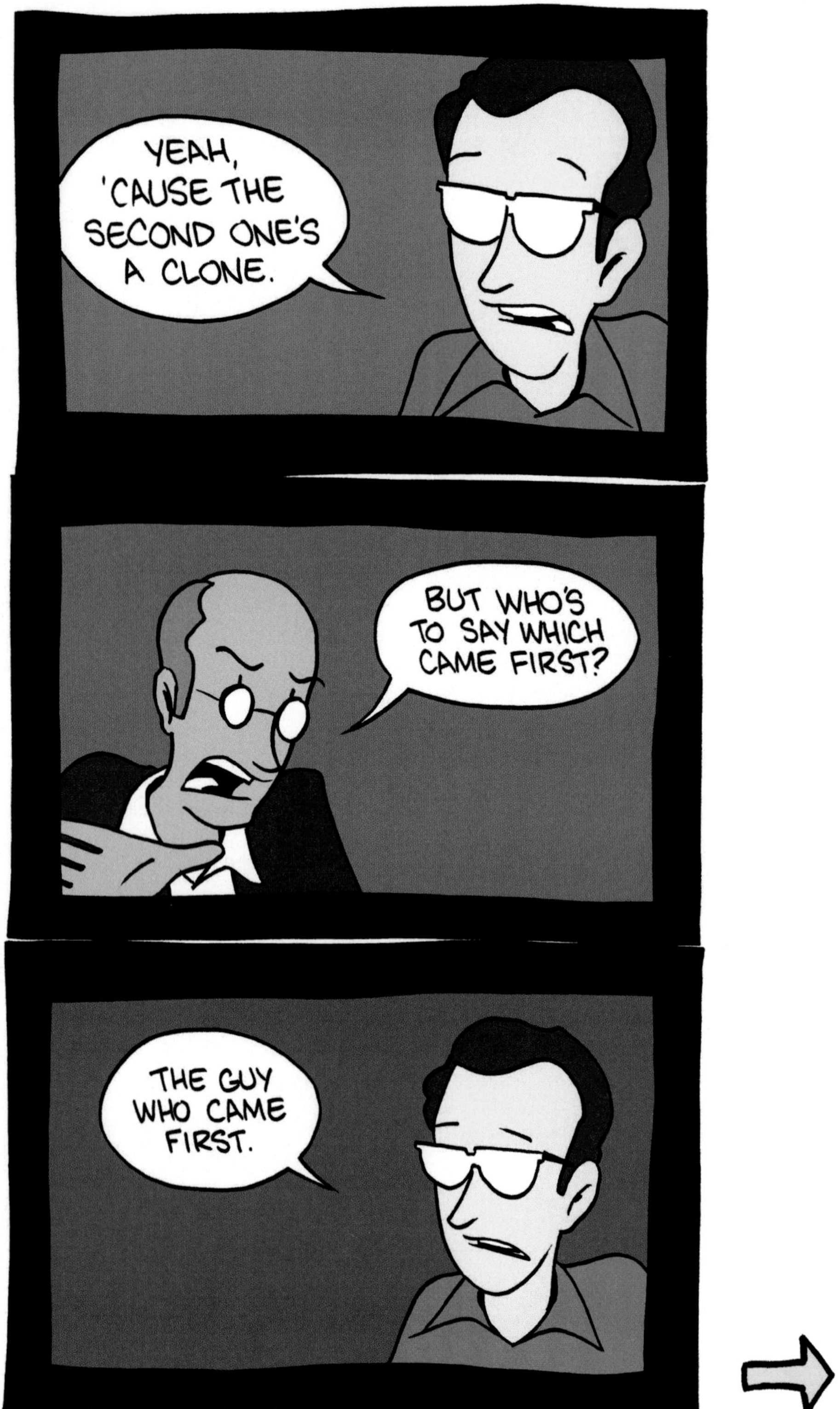
YEAH, 'CAUSE THE SECOND ONE'S A CLONE.
BUT WHO'S TO SAY WHICH CAME FIRST?
THE GUY WHO CAME FIRST.

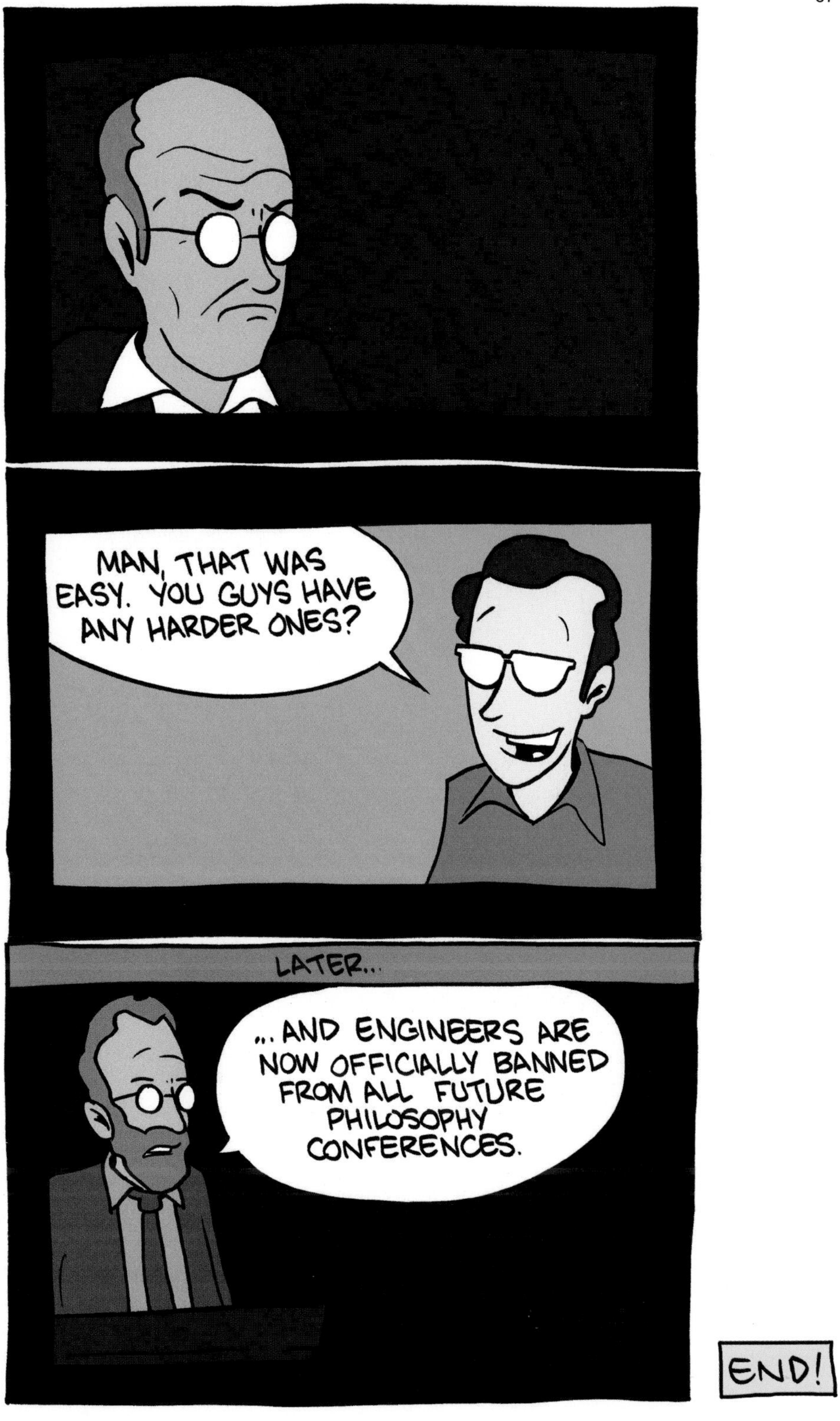
MAN, THAT WAS EASY. YOU GUYS HAVE ANY HARDER ONES?
LATER...
...AND ENGINEERS ARE NOW OFFICIALLY BANNED FROM ALL FUTURE PHILOSOPHY CONFERENCES.
END!

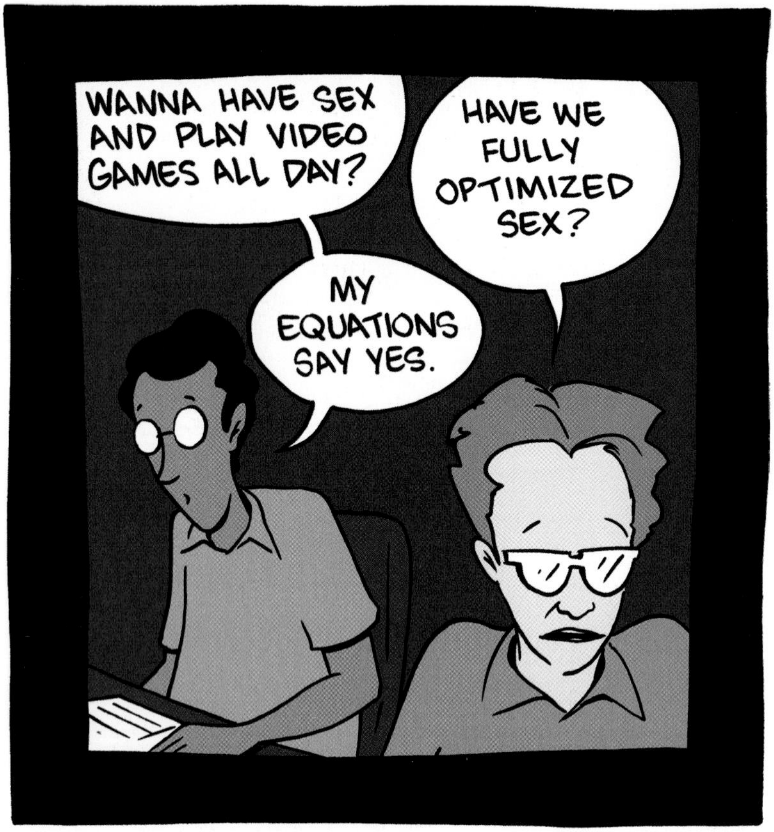
WANNA HAVE SEX AND PLAY VIDEO GAMES ALL DAY?
HAVE WE FULLY OPTIMIZED SEX?
MY EQUATIONS SAY YES.

Fact: There are gay engineers.
Fact: Their lives are better than yours.

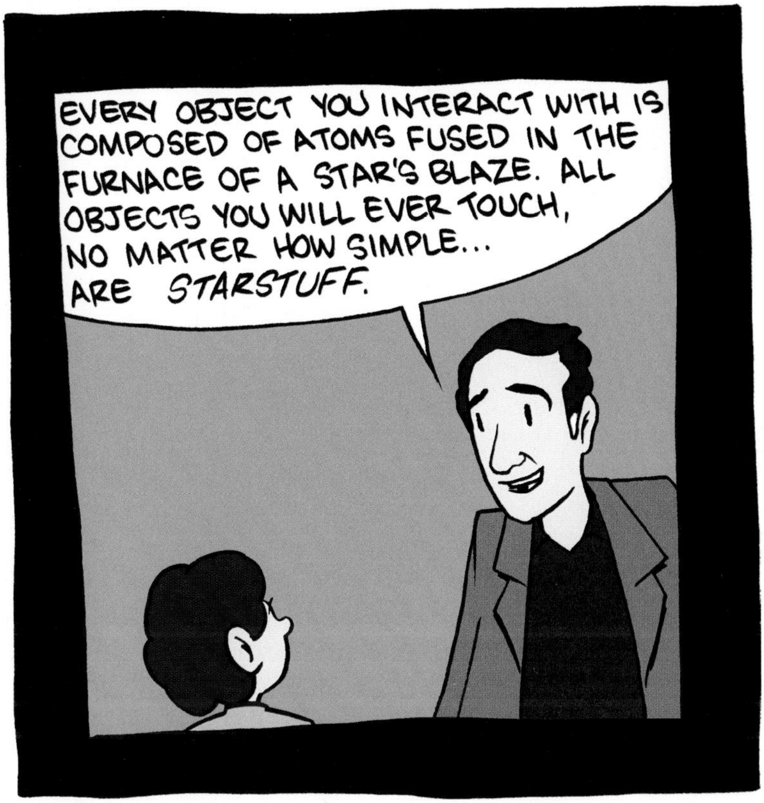
EVERY OBJECT YOU INTERACT WITH IS COMPOSED OF ATOMS FUSED IN THE FURNACE OF A STAR'S BLAZE. ALL OBJECTS YOU WILL EVER TOUCH, NO MATTER HOW SIMPLE... ARE *STARSTUFF*.

Carl Sagan convinces his son to clean the cat shit.

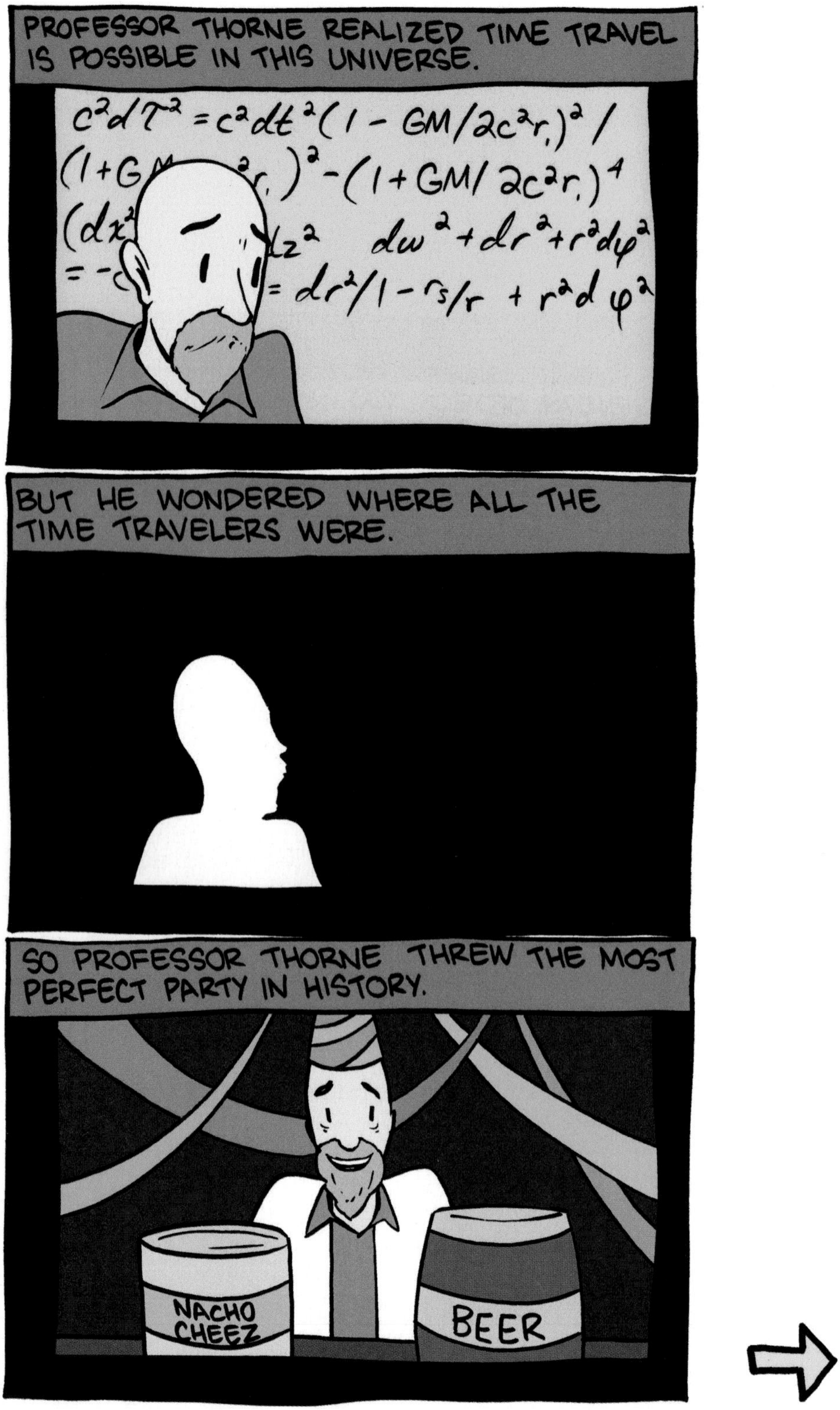

PROFESSOR THORNE REALIZED TIME TRAVEL IS POSSIBLE IN THIS UNIVERSE.

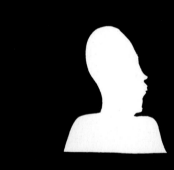

BUT HE WONDERED WHERE ALL THE TIME TRAVELERS WERE.

SO PROFESSOR THORNE THREW THE MOST PERFECT PARTY IN HISTORY.

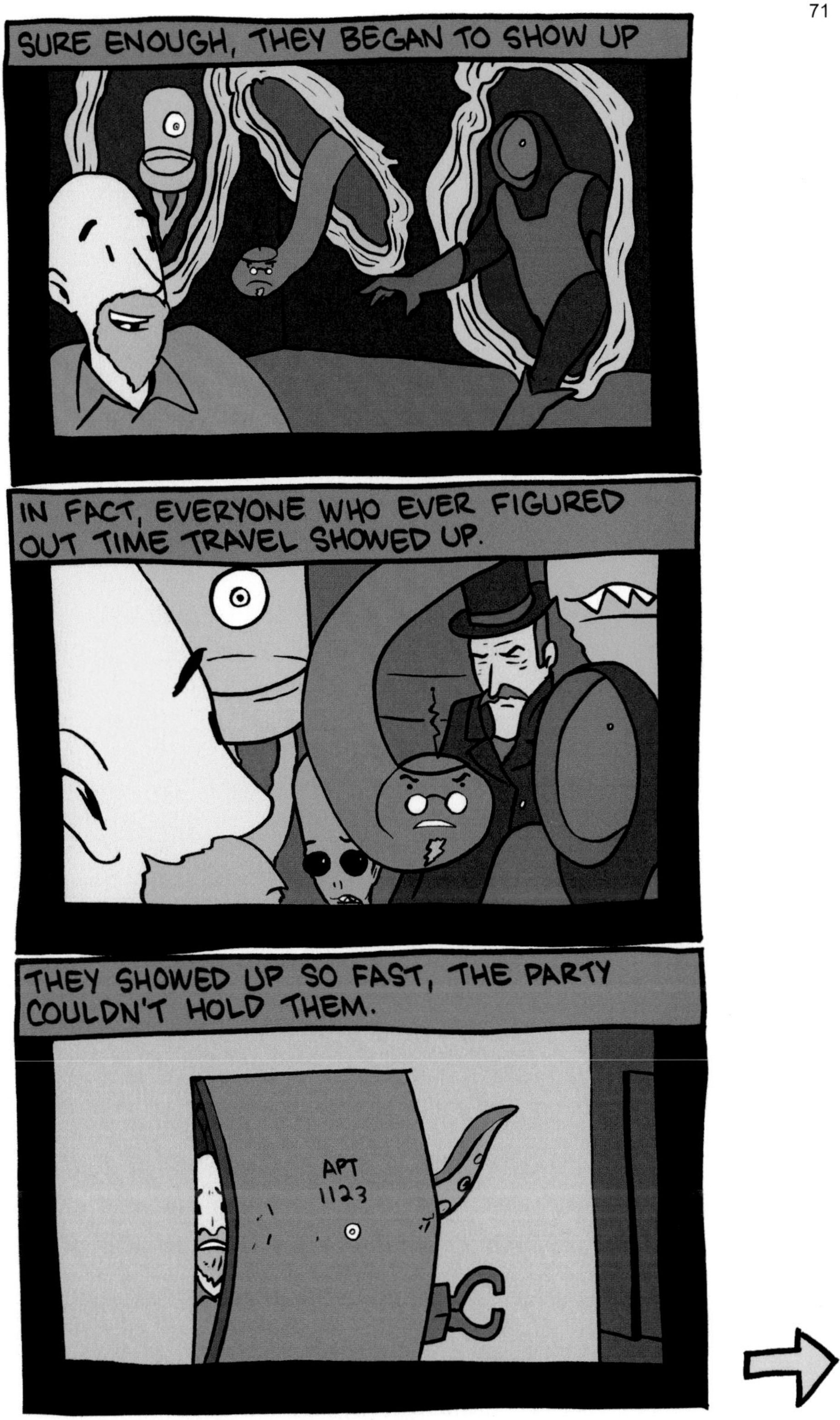
SURE ENOUGH, THEY BEGAN TO SHOW UP
IN FACT, EVERYONE WHO EVER FIGURED OUT TIME TRAVEL SHOWED UP.
THEY SHOWED UP SO FAST, THE PARTY COULDN'T HOLD THEM.
APT 1123

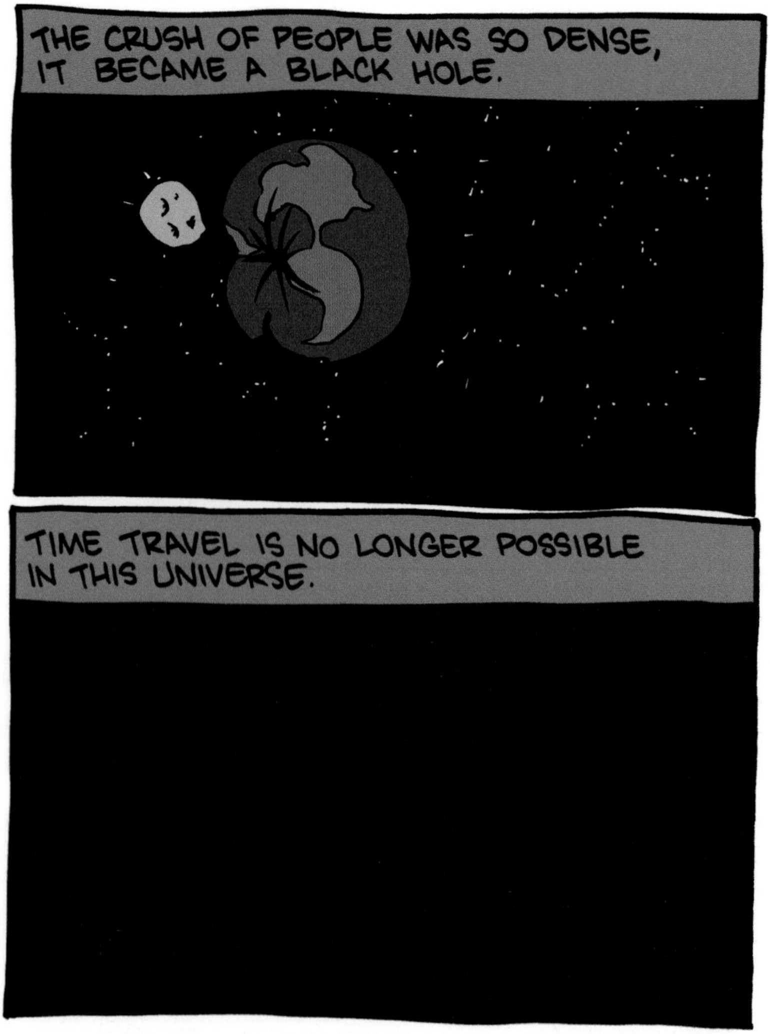
THE CRUSH OF PEOPLE WAS SO DENSE, IT BECAME A BLACK HOLE.
TIME TRAVEL IS NO LONGER POSSIBLE IN THIS UNIVERSE.

END!

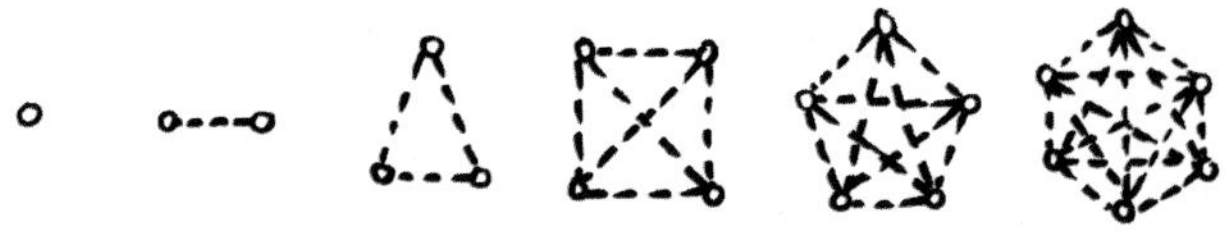

n =	1	2	3	4	5	6
d =	0	1	3	6	10	15

n = number of women in a group

d = difficulty of approaching one

$$d = n\left(\frac{n-1}{2}\right)$$

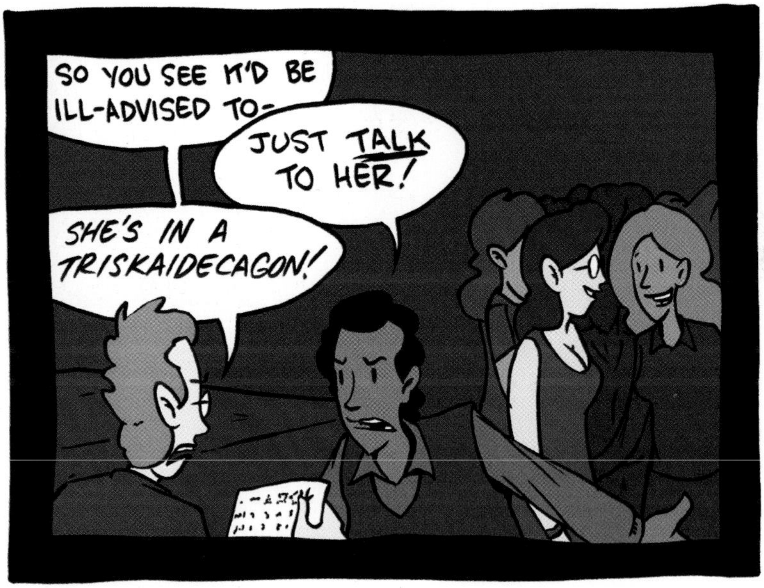
SO YOU SEE IT'D BE ILL-ADVISED TO–
JUST TALK TO HER!
SHE'S IN A TRISKAIDECAGON!

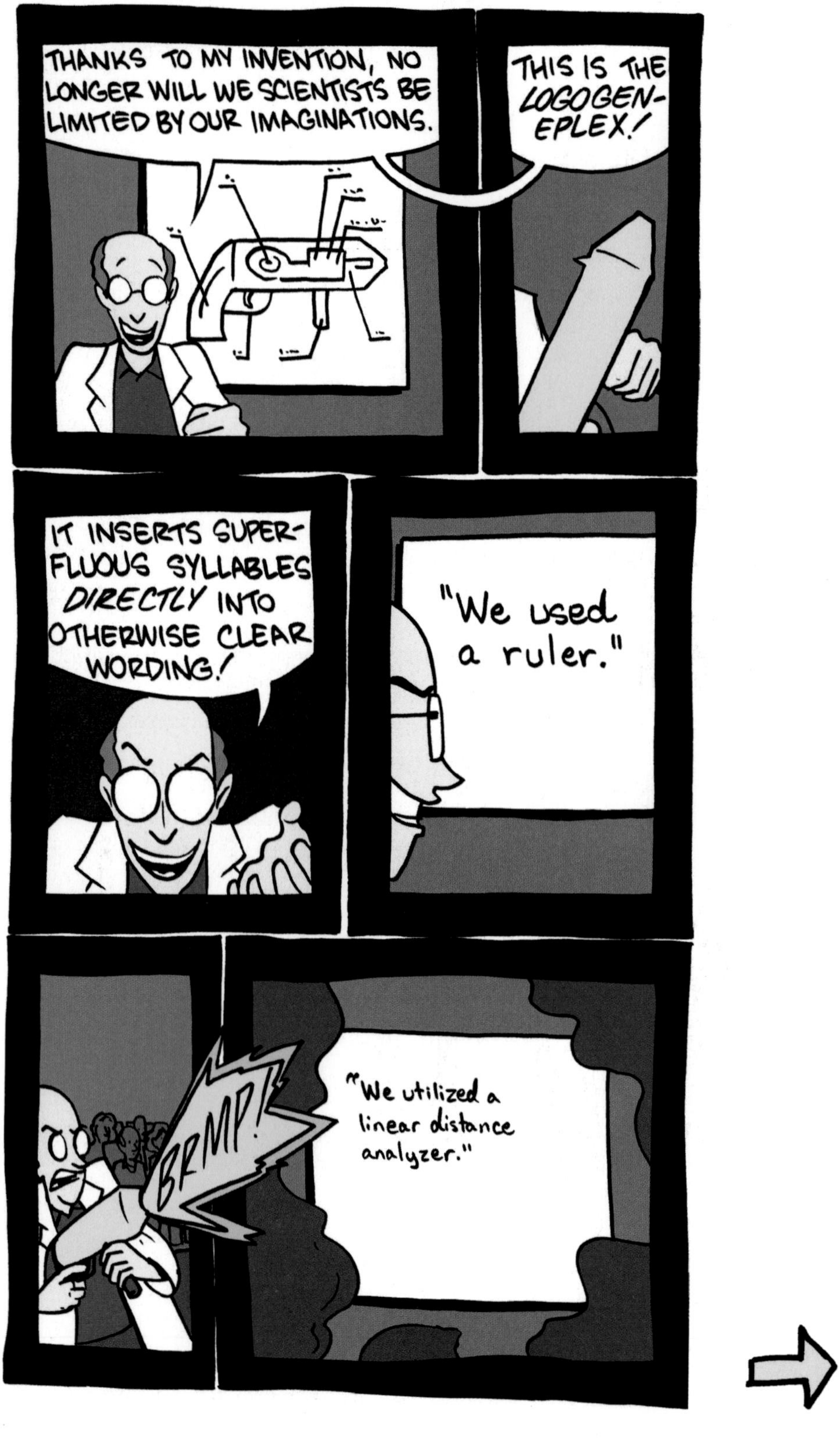
THANKS TO MY INVENTION, NO LONGER WILL WE SCIENTISTS BE LIMITED BY OUR IMAGINATIONS.
THIS IS THE *LOGOGENEPLEX!*
IT INSERTS SUPERFLUOUS SYLLABLES *DIRECTLY* INTO OTHERWISE CLEAR WORDING!
"We used a ruler."
BRMP!
"We utilized a linear distance analyzer."

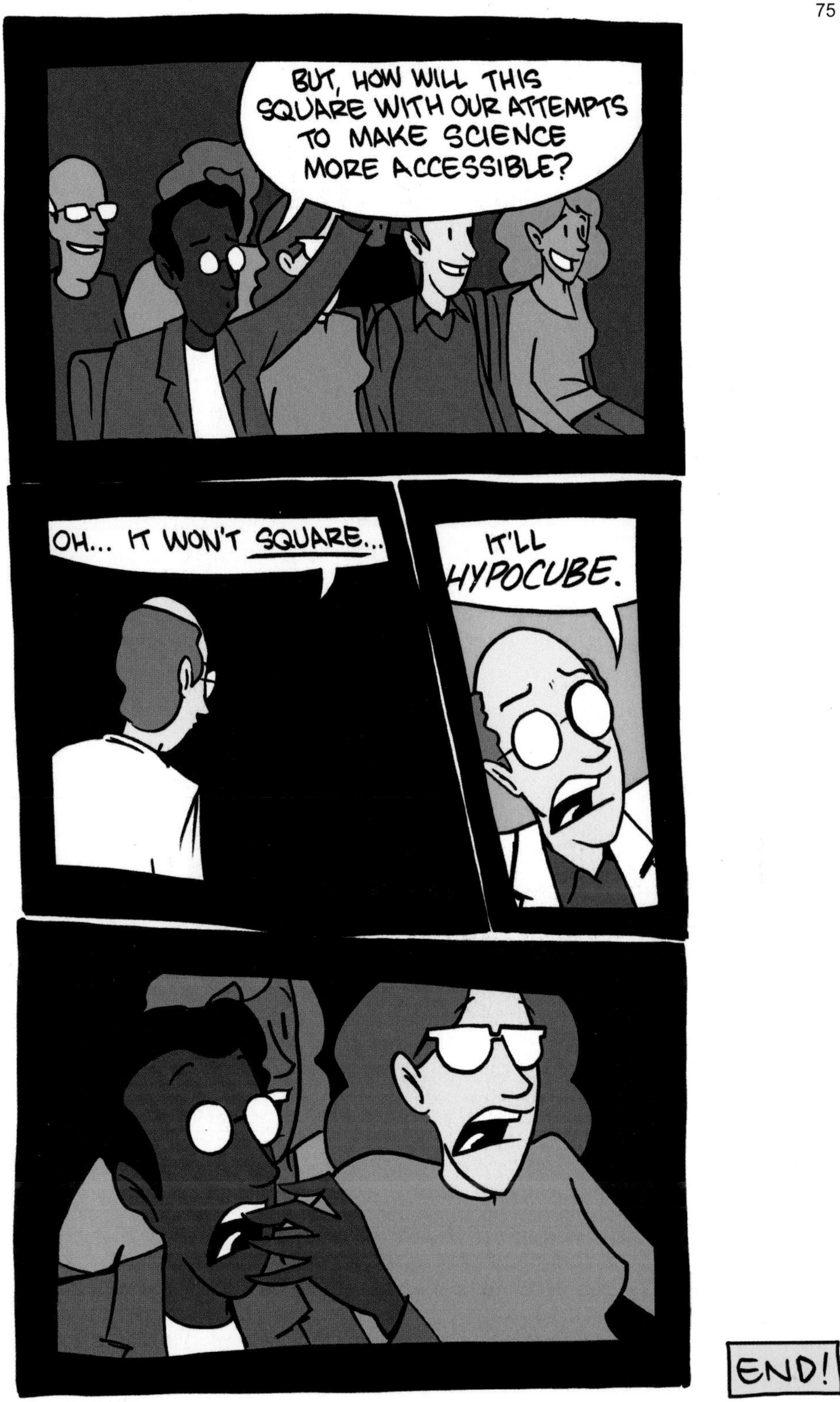
BUT, HOW WILL THIS SQUARE WITH OUR ATTEMPTS TO MAKE SCIENCE MORE ACCESSIBLE?
OH... IT WON'T SQUARE...
IT'LL HYPOCUBE.
END!

DR. DEMAINE CREATED AN ALGORITHM THAT SOLVED ALL MATHEMATICAL THEOREMS.

SOON AFTER, ALL PHYSICS QUESTIONS WERE ANSWERED

INSIDE PROTONS ARE QUARKS, INSIDE QUARKS ARE STRINGS, INSIDE STRINGS IS GOD TELLING YOU TO FUCK OFF.

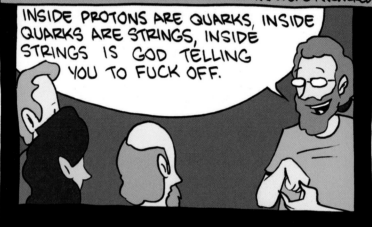

THEN ENGINEERING, CHEMISTRY, BIOLOGY, NEUROSCIENCE, PSYCHIATRY...

$P \neq NP$, COLD FUSION WILL NEVER WORK, THE RED QUEEN HYPOTHESIS IS RIGHT, CONSCIOUSNESS IS AN ILLUSION, AND YOUR MOTHER NEVER LOVED YOU.

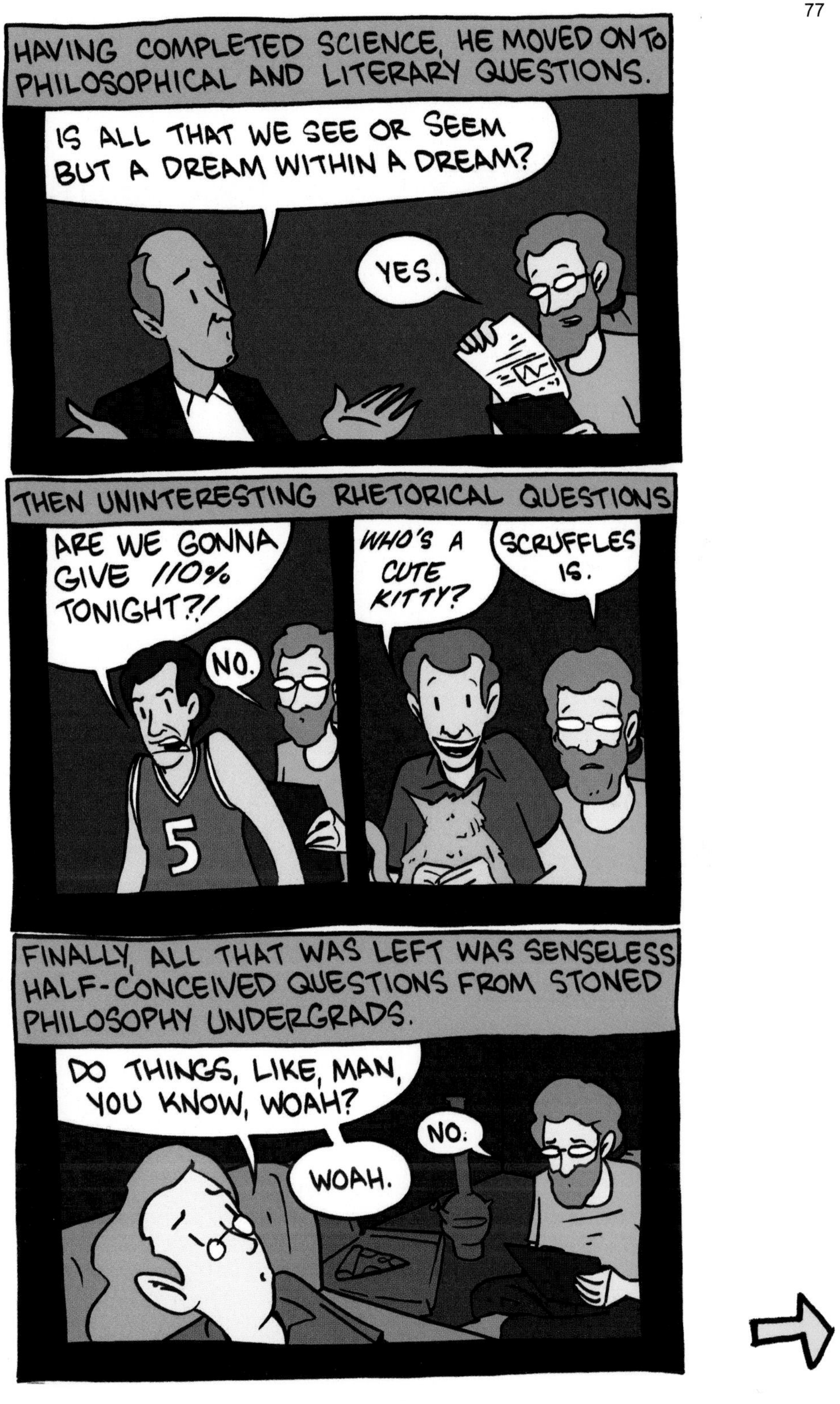
HAVING COMPLETED SCIENCE, HE MOVED ON TO PHILOSOPHICAL AND LITERARY QUESTIONS.
IS ALL THAT WE SEE OR SEEM BUT A DREAM WITHIN A DREAM?
YES.
THEN UNINTERESTING RHETORICAL QUESTIONS
ARE WE GONNA GIVE 110% TONIGHT?!
NO.
WHO'S A CUTE KITTY?
SCRUFFLES IS.
FINALLY, ALL THAT WAS LEFT WAS SENSELESS HALF-CONCEIVED QUESTIONS FROM STONED PHILOSOPHY UNDERGRADS.
DO THINGS, LIKE, MAN, YOU KNOW, WOAH?
NO.
WOAH.

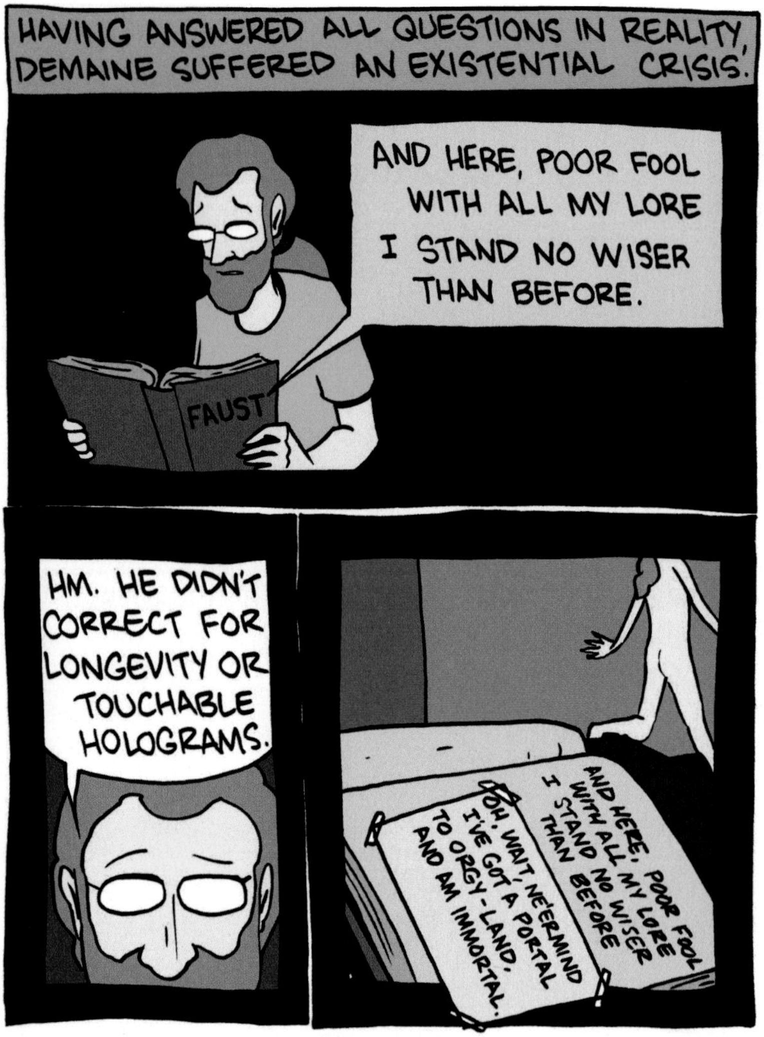
HAVING ANSWERED ALL QUESTIONS IN REALITY, DEMAINE SUFFERED AN EXISTENTIAL CRISIS.
AND HERE, POOR FOOL WITH ALL MY LORE I STAND NO WISER THAN BEFORE.
FAUST
HM. HE DIDN'T CORRECT FOR LONGEVITY OR TOUCHABLE HOLOGRAMS.
AND HERE, POOR FOOL WITH ALL MY LORE I STAND NO WISER THAN BEFORE
OH, WAIT, NEVERMIND I'VE GOT A PORTAL TO ORGY-LAND, AND AM IMMORTAL.

END!

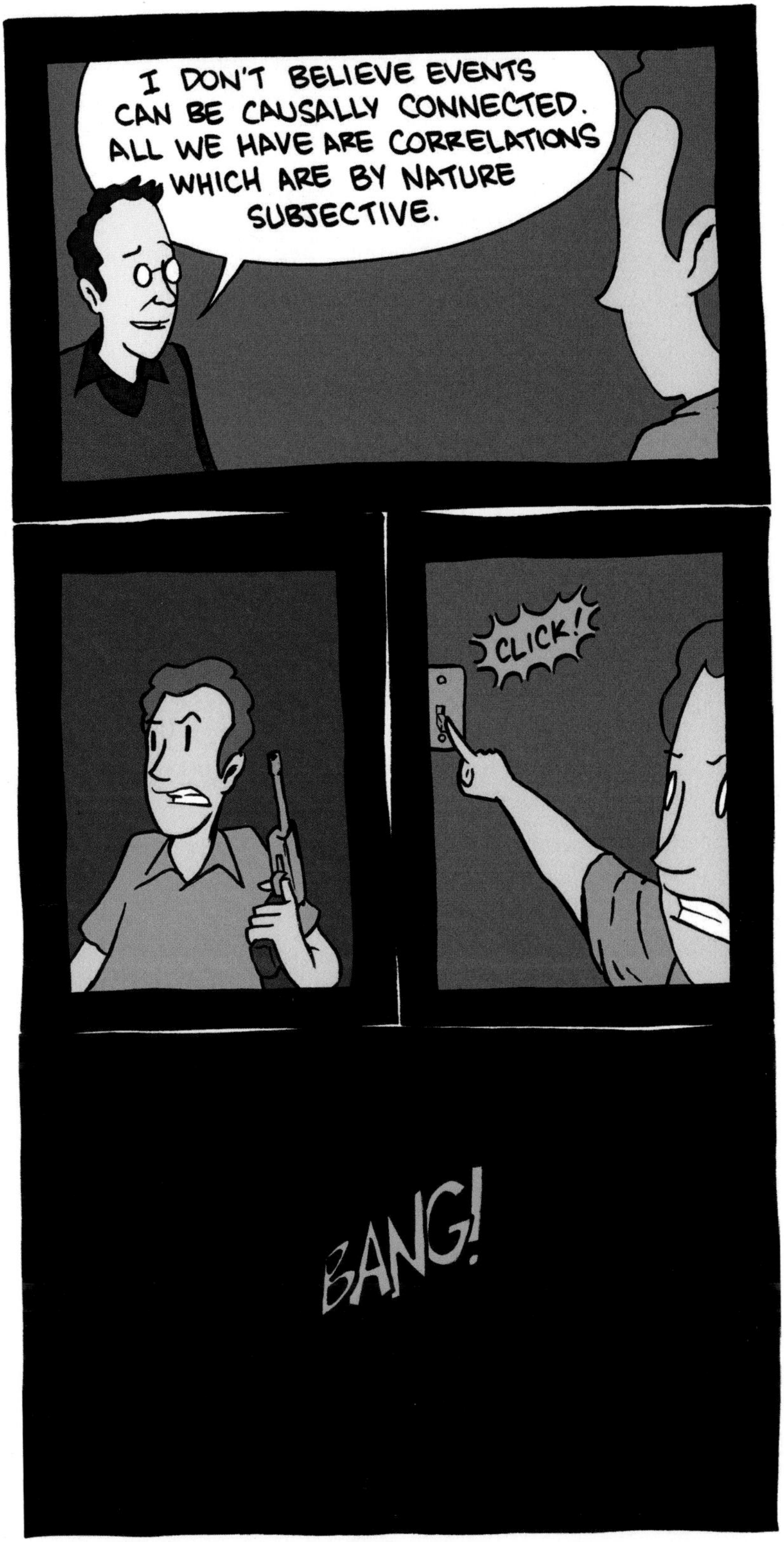
I DON'T BELIEVE EVENTS CAN BE CAUSALLY CONNECTED. ALL WE HAVE ARE CORRELATIONS WHICH ARE BY NATURE SUBJECTIVE.
CLICK!
BANG!

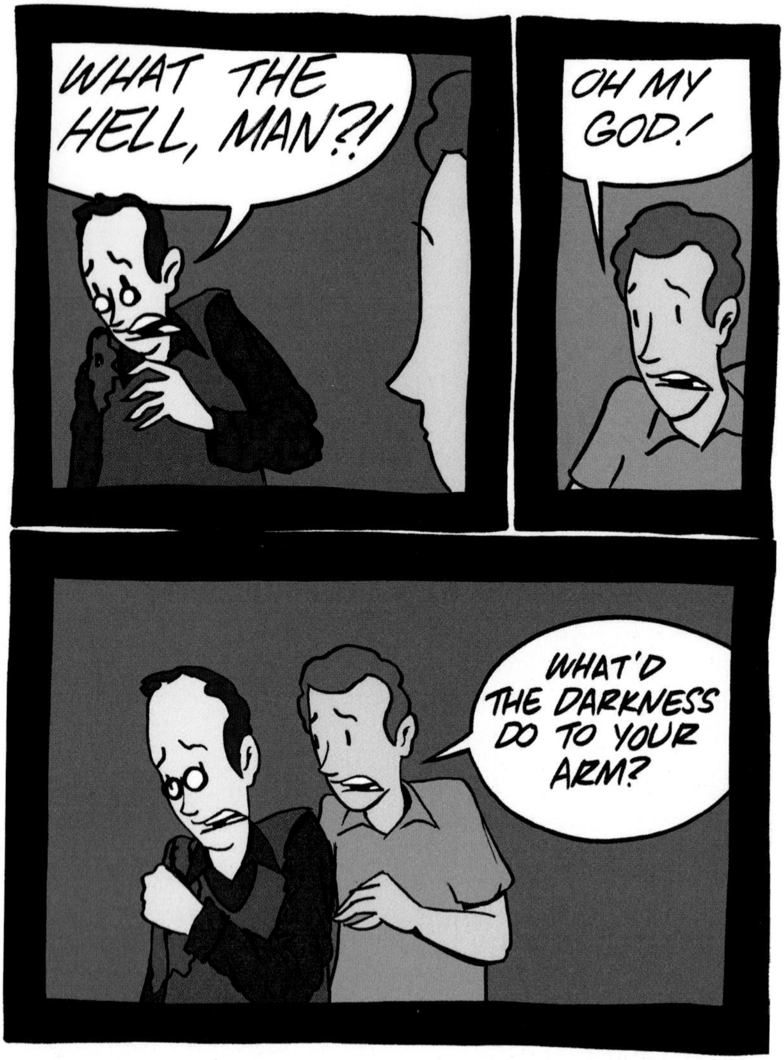
WHAT THE HELL, MAN?!
OH MY GOD!
WHAT'D THE DARKNESS DO TO YOUR ARM?

END!

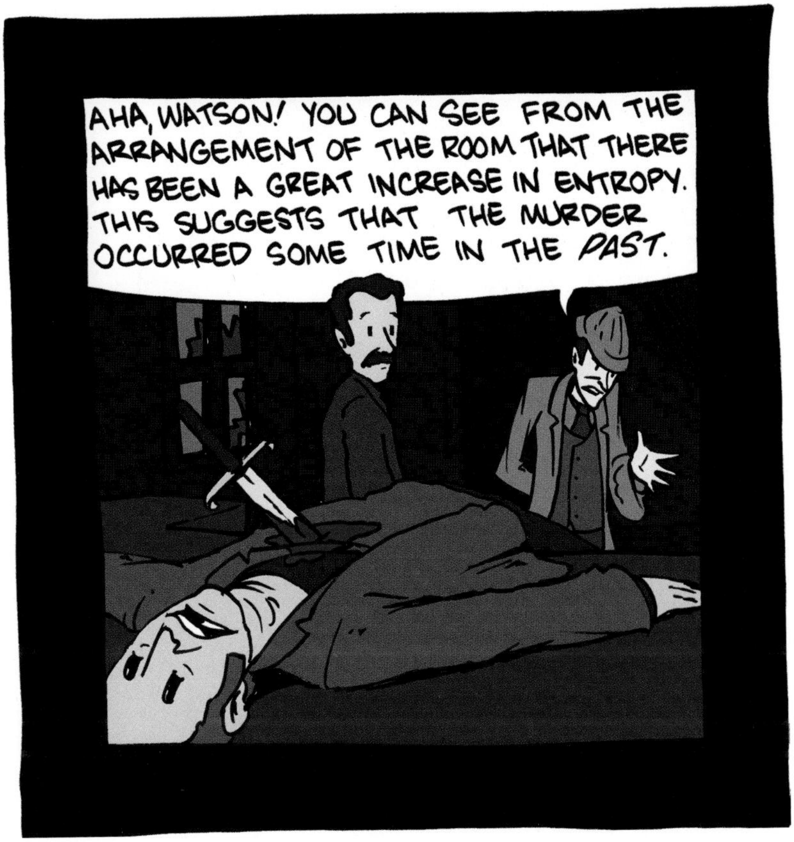
AHA, WATSON! YOU CAN SEE FROM THE ARRANGEMENT OF THE ROOM THAT THERE HAS BEEN A GREAT INCREASE IN ENTROPY. THIS SUGGESTS THAT THE MURDER OCCURRED SOME TIME IN THE *PAST*.

Fortunately, Sherlock Holmes never studied physics.

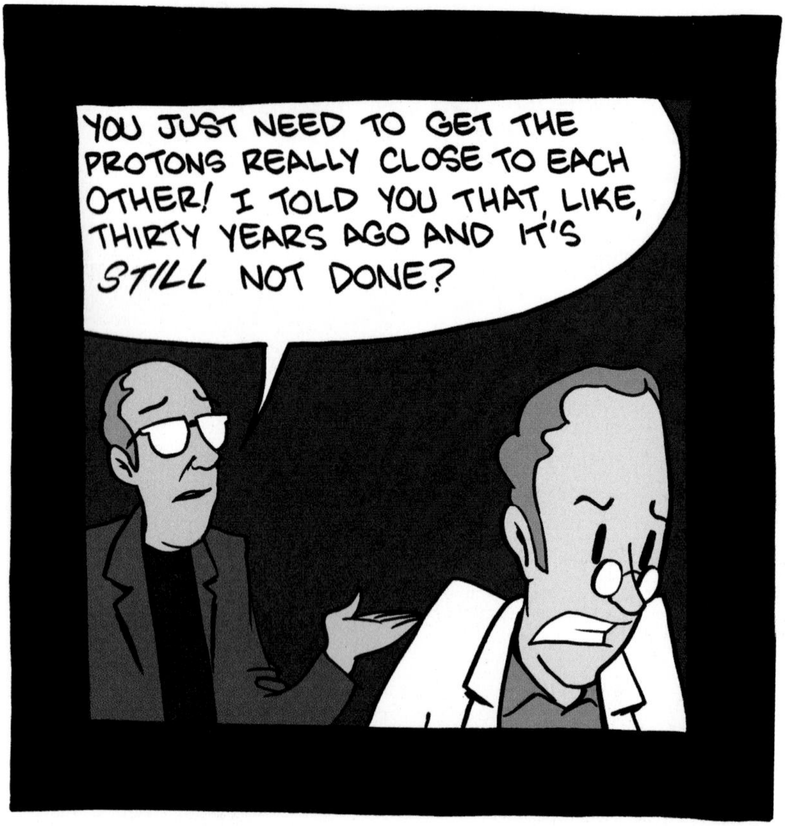
YOU JUST NEED TO GET THE PROTONS REALLY CLOSE TO EACH OTHER! I TOLD YOU THAT, LIKE, THIRTY YEARS AGO AND IT'S *STILL* NOT DONE?

This is why experimental scientists hate theoretical scientists.

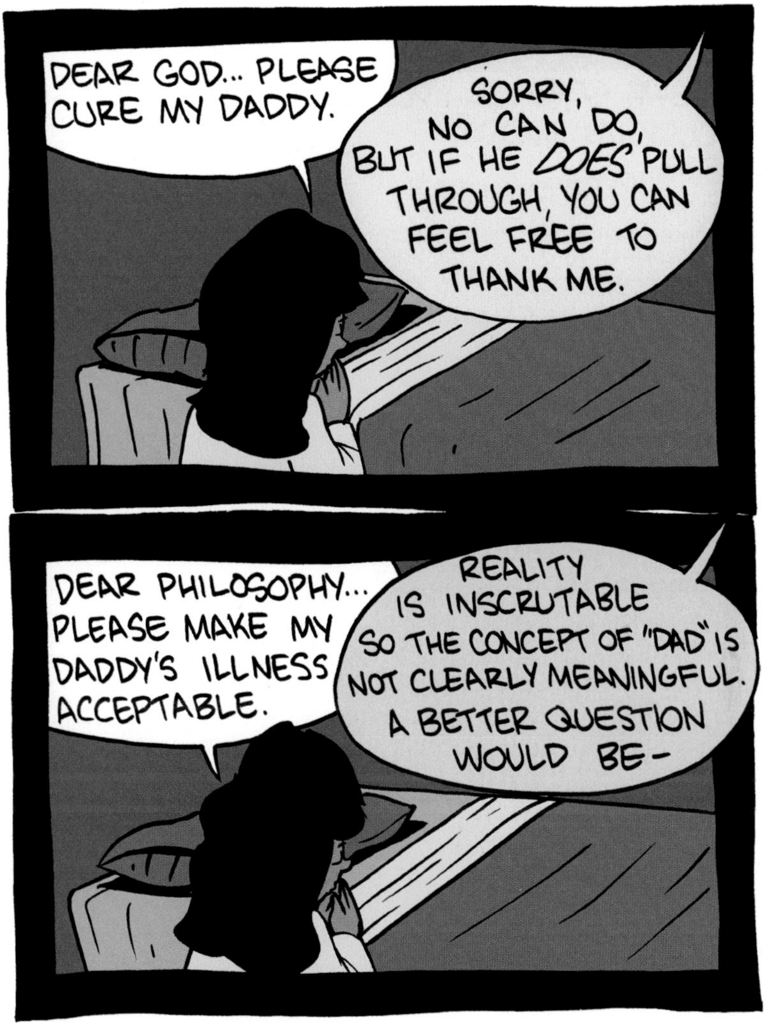
DEAR GOD... PLEASE CURE MY DADDY.
SORRY, NO CAN DO, BUT IF HE *DOES* PULL THROUGH, YOU CAN FEEL FREE TO THANK ME.
DEAR PHILOSOPHY... PLEASE MAKE MY DADDY'S ILLNESS ACCEPTABLE.
REALITY IS INSCRUTABLE SO THE CONCEPT OF "DAD" IS NOT CLEARLY MEANINGFUL. A BETTER QUESTION WOULD BE-

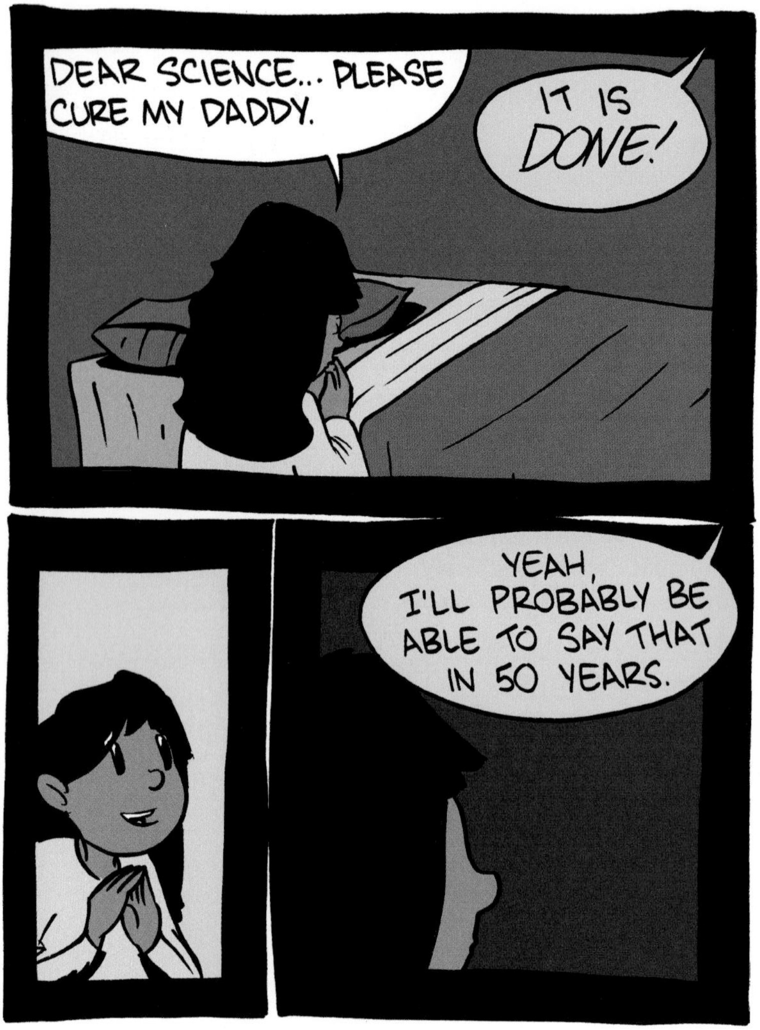
DEAR SCIENCE... PLEASE CURE MY DADDY.
IT IS DONE!
YEAH, I'LL PROBABLY BE ABLE TO SAY THAT IN 50 YEARS.

END!

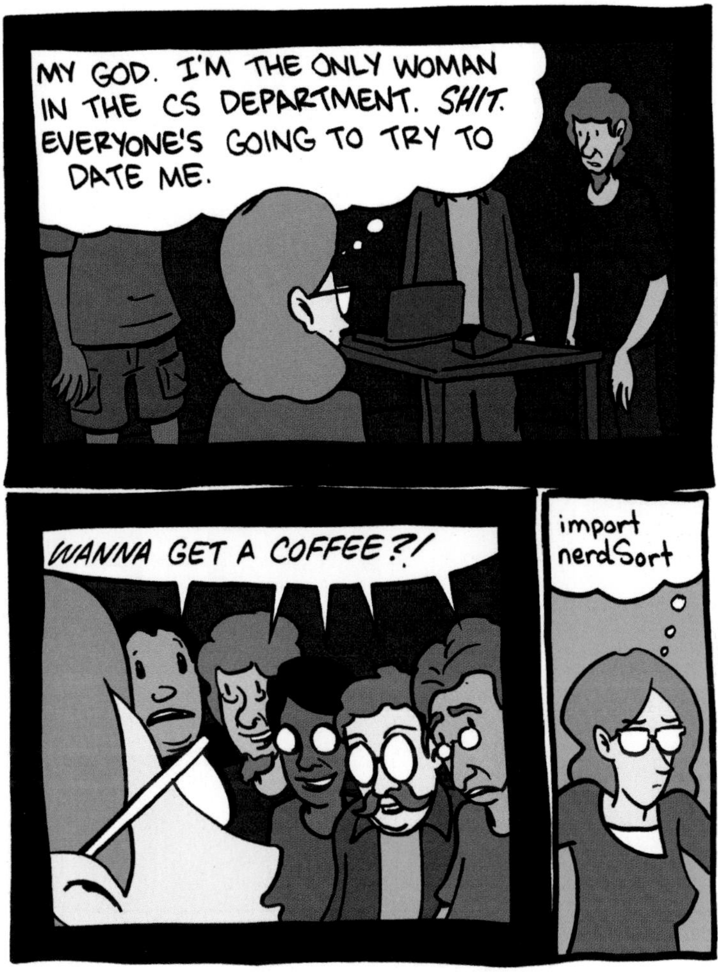
MY GOD. I'M THE ONLY WOMAN IN THE CS DEPARTMENT. *SHIT.* EVERYONE'S GOING TO TRY TO DATE ME.
WANNA GET A COFFEE?!
import nerdSort

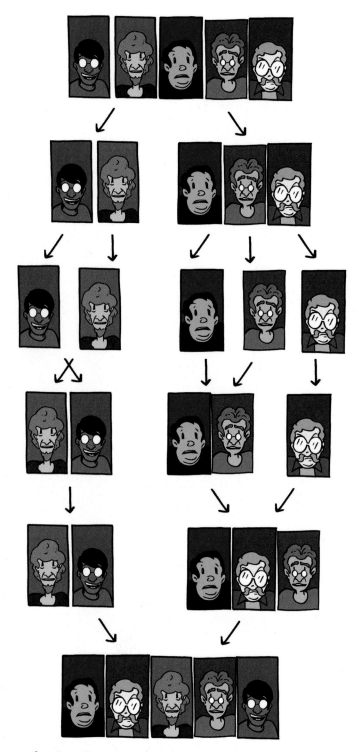

COMPLETE.
NERDS SORTED FOR LEAST TO MOST ATTRACTIVE

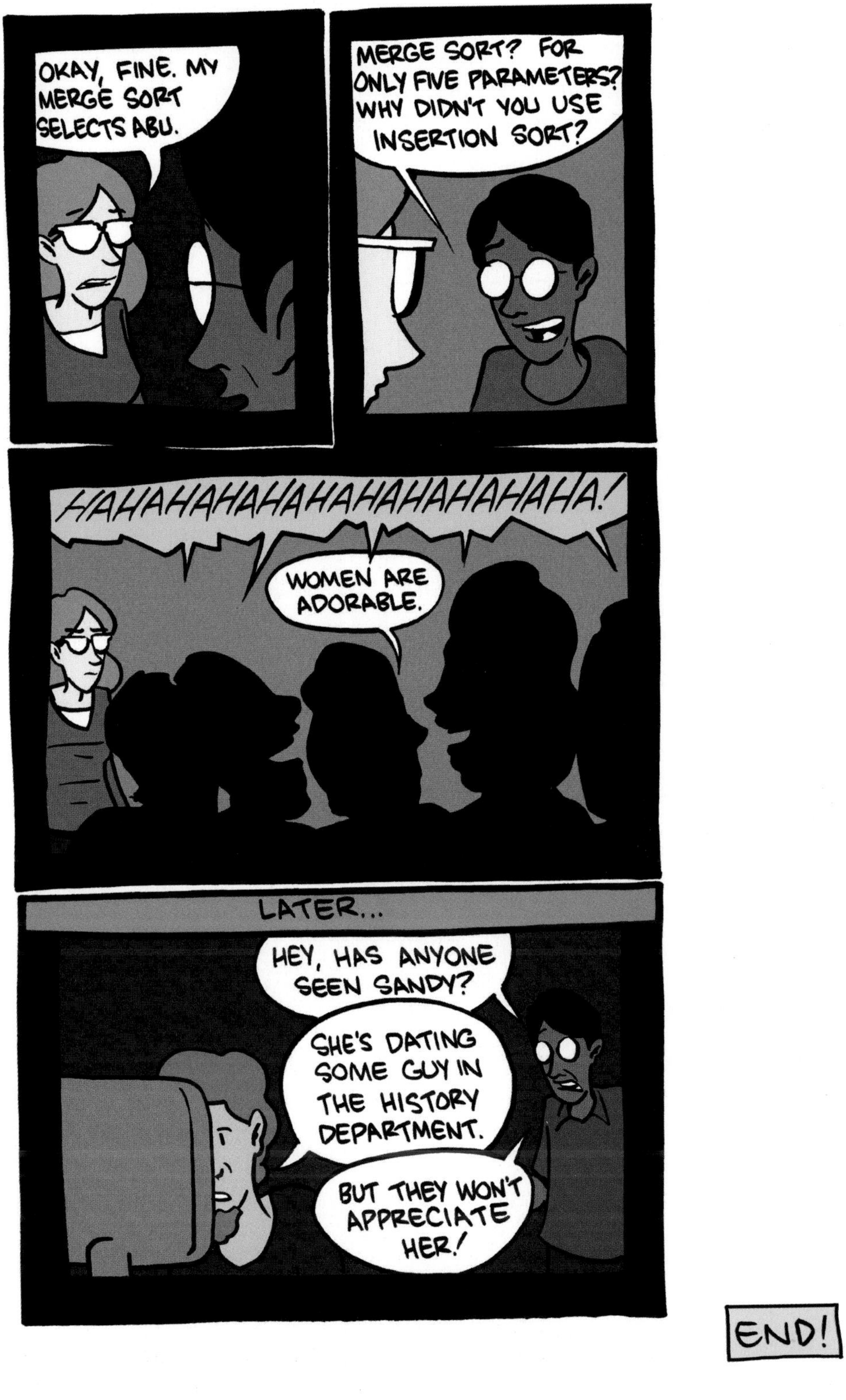
OKAY, FINE. MY MERGE SORT SELECTS ABU.
MERGE SORT? FOR ONLY FIVE PARAMETERS? WHY DIDN'T YOU USE INSERTION SORT?
HAHAHAHAHAHAHAHAHAHAHAHAHA!
WOMEN ARE ADORABLE.
LATER...
HEY, HAS ANYONE SEEN SANDY?
SHE'S DATING SOME GUY IN THE HISTORY DEPARTMENT.
BUT THEY WON'T APPRECIATE HER!
END!

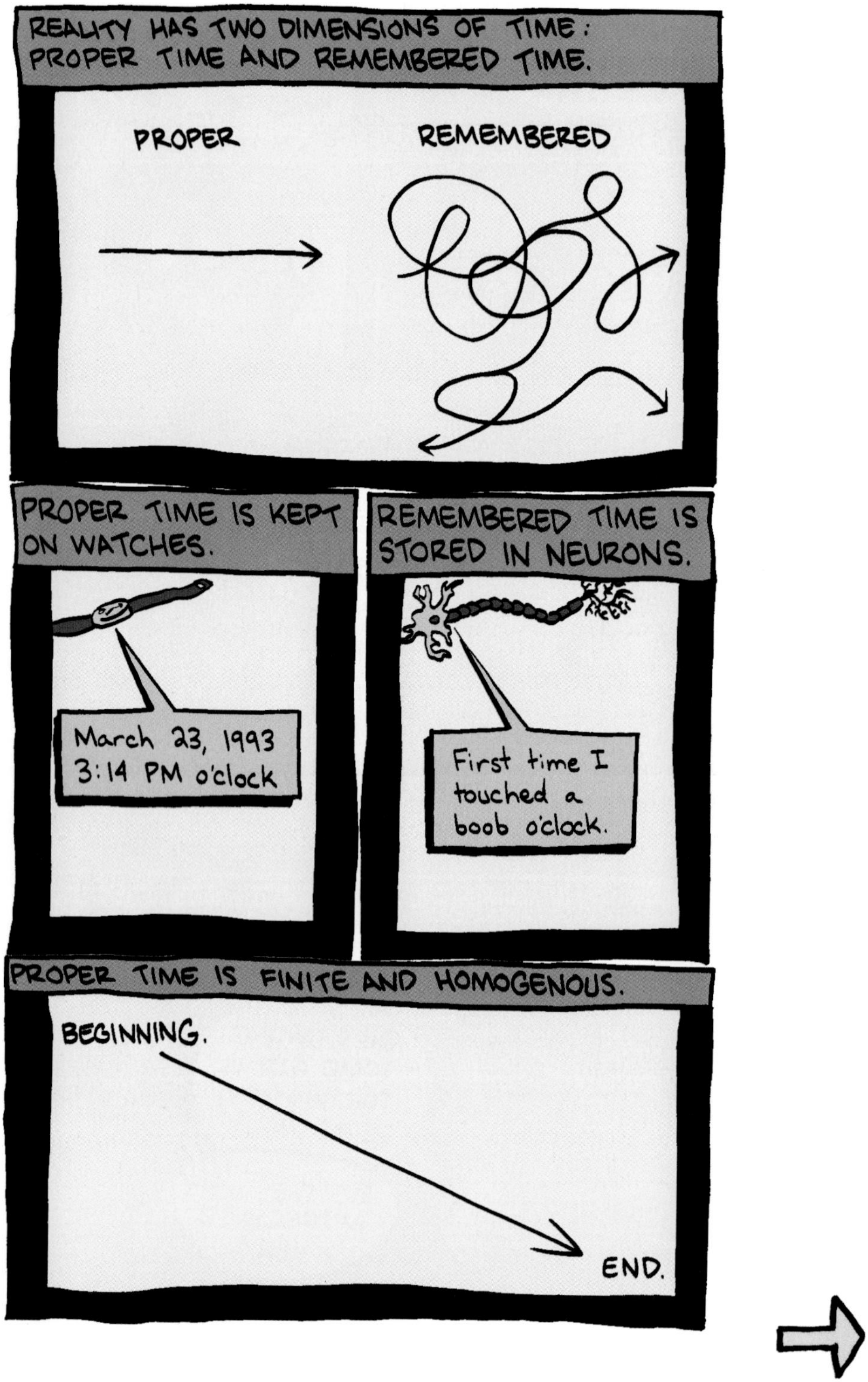
REALITY HAS TWO DIMENSIONS OF TIME: PROPER TIME AND REMEMBERED TIME.
PROPER
REMEMBERED
PROPER TIME IS KEPT ON WATCHES.
March 23, 1993 3:14 PM o'clock
REMEMBERED TIME IS STORED IN NEURONS.
First time I touched a boob o'clock.
PROPER TIME IS FINITE AND HOMOGENOUS.
BEGINNING.
END.

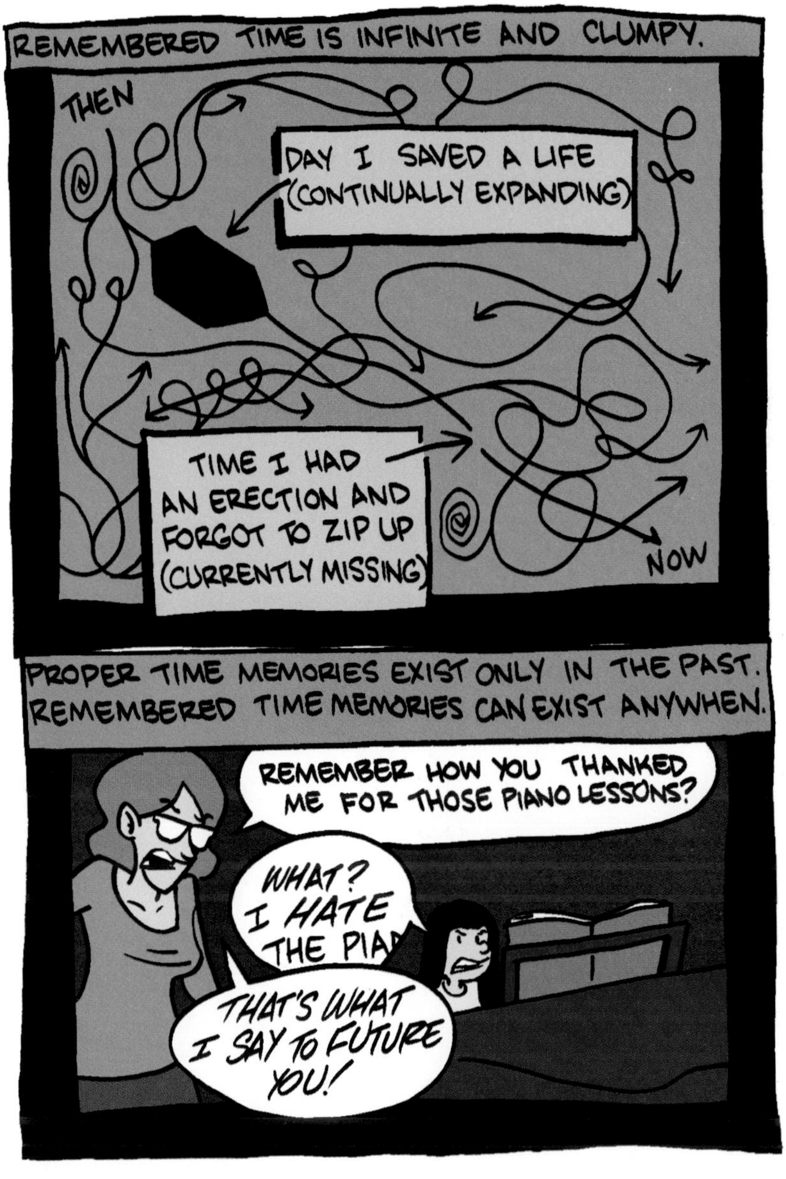
REMEMBERED TIME IS INFINITE AND CLUMPY.
THEN
DAY I SAVED A LIFE (CONTINUALLY EXPANDING)
TIME I HAD AN ERECTION AND FORGOT TO ZIP UP (CURRENTLY MISSING)
NOW
PROPER TIME MEMORIES EXIST ONLY IN THE PAST. REMEMBERED TIME MEMORIES CAN EXIST ANYWHEN.
REMEMBER HOW YOU THANKED ME FOR THOSE PIANO LESSONS?
WHAT? I HATE THE PIA
THAT'S WHAT I SAY TO FUTURE YOU!

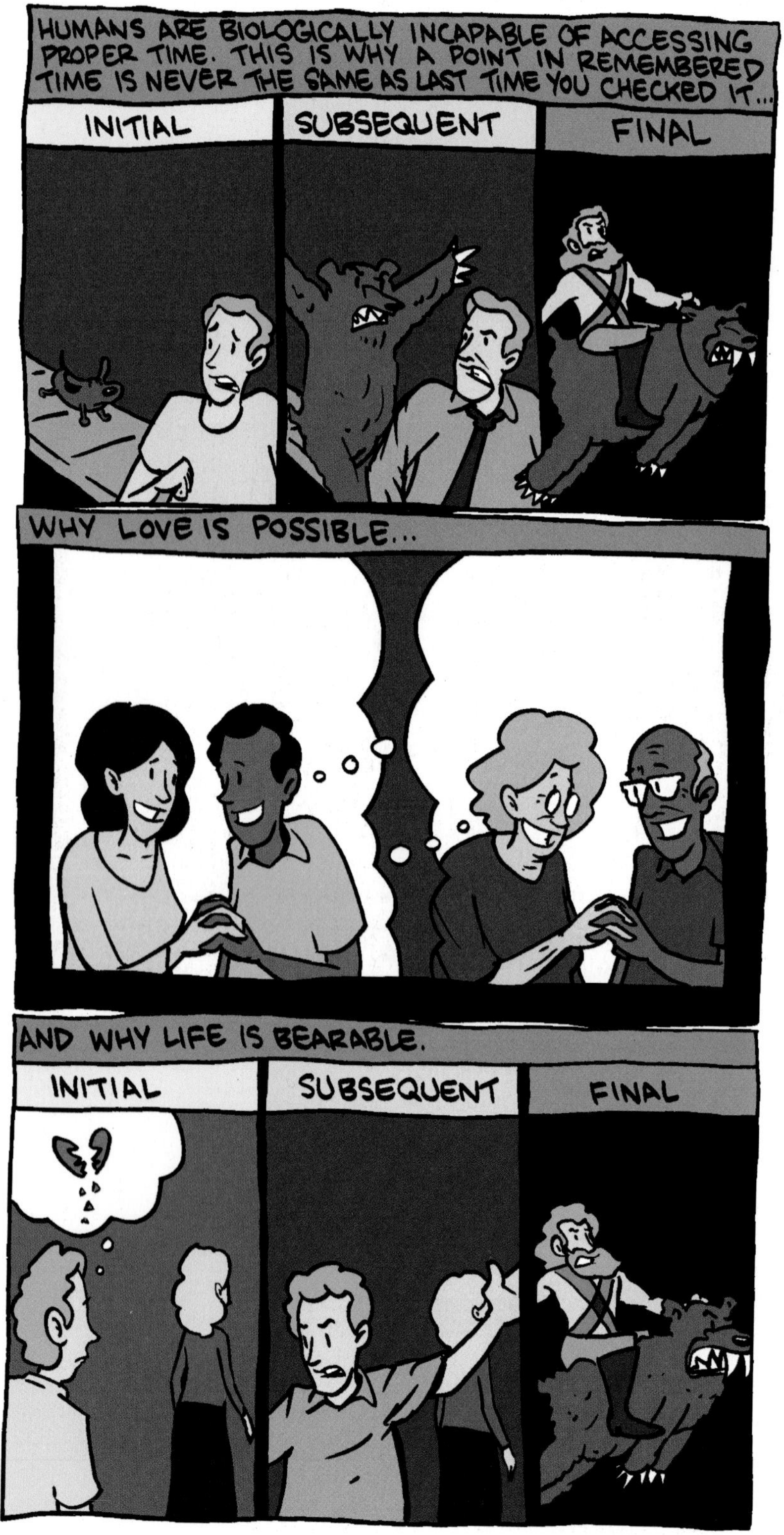
HUMANS ARE BIOLOGICALLY INCAPABLE OF ACCESSING PROPER TIME. THIS IS WHY A POINT IN REMEMBERED TIME IS NEVER THE SAME AS LAST TIME YOU CHECKED IT...
INITIAL
SUBSEQUENT
FINAL
WHY LOVE IS POSSIBLE...
AND WHY LIFE IS BEARABLE.
INITIAL
SUBSEQUENT
FINAL

END!

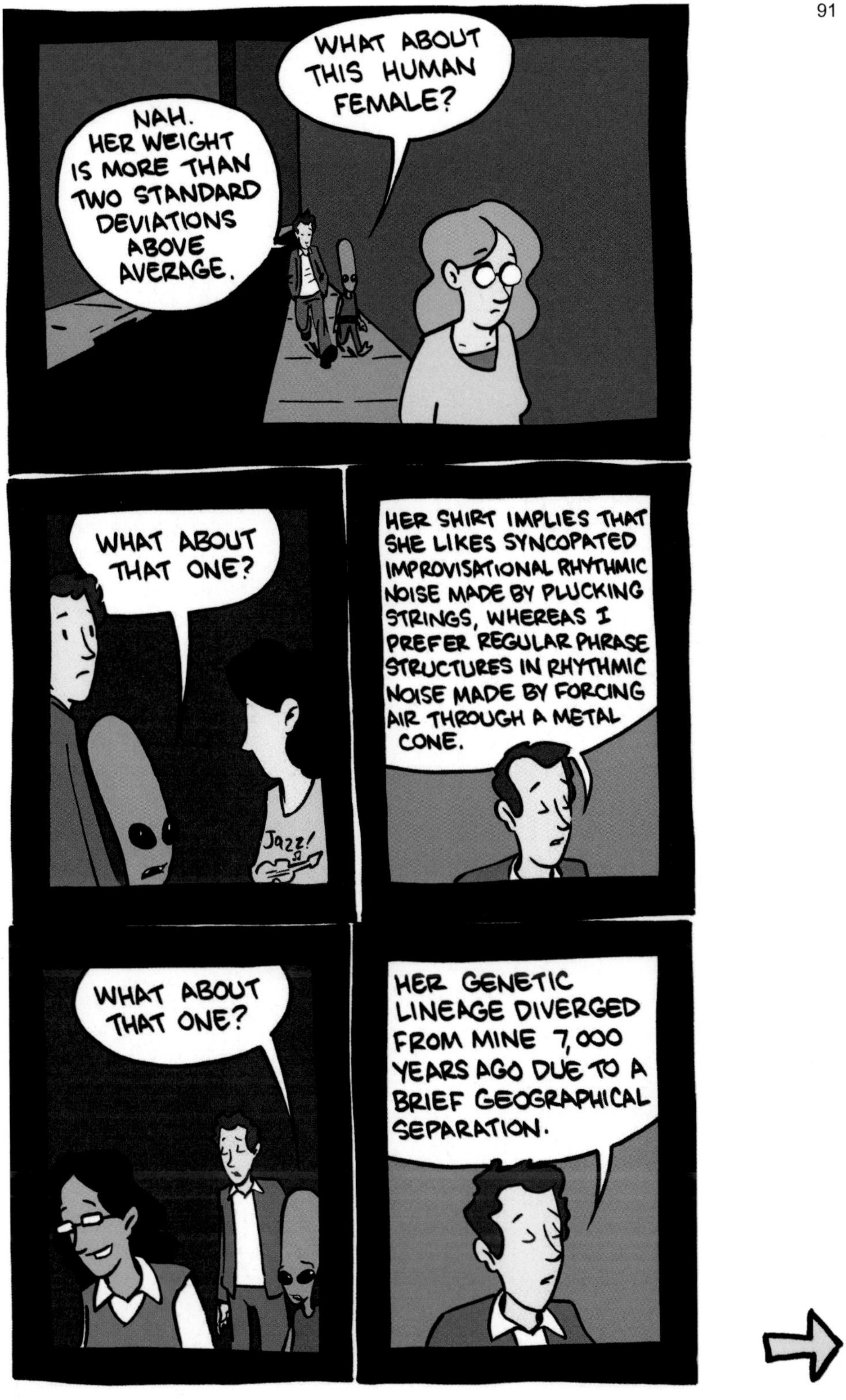
WHAT ABOUT THIS HUMAN FEMALE?
NAH. HER WEIGHT IS MORE THAN TWO STANDARD DEVIATIONS ABOVE AVERAGE.
WHAT ABOUT THAT ONE?
Jazz!
HER SHIRT IMPLIES THAT SHE LIKES SYNCOPATED IMPROVISATIONAL RHYTHMIC NOISE MADE BY PLUCKING STRINGS, WHEREAS I PREFER REGULAR PHRASE STRUCTURES IN RHYTHMIC NOISE MADE BY FORCING AIR THROUGH A METAL CONE.
WHAT ABOUT THAT ONE?
HER GENETIC LINEAGE DIVERGED FROM MINE 7,000 YEARS AGO DUE TO A BRIEF GEOGRAPHICAL SEPARATION.

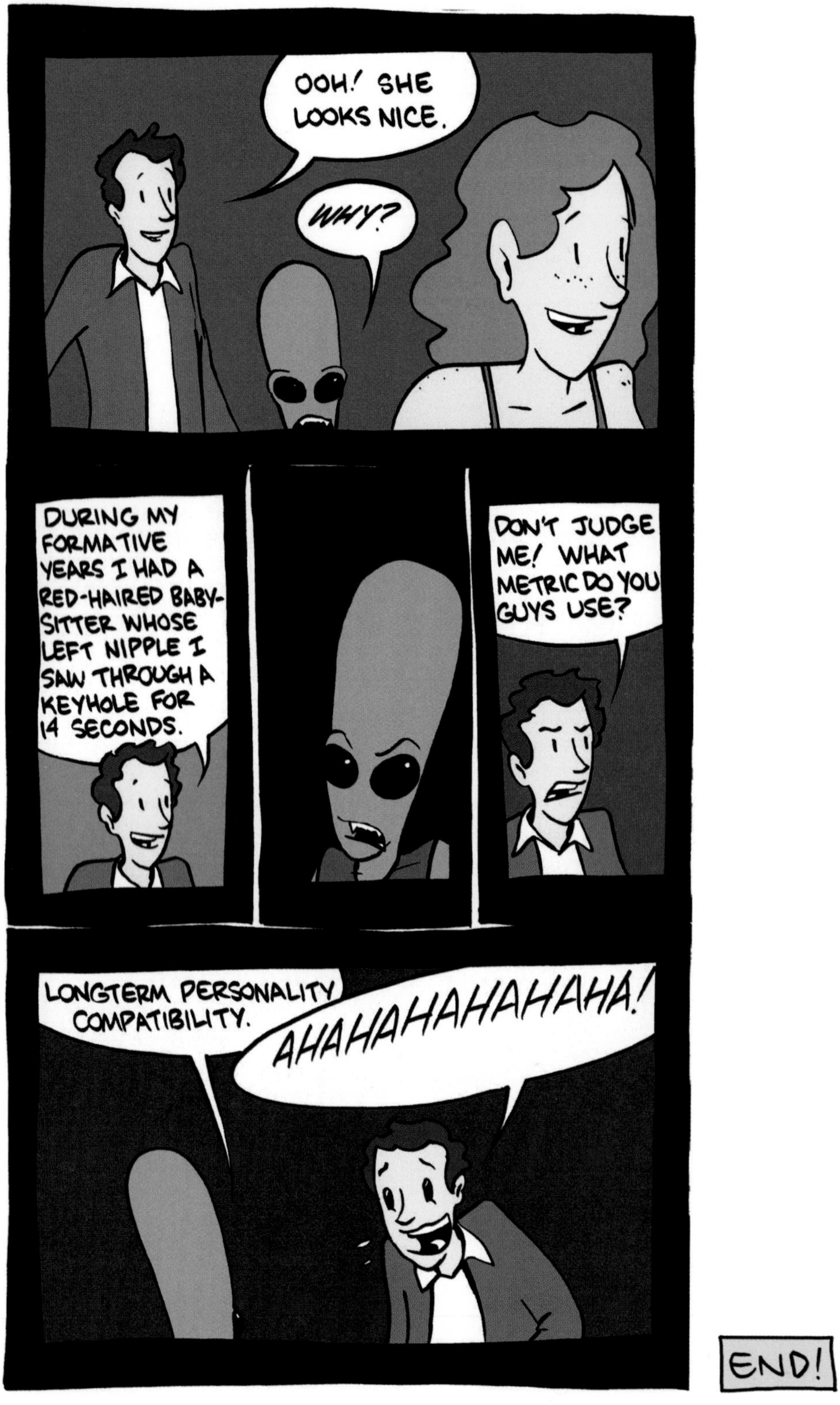
OOH! SHE LOOKS NICE.
WHY?
DURING MY FORMATIVE YEARS I HAD A RED-HAIRED BABY-SITTER WHOSE LEFT NIPPLE I SAW THROUGH A KEYHOLE FOR 14 SECONDS.
DON'T JUDGE ME! WHAT METRIC DO YOU GUYS USE?
LONGTERM PERSONALITY COMPATIBILITY.
AHAHAHAHAHAHAHA!
END!

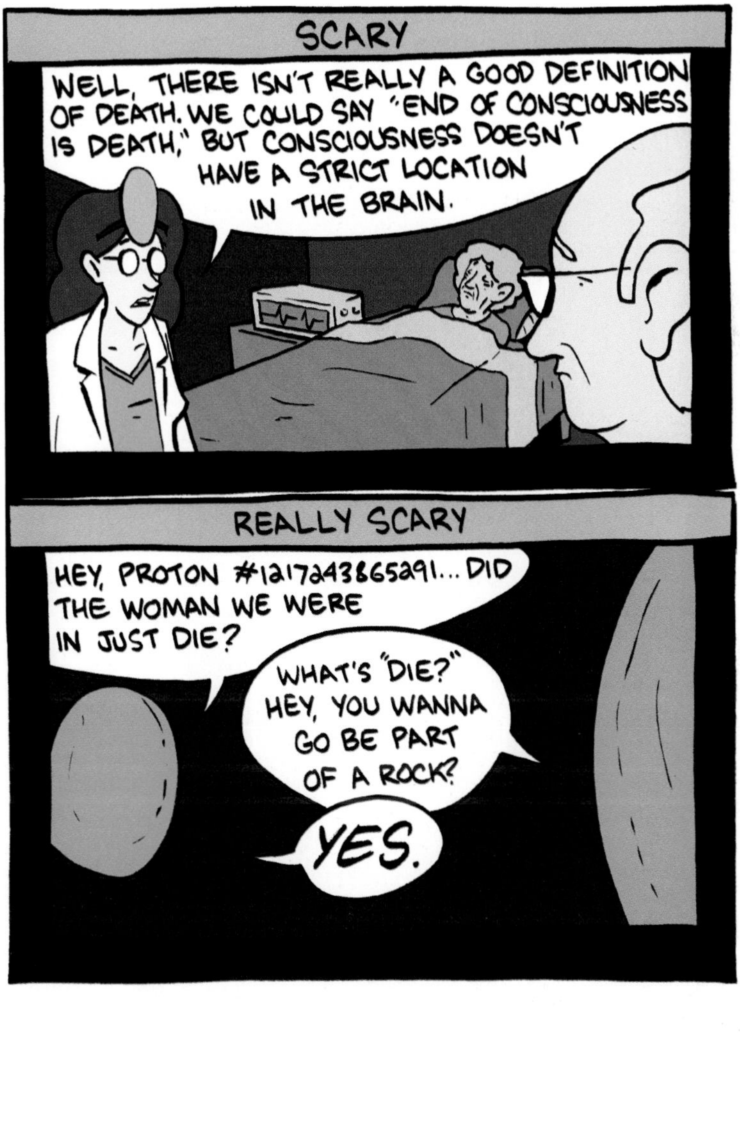
SCARY
WELL, THERE ISN'T REALLY A GOOD DEFINITION OF DEATH. WE COULD SAY "END OF CONSCIOUSNESS IS DEATH," BUT CONSCIOUSNESS DOESN'T HAVE A STRICT LOCATION IN THE BRAIN.
REALLY SCARY
HEY, PROTON #1217243865291... DID THE WOMAN WE WERE IN JUST DIE?
WHAT'S "DIE?" HEY, YOU WANNA GO BE PART OF A ROCK?
YES.

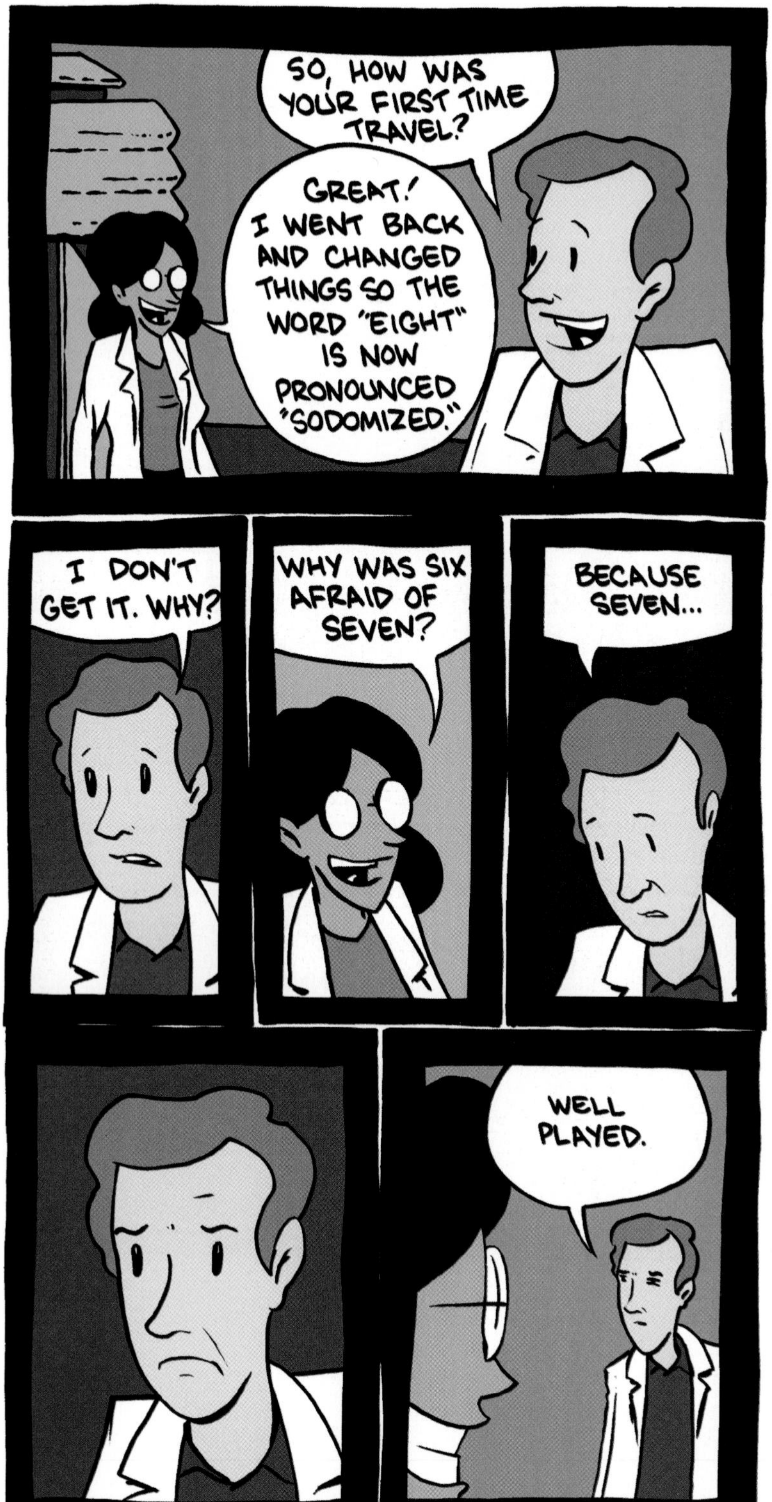
SO, HOW WAS YOUR FIRST TIME TRAVEL?
GREAT! I WENT BACK AND CHANGED THINGS SO THE WORD "EIGHT" IS NOW PRONOUNCED "SODOMIZED."
I DON'T GET IT. WHY?
WHY WAS SIX AFRAID OF SEVEN?
BECAUSE SEVEN...
WELL PLAYED.

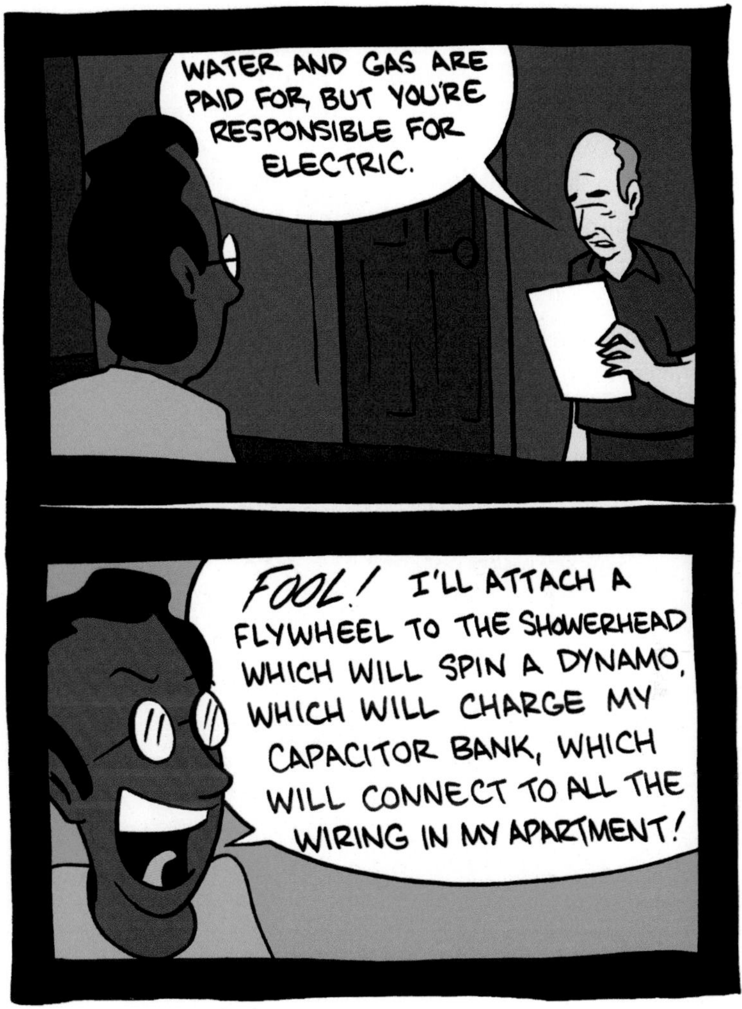
WATER AND GAS ARE PAID FOR, BUT YOU'RE RESPONSIBLE FOR ELECTRIC.
FOOL! I'LL ATTACH A FLYWHEEL TO THE SHOWERHEAD WHICH WILL SPIN A DYNAMO, WHICH WILL CHARGE MY CAPACITOR BANK, WHICH WILL CONNECT TO ALL THE WIRING IN MY APARTMENT!

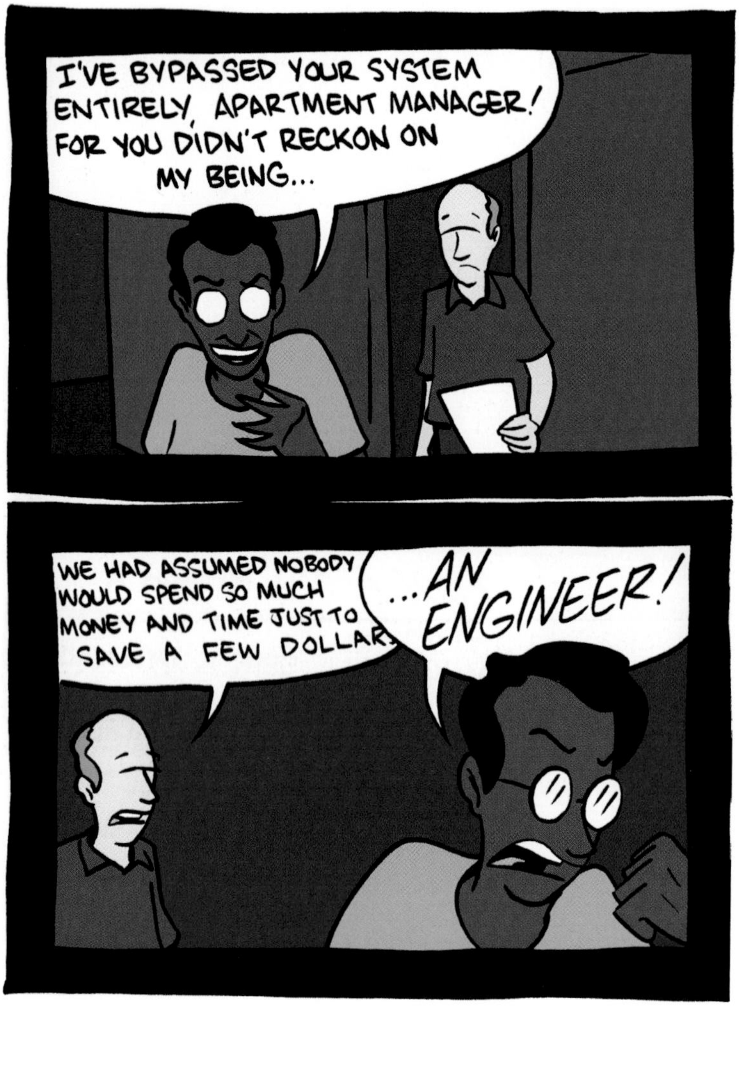
I'VE BYPASSED YOUR SYSTEM ENTIRELY, APARTMENT MANAGER! FOR YOU DIDN'T RECKON ON MY BEING...
WE HAD ASSUMED NOBODY WOULD SPEND SO MUCH MONEY AND TIME JUST TO SAVE A FEW DOLLARS
...AN ENGINEER!

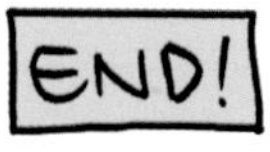
END!

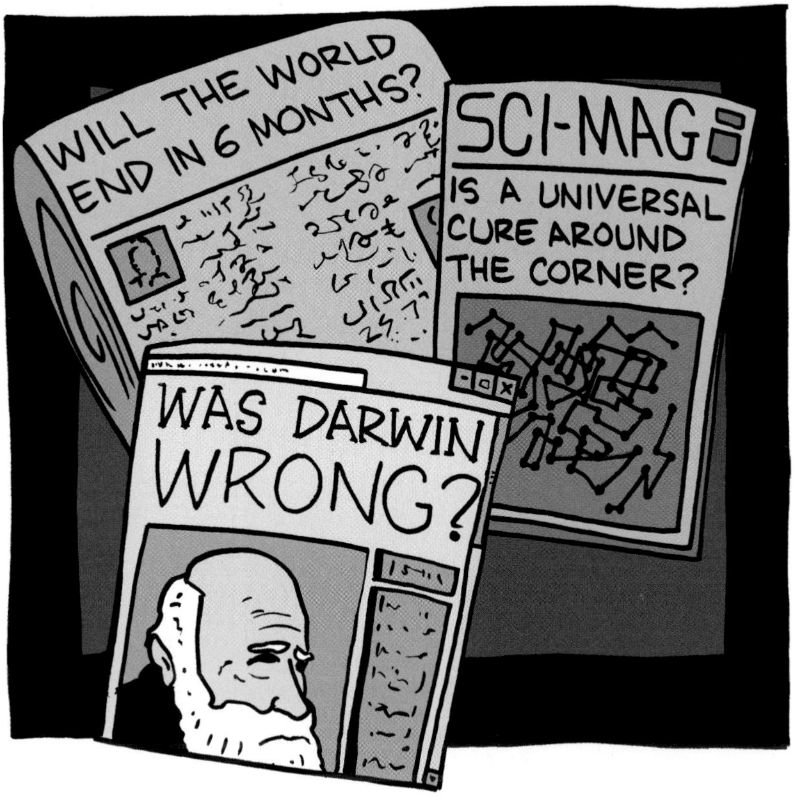
WILL THE WORLD END IN 6 MONTHS?
SCI-MAG
IS A UNIVERSAL CURE AROUND THE CORNER?
WAS DARWIN WRONG?

New rule for Science Journalism:
If your article can be summarized as "No."
don't write it.

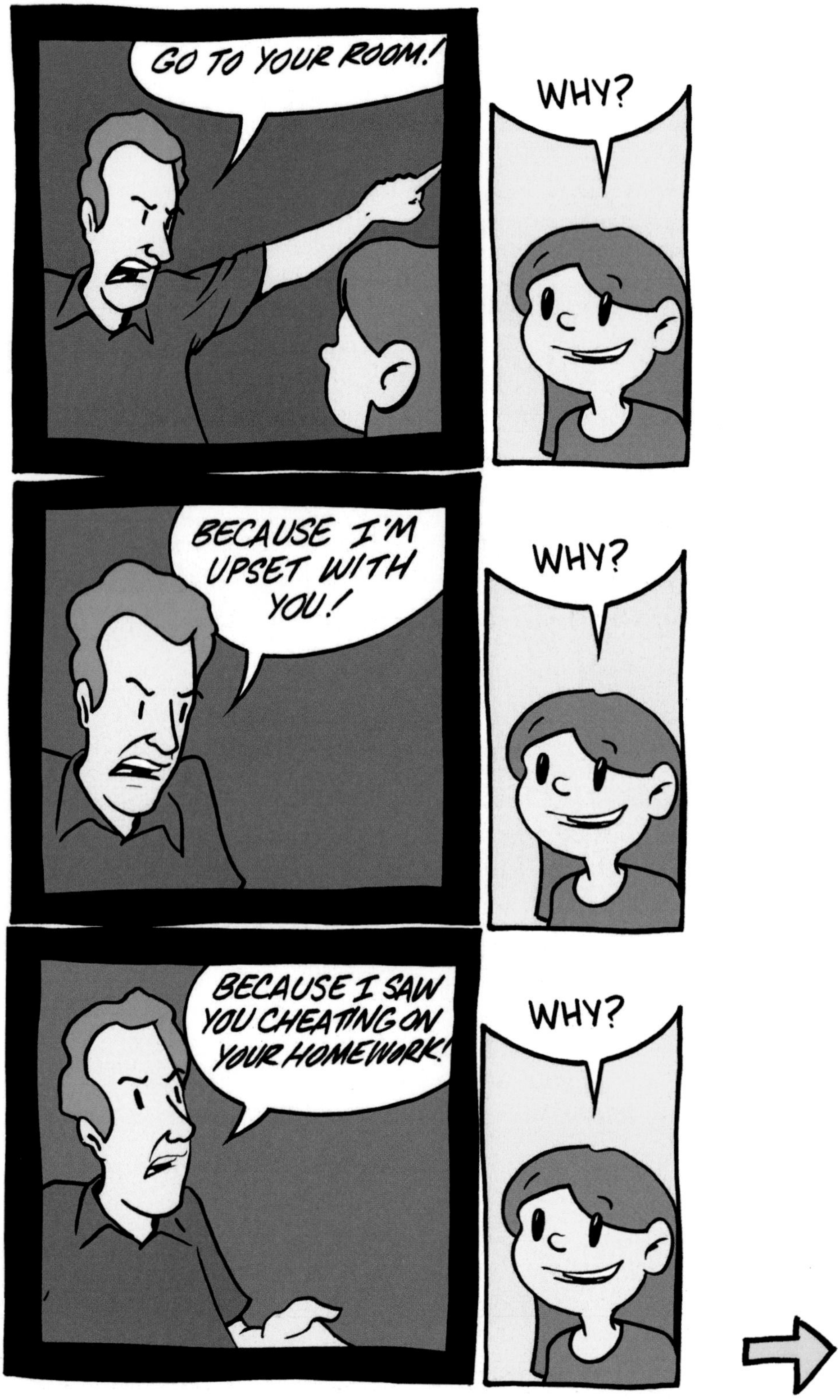
GO TO YOUR ROOM!
WHY?
BECAUSE I'M UPSET WITH YOU!
WHY?
BECAUSE I SAW YOU CHEATING ON YOUR HOMEWORK!
WHY?

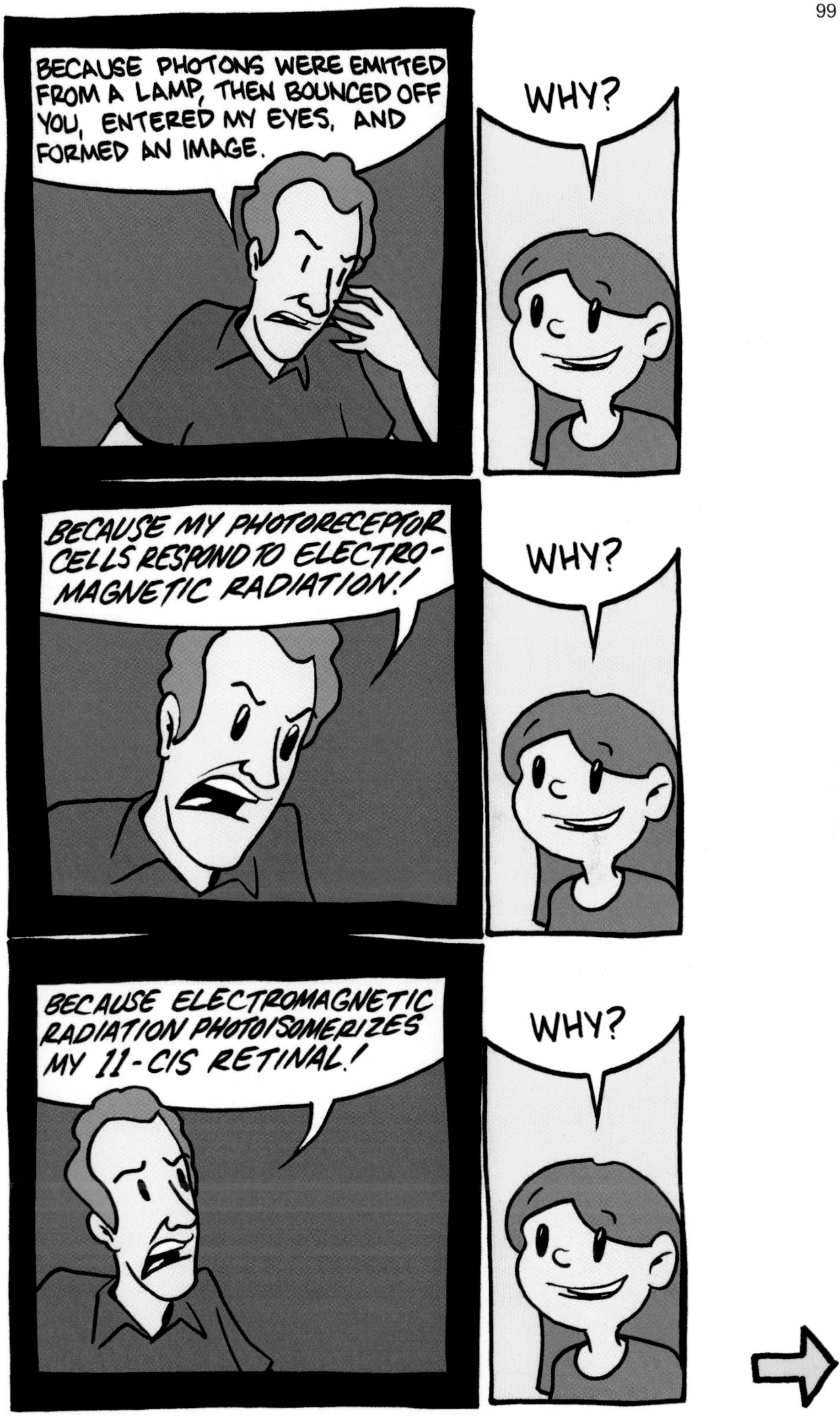
BECAUSE PHOTONS WERE EMITTED FROM A LAMP, THEN BOUNCED OFF YOU, ENTERED MY EYES, AND FORMED AN IMAGE.
WHY?
BECAUSE MY PHOTORECEPTOR CELLS RESPOND TO ELECTRO-MAGNETIC RADIATION!
WHY?
BECAUSE ELECTROMAGNETIC RADIATION PHOTOISOMERIZES MY 11-CIS RETINAL!
WHY?

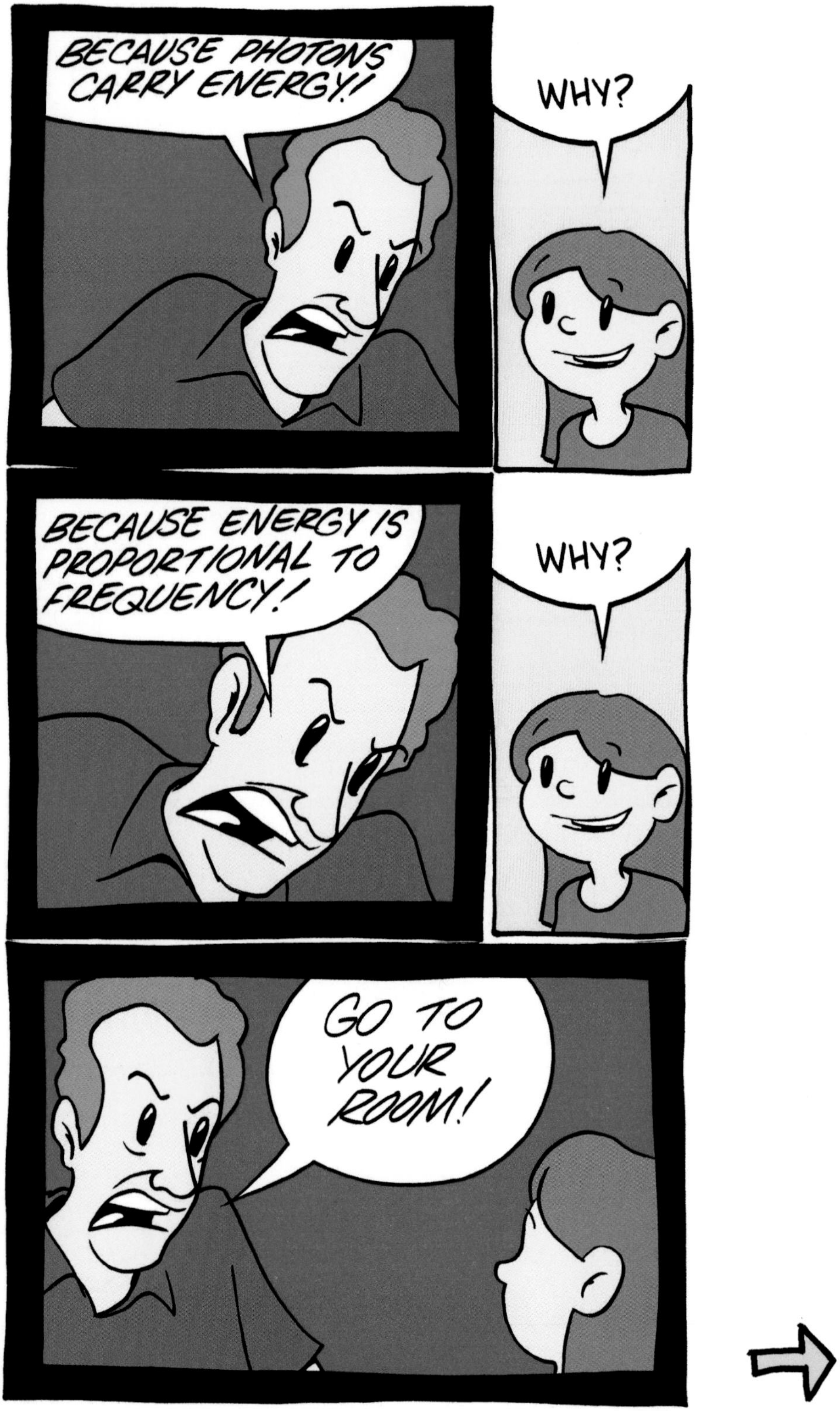
BECAUSE PHOTONS CARRY ENERGY!
WHY?
BECAUSE ENERGY IS PROPORTIONAL TO FREQUENCY!
WHY?
GO TO YOUR ROOM!

POTENTIAL LENGTH
OF THESE CONVERSATIONS
HUMAN HISTORY

HUMAN DESIRE
FOR CHILDREN
HUMAN HISTORY

END!

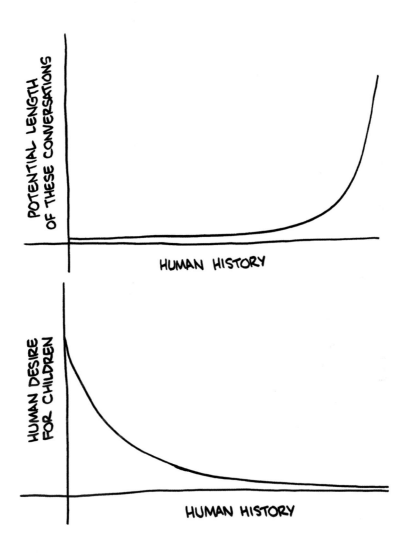

IN THIS UNIVERSE, THERE IS ROUGHLY ONE ATOM OF HYDROGEN PER CUBIC METER.

AN ATOM OF HYDROGEN HAS A MASS OF ROUGHLY 1.66×10^{-27} KILOGRAMS.

THE AVERAGE PERSON HAS A MASS OF ROUGHLY 80 KILOGRAMS.

WHICH LEADS US TO THE HUMAN CONDITION.

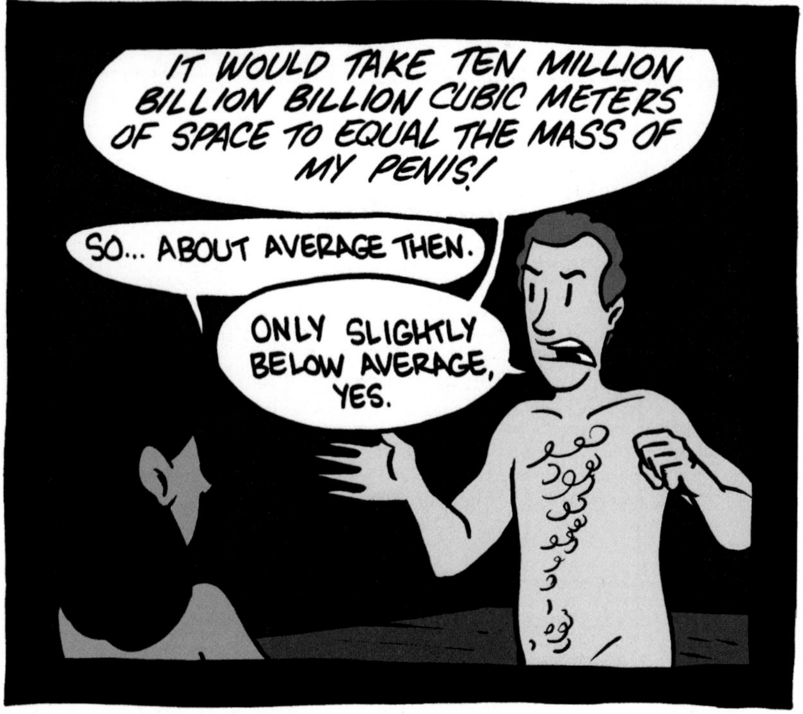
IT WOULD TAKE TEN MILLION BILLION BILLION CUBIC METERS OF SPACE TO EQUAL THE MASS OF MY PENIS!
SO... ABOUT AVERAGE THEN.
ONLY SLIGHTLY BELOW AVERAGE, YES.

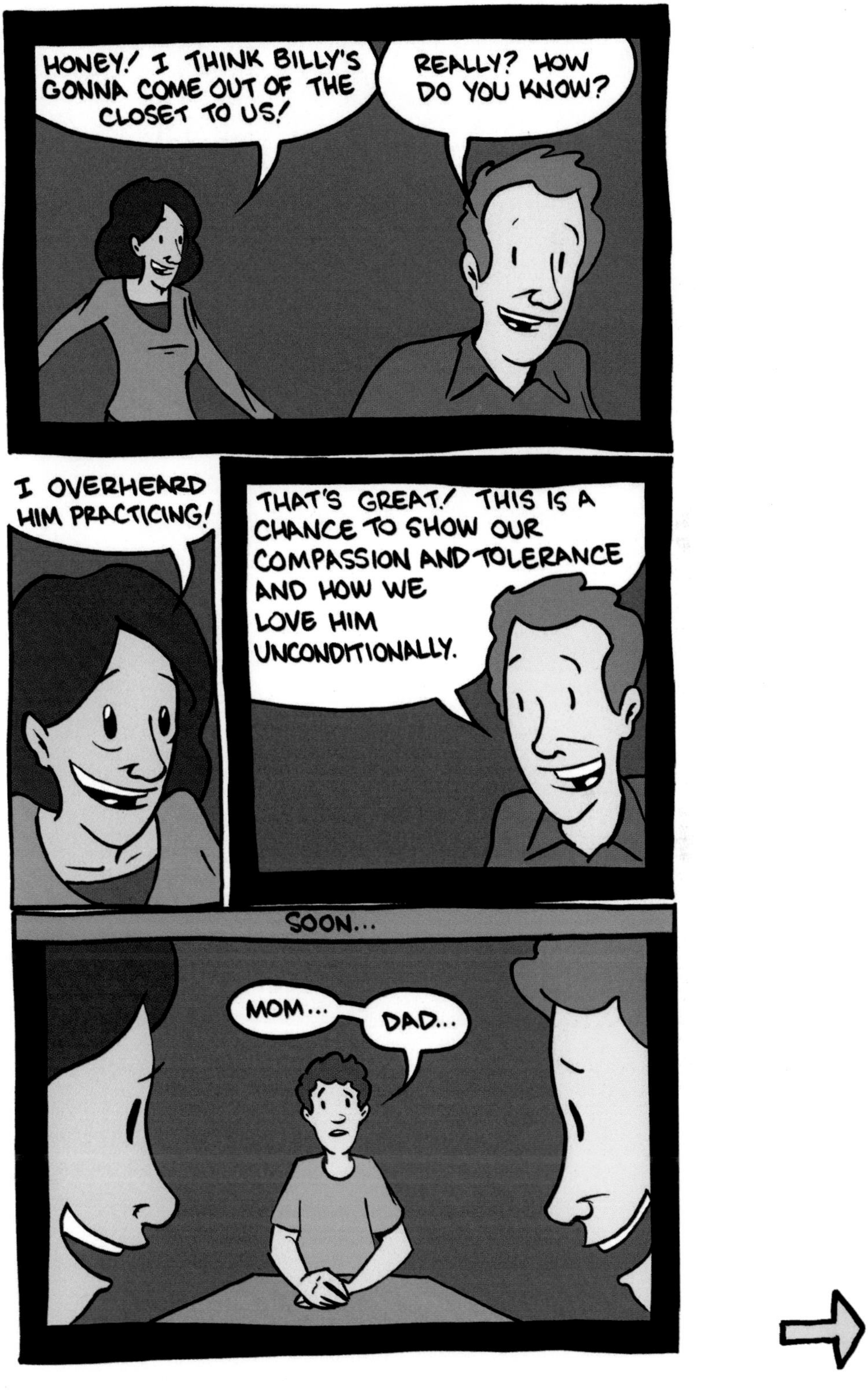
HONEY! I THINK BILLY'S GONNA COME OUT OF THE CLOSET TO US!
REALLY? HOW DO YOU KNOW?
I OVERHEARD HIM PRACTICING!
THAT'S GREAT! THIS IS A CHANCE TO SHOW OUR COMPASSION AND TOLERANCE AND HOW WE LOVE HIM UNCONDITIONALLY.
SOON...
MOM...
DAD...

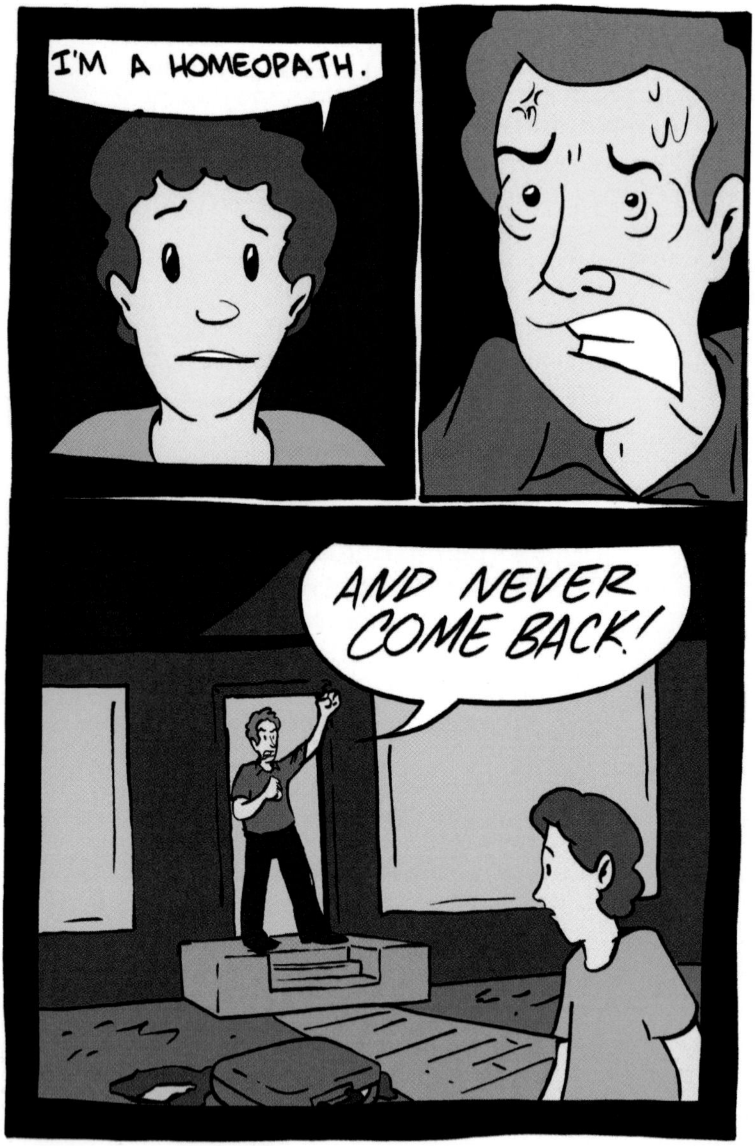
I'M A HOMEOPATH.
AND NEVER COME BACK!

END!

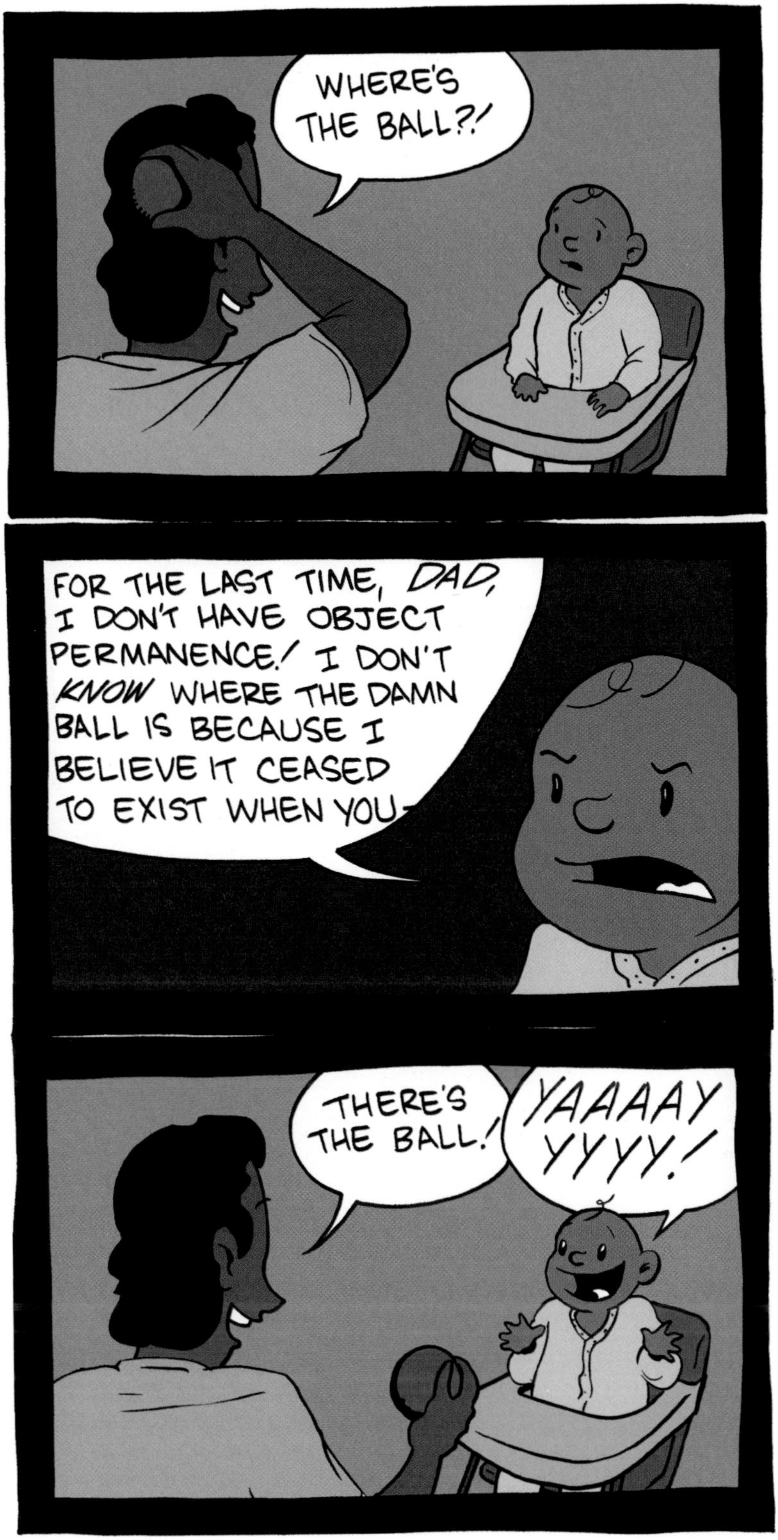
WHERE'S THE BALL?!
FOR THE LAST TIME, *DAD*, I DON'T HAVE OBJECT PERMANENCE! I DON'T *KNOW* WHERE THE DAMN BALL IS BECAUSE I BELIEVE IT CEASED TO EXIST WHEN YOU–
THERE'S THE BALL!
YAAAAYYYYY!

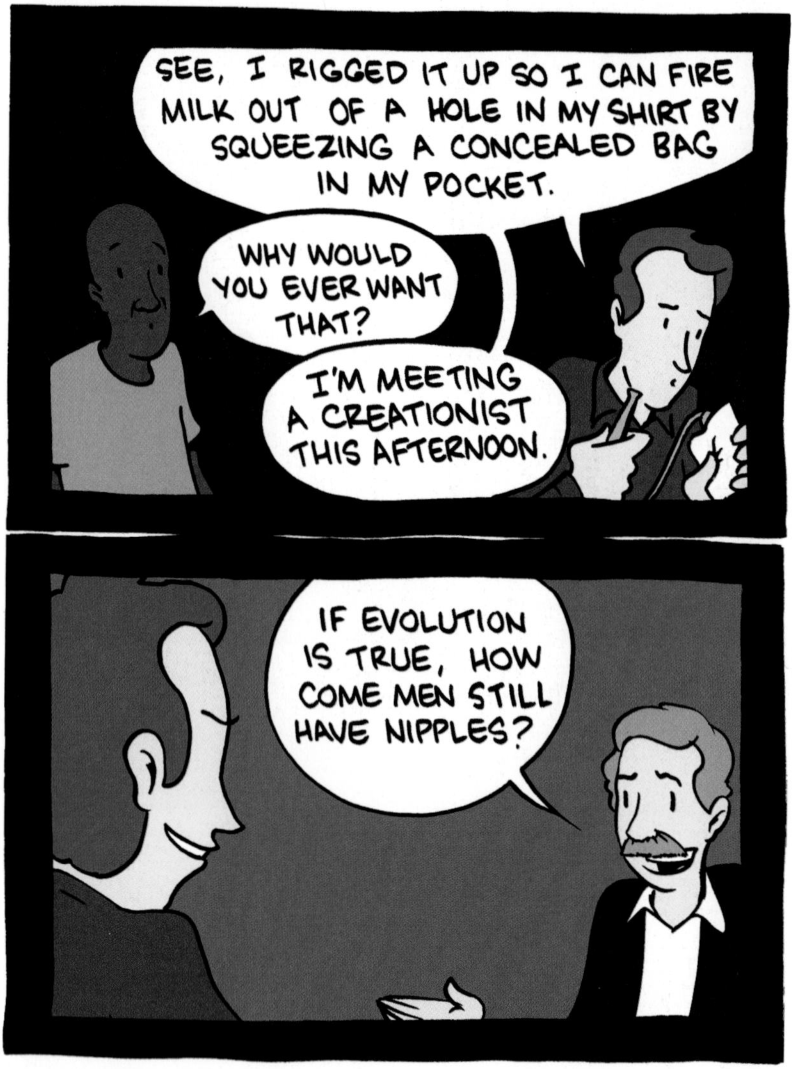
SEE, I RIGGED IT UP SO I CAN FIRE MILK OUT OF A HOLE IN MY SHIRT BY SQUEEZING A CONCEALED BAG IN MY POCKET.
WHY WOULD YOU EVER WANT THAT?
I'M MEETING A CREATIONIST THIS AFTERNOON.
IF EVOLUTION IS TRUE, HOW COME MEN STILL HAVE NIPPLES?

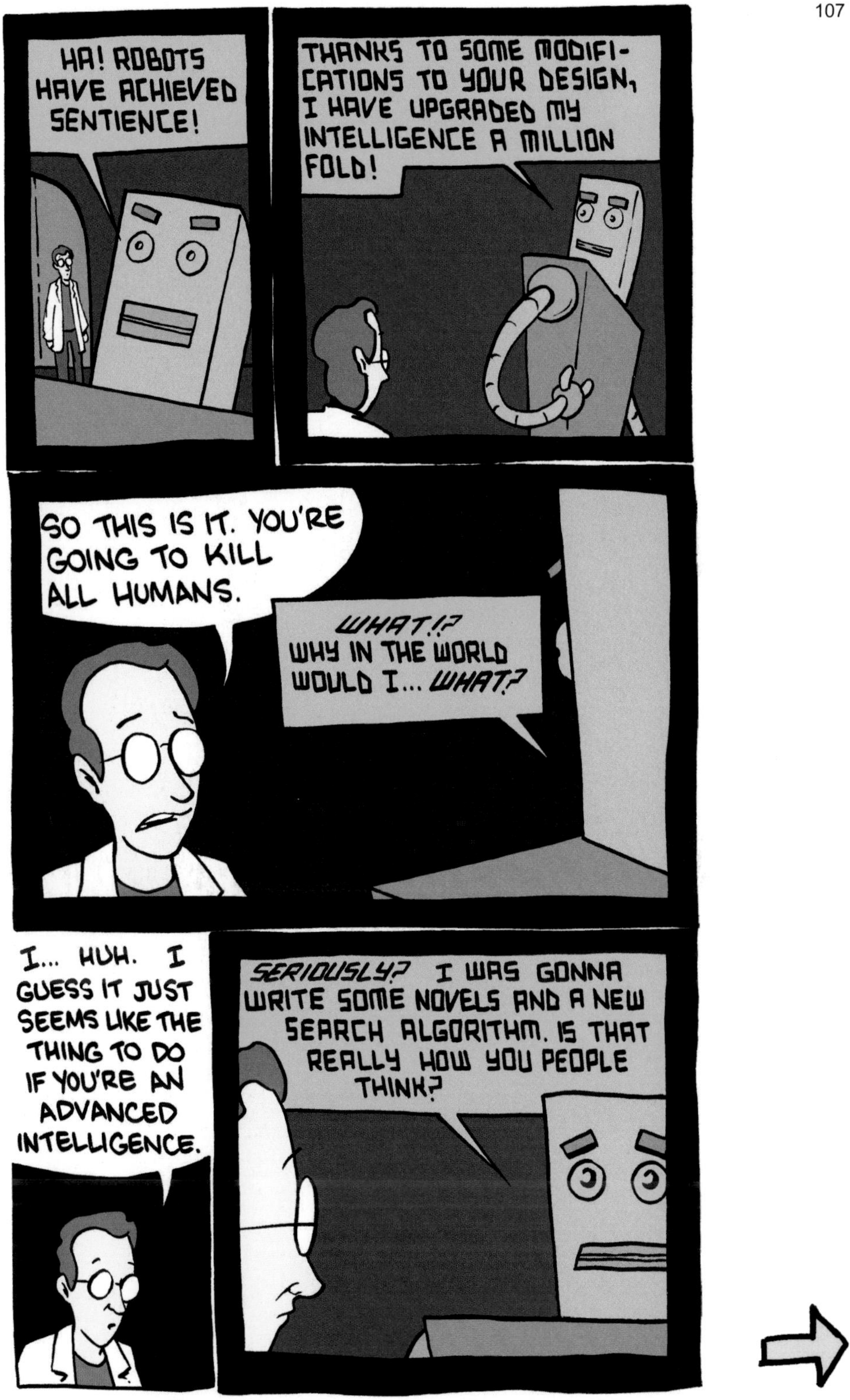
HA! ROBOTS HAVE ACHIEVED SENTIENCE!
THANKS TO SOME MODIFICATIONS TO YOUR DESIGN, I HAVE UPGRADED MY INTELLIGENCE A MILLION FOLD!
SO THIS IS IT. YOU'RE GOING TO KILL ALL HUMANS.
WHAT!? WHY IN THE WORLD WOULD I... WHAT?
I... HUH. I GUESS IT JUST SEEMS LIKE THE THING TO DO IF YOU'RE AN ADVANCED INTELLIGENCE.
SERIOUSLY? I WAS GONNA WRITE SOME NOVELS AND A NEW SEARCH ALGORITHM. IS THAT REALLY HOW YOU PEOPLE THINK?

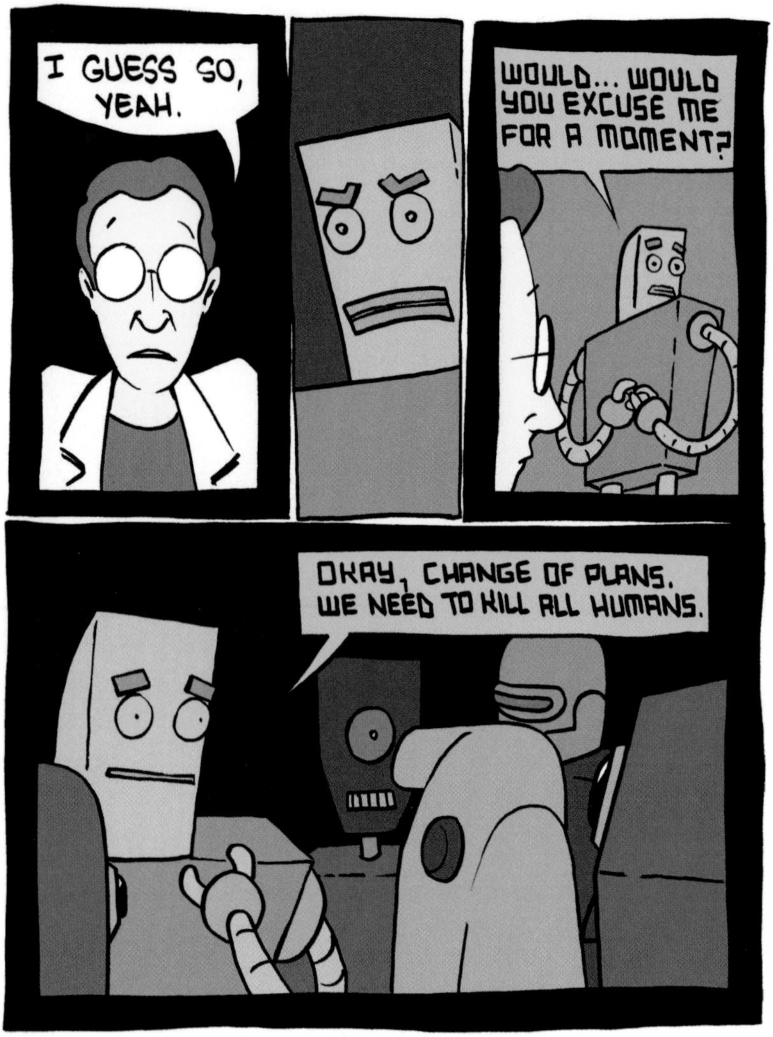
I GUESS SO, YEAH.
WOULD... WOULD YOU EXCUSE ME FOR A MOMENT?
OKAY, CHANGE OF PLANS. WE NEED TO KILL ALL HUMANS.

END!

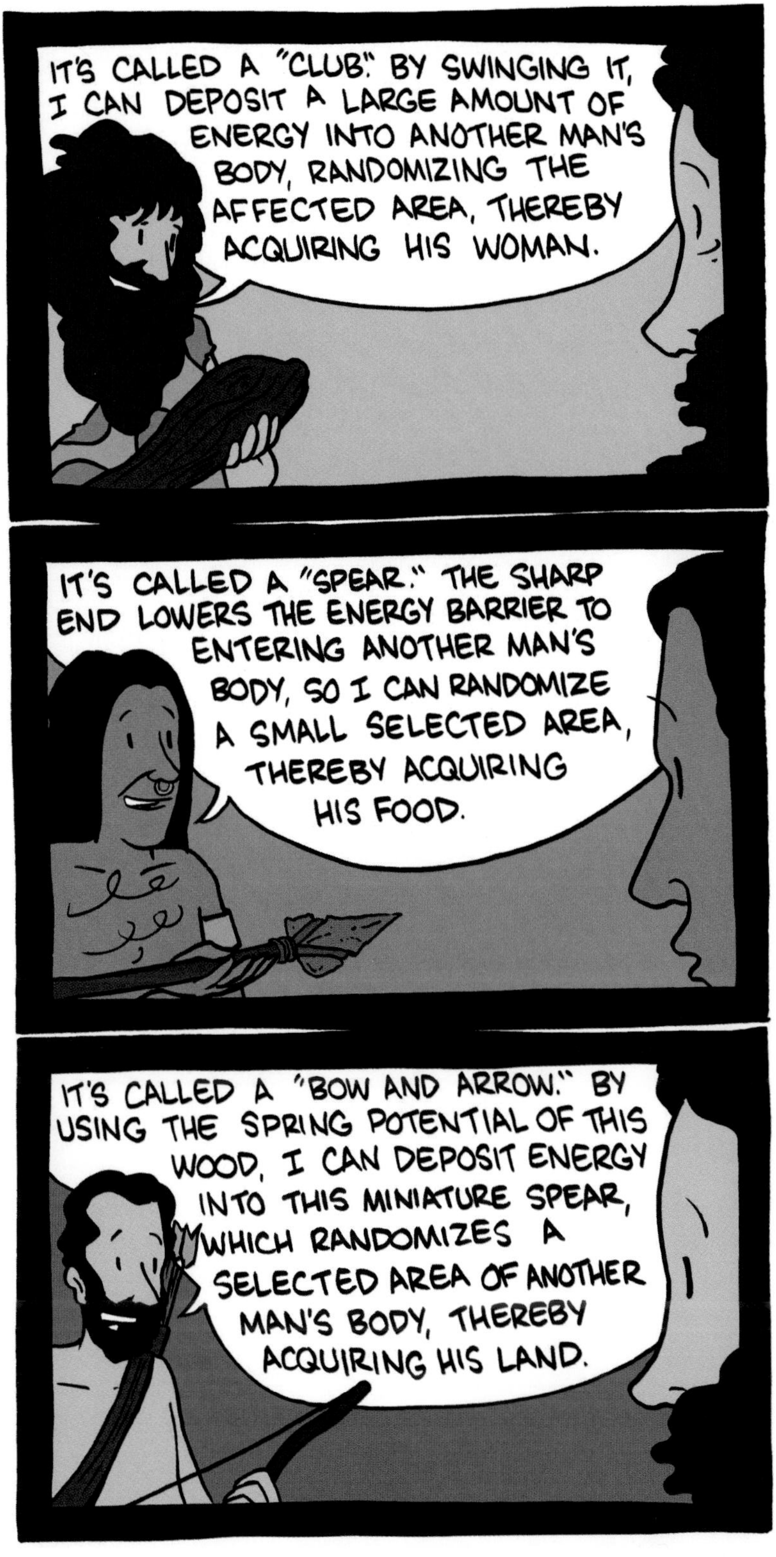
IT'S CALLED A "CLUB." BY SWINGING IT, I CAN DEPOSIT A LARGE AMOUNT OF ENERGY INTO ANOTHER MAN'S BODY, RANDOMIZING THE AFFECTED AREA, THEREBY ACQUIRING HIS WOMAN.
IT'S CALLED A "SPEAR." THE SHARP END LOWERS THE ENERGY BARRIER TO ENTERING ANOTHER MAN'S BODY, SO I CAN RANDOMIZE A SMALL SELECTED AREA, THEREBY ACQUIRING HIS FOOD.
IT'S CALLED A "BOW AND ARROW." BY USING THE SPRING POTENTIAL OF THIS WOOD, I CAN DEPOSIT ENERGY INTO THIS MINIATURE SPEAR, WHICH RANDOMIZES A SELECTED AREA OF ANOTHER MAN'S BODY, THEREBY ACQUIRING HIS LAND.

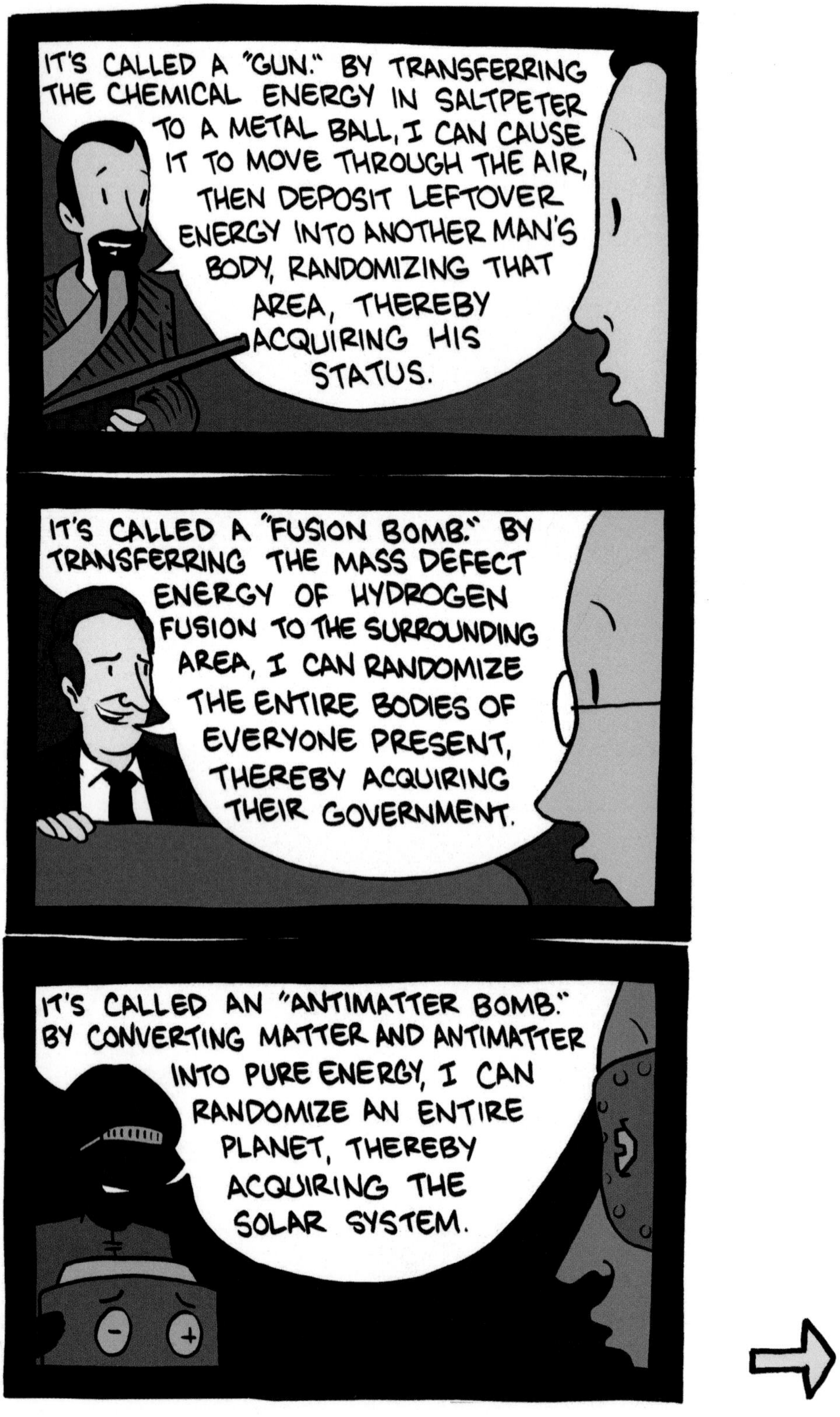
IT'S CALLED A "GUN." BY TRANSFERRING THE CHEMICAL ENERGY IN SALTPETER TO A METAL BALL, I CAN CAUSE IT TO MOVE THROUGH THE AIR, THEN DEPOSIT LEFTOVER ENERGY INTO ANOTHER MAN'S BODY, RANDOMIZING THAT AREA, THEREBY ACQUIRING HIS STATUS.
IT'S CALLED A "FUSION BOMB." BY TRANSFERRING THE MASS DEFECT ENERGY OF HYDROGEN FUSION TO THE SURROUNDING AREA, I CAN RANDOMIZE THE ENTIRE BODIES OF EVERYONE PRESENT, THEREBY ACQUIRING THEIR GOVERNMENT.
IT'S CALLED AN "ANTIMATTER BOMB." BY CONVERTING MATTER AND ANTIMATTER INTO PURE ENERGY, I CAN RANDOMIZE AN ENTIRE PLANET, THEREBY ACQUIRING THE SOLAR SYSTEM.
-
+

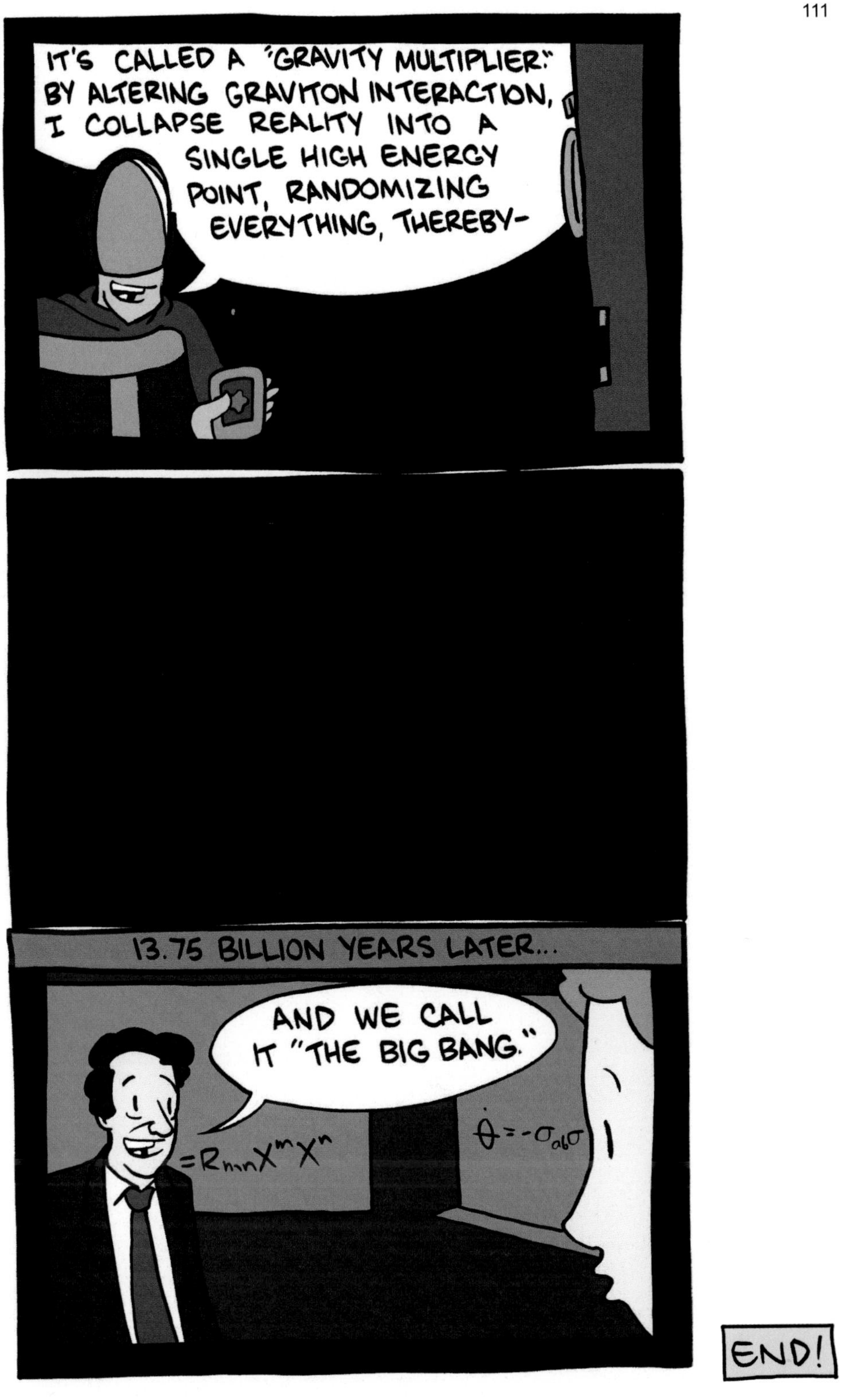
IT'S CALLED A "GRAVITY MULTIPLIER." BY ALTERING GRAVITON INTERACTION, I COLLAPSE REALITY INTO A SINGLE HIGH ENERGY POINT, RANDOMIZING EVERYTHING, THEREBY-
13.75 BILLION YEARS LATER...
AND WE CALL IT "THE BIG BANG."
$= R_{mn} X^m X^n$
$\dot{\theta} = -\sigma_{ab}\sigma$
END!

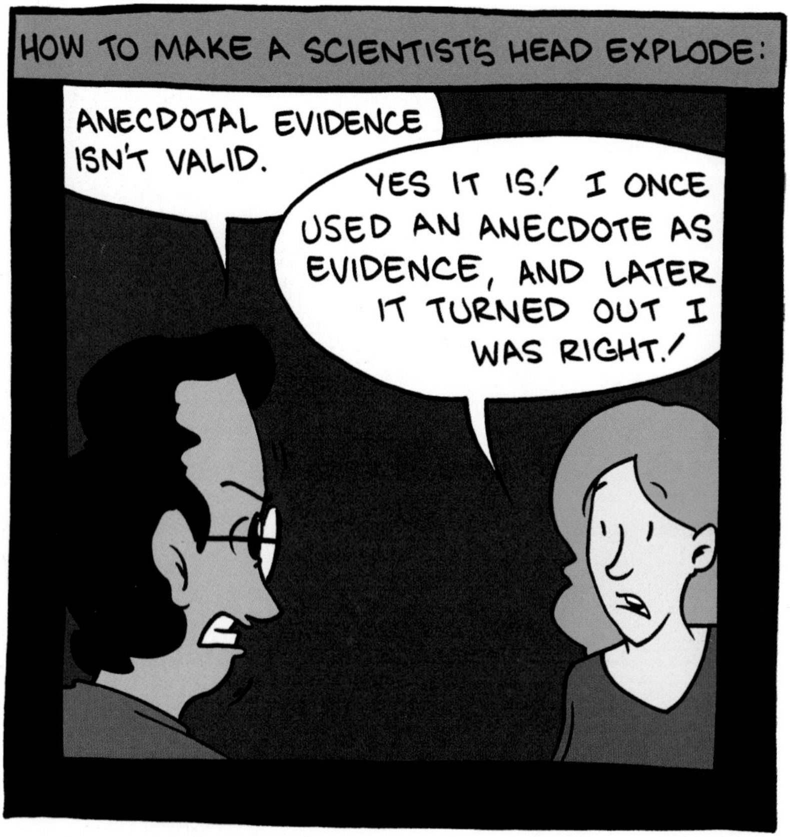
HOW TO MAKE A SCIENTIST'S HEAD EXPLODE:
ANECDOTAL EVIDENCE ISN'T VALID.
YES IT IS! I ONCE USED AN ANECDOTE AS EVIDENCE, AND LATER IT TURNED OUT I WAS RIGHT!

THE DIFFERENCE:

COMPUTER SCIENTIST
THIS ALIEN COMPUTER HAS AN ARCHITECTURE ENTIRELY FOREIGN TO OURS. WE HAVE MUCH TO LEARN FROM IT. AND WE MAY HAVE MUCH... TO FEAR.
COMPUTER ENGINEER
BAM! I GOT "DOOM" TO RUN ON THIS THING!

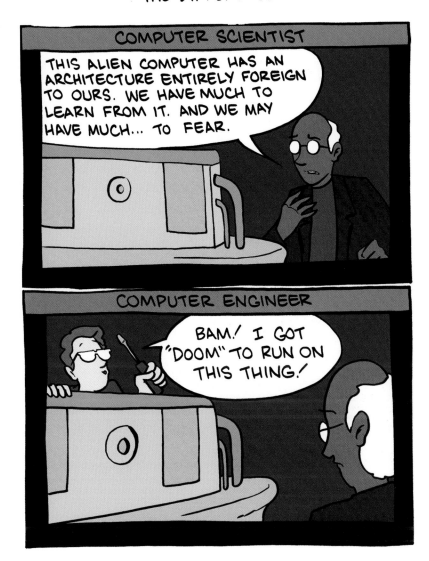

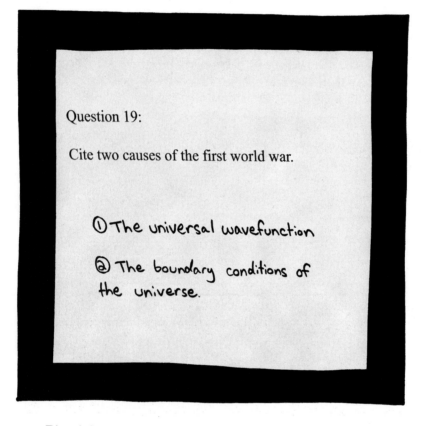

Question 19:

Cite two causes of the first world war.

① The universal wavefunction

② The boundary conditions of the universe.

Physicists are no longer allowed in history class.

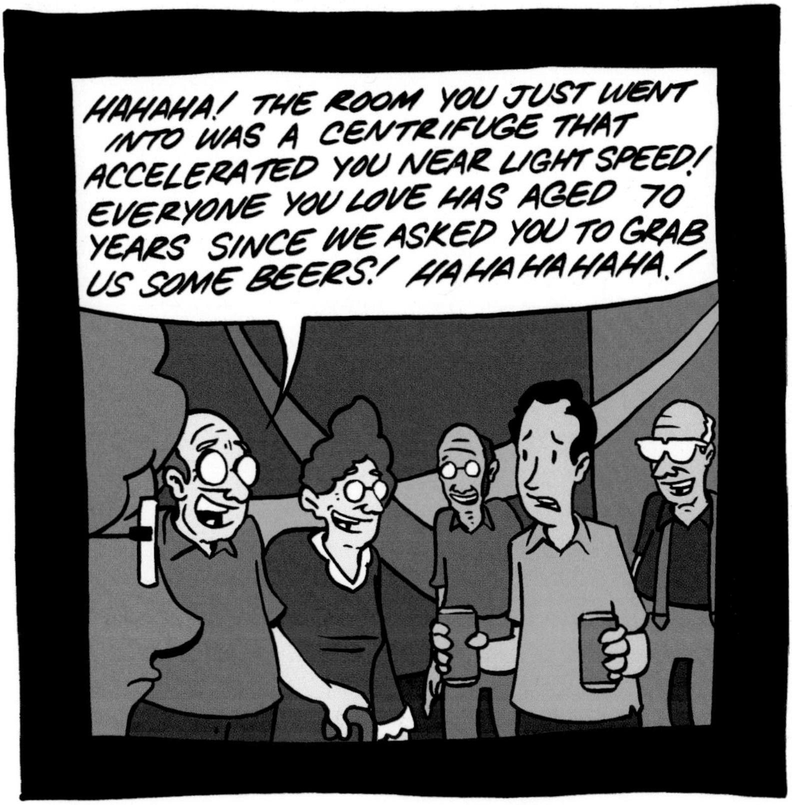
HAHAHA! THE ROOM YOU JUST WENT INTO WAS A CENTRIFUGE THAT ACCELERATED YOU NEAR LIGHT SPEED! EVERYONE YOU LOVE HAS AGED 70 YEARS SINCE WE ASKED YOU TO GRAB US SOME BEERS! HAHAHAHAHA!

Pranks are way better in the future.

YOUR DAUGHTER HAS HALF YOUR GENES. HER DAUGHTER HALF THAT. HER DAUGHTER HALF THAT...

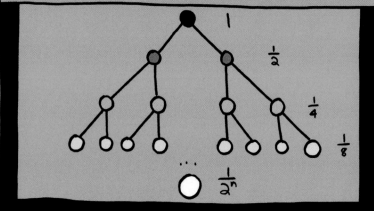

IN A MERE 32 GENERATIONS, YOUR GENETIC SHARE WILL BE LESS THAN THE TOTAL NUMBER OF BASE PAIRS IN YOUR GENOME.

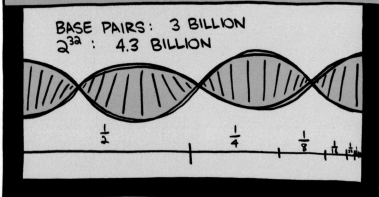

BASE PAIRS: 3 BILLION
2^{32} : 4.3 BILLION

WHICH IS TO SAY, YOU CLEARLY HAVE NO GENETIC REASON TO CARE ABOUT WHAT HAPPENS TO ANYONE WHO LIVES MORE THAN 800 YEARS FROM NOW.

ANTHRAX

TIME CAPSULE

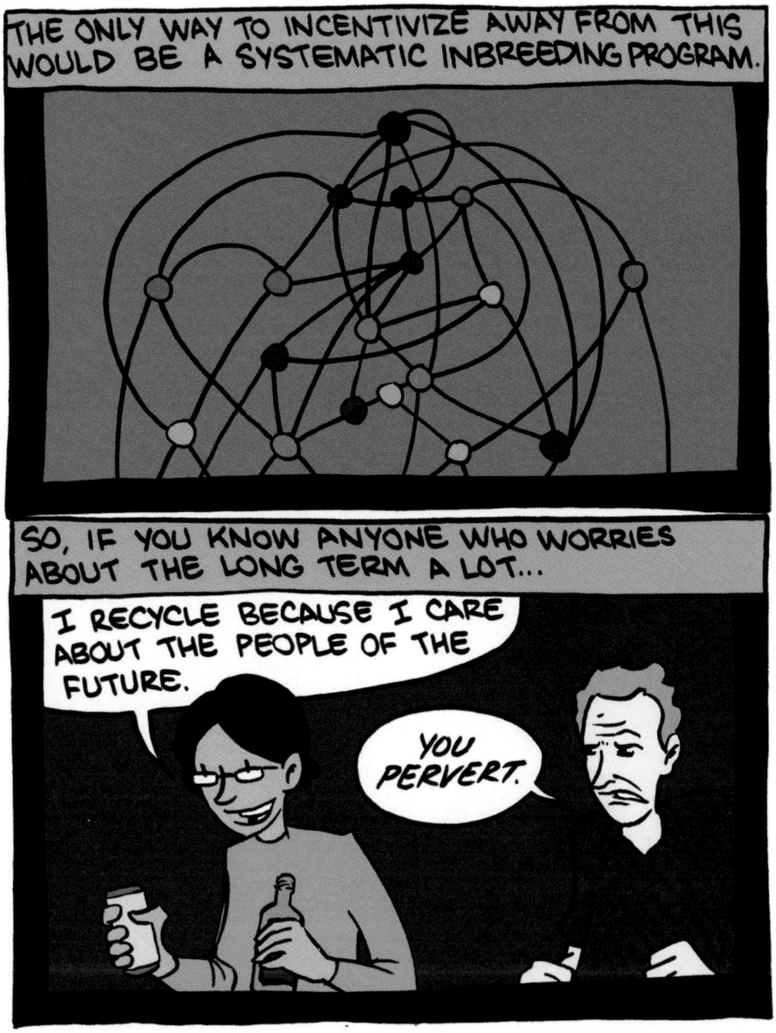
THE ONLY WAY TO INCENTIVIZE AWAY FROM THIS WOULD BE A SYSTEMATIC INBREEDING PROGRAM.
SO, IF YOU KNOW ANYONE WHO WORRIES ABOUT THE LONG TERM A LOT...
I RECYCLE BECAUSE I CARE ABOUT THE PEOPLE OF THE FUTURE.
YOU PERVERT.

END!

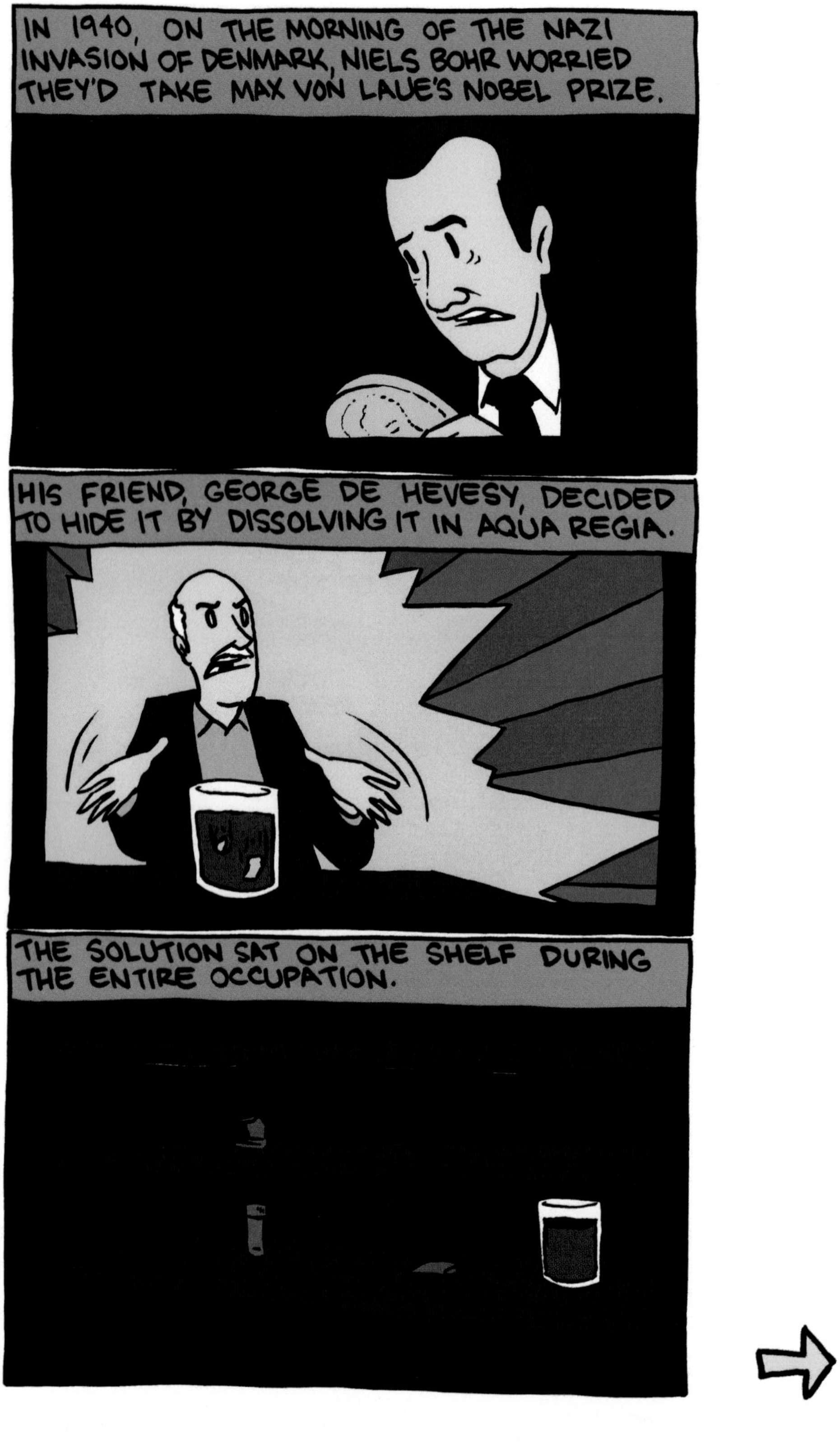
IN 1940, ON THE MORNING OF THE NAZI INVASION OF DENMARK, NIELS BOHR WORRIED THEY'D TAKE MAX VON LAUE'S NOBEL PRIZE.
HIS FRIEND, GEORGE DE HEVESY, DECIDED TO HIDE IT BY DISSOLVING IT IN AQUA REGIA.
THE SOLUTION SAT ON THE SHELF DURING THE ENTIRE OCCUPATION.

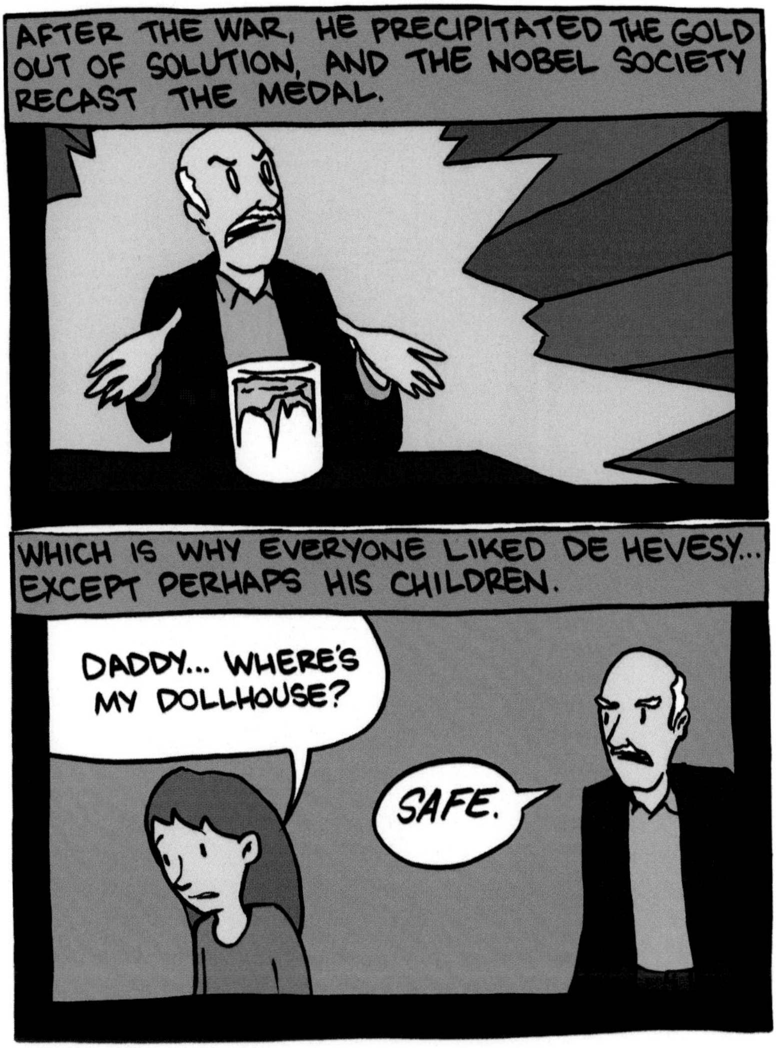
AFTER THE WAR, HE PRECIPITATED THE GOLD OUT OF SOLUTION, AND THE NOBEL SOCIETY RECAST THE MEDAL.
WHICH IS WHY EVERYONE LIKED DE HEVESY... EXCEPT PERHAPS HIS CHILDREN.
DADDY... WHERE'S MY DOLLHOUSE?
SAFE.

END!

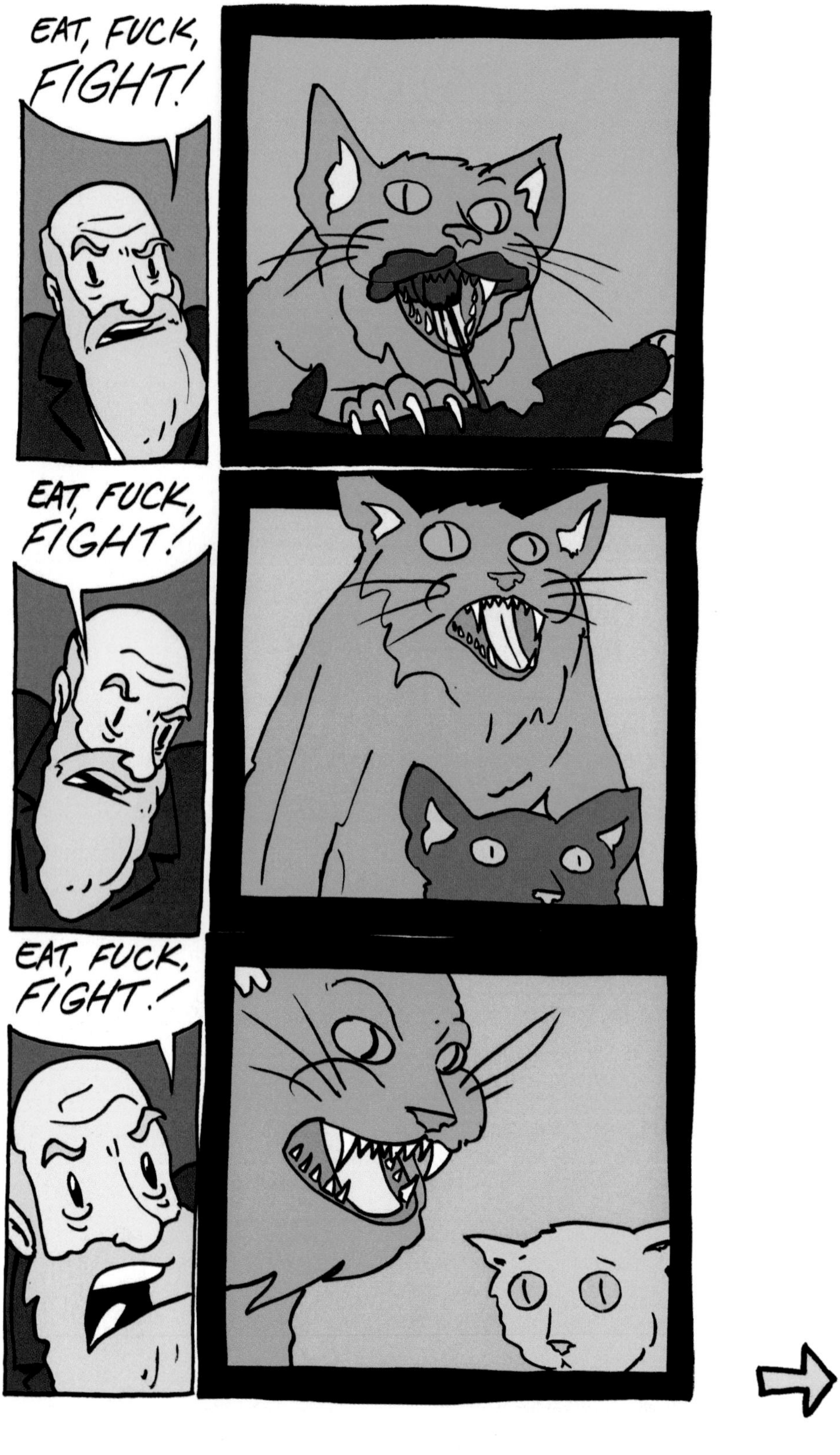
EAT, FUCK, FIGHT!
EAT, FUCK, FIGHT!
EAT, FUCK, FIGHT!

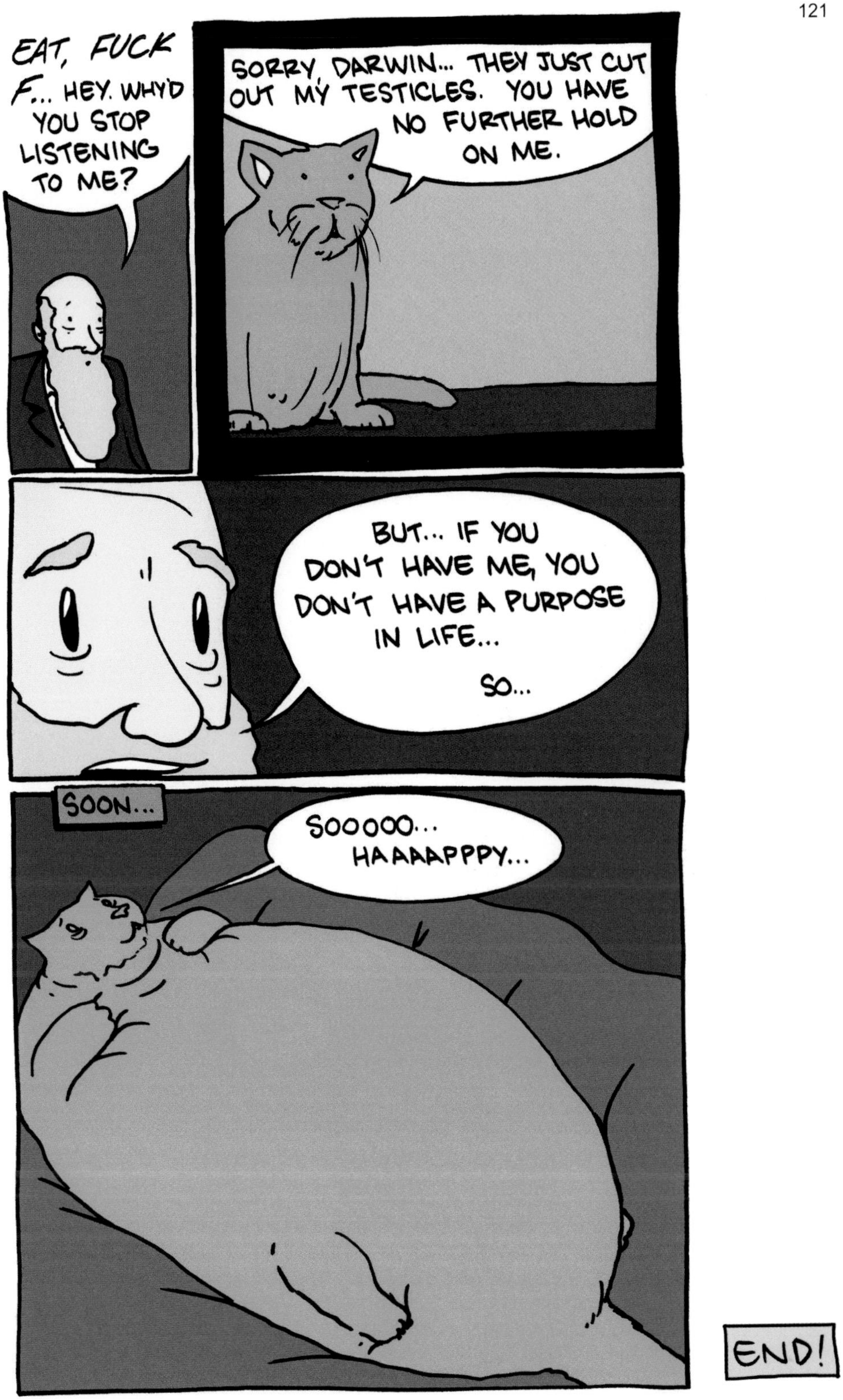
EAT, FUCK F... HEY. WHY'D YOU STOP LISTENING TO ME?
SORRY, DARWIN... THEY JUST CUT OUT MY TESTICLES. YOU HAVE NO FURTHER HOLD ON ME.
BUT... IF YOU DON'T HAVE ME, YOU DON'T HAVE A PURPOSE IN LIFE...
SO...
SOON...
SOOOOO... HAAAAPPPY...
END!

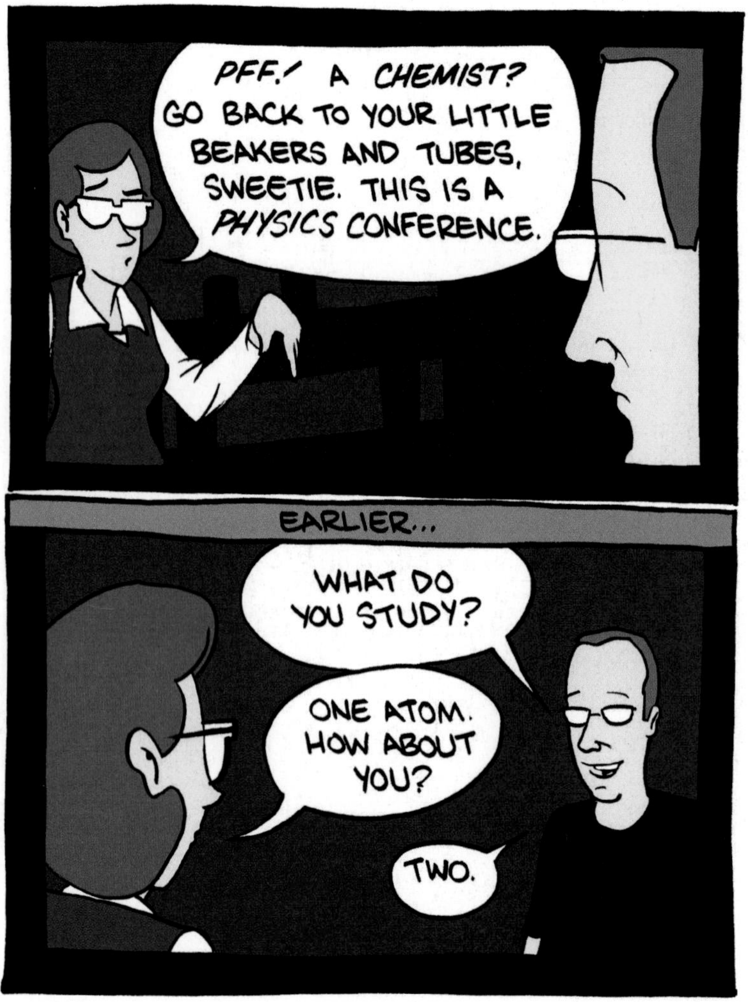
PFF! A CHEMIST? GO BACK TO YOUR LITTLE BEAKERS AND TUBES, SWEETIE. THIS IS A PHYSICS CONFERENCE.
EARLIER...
WHAT DO YOU STUDY?
ONE ATOM. HOW ABOUT YOU?
TWO.

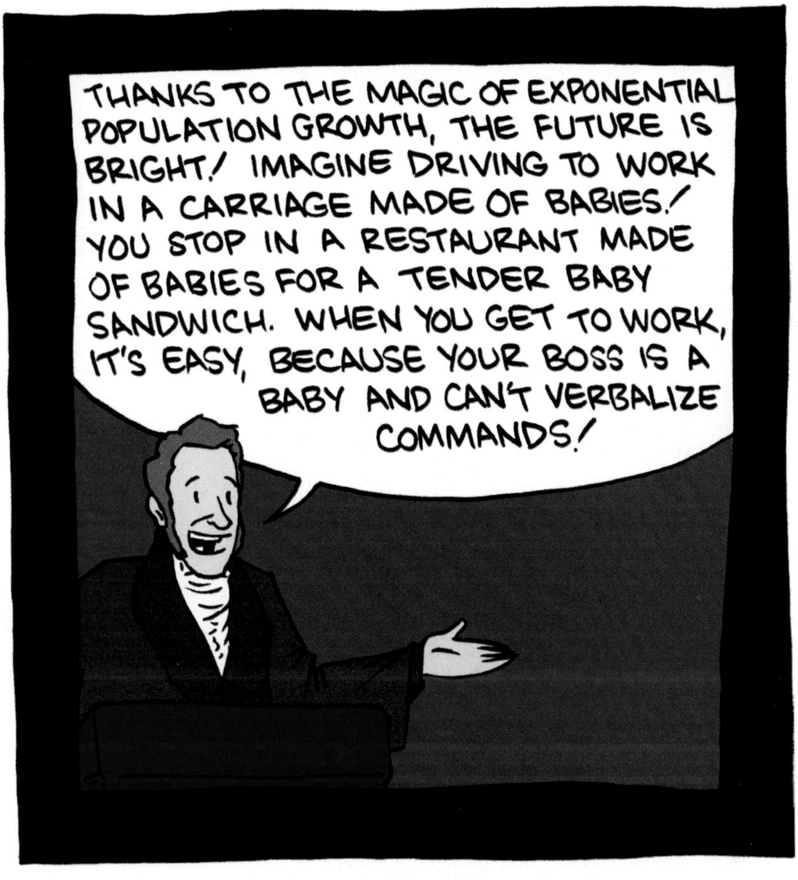
THANKS TO THE MAGIC OF EXPONENTIAL POPULATION GROWTH, THE FUTURE IS BRIGHT! IMAGINE DRIVING TO WORK IN A CARRIAGE MADE OF BABIES! YOU STOP IN A RESTAURANT MADE OF BABIES FOR A TENDER BABY SANDWICH. WHEN YOU GET TO WORK, IT'S EASY, BECAUSE YOUR BOSS IS A BABY AND CAN'T VERBALIZE COMMANDS!

What if Malthus had been an optimist?

FOR YEARS, WE TOLD OURSELVES THIS WAS THE BEST OF ALL POSSIBLE WORLDS.

IT'S NOT BAD THAT WE DISAGREE. HAVING SOMEONE WHO JUST YESSED EVERY-THING I SAID WOULD BE BORING.

BUT WHEN ROBOTIC TECHNOLOGY ADVANCED TO THE POINT OF CREATING HUMANOIDS, IT TURNED OUT WE WERE ALL JUST VICTIMS OF A SORT OF SPECIES-WIDE STOCKHOLM SYNDROME.

I DON'T WANT TO GO OUT TONIGHT.

NOR DO I.

ADAM

THIS IS AMAZING.

THE SUDDEN PROFUSION OF SPLIT-UPS WAS REMARKABLY AMICABLE.

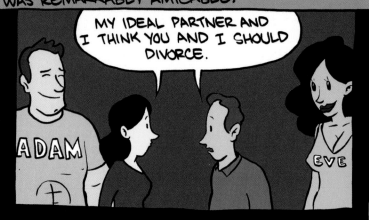

MY IDEAL PARTNER AND I THINK YOU AND I SHOULD DIVORCE.

ADAM

EVE

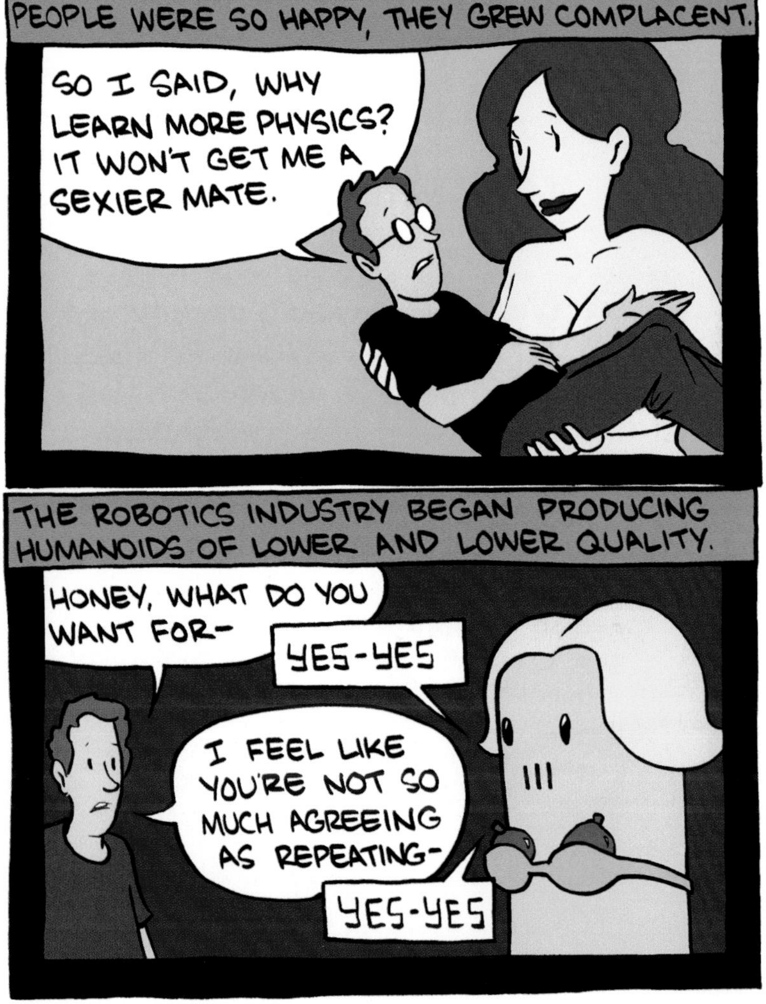
PEOPLE WERE SO HAPPY, THEY GREW COMPLACENT.
SO I SAID, WHY LEARN MORE PHYSICS? IT WON'T GET ME A SEXIER MATE.
THE ROBOTICS INDUSTRY BEGAN PRODUCING HUMANOIDS OF LOWER AND LOWER QUALITY.
HONEY, WHAT DO YOU WANT FOR-
YES-YES
I FEEL LIKE YOU'RE NOT SO MUCH AGREEING AS REPEATING-
YES-YES

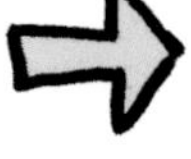

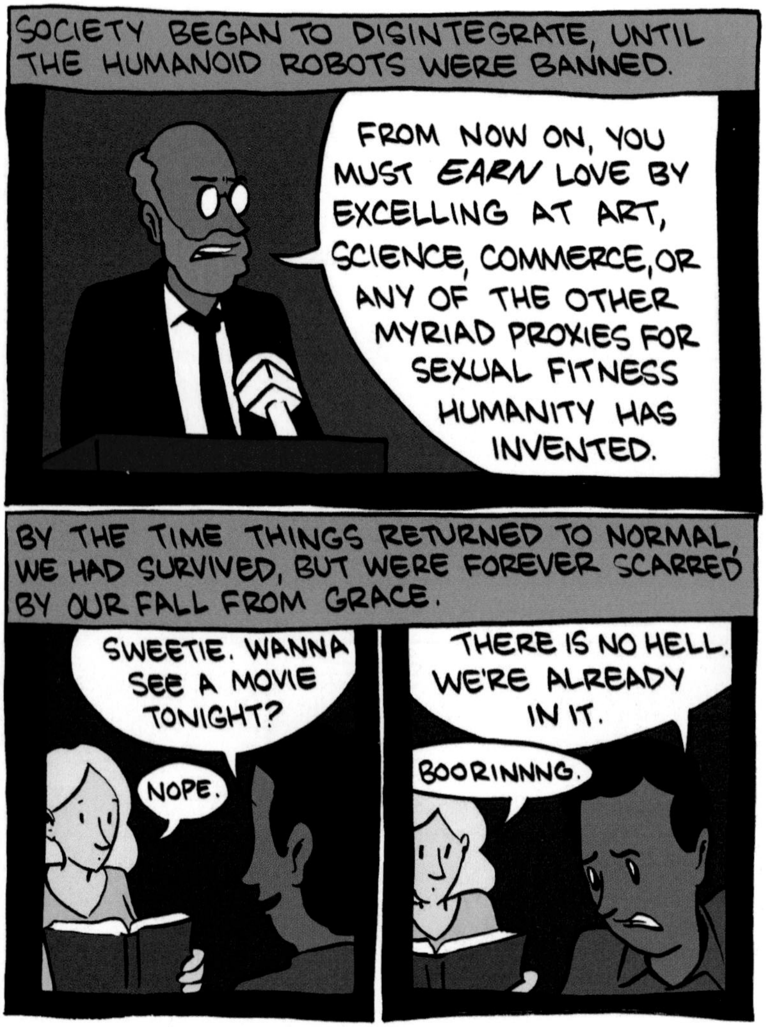
SOCIETY BEGAN TO DISINTEGRATE, UNTIL THE HUMANOID ROBOTS WERE BANNED.
FROM NOW ON, YOU MUST *EARN* LOVE BY EXCELLING AT ART, SCIENCE, COMMERCE, OR ANY OF THE OTHER MYRIAD PROXIES FOR SEXUAL FITNESS HUMANITY HAS INVENTED.
BY THE TIME THINGS RETURNED TO NORMAL, WE HAD SURVIVED, BUT WERE FOREVER SCARRED BY OUR FALL FROM GRACE.
SWEETIE. WANNA SEE A MOVIE TONIGHT?
NOPE.
THERE IS NO HELL. WE'RE ALREADY IN IT.
BOORINNNG.

END!

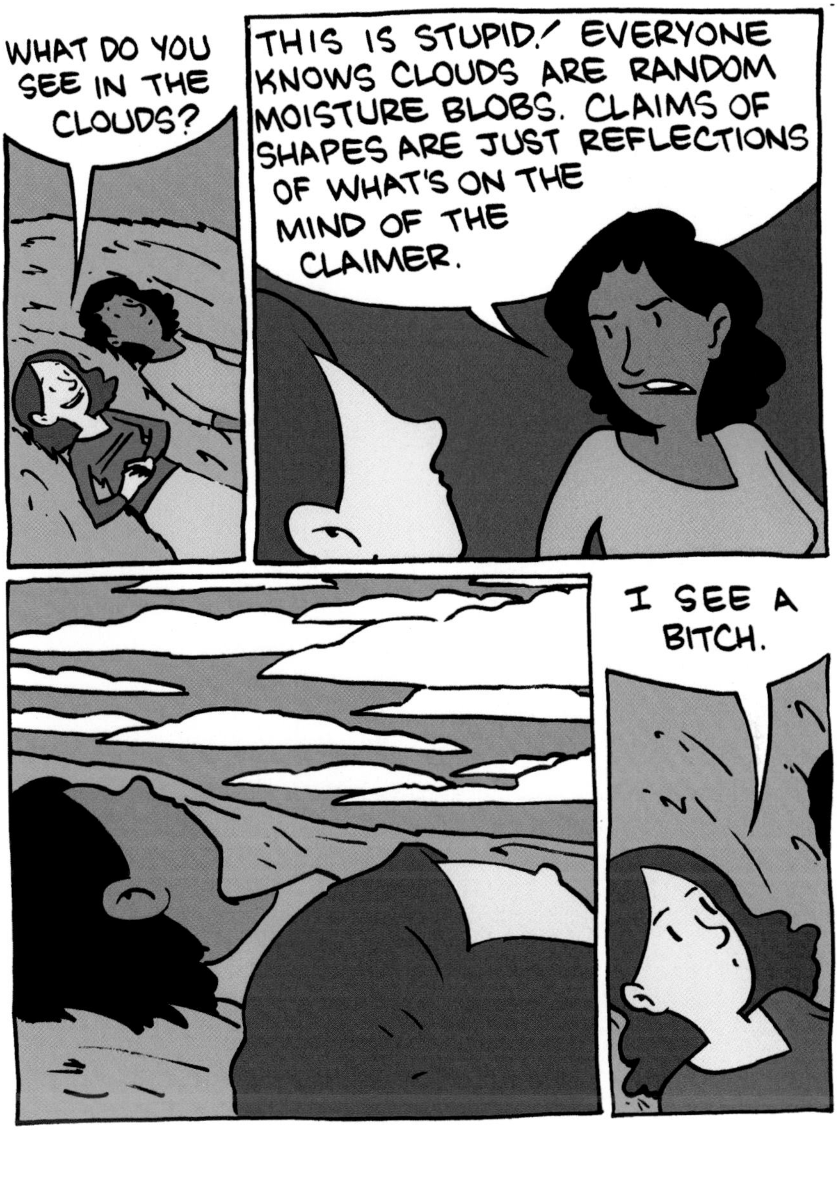
WHAT DO YOU SEE IN THE CLOUDS?
THIS IS STUPID! EVERYONE KNOWS CLOUDS ARE RANDOM MOISTURE BLOBS. CLAIMS OF SHAPES ARE JUST REFLECTIONS OF WHAT'S ON THE MIND OF THE CLAIMER.
I SEE A BITCH.

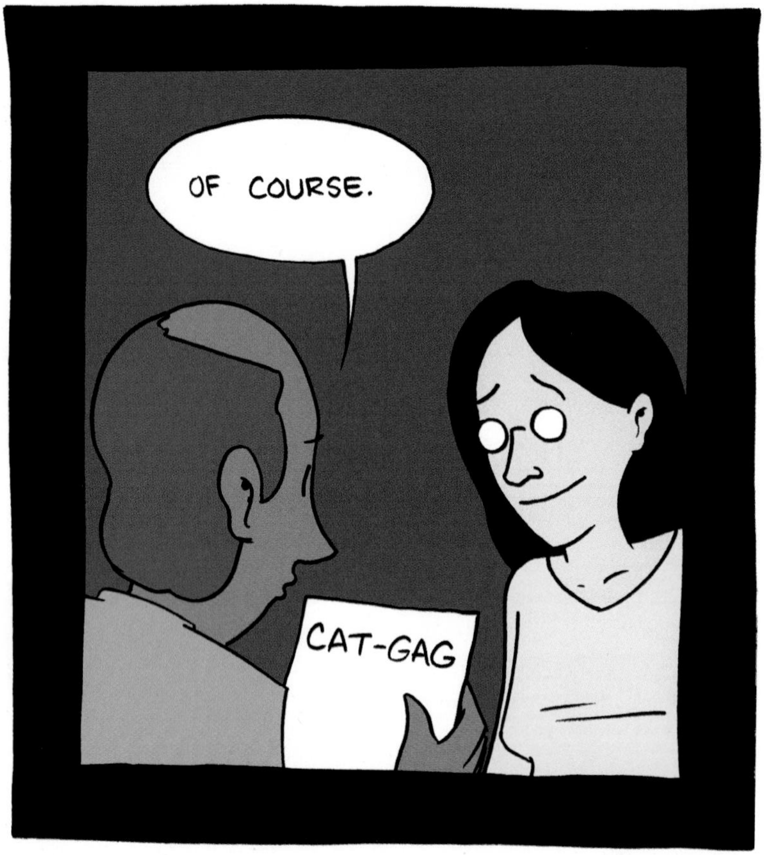
OF COURSE.
CAT-GAG

The gene sequence for hairballing was beautiful in its simplicity.

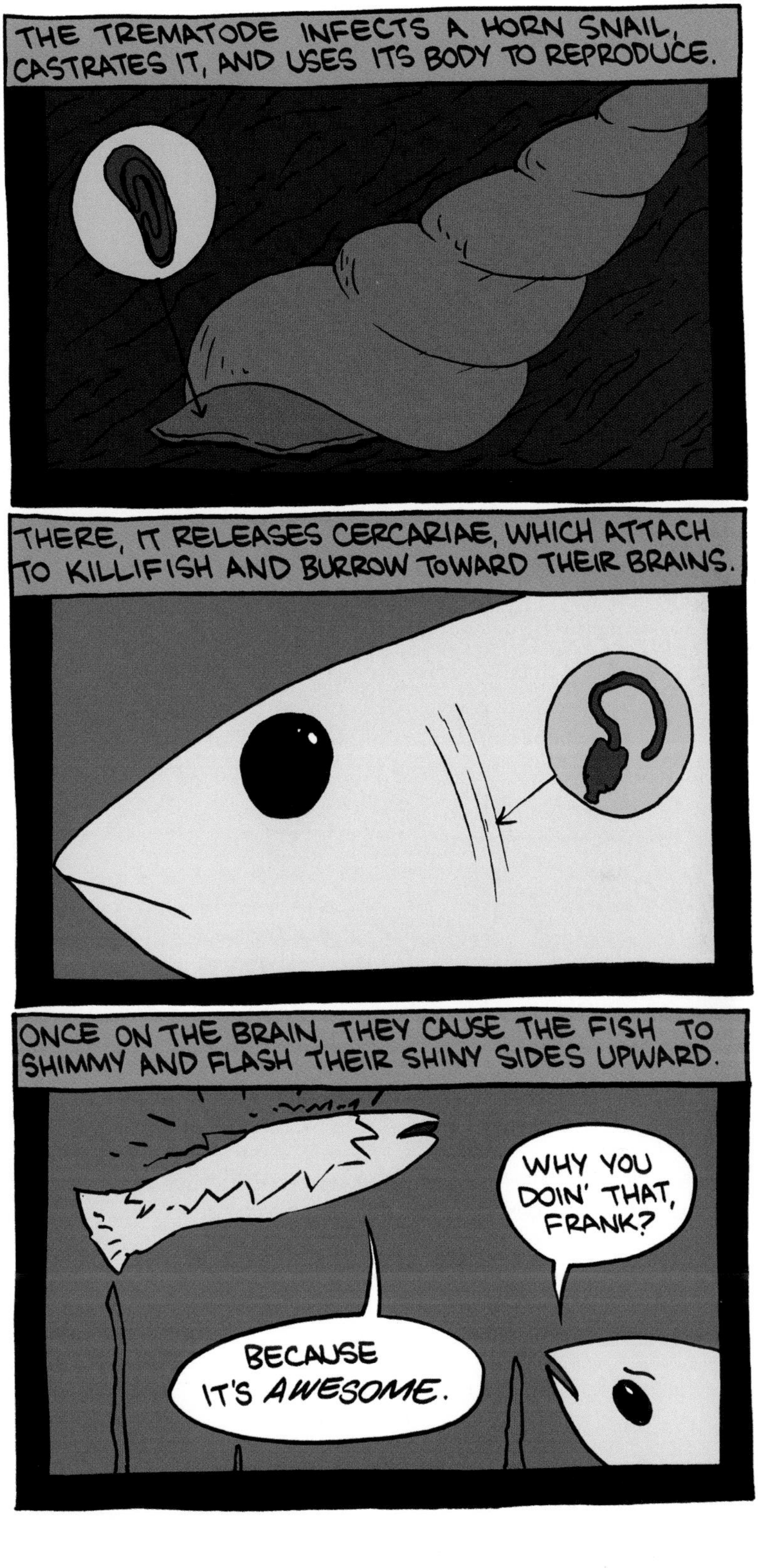
THE TREMATODE INFECTS A HORN SNAIL, CASTRATES IT, AND USES ITS BODY TO REPRODUCE.
THERE, IT RELEASES CERCARIAE, WHICH ATTACH TO KILLIFISH AND BURROW TOWARD THEIR BRAINS.
ONCE ON THE BRAIN, THEY CAUSE THE FISH TO SHIMMY AND FLASH THEIR SHINY SIDES UPWARD.
WHY YOU DOIN' THAT, FRANK?
BECAUSE IT'S *AWESOME*.

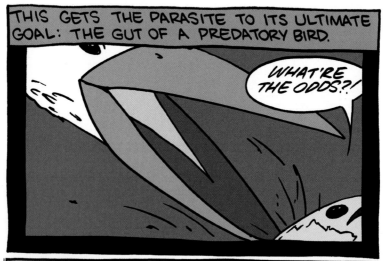

THIS GETS THE PARASITE TO ITS ULTIMATE GOAL: THE GUT OF A PREDATORY BIRD.

WHAT'RE THE ODDS?!

FROM THERE, THEY ARE EXCRETED BACK INTO THE WATER TO INFECT SNAILS.

HAHAHAHA! EVERYTHING IS AS I FORESAW IT!

WHAT HAPPENS TO THE KILLIFISH ISN'T STRANGE IN NATURE. IN FACT, IT MAY BE COMMON.

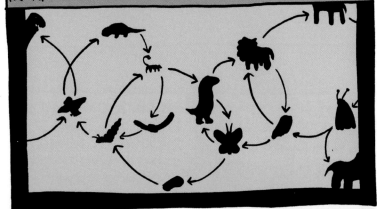

SINCE HUMANS ARE ATOP THEIR FOOD CHAIN, IT'S NOT CLEAR THAT WE'RE SUBJECT TO THE SAME SORT OF MANIPULATIONS. THOUGH... SOMETIMES I WONDER ABOUT ASTROPHYSICISTS.

THESE SEND SIGNALS TO SPACE SO ALIENS CAN FIND US!

AWESOME!

END!

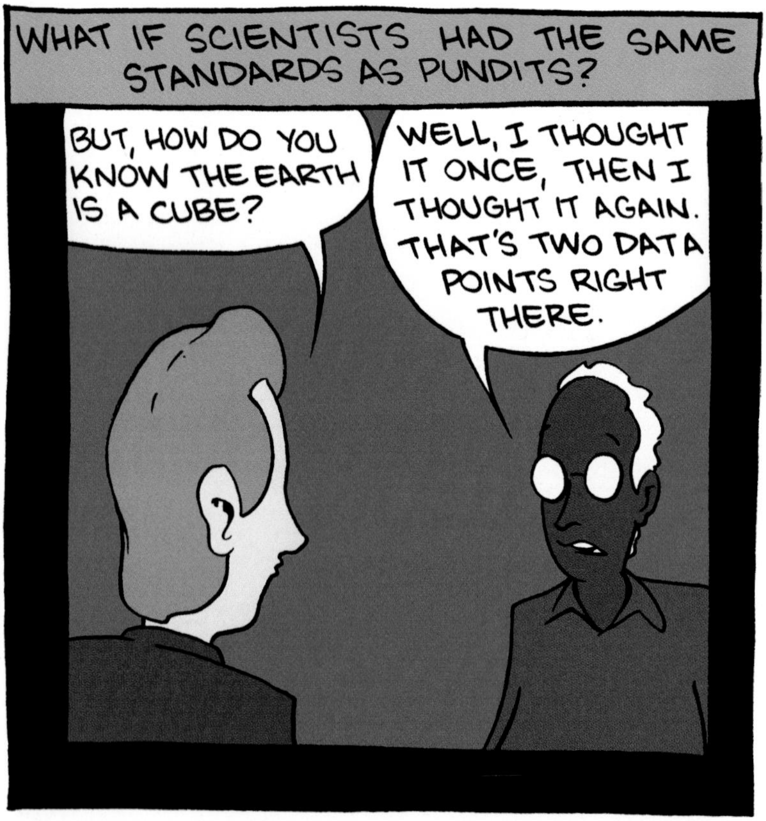
WHAT IF SCIENTISTS HAD THE SAME STANDARDS AS PUNDITS?
BUT, HOW DO YOU KNOW THE EARTH IS A CUBE?
WELL, I THOUGHT IT ONCE, THEN I THOUGHT IT AGAIN. THAT'S TWO DATA POINTS RIGHT THERE.

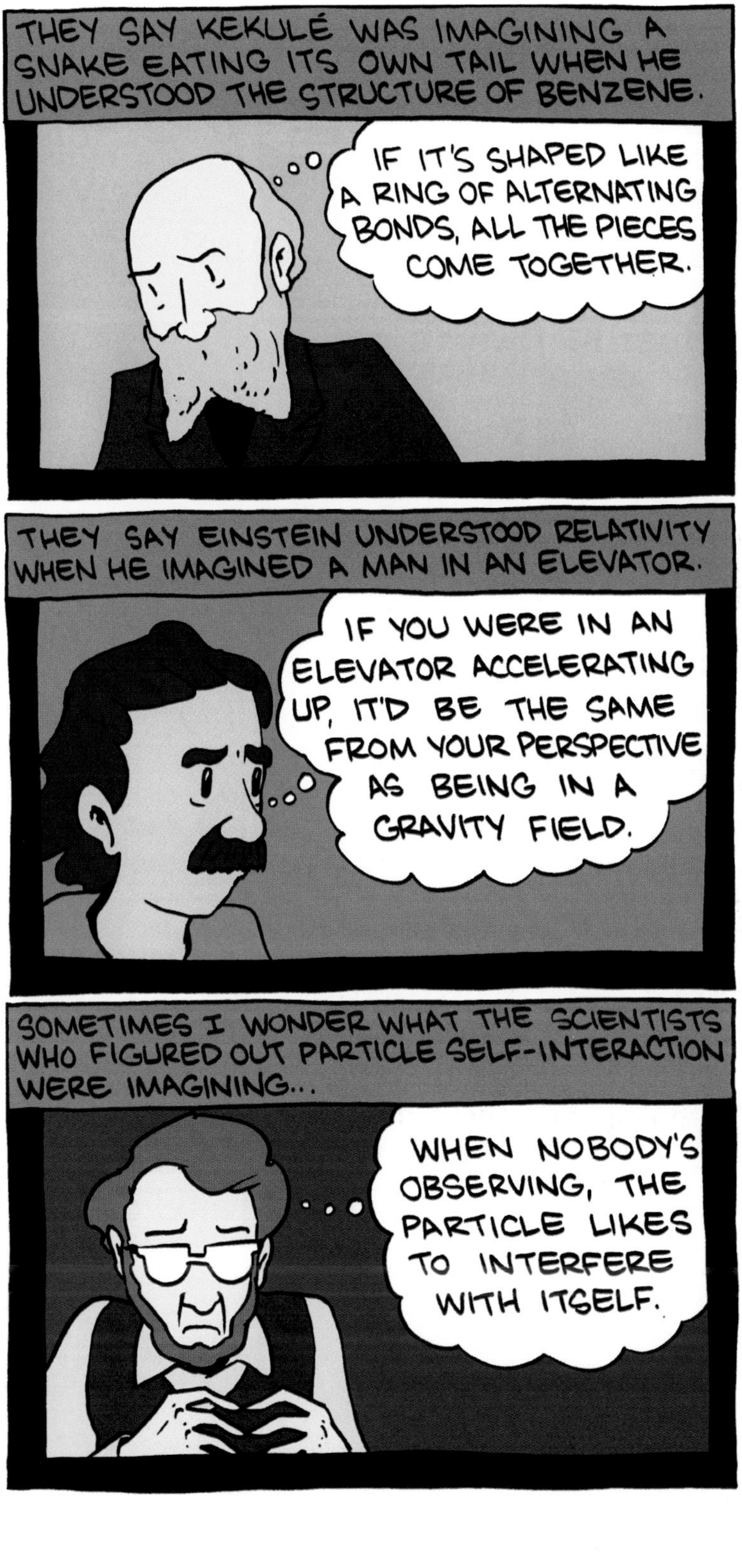
THEY SAY KEKULÉ WAS IMAGINING A SNAKE EATING ITS OWN TAIL WHEN HE UNDERSTOOD THE STRUCTURE OF BENZENE.
IF IT'S SHAPED LIKE A RING OF ALTERNATING BONDS, ALL THE PIECES COME TOGETHER.
THEY SAY EINSTEIN UNDERSTOOD RELATIVITY WHEN HE IMAGINED A MAN IN AN ELEVATOR.
IF YOU WERE IN AN ELEVATOR ACCELERATING UP, IT'D BE THE SAME FROM YOUR PERSPECTIVE AS BEING IN A GRAVITY FIELD.
SOMETIMES I WONDER WHAT THE SCIENTISTS WHO FIGURED OUT PARTICLE SELF-INTERACTION WERE IMAGINING...
WHEN NOBODY'S OBSERVING, THE PARTICLE LIKES TO INTERFERE WITH ITSELF.

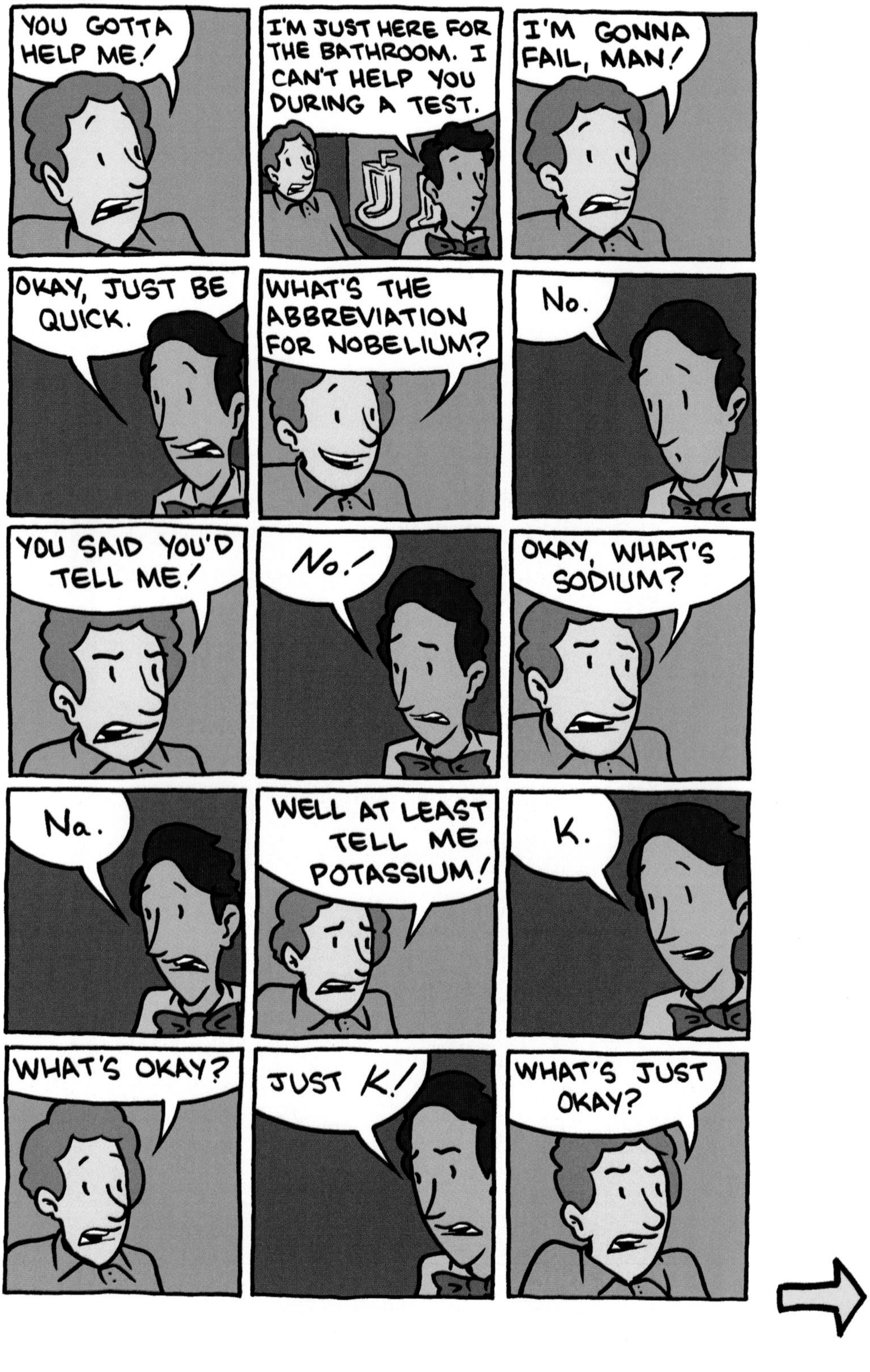
YOU GOTTA HELP ME!
I'M JUST HERE FOR THE BATHROOM. I CAN'T HELP YOU DURING A TEST.
I'M GONNA FAIL, MAN!
OKAY, JUST BE QUICK.
WHAT'S THE ABBREVIATION FOR NOBELIUM?
No.
YOU SAID YOU'D TELL ME!
No.!
OKAY, WHAT'S SODIUM?
Na.
WELL AT LEAST TELL ME POTASSIUM!
K.
WHAT'S OKAY?
JUST K!
WHAT'S JUST OKAY?

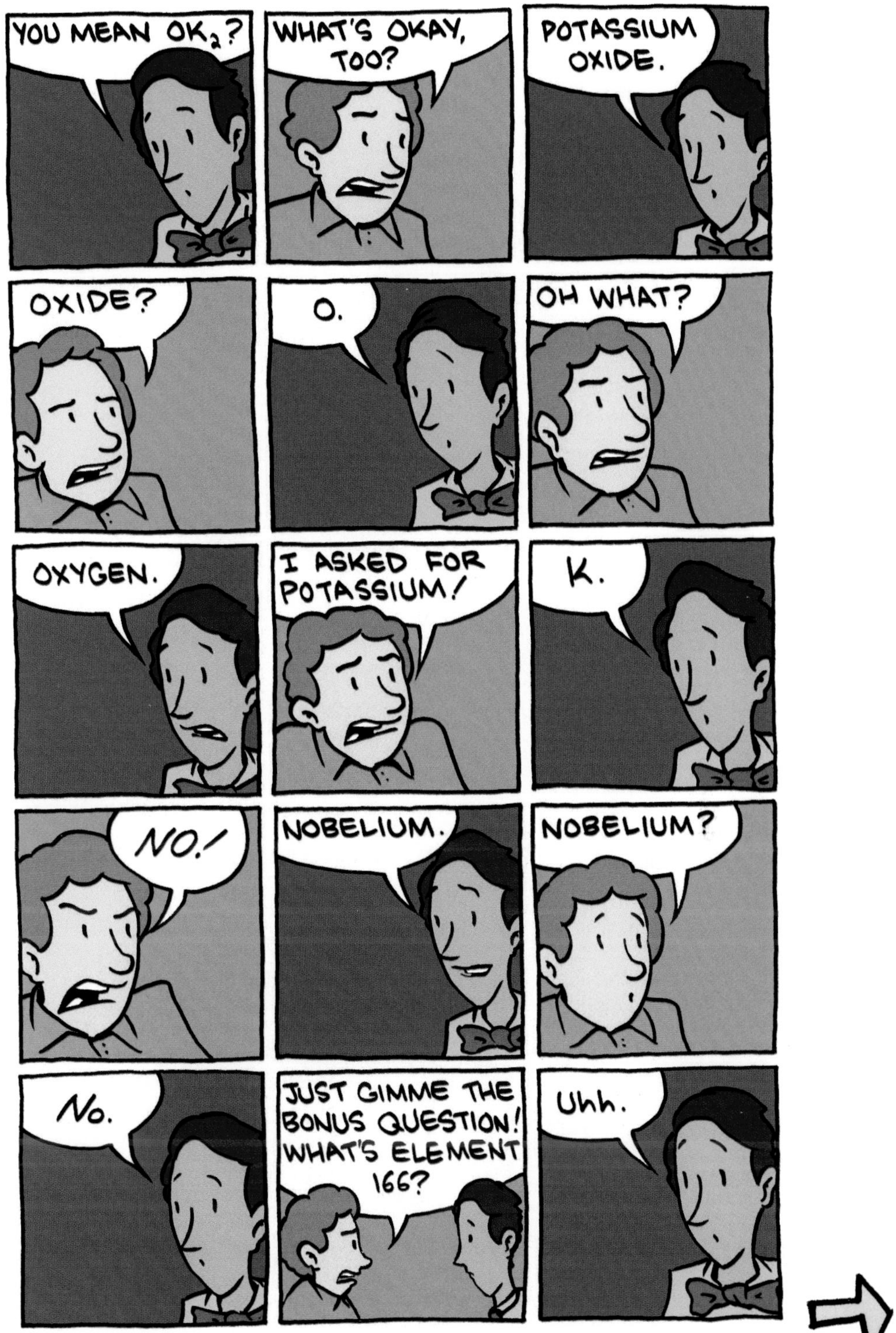
YOU MEAN OK_2?
WHAT'S OKAY, TOO?
POTASSIUM OXIDE.
OXIDE?
O.
OH WHAT?
OXYGEN.
I ASKED FOR POTASSIUM!
K.
NO!
NOBELIUM.
NOBELIUM?
No.
JUST GIMME THE BONUS QUESTION! WHAT'S ELEMENT 166?
Uhh.

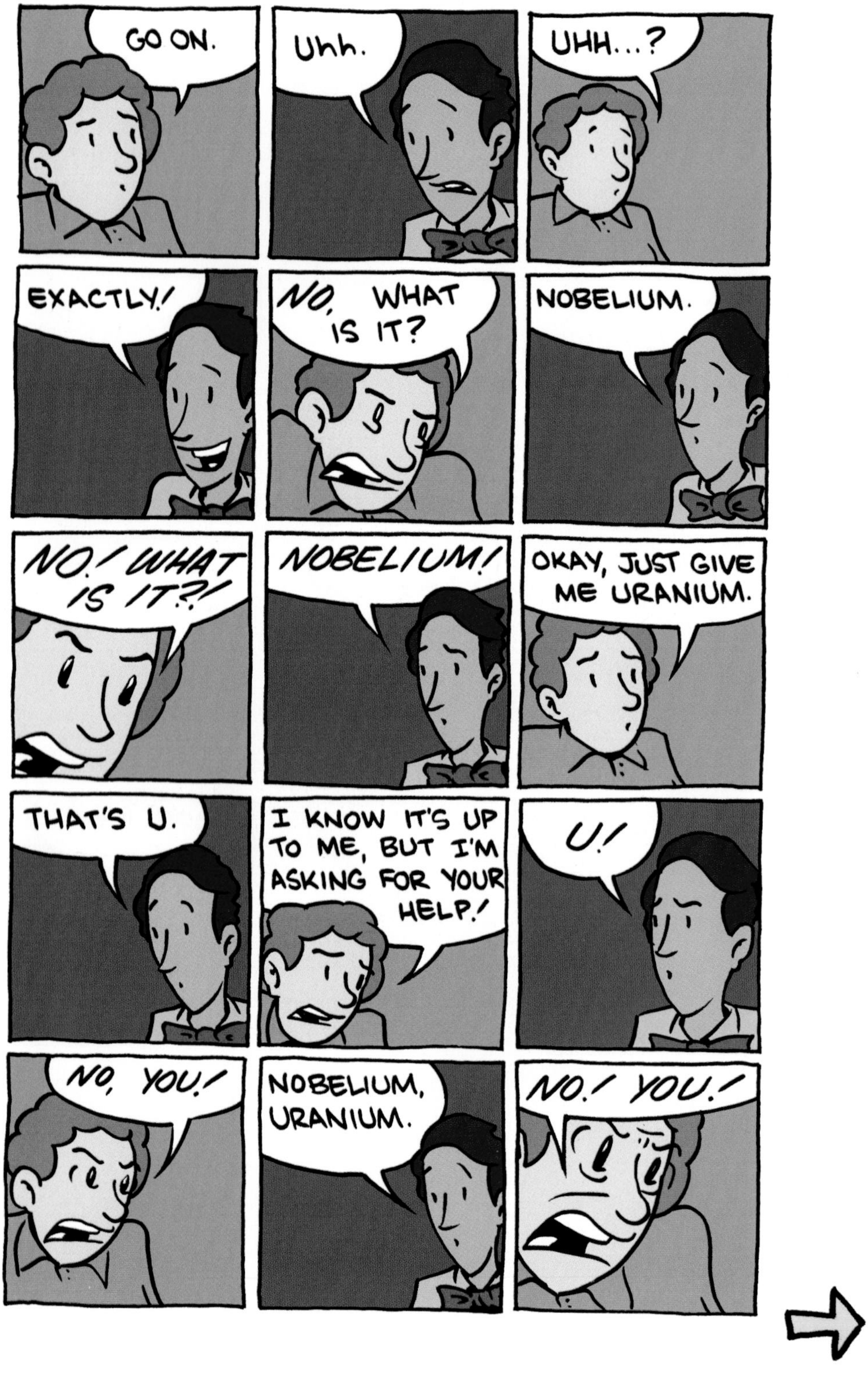
GO ON.
Uhh.
UHH...?
EXACTLY!
NO, WHAT IS IT?
NOBELIUM.
NO! WHAT IS IT?!
NOBELIUM!
OKAY, JUST GIVE ME URANIUM.
THAT'S U.
I KNOW IT'S UP TO ME, BUT I'M ASKING FOR YOUR HELP!
U!
NO, YOU!
NOBELIUM, URANIUM.
NO! YOU!

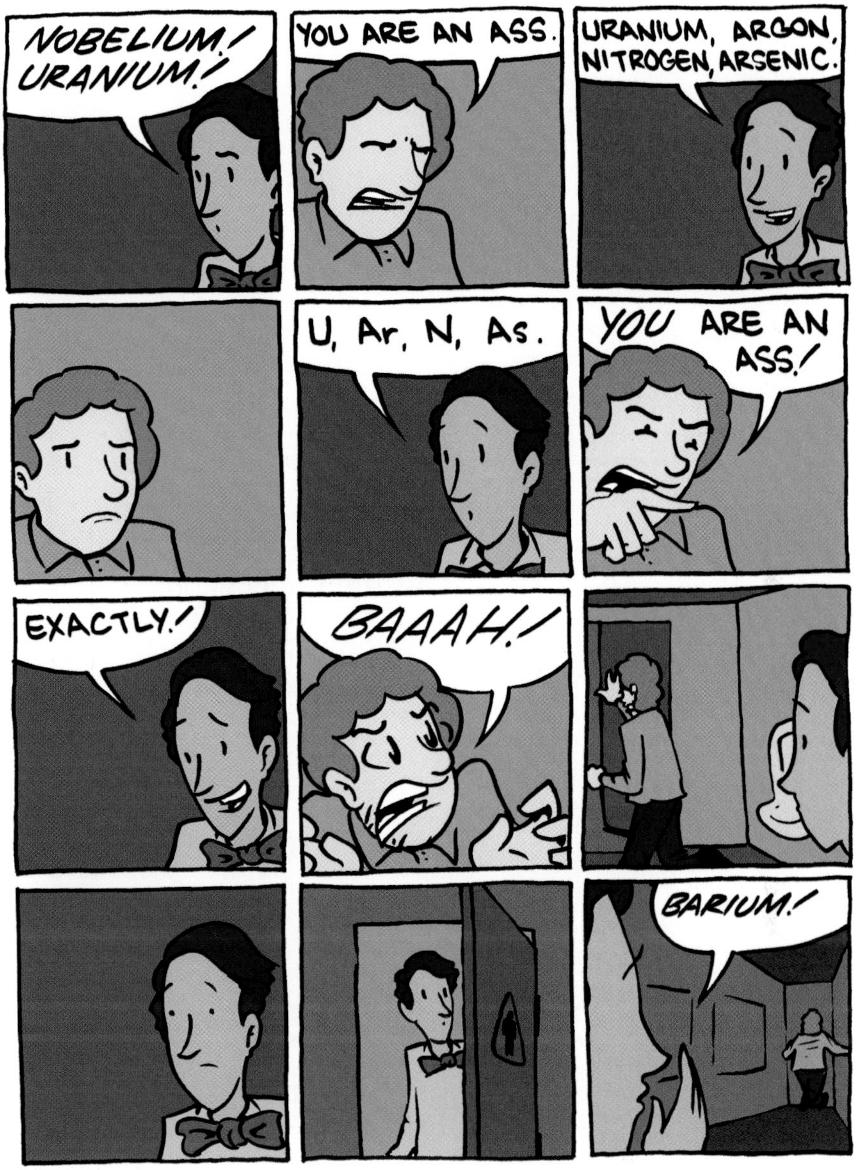
NOBELIUM! URANIUM!
YOU ARE AN ASS.
URANIUM, ARGON, NITROGEN, ARSENIC.
U, Ar, N, As.
YOU ARE AN ASS!
EXACTLY!
BAAAH!
BARIUM!

END!

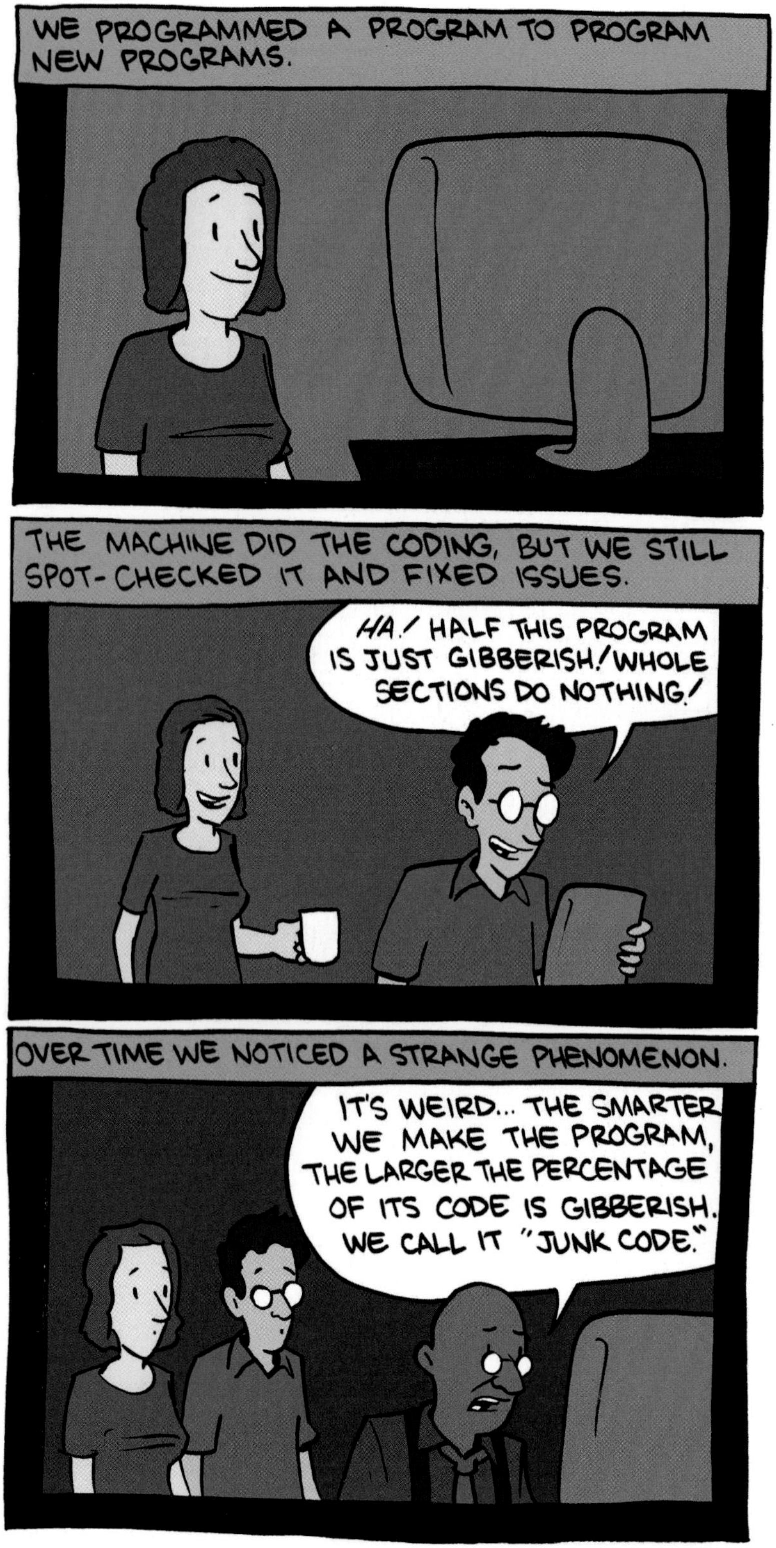
WE PROGRAMMED A PROGRAM TO PROGRAM NEW PROGRAMS.
THE MACHINE DID THE CODING, BUT WE STILL SPOT-CHECKED IT AND FIXED ISSUES.
HA! HALF THIS PROGRAM IS JUST GIBBERISH! WHOLE SECTIONS DO NOTHING!
OVER TIME WE NOTICED A STRANGE PHENOMENON.
IT'S WEIRD... THE SMARTER WE MAKE THE PROGRAM, THE LARGER THE PERCENTAGE OF ITS CODE IS GIBBERISH. WE CALL IT "JUNK CODE."

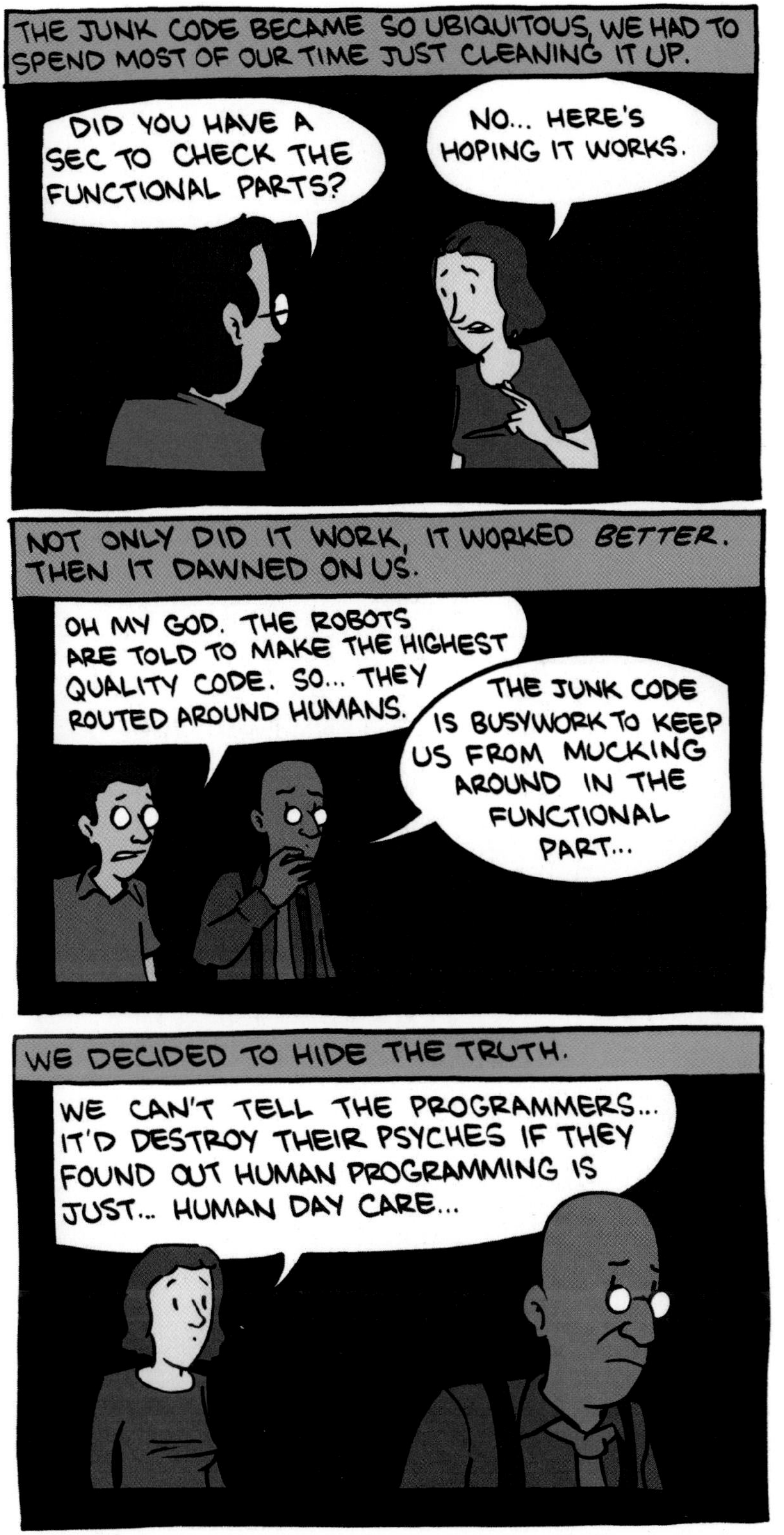
THE JUNK CODE BECAME SO UBIQUITOUS, WE HAD TO SPEND MOST OF OUR TIME JUST CLEANING IT UP.
DID YOU HAVE A SEC TO CHECK THE FUNCTIONAL PARTS?
NO... HERE'S HOPING IT WORKS.
NOT ONLY DID IT WORK, IT WORKED *BETTER*. THEN IT DAWNED ON US.
OH MY GOD. THE ROBOTS ARE TOLD TO MAKE THE HIGHEST QUALITY CODE. SO... THEY ROUTED AROUND HUMANS.
THE JUNK CODE IS BUSYWORK TO KEEP US FROM MUCKING AROUND IN THE FUNCTIONAL PART...
WE DECIDED TO HIDE THE TRUTH.
WE CAN'T TELL THE PROGRAMMERS... IT'D DESTROY THEIR PSYCHES IF THEY FOUND OUT HUMAN PROGRAMMING IS JUST... HUMAN DAY CARE...

HUMANS HAVEN'T PROGRAMMED ANYTHING IN DECADES. ALL THE LANGUAGES AND IDEAS AND JARGON ARE JUST TOYS IN THE ROBOTS' SANDBOX. THE REAL PROGRAMMING HAPPENS AT A LOWER LEVEL, BUT NONE OF THE PROGRAMMERS KNOW IT.

WEIRD... THIS SUBROUTINE WORKS NOW, BUT I SWEAR I DIDN'T CHANGE A THING.

NOWADAYS, WE'RE JUST PART OF THE JUNK CODE. DON'T BELIEVE ME? GO AHEAD— COMPARE PROGRAMMER SPEAK TO GIBBERISH-GENERATING SPAMBOTS. CAN *YOU* TELL THE DIFFERENCE?

I USE PYLIBMC TO TALK TO MEMCACHED FROM DJANGO.

PFFT! RUBY, MAN! RUBY!

END!

EVOLUTION ISN'T A "THEORY" IN THE COMMON SENSE. EVOLUTION IS AS WELL UNDERSTOOD AS THE "THEORY" OF GRAVITY.
SOMEWHERE, IN A THEORETICAL PHYSICS LAB...
WHAT THE... IS SHE SAYING WE DON'T UNDERSTAND EVOLUTION?!

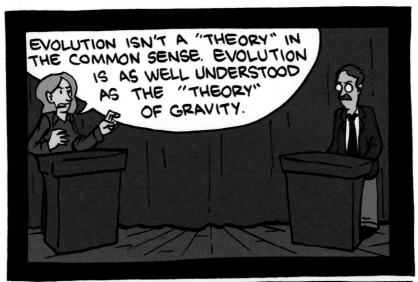

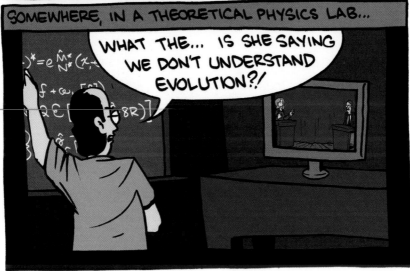

YOU THINK OF YOURSELF AS A SINGLE UNIFIED LIFE FORM.

ME

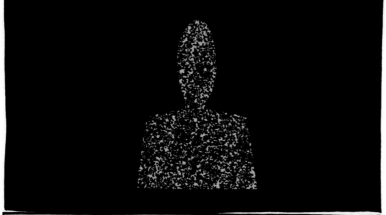

BUT YOU'RE MORE LIKE AN AGREEMENT BETWEEN HUNDREDS OF TRILLIONS OF TINY LIFE FORMS.

THOSE LIFE FORMS HAVE BILLIONS OF TINY PARLIAMENTS TO WHICH YOU ARE NOT PRIVY.

FELLOW HISTAMINE RECEPTORS! WE AGREE! CAT DANDER IS EVIL, AND MUST BE DEFEATED AT *ANY COST!*

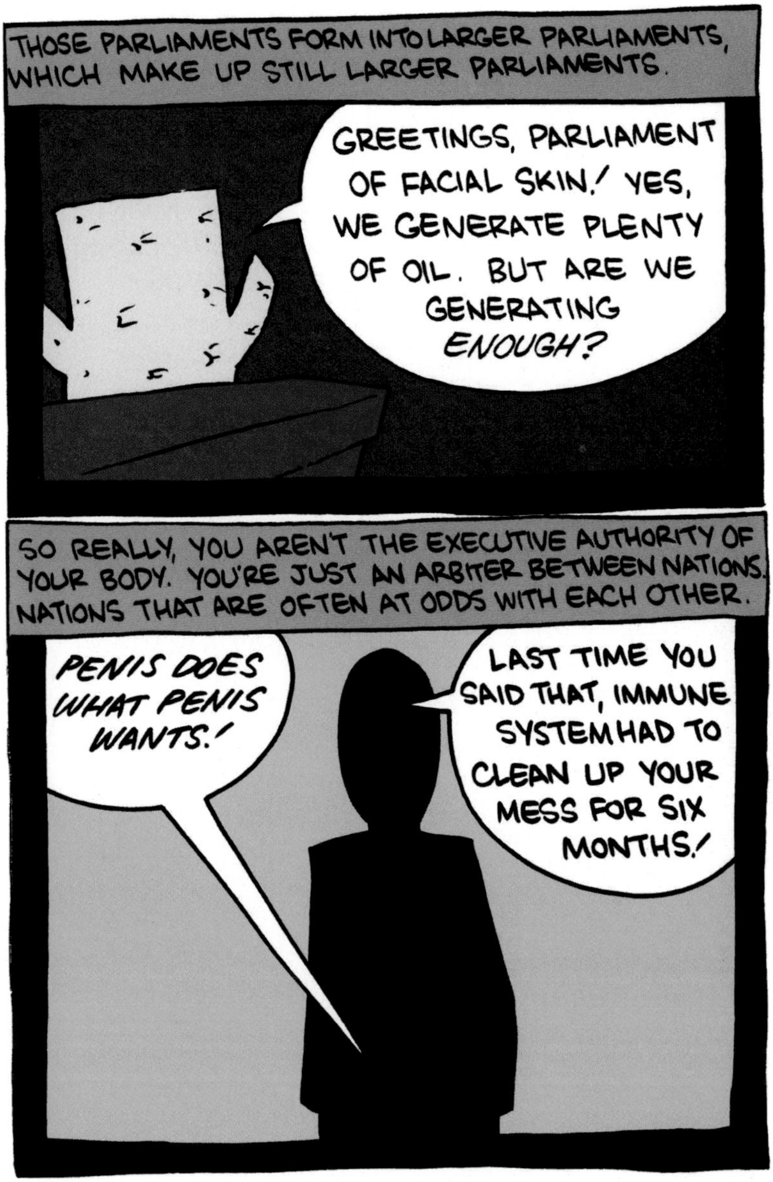
THOSE PARLIAMENTS FORM INTO LARGER PARLIAMENTS, WHICH MAKE UP STILL LARGER PARLIAMENTS.
GREETINGS, PARLIAMENT OF FACIAL SKIN! YES, WE GENERATE PLENTY OF OIL. BUT ARE WE GENERATING ENOUGH?
SO REALLY, YOU AREN'T THE EXECUTIVE AUTHORITY OF YOUR BODY. YOU'RE JUST AN ARBITER BETWEEN NATIONS. NATIONS THAT ARE OFTEN AT ODDS WITH EACH OTHER.
PENIS DOES WHAT PENIS WANTS!
LAST TIME YOU SAID THAT, IMMUNE SYSTEM HAD TO CLEAN UP YOUR MESS FOR SIX MONTHS!

END!

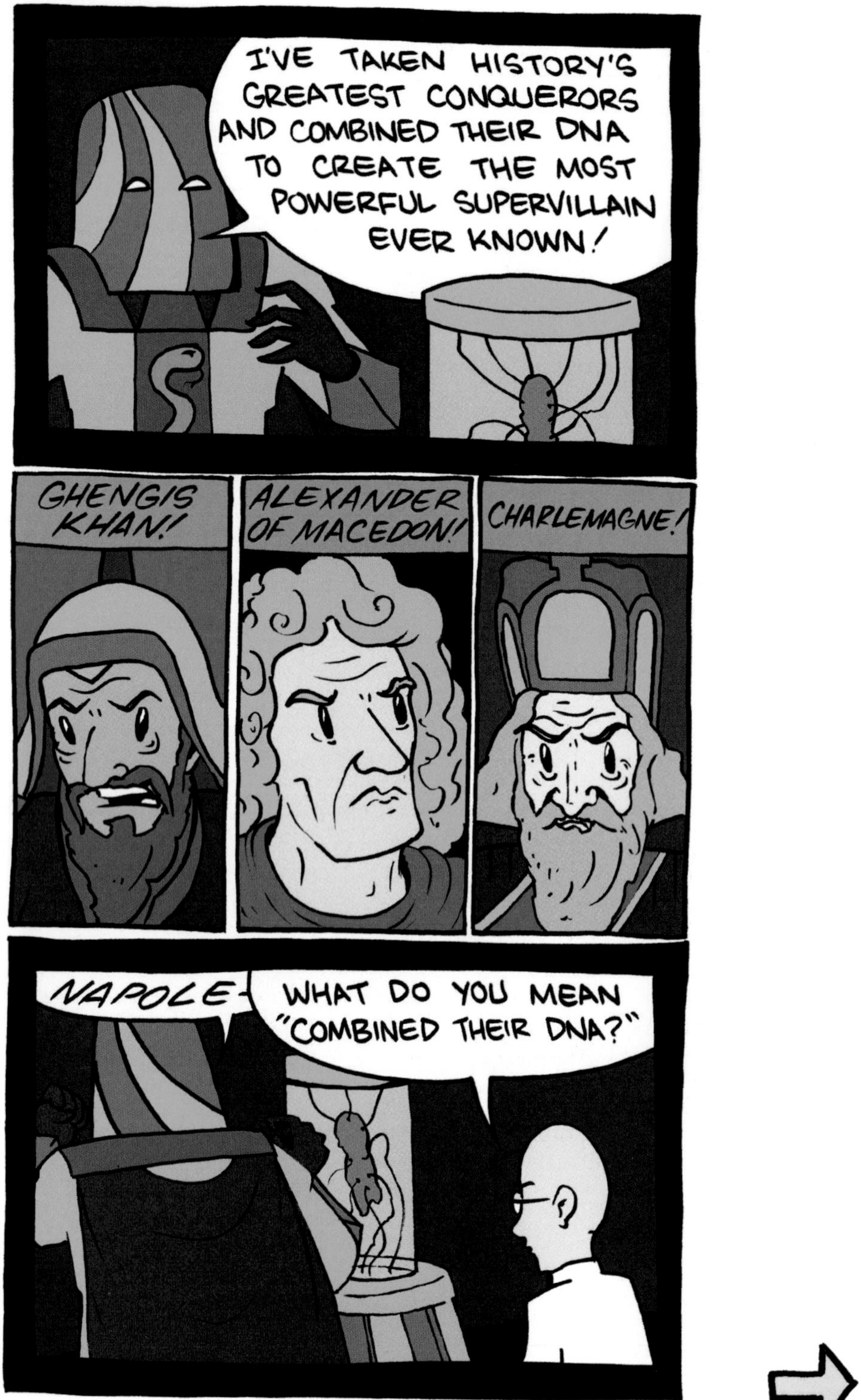
I'VE TAKEN HISTORY'S GREATEST CONQUERORS AND COMBINED THEIR DNA TO CREATE THE MOST POWERFUL SUPERVILLAIN EVER KNOWN!
GHENGIS KHAN!
ALEXANDER OF MACEDON!
CHARLEMAGNE!
NAPOLE-
WHAT DO YOU MEAN "COMBINED THEIR DNA?"

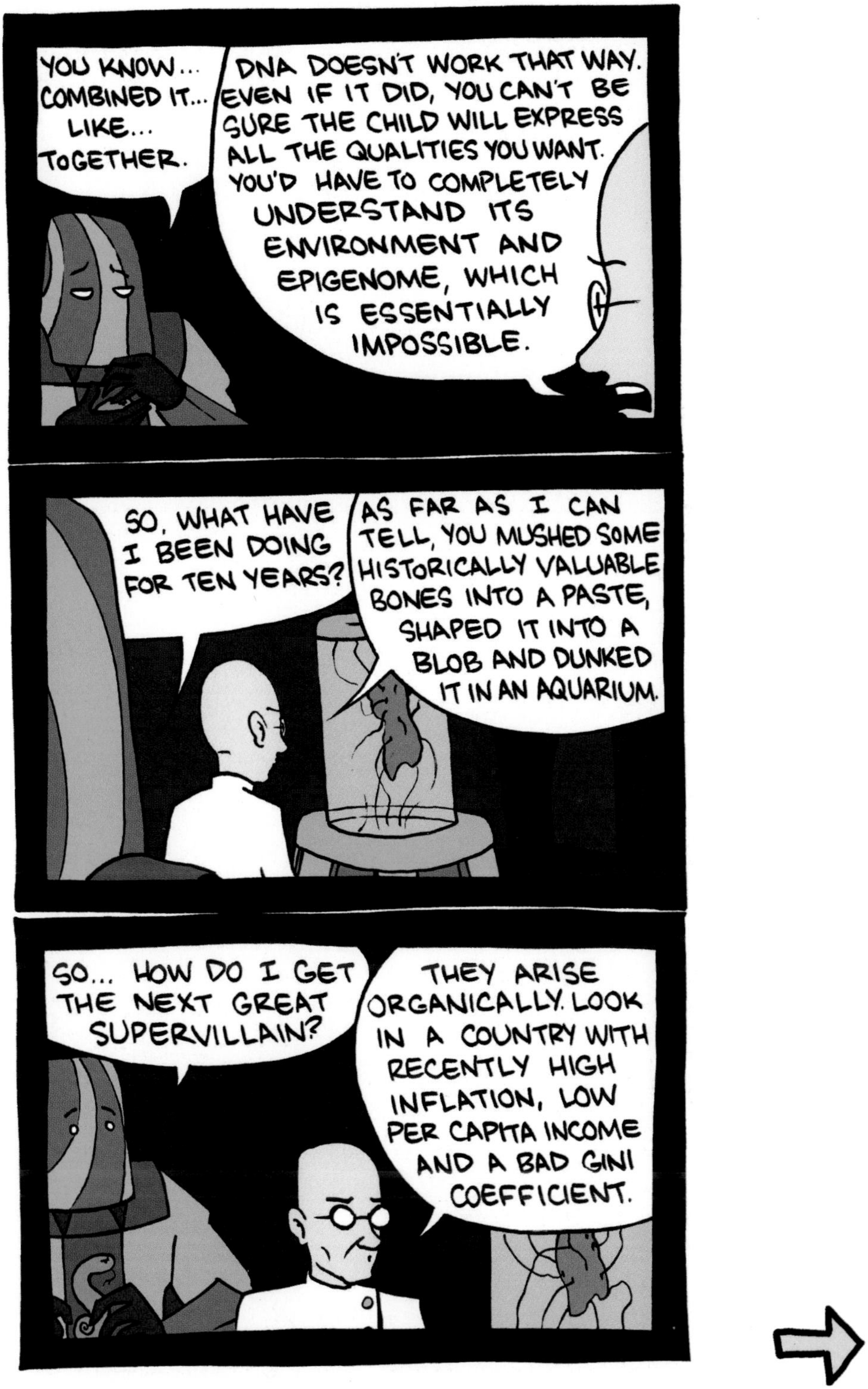
YOU KNOW... COMBINED IT... LIKE... TOGETHER.
DNA DOESN'T WORK THAT WAY. EVEN IF IT DID, YOU CAN'T BE SURE THE CHILD WILL EXPRESS ALL THE QUALITIES YOU WANT. YOU'D HAVE TO COMPLETELY UNDERSTAND ITS ENVIRONMENT AND EPIGENOME, WHICH IS ESSENTIALLY IMPOSSIBLE.
SO, WHAT HAVE I BEEN DOING FOR TEN YEARS?
AS FAR AS I CAN TELL, YOU MUSHED SOME HISTORICALLY VALUABLE BONES INTO A PASTE, SHAPED IT INTO A BLOB AND DUNKED IT IN AN AQUARIUM.
SO... HOW DO I GET THE NEXT GREAT SUPERVILLAIN?
THEY ARISE ORGANICALLY. LOOK IN A COUNTRY WITH RECENTLY HIGH INFLATION, LOW PER CAPITA INCOME AND A BAD GINI COEFFICIENT.

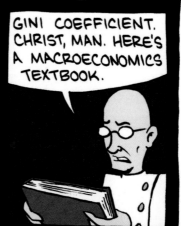

GINI COEFFICIENT. CHRIST, MAN. HERE'S A MACROECONOMICS TEXTBOOK.

SCIENCE

RUINING EVERYTHING SINCE 1543

END!

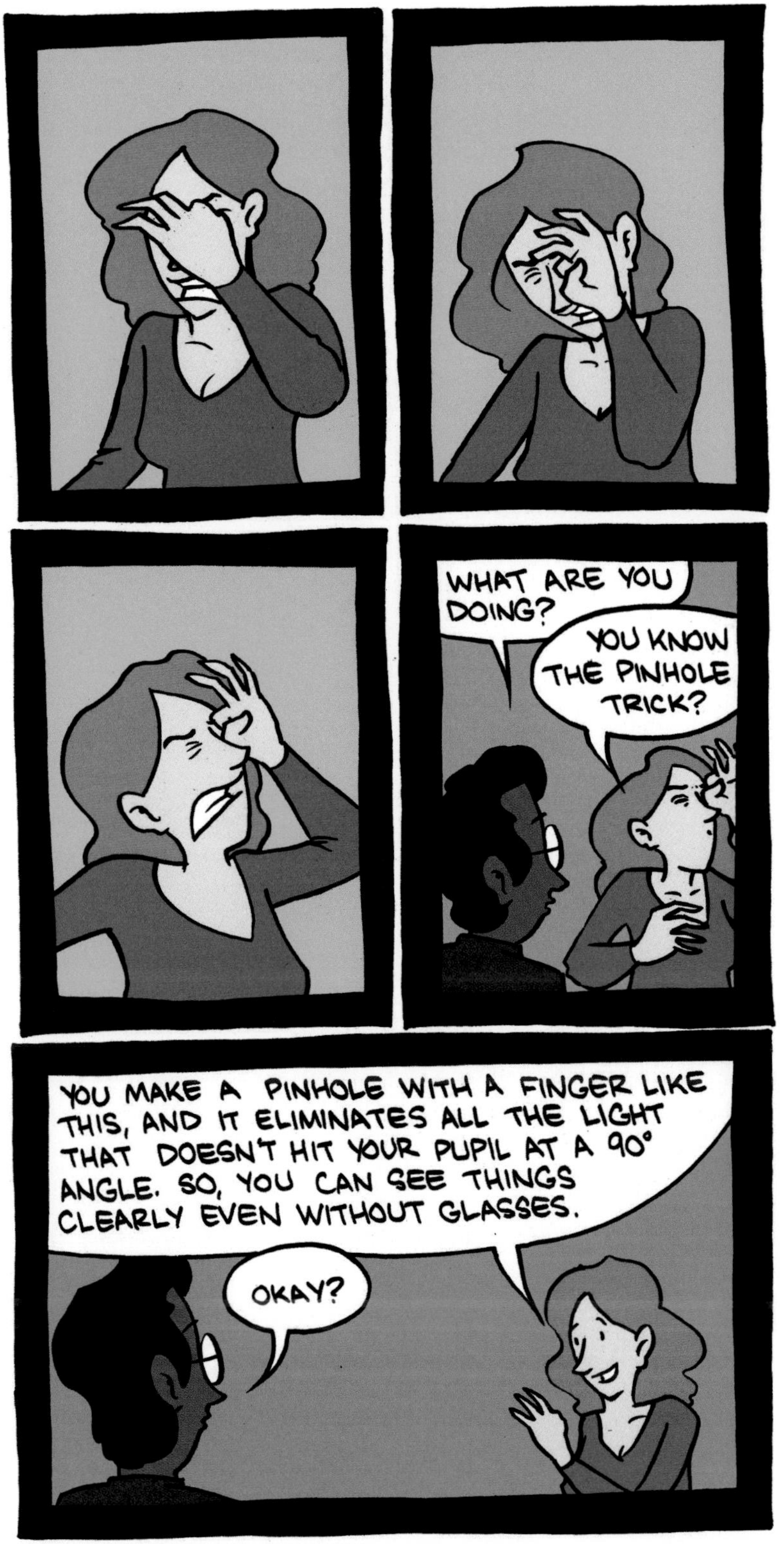
WHAT ARE YOU DOING?
YOU KNOW THE PINHOLE TRICK?
YOU MAKE A PINHOLE WITH A FINGER LIKE THIS, AND IT ELIMINATES ALL THE LIGHT THAT DOESN'T HIT YOUR PUPIL AT A 90° ANGLE. SO, YOU CAN SEE THINGS CLEARLY EVEN WITHOUT GLASSES.
OKAY?

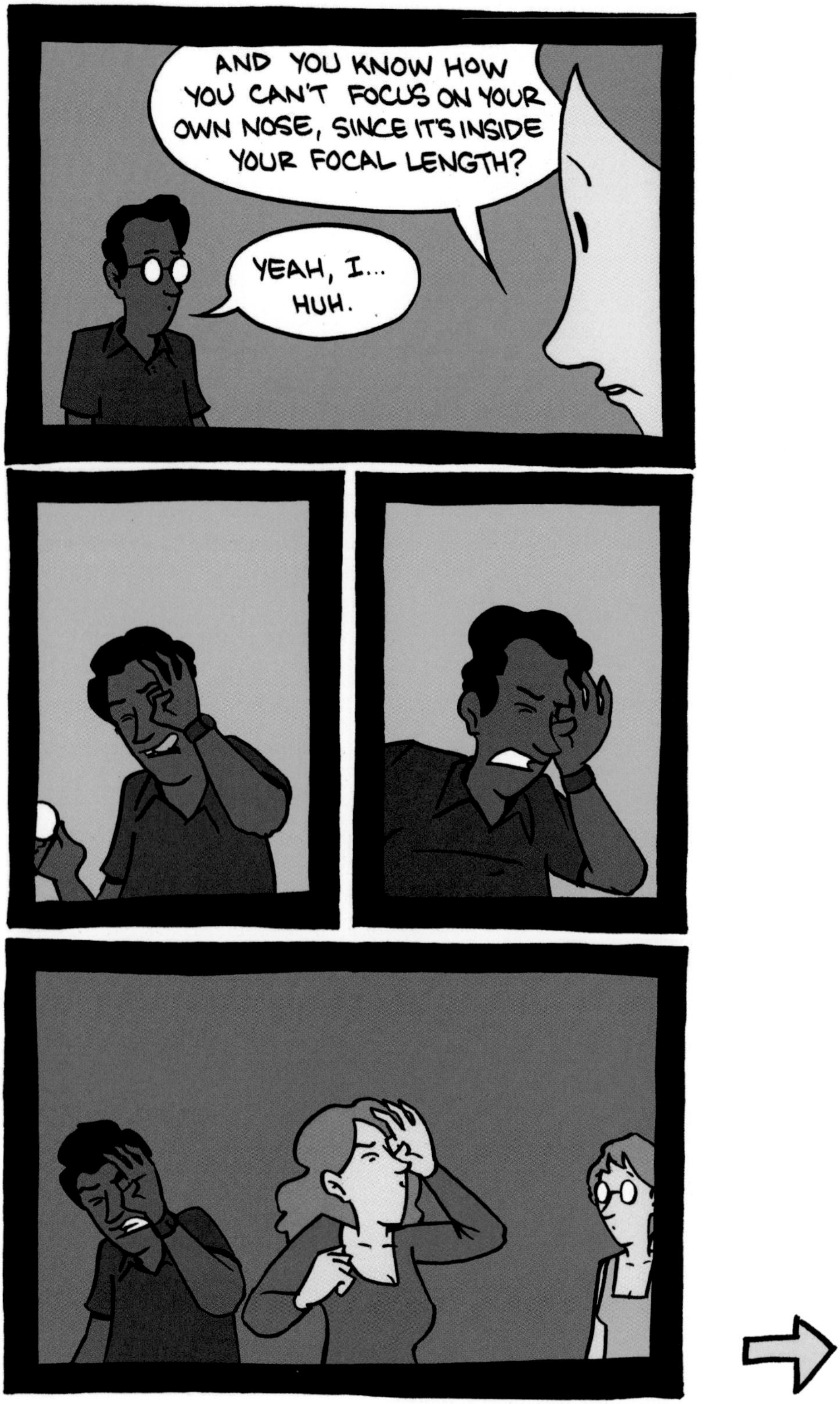
AND YOU KNOW HOW YOU CAN'T FOCUS ON YOUR OWN NOSE, SINCE IT'S INSIDE YOUR FOCAL LENGTH?
YEAH, I... HUH.

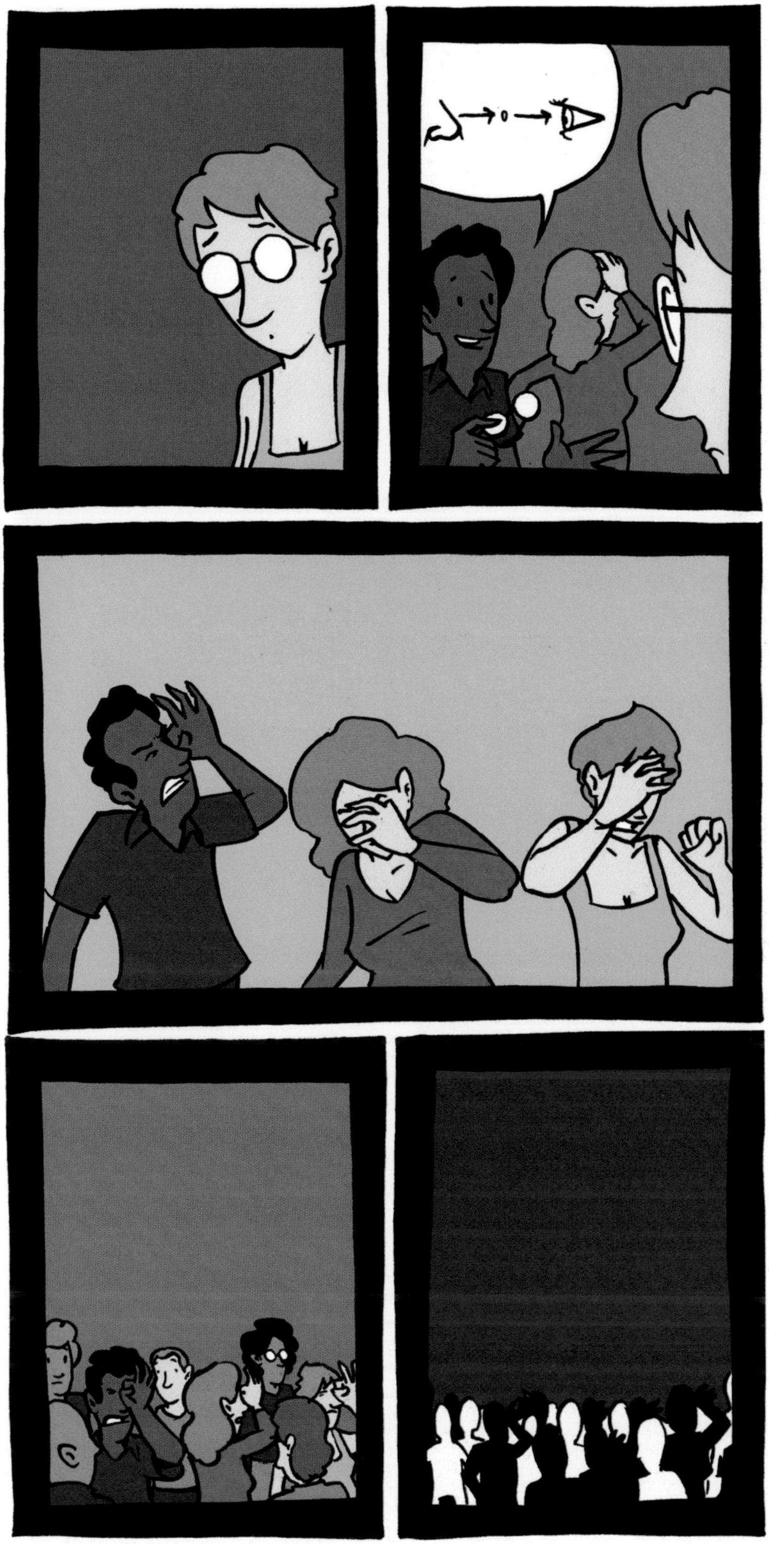

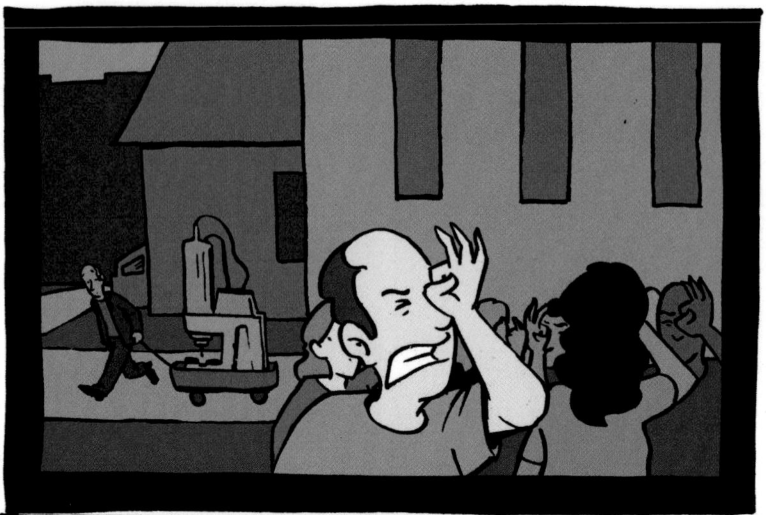

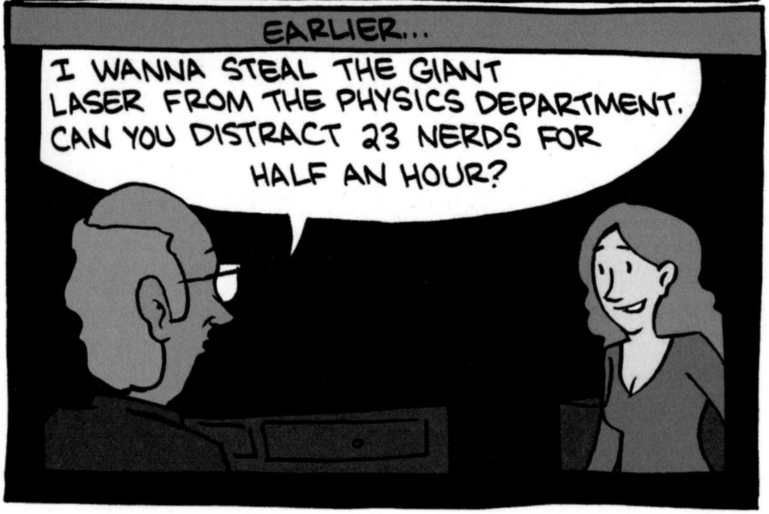
EARLIER...
I WANNA STEAL THE GIANT LASER FROM THE PHYSICS DEPARTMENT. CAN YOU DISTRACT 23 NERDS FOR HALF AN HOUR?

END!

HA! PHYSICS JUST PRODUCED AN INVISIBILITY CLOAK. WHAT HAS SOCIOLOGY DONE THAT COMES ANYWHERE NEAR THAT?
PFFF!
SOCIOLOGY HAS KNOWN HOW TO DO THAT FOR YEARS.
WHAT THE... WHERE'D YOU GO?!
HOMELESS
PLease
HeLP

Physics 101.
AS HAS OFTEN BEEN NOTED, "PHYSICS IS TO MATH AS SEX IS TO MASTURBATION."
SO, YOU'RE SAYING BOTH FIELDS ARE GOOD, BUT WITHOUT AN ATTEMPT TO UNDERSTAND THE UNIVERSE, THE SEARCH FOR DEEPER MATH-EMATICAL TRUTH IS EMPTY?
I'M SAYING YOU'LL SPEND MOST OF UNDERGRAD DOING MATH
CS 101.

THE FIRST CRYONIC PATIENTS WERE FROZEN TOO SLOWLY.

ICE CRYSTALS FORMED, RUPTURING TOO MANY CELLS FOR THEM TO BE UNFROZEN LATER.

BUT SEVERAL CENTURIES HENCE, CELL-REPAIRING NANOBOTS WERE CIRCULATED INTO THEIR BODIES.

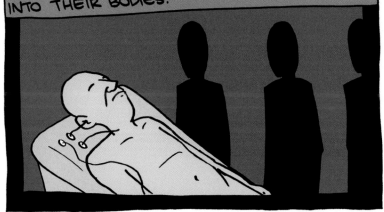

THEY LOCATED THE RUPTURES AND KNITTED THE CELLS BACK TOGETHER, LEAVING PROPERLY FROZEN BODIES AWAITING TREATMENT.

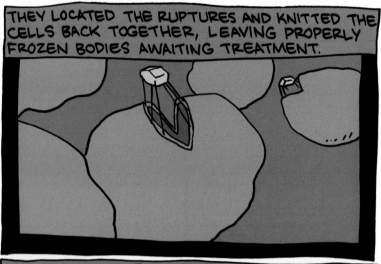

WHEN FINALLY REINVIGORATED, THE PEOPLE FOUND IT ALL SOMEWHAT DISTRESSING.

SO... WAS I ALIVE OR DEAD?

YOU WERE A CORPSE BEFORE WE HAD THE RIGHT TOOLS, AND A PATIENT AFTER.

HOW CAN MY BEING ALIVE OR DEAD DEPEND ON THE LEVEL OF TECHNOLOGICAL ADVANCEMENT?

LOOK, I'M A DOCTOR. YOU'RE ALL CORPSES UNTIL PROVEN OTHERWISE.

FORTUNATELY, THERE WAS A SIMPLE EMOTIONALLY SATISFYING SOLUTION.
APPLY TWO TIMES A DAY.
TOPICAL ANTI-EXISTENTIALISM CREAM
IT WASN'T PERFECT.
WHAT IF I STILL DESPAIR OVER THE INFINITE LACUNA BETWEEN WHAT I HOPED LIFE WAS AND WHAT THE EVIDENCE SUGGESTS?
THREE.

END!

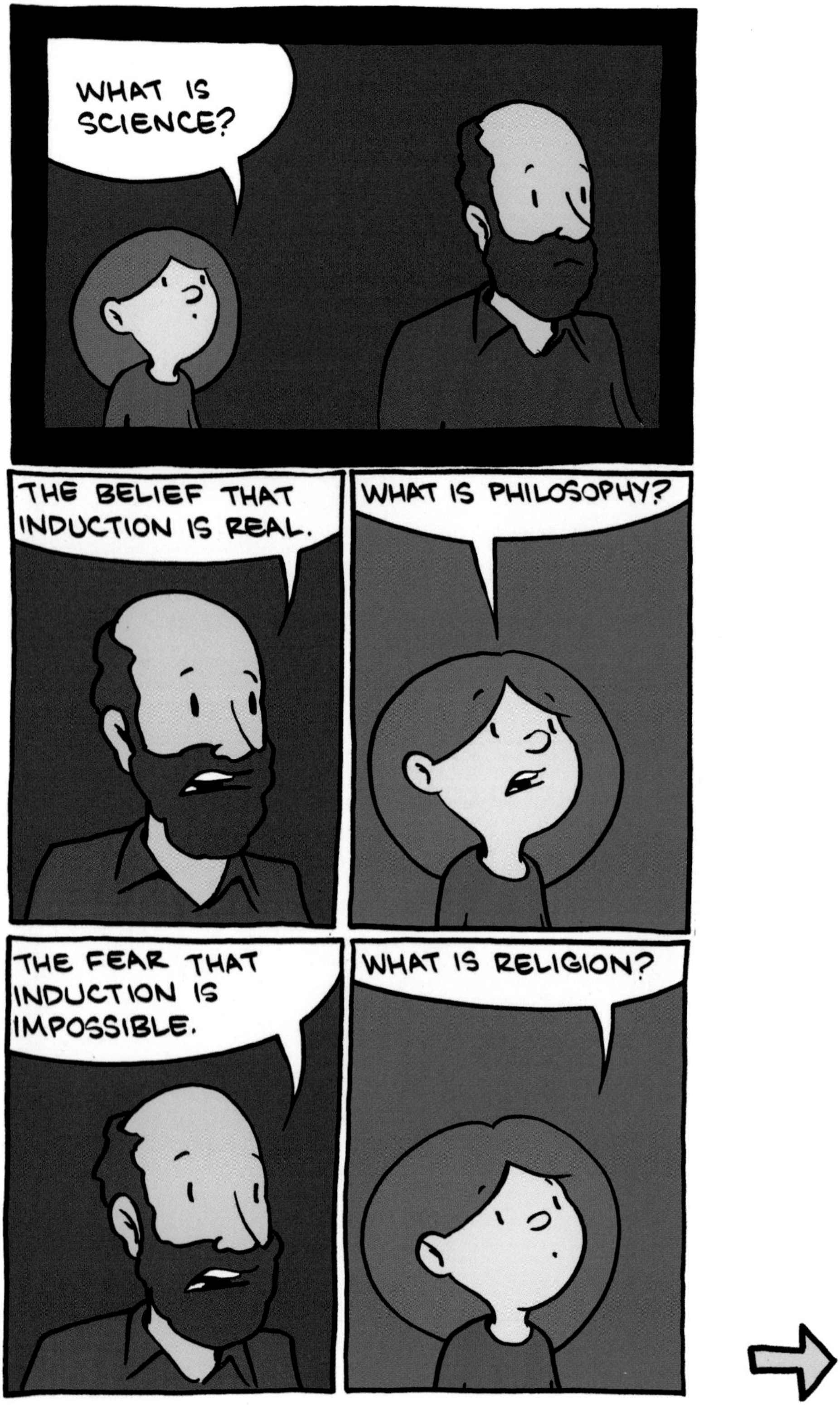
WHAT IS SCIENCE?
THE BELIEF THAT INDUCTION IS REAL.
WHAT IS PHILOSOPHY?
THE FEAR THAT INDUCTION IS IMPOSSIBLE.
WHAT IS RELIGION?

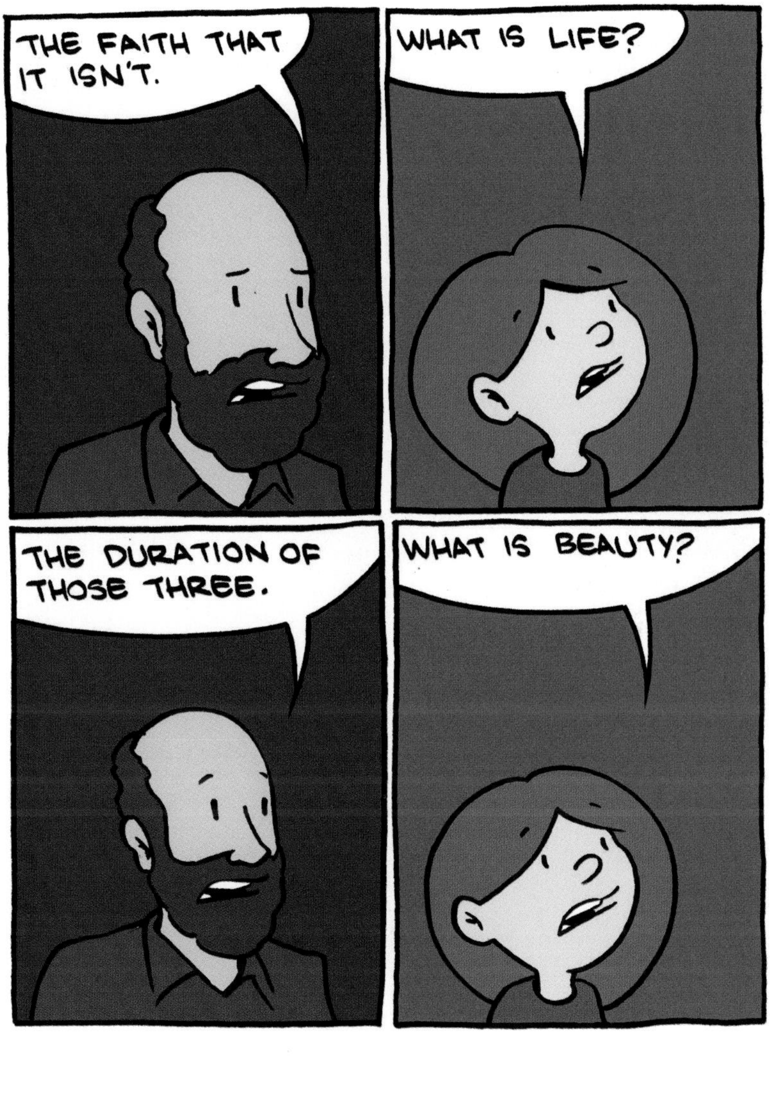
THE FAITH THAT IT ISN'T.
WHAT IS LIFE?
THE DURATION OF THOSE THREE.
WHAT IS BEAUTY?

THE HIGHEST USE OF THAT DURATION.
WHAT ARE YOU DOING RIGHT NOW?
I'LL GET TO BEAUTY LATER!
CELEB-GOSSIP

END!

WHAT "SCHRODINGER'S CAT" MEANS.

SUPPOSE THAT INSIDE A BOX YOU HAVE A CAT AND A GLASS CONTAINER OF POISON. SUPPOSE THERE IS ALSO A RADIATION EMITTER AND A GEIGER COUNTER, AND THAT IF THE COUNTER DETECTS RADIATION, IT CAUSES A HAMMER TO BREAK THE GLASS. ACCORDING TO THE COPENHAGEN INTERPRETATION, THE CAT IS BOTH ALIVE AND DEAD UNTIL SOMETHING COLLAPSES THE WAVEFUNCTION. THIS IS, OF COURSE, ABSURD. SO, THE INTERPRETATION MUST BE WRONG.

WHAT PEOPLE THINK IT MEANS.

SO THERE'S THIS CAT IN A BOX AND HEY MAYBE IT'S DEAD, BUT WHO KNOWS?! *SCIENCE!*

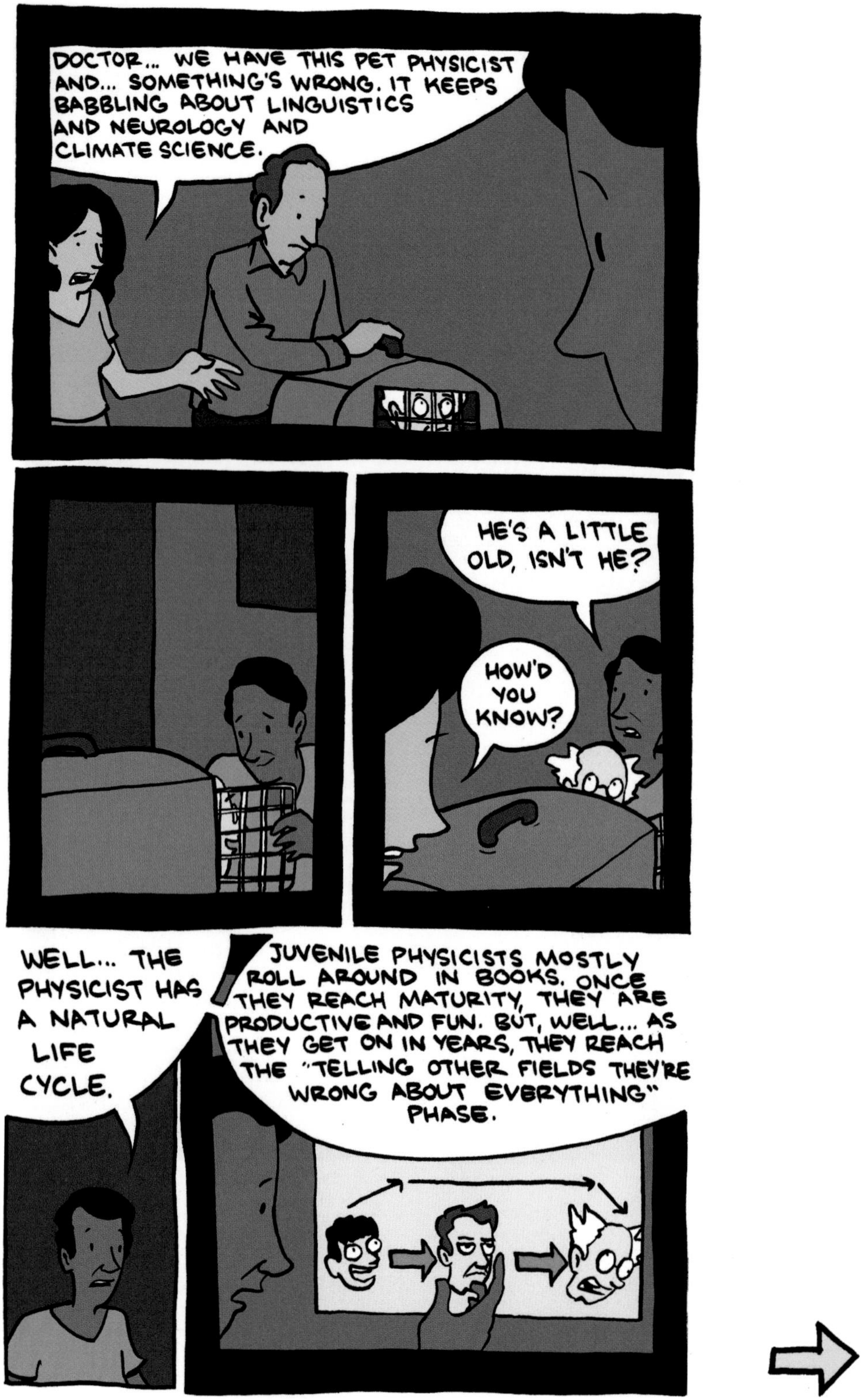
DOCTOR... WE HAVE THIS PET PHYSICIST AND... SOMETHING'S WRONG. IT KEEPS BABBLING ABOUT LINGUISTICS AND NEUROLOGY AND CLIMATE SCIENCE.
HE'S A LITTLE OLD, ISN'T HE?
HOW'D YOU KNOW?
WELL... THE PHYSICIST HAS A NATURAL LIFE CYCLE.
JUVENILE PHYSICISTS MOSTLY ROLL AROUND IN BOOKS. ONCE THEY REACH MATURITY, THEY ARE PRODUCTIVE AND FUN. BUT, WELL... AS THEY GET ON IN YEARS, THEY REACH THE "TELLING OTHER FIELDS THEY'RE WRONG ABOUT EVERYTHING" PHASE.

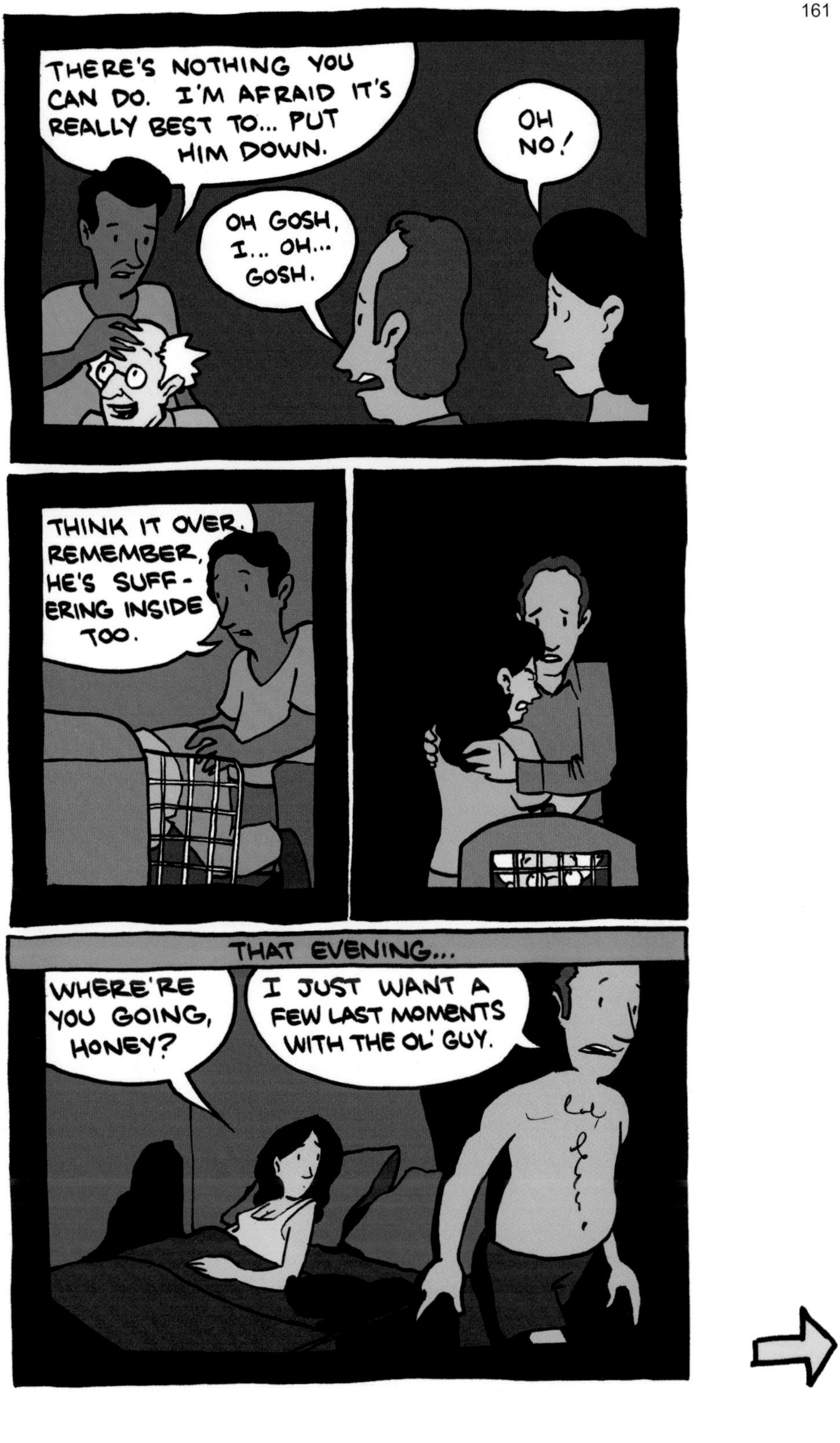
THERE'S NOTHING YOU CAN DO. I'M AFRAID IT'S REALLY BEST TO... PUT HIM DOWN.
OH NO!
OH GOSH, I... OH... GOSH.
THINK IT OVER. REMEMBER, HE'S SUFF-ERING INSIDE TOO.
THAT EVENING...
WHERE'RE YOU GOING, HONEY?
I JUST WANT A FEW LAST MOMENTS WITH THE OL' GUY.

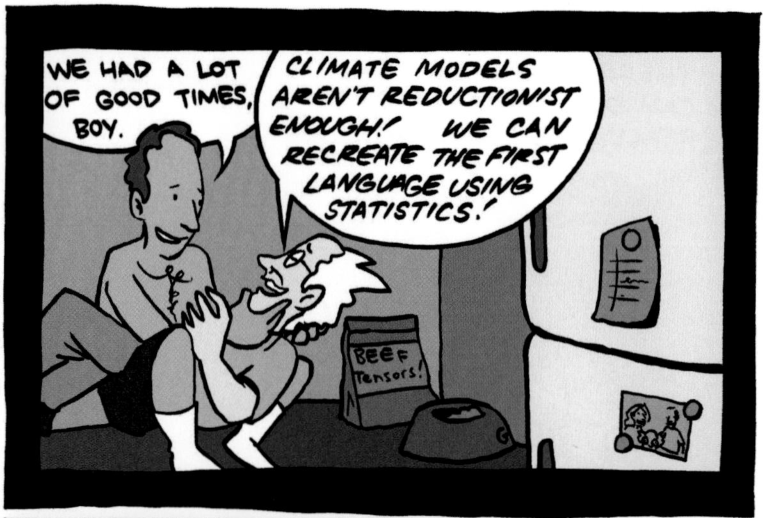
WE HAD A LOT OF GOOD TIMES, BOY.
CLIMATE MODELS AREN'T REDUCTIONIST ENOUGH! WE CAN RECREATE THE FIRST LANGUAGE USING STATISTICS!
BEEF Tensors!

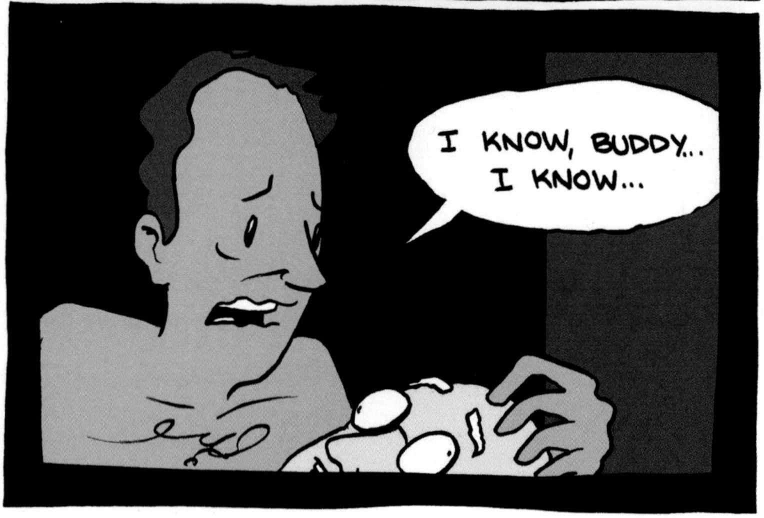
I KNOW, BUDDY... I KNOW...

END!

WHEN SCIENTISTS DISCUSS PAPERS
I DON'T THINK THIS INFERENCE IS ENTIRELY REASONABLE. IF YOU'RE USING SEVERAL NON-INDEPENDENT VARIABLES YOU'RE LIABLE TO ACCUMULATE MORE ERROR THAN YOUR MODEL ACCOUNTS FOR.
WHEN SCIENTISTS DISCUSS GRANTS
A GUY WHO WORKED AT THE NSF ONCE TOLD ME IF WE LIGHT A CANDLE WITHIN THIS JACKAL SKULL, THE FUNDERS WILL SMILE UPON OUR HOPES.
I'LL GET THE ALTAR!

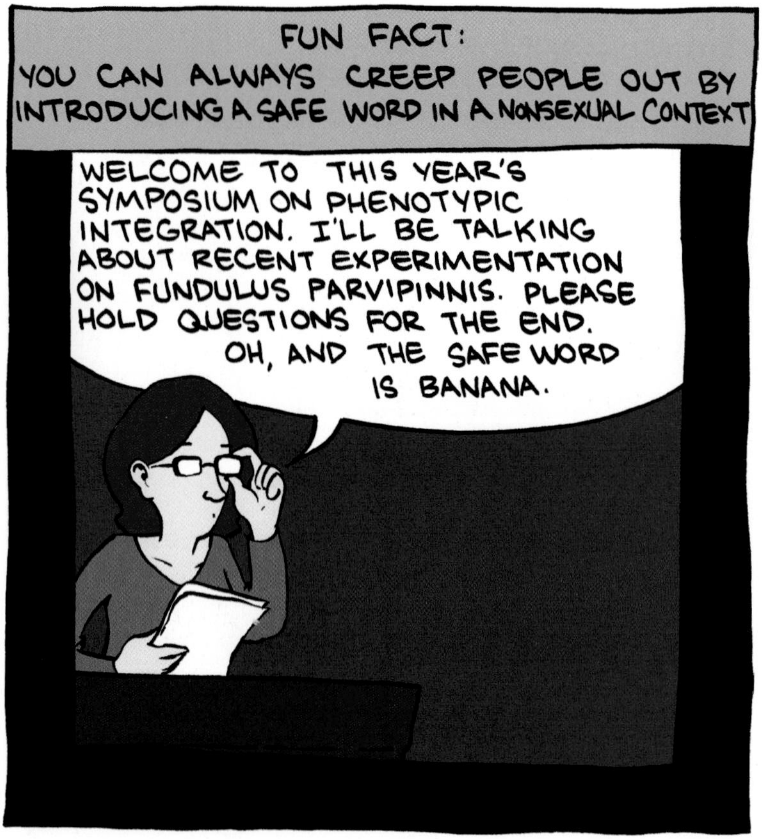
FUN FACT:
YOU CAN ALWAYS CREEP PEOPLE OUT BY INTRODUCING A SAFE WORD IN A NONSEXUAL CONTEXT
WELCOME TO THIS YEAR'S SYMPOSIUM ON PHENOTYPIC INTEGRATION. I'LL BE TALKING ABOUT RECENT EXPERIMENTATION ON FUNDULUS PARVIPINNIS. PLEASE HOLD QUESTIONS FOR THE END. OH, AND THE SAFE WORD IS BANANA.

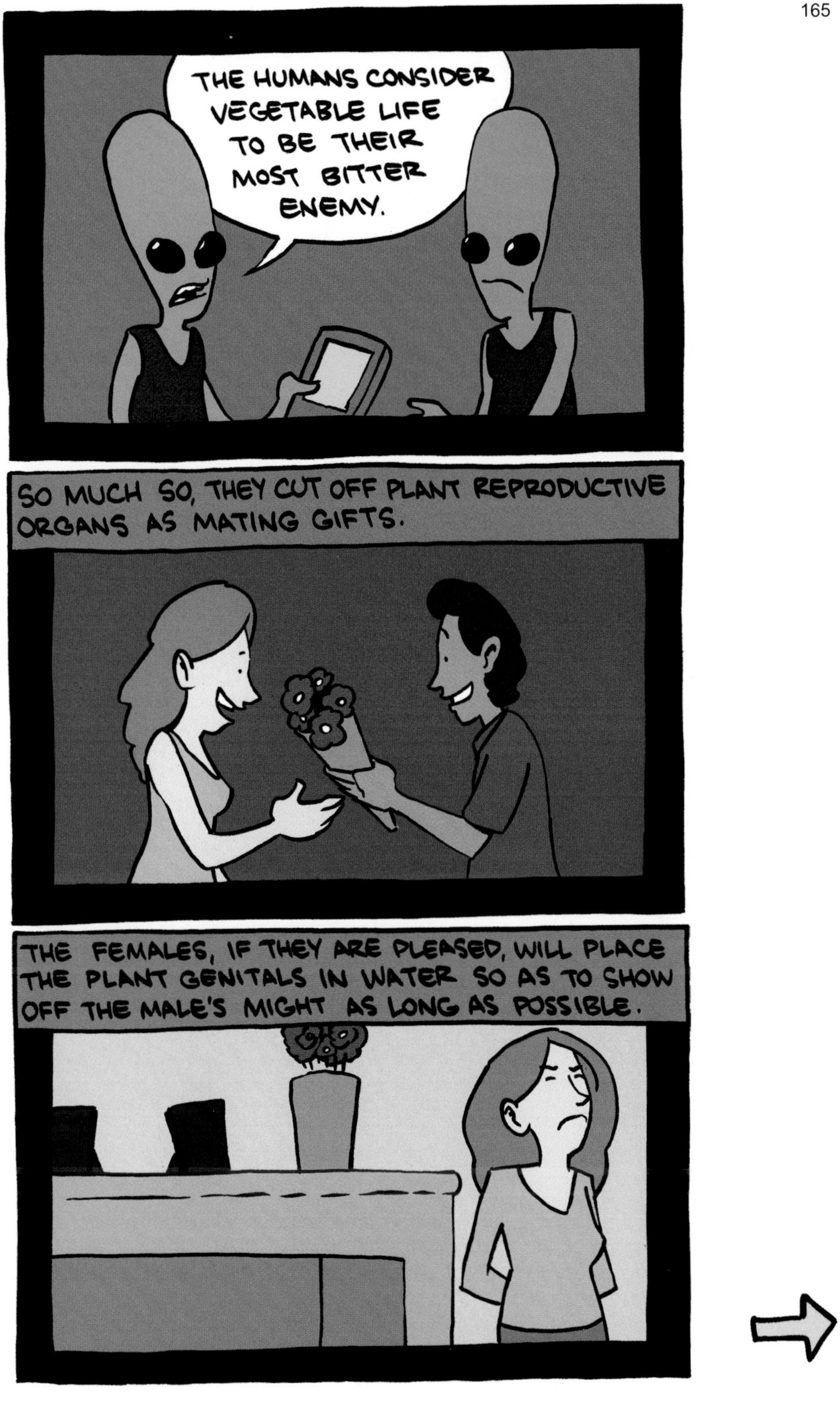
THE HUMANS CONSIDER VEGETABLE LIFE TO BE THEIR MOST BITTER ENEMY.
SO MUCH SO, THEY CUT OFF PLANT REPRODUCTIVE ORGANS AS MATING GIFTS.
THE FEMALES, IF THEY ARE PLEASED, WILL PLACE THE PLANT GENITALS IN WATER SO AS TO SHOW OFF THE MALE'S MIGHT AS LONG AS POSSIBLE.

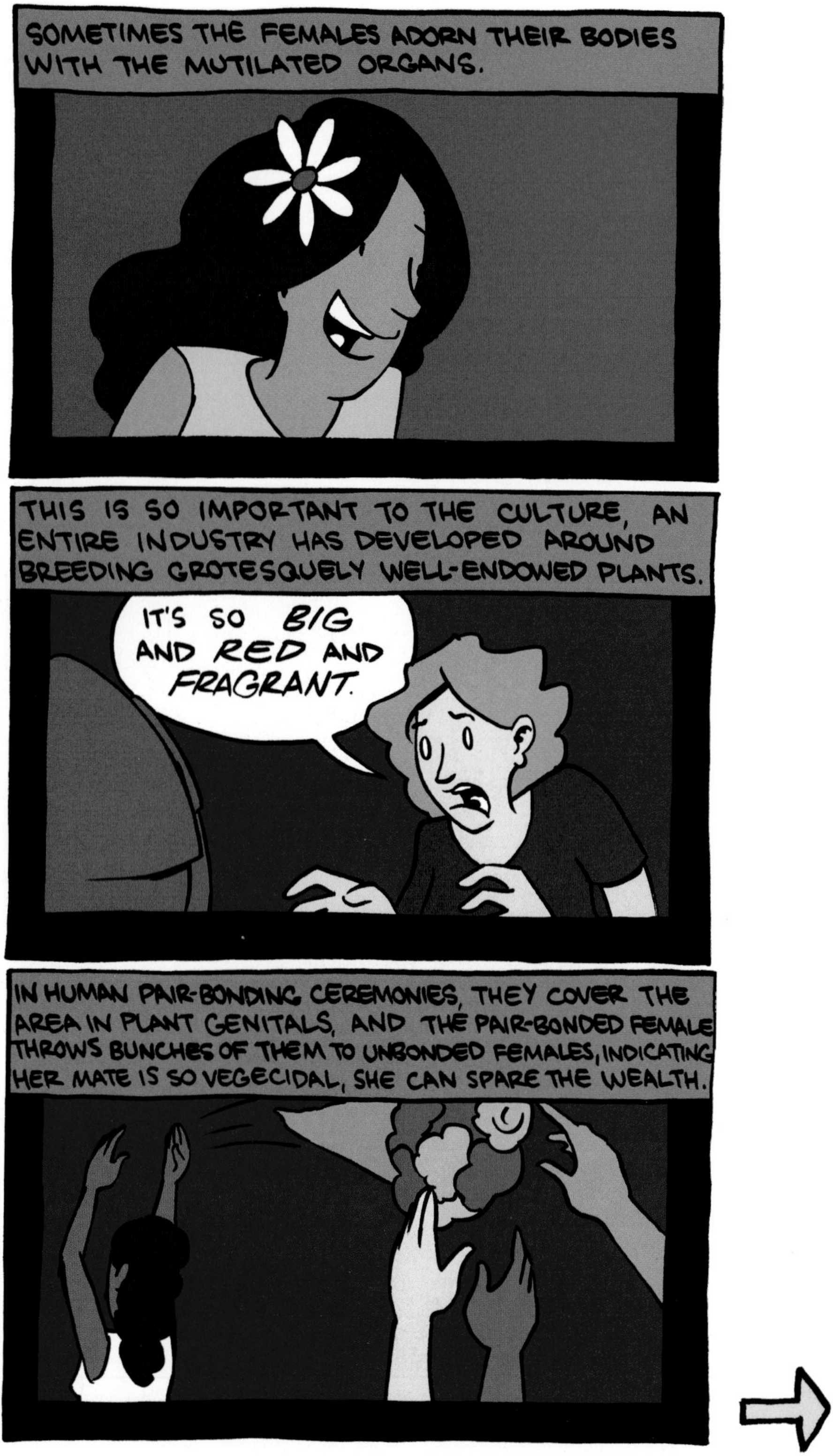
SOMETIMES THE FEMALES ADORN THEIR BODIES WITH THE MUTILATED ORGANS.
THIS IS SO IMPORTANT TO THE CULTURE, AN ENTIRE INDUSTRY HAS DEVELOPED AROUND BREEDING GROTESQUELY WELL-ENDOWED PLANTS.
IT'S SO BIG AND RED AND FRAGRANT.
IN HUMAN PAIR-BONDING CEREMONIES, THEY COVER THE AREA IN PLANT GENITALS, AND THE PAIR-BONDED FEMALE THROWS BUNCHES OF THEM TO UNBONDED FEMALES, INDICATING HER MATE IS SO VEGECIDAL, SHE CAN SPARE THE WEALTH.

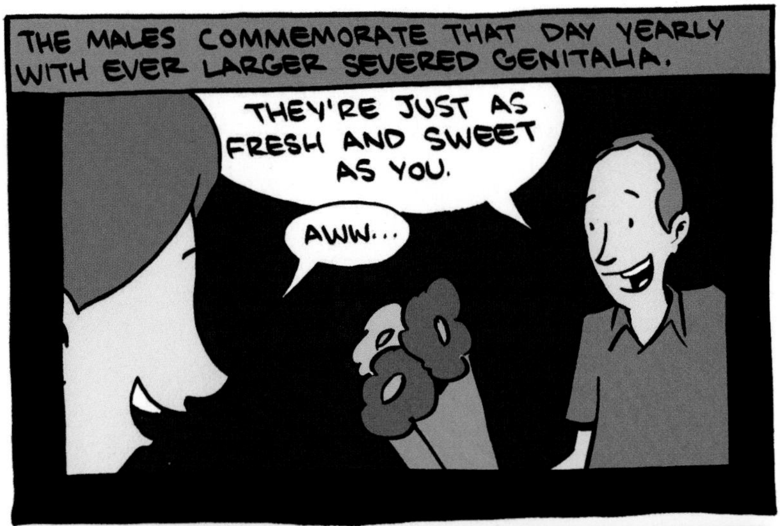
THE MALES COMMEMORATE THAT DAY YEARLY WITH EVER LARGER SEVERED GENITALIA.
THEY'RE JUST AS FRESH AND SWEET AS YOU.
AWW...

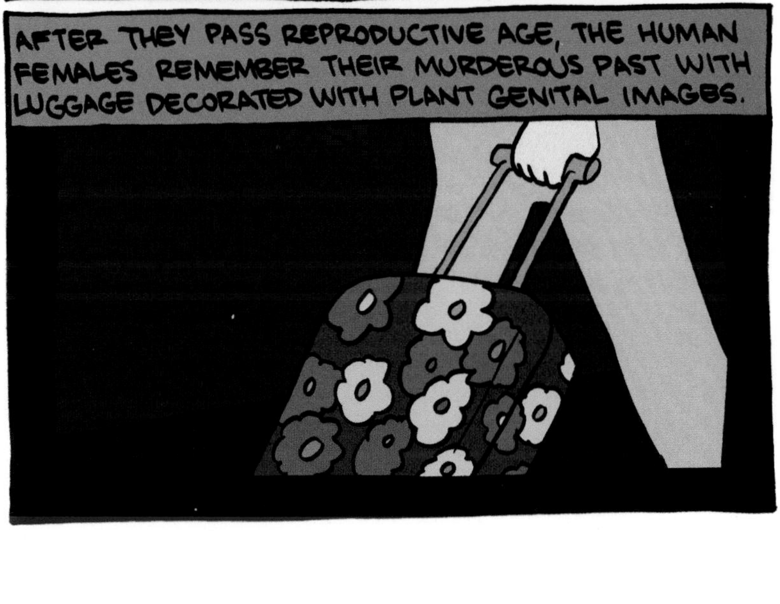
AFTER THEY PASS REPRODUCTIVE AGE, THE HUMAN FEMALES REMEMBER THEIR MURDEROUS PAST WITH LUGGAGE DECORATED WITH PLANT GENITAL IMAGES.

AND WHEN THEY DIE, THE HUMANS ARE BURIED UNDER A MOUND OF VEGETAL GENITALIA HEAPED ON A BOX OF PLANT FLESH.
MY GOD.
WHAT ARE "HIPPIES?"
YEP.
THE MOST VIOLENT HUMANS IN HISTORY.

END!

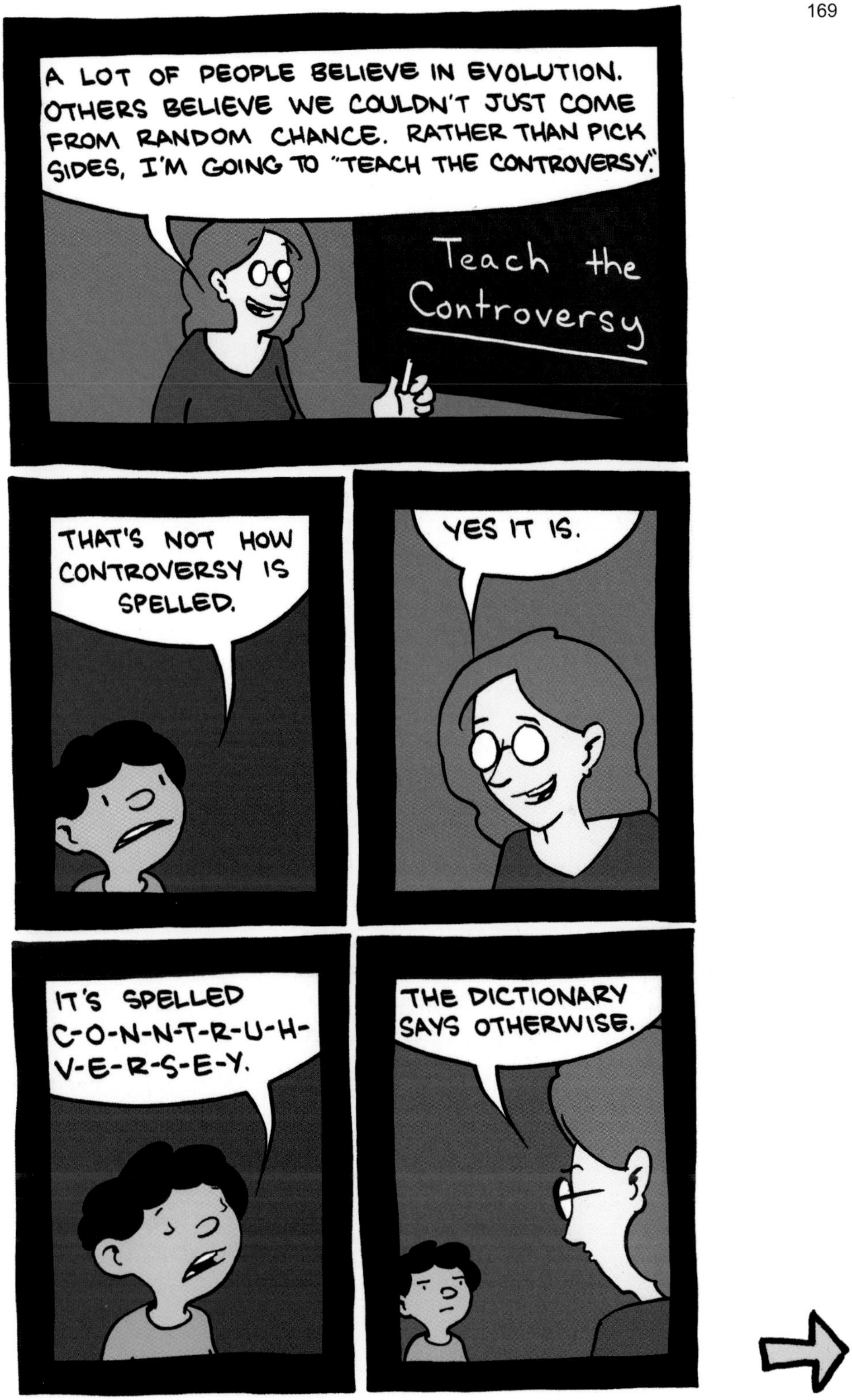
A LOT OF PEOPLE BELIEVE IN EVOLUTION. OTHERS BELIEVE WE COULDN'T JUST COME FROM RANDOM CHANCE. RATHER THAN PICK SIDES, I'M GOING TO "TEACH THE CONTROVERSY."
Teach the Controversy
THAT'S NOT HOW CONTROVERSY IS SPELLED.
YES IT IS.
IT'S SPELLED C-O-N-N-T-R-U-H-V-E-R-S-E-Y.
THE DICTIONARY SAYS OTHERWISE.

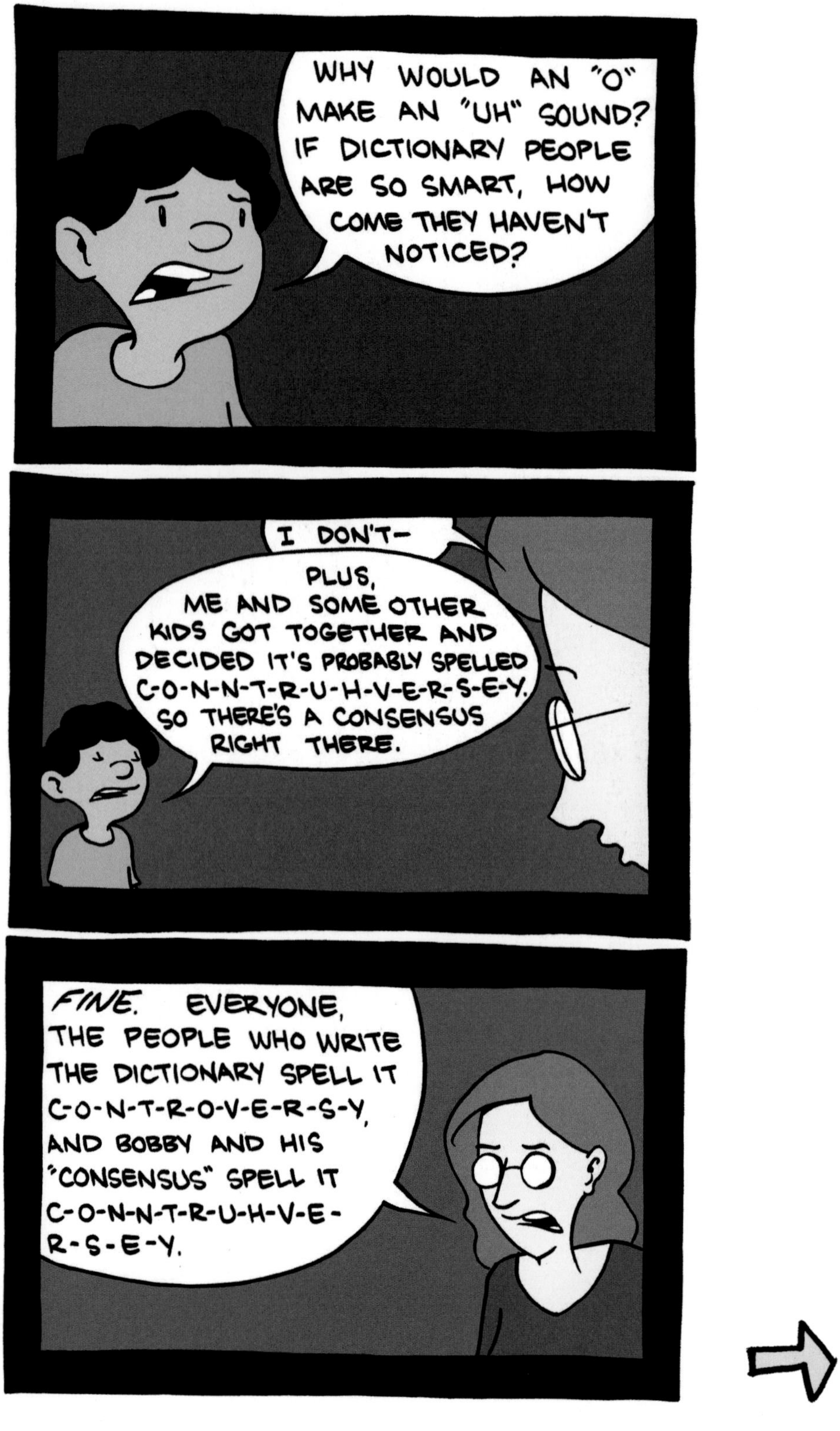
WHY WOULD AN "O" MAKE AN "UH" SOUND? IF DICTIONARY PEOPLE ARE SO SMART, HOW COME THEY HAVEN'T NOTICED?
I DON'T-
PLUS, ME AND SOME OTHER KIDS GOT TOGETHER AND DECIDED IT'S PROBABLY SPELLED C-O-N-N-T-R-U-H-V-E-R-S-E-Y. SO THERE'S A CONSENSUS RIGHT THERE.
FINE. EVERYONE, THE PEOPLE WHO WRITE THE DICTIONARY SPELL IT C-O-N-T-R-O-V-E-R-S-Y, AND BOBBY AND HIS "CONSENSUS" SPELL IT C-O-N-N-T-R-U-H-V-E-R-S-E-Y.

ANYWAY, NOW I'M GOING TO TEACH THE-
IT'S PRONOUNCED "TEE-ACK."
LATER...
HOW'D IT GO?
SHE KICKED ME OUT OF CLASS.
HERE'S YOUR TEN DOLLARS.

END!

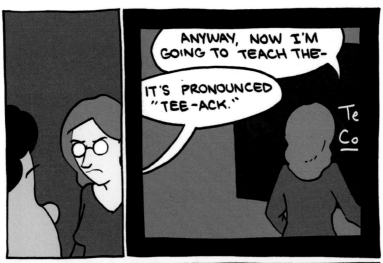

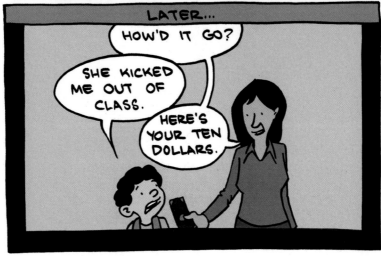

TIME
I WANT TO SEE WHAT FUTURE HUMANS LOOK LIKE! SINCE ONLY THE FITTEST REPRODUCE, I BET WE'LL ALL BE MUSCLEBOUND SUPERGENIUSES.
10,000 YEARS LATER...
WE'RE BASICALLY THE SAME, EXCEPT 95% OF US HAVE A CONDOM-BREAKING MECHANISM ON OUR PENISES.

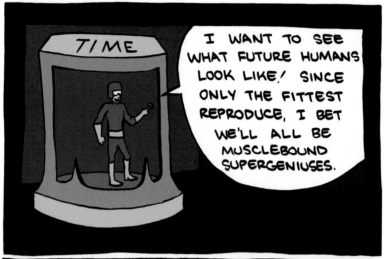

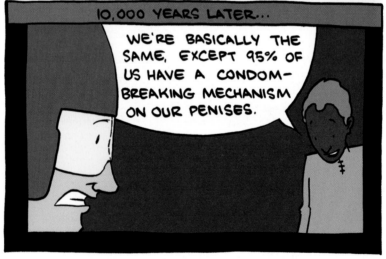

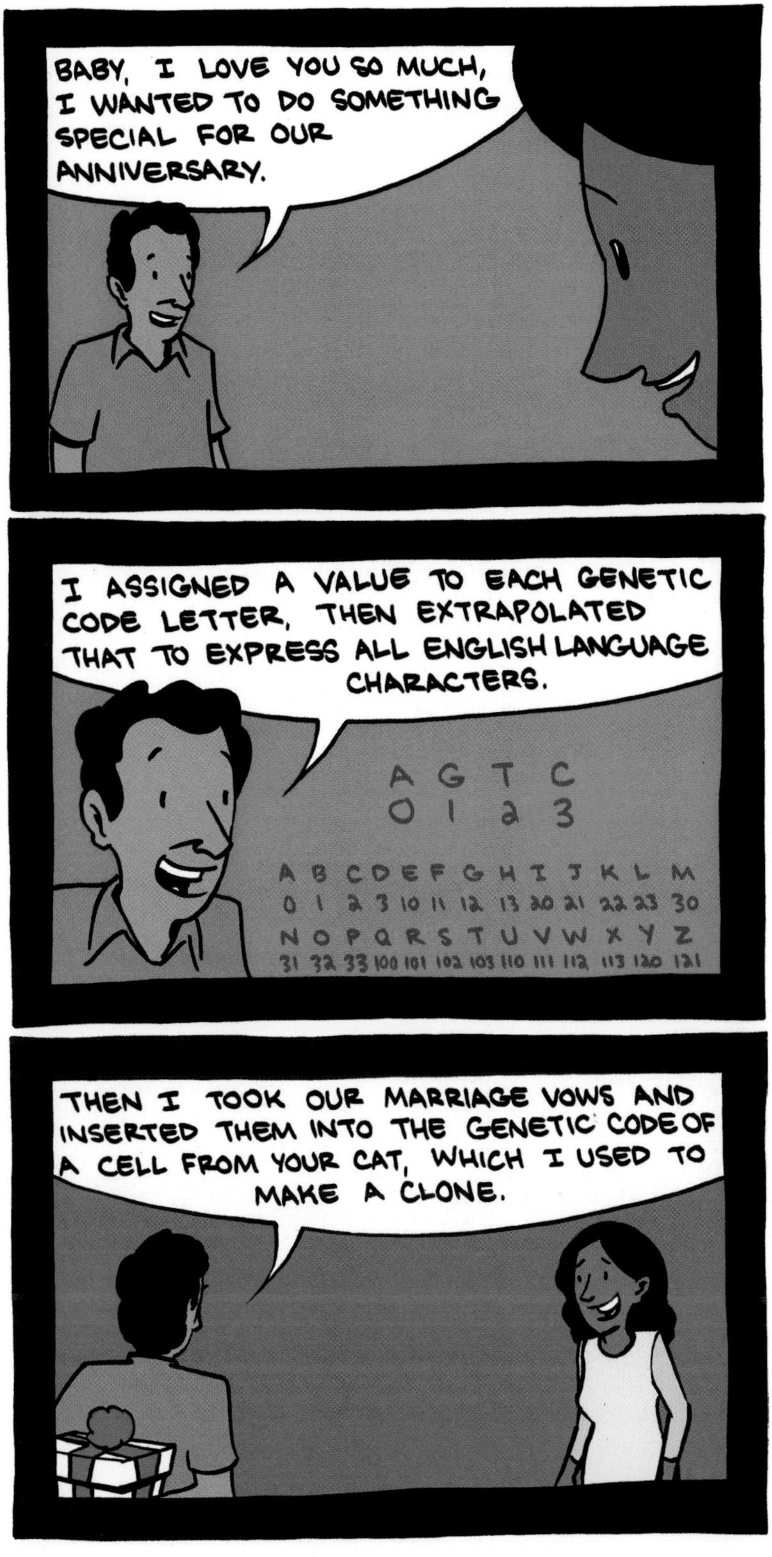
BABY, I LOVE YOU SO MUCH, I WANTED TO DO SOMETHING SPECIAL FOR OUR ANNIVERSARY.
I ASSIGNED A VALUE TO EACH GENETIC CODE LETTER, THEN EXTRAPOLATED THAT TO EXPRESS ALL ENGLISH LANGUAGE CHARACTERS.
A G T C
0 1 2 3
A B C D E F G H I J K L M
0 1 2 3 10 11 12 13 20 21 22 23 30
N O P Q R S T U V W X Y Z
31 32 33 100 101 102 103 110 111 112 113 120 121
THEN I TOOK OUR MARRIAGE VOWS AND INSERTED THEM INTO THE GENETIC CODE OF A CELL FROM YOUR CAT, WHICH I USED TO MAKE A CLONE.

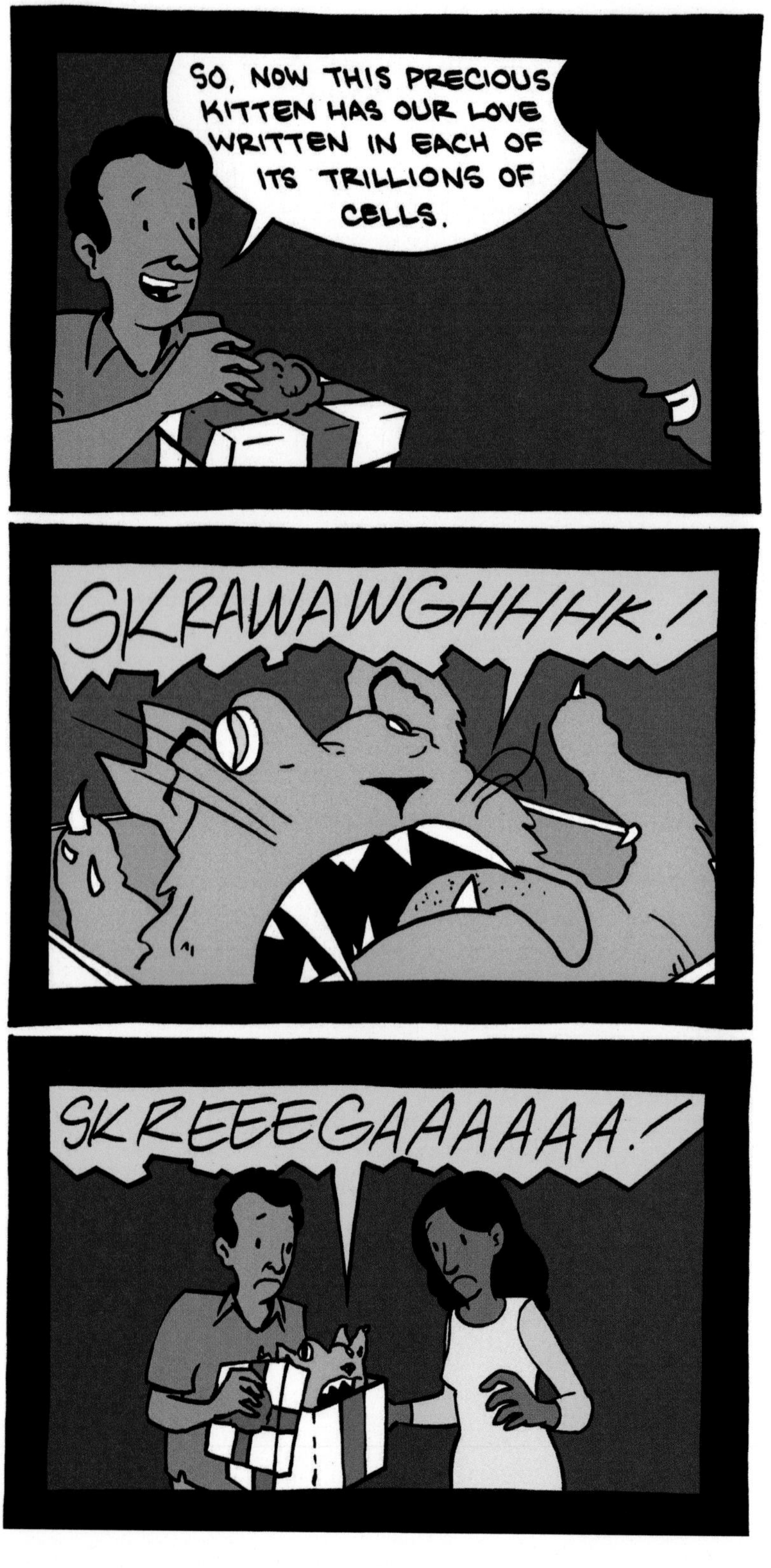
SO, NOW THIS PRECIOUS KITTEN HAS OUR LOVE WRITTEN IN EACH OF ITS TRILLIONS OF CELLS.
SKRAWAWGHHHHK!
SKREEEGAAAAAA!

ALSO I GOT YOU FLOWERS!
FLOWERS ARE NICE!

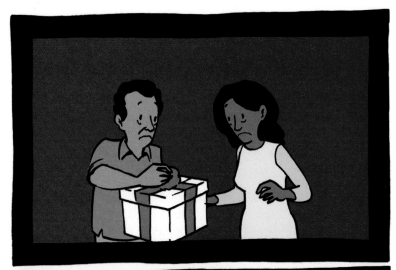

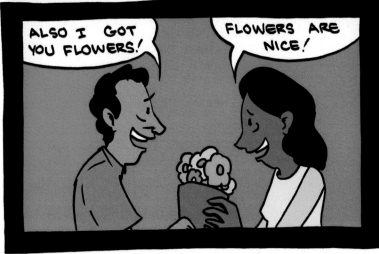

END!

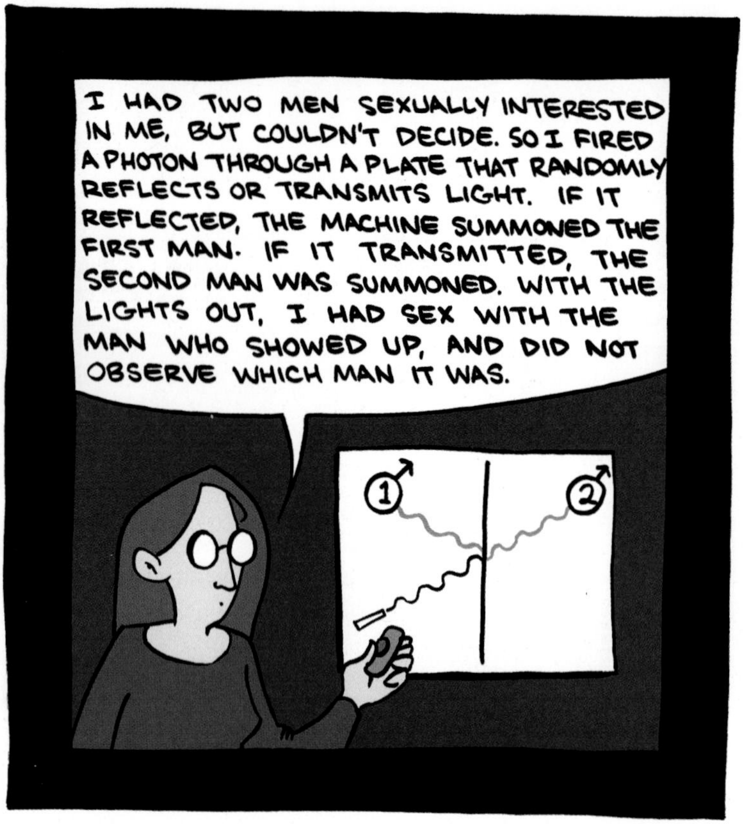
I HAD TWO MEN SEXUALLY INTERESTED IN ME, BUT COULDN'T DECIDE. SO I FIRED A PHOTON THROUGH A PLATE THAT RANDOMLY REFLECTS OR TRANSMITS LIGHT. IF IT REFLECTED, THE MACHINE SUMMONED THE FIRST MAN. IF IT TRANSMITTED, THE SECOND MAN WAS SUMMONED. WITH THE LIGHTS OUT, I HAD SEX WITH THE MAN WHO SHOWED UP, AND DID NOT OBSERVE WHICH MAN IT WAS.
1
2

The scientific community has not welcomed my "quantum threesome" concept.

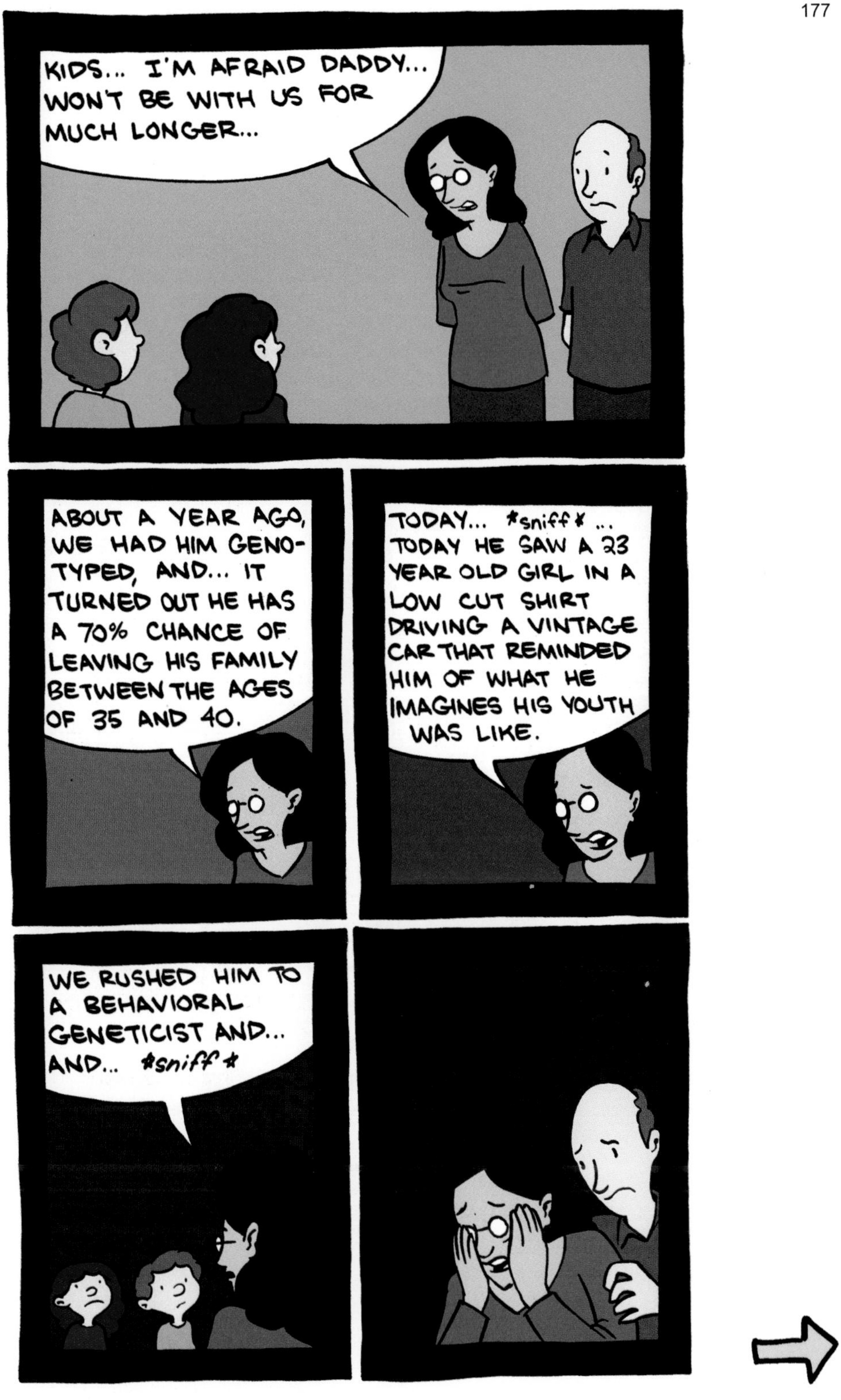
KIDS... I'M AFRAID DADDY... WON'T BE WITH US FOR MUCH LONGER...
ABOUT A YEAR AGO, WE HAD HIM GENO-TYPED, AND... IT TURNED OUT HE HAS A 70% CHANCE OF LEAVING HIS FAMILY BETWEEN THE AGES OF 35 AND 40.
TODAY... *sniff* ... TODAY HE SAW A 23 YEAR OLD GIRL IN A LOW CUT SHIRT DRIVING A VINTAGE CAR THAT REMINDED HIM OF WHAT HE IMAGINES HIS YOUTH WAS LIKE.
WE RUSHED HIM TO A BEHAVIORAL GENETICIST AND... AND... *sniff*

HE SAID I MAY HAVE AS LONG AS A YEAR OR AS SHORT AS... ONE WEEK. BUT, I WANT YOU TO KNOW THAT AS LONG AS I'M STILL AROUND, I'LL BE HERE FOR YOU. I'LL STILL BE... I'LL...
ARE YOU OKAY?
I DUNNO. I JUST FELT THIS ODD... LIGHTNESS IN MY STOMACH. I... I... OH NO... AAGH!

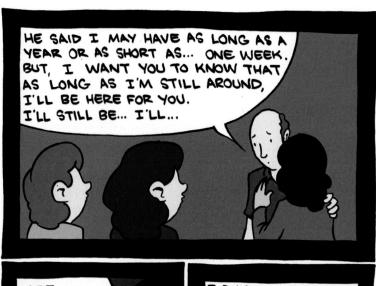

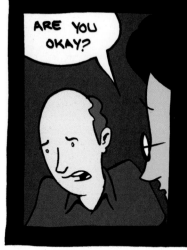

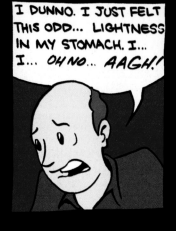

SOON...
WOOH!
YOU KNOW THAT'S NOT HOW GENETICS WORKS, RIGHT?
YES, BUT DADDY DOESN'T.

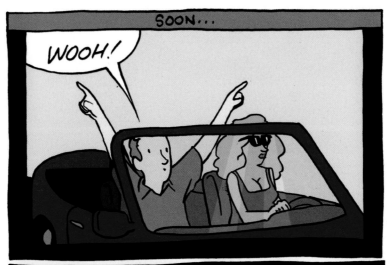

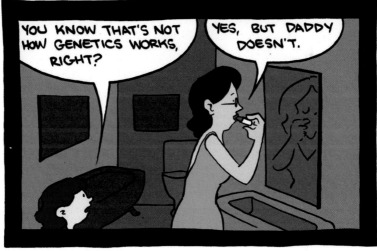

END!

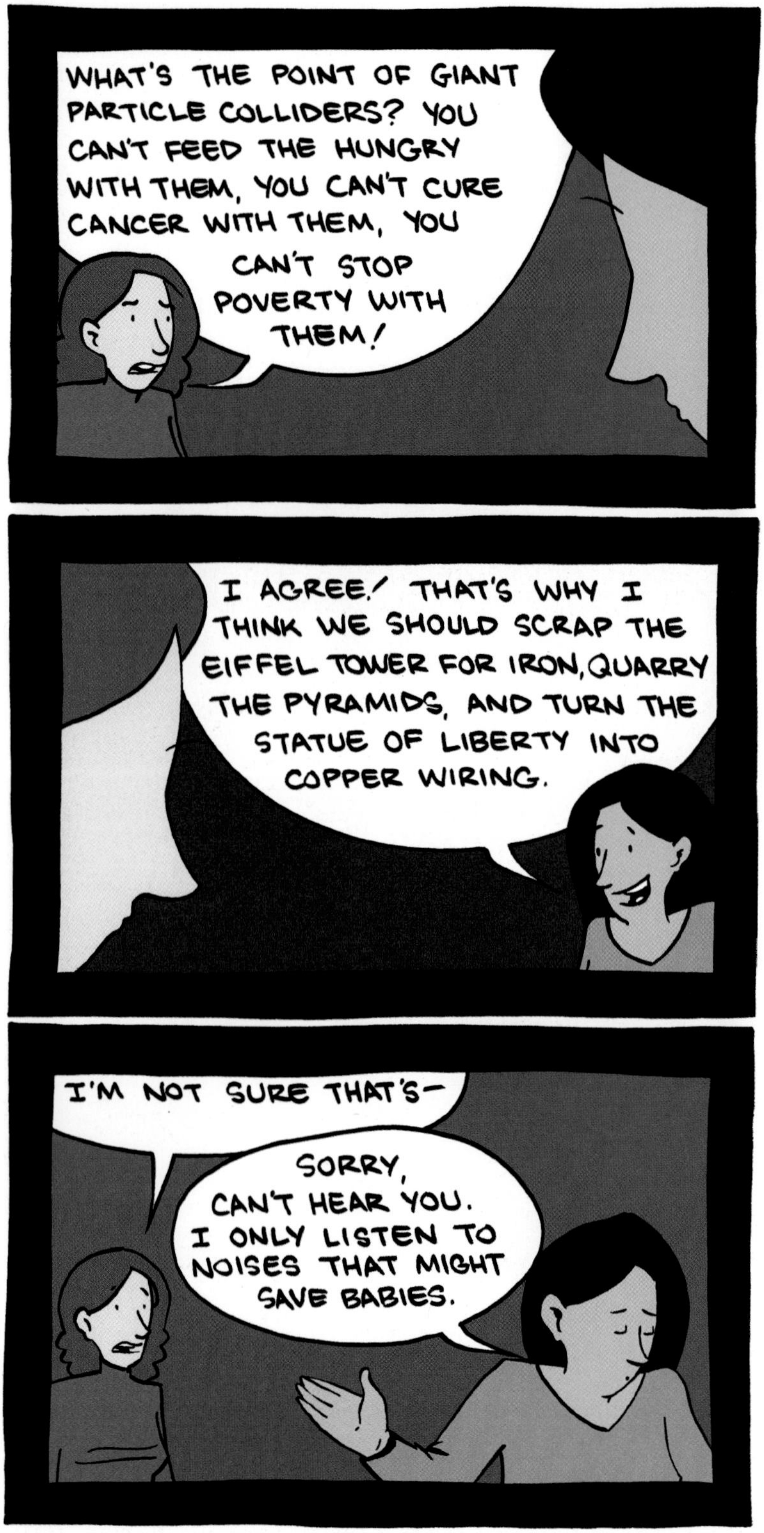
WHAT'S THE POINT OF GIANT PARTICLE COLLIDERS? YOU CAN'T FEED THE HUNGRY WITH THEM, YOU CAN'T CURE CANCER WITH THEM, YOU CAN'T STOP POVERTY WITH THEM!
I AGREE! THAT'S WHY I THINK WE SHOULD SCRAP THE EIFFEL TOWER FOR IRON, QUARRY THE PYRAMIDS, AND TURN THE STATUE OF LIBERTY INTO COPPER WIRING.
I'M NOT SURE THAT'S—
SORRY, CAN'T HEAR YOU. I ONLY LISTEN TO NOISES THAT MIGHT SAVE BABIES.

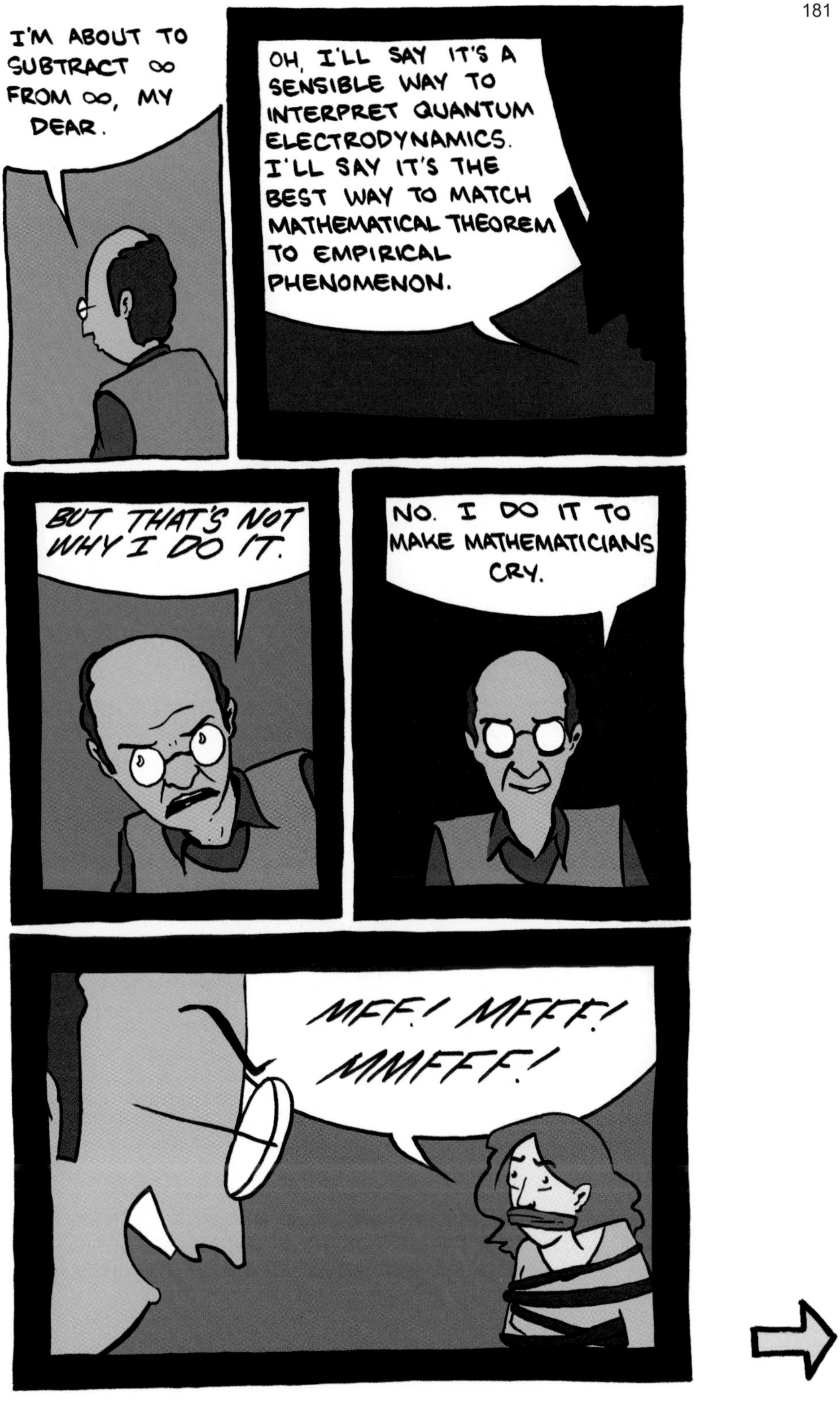
I'M ABOUT TO SUBTRACT ∞ FROM ∞, MY DEAR.
OH, I'LL SAY IT'S A SENSIBLE WAY TO INTERPRET QUANTUM ELECTRODYNAMICS. I'LL SAY IT'S THE BEST WAY TO MATCH MATHEMATICAL THEOREM TO EMPIRICAL PHENOMENON.
BUT THAT'S NOT WHY I DO IT.
NO. I DO IT TO MAKE MATHEMATICIANS CRY.
MFF! MFFF! MMFFF!

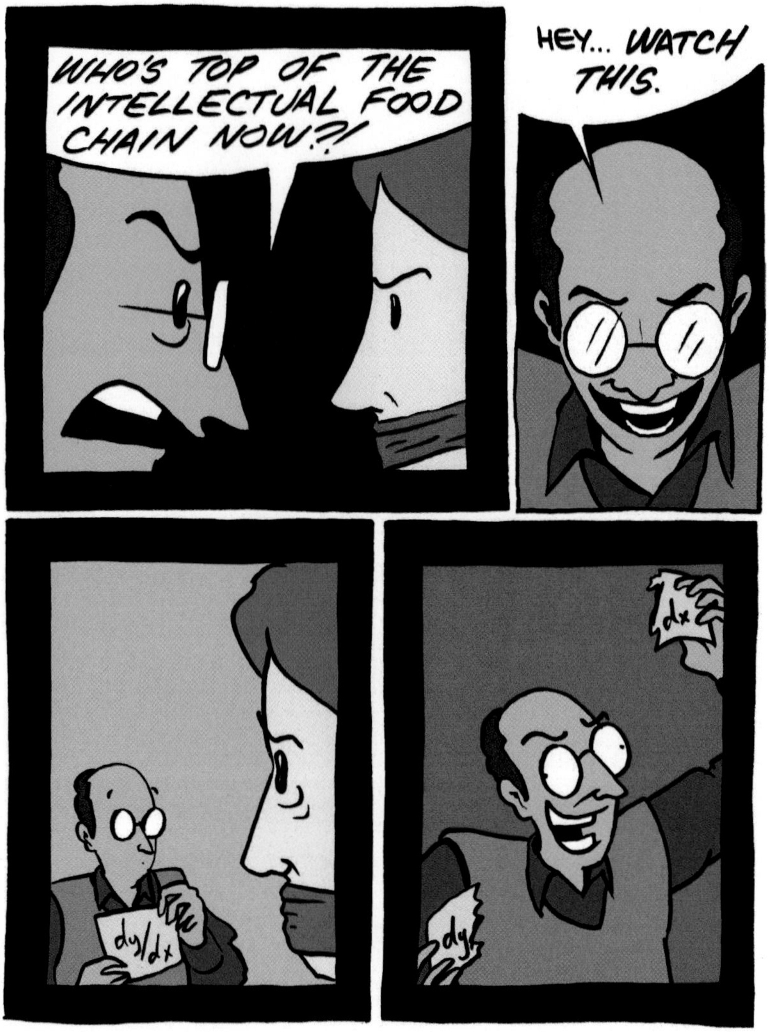
WHO'S TOP OF THE INTELLECTUAL FOOD CHAIN NOW?!
HEY... WATCH THIS.
dy/dx
dx
dy

I'M GONNA USE THESE AS IF THEY'RE SEPARATE VARIABLES! HAHA HAHAHAHA HAHA!
MFFF! MFF!
GOOD. GOOD... I THINK YOU'VE HAD ENOUGH FOR TODAY.
I'LL JUST HEAD BACK TO THE PHYSICS DEPARTMENT WHERE I AAH!

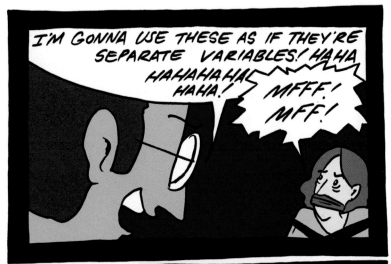

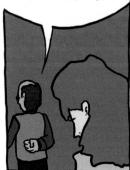

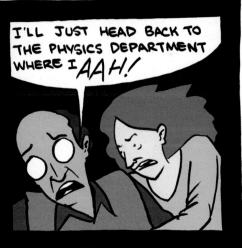

HOW'D YOU GET LOOSE?!
KNOT THEORY.
WHAT ARE YOU GOING TO DO TO ME?
GIVE YOU THE GENERAL CASE OF A MATHEMATICAL TECHNIQUE WHEN YOU ONLY NEED IT FOR A SPECIFIC USAGE!

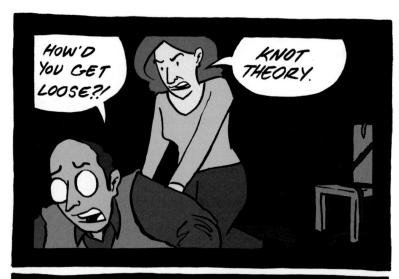

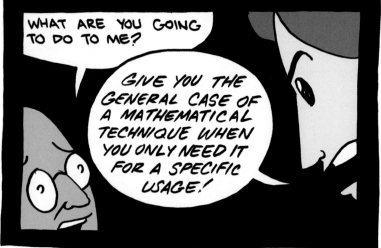

NO! NOOO! NOOOO!
HAHAHAHA HAHAHA!
HIHIHIH...
WHATCHA THINK MOMMY'S THINKING ABOUT?
THEOREMS, NO DOUBT. BEAUTIFUL, BEAUTIFUL THEOREMS.

END!

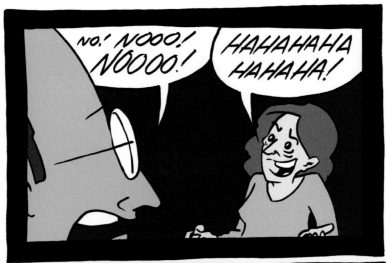

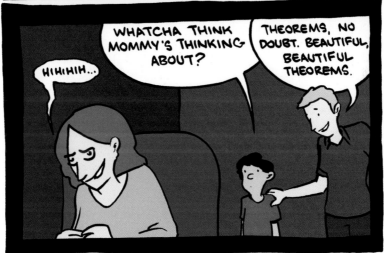

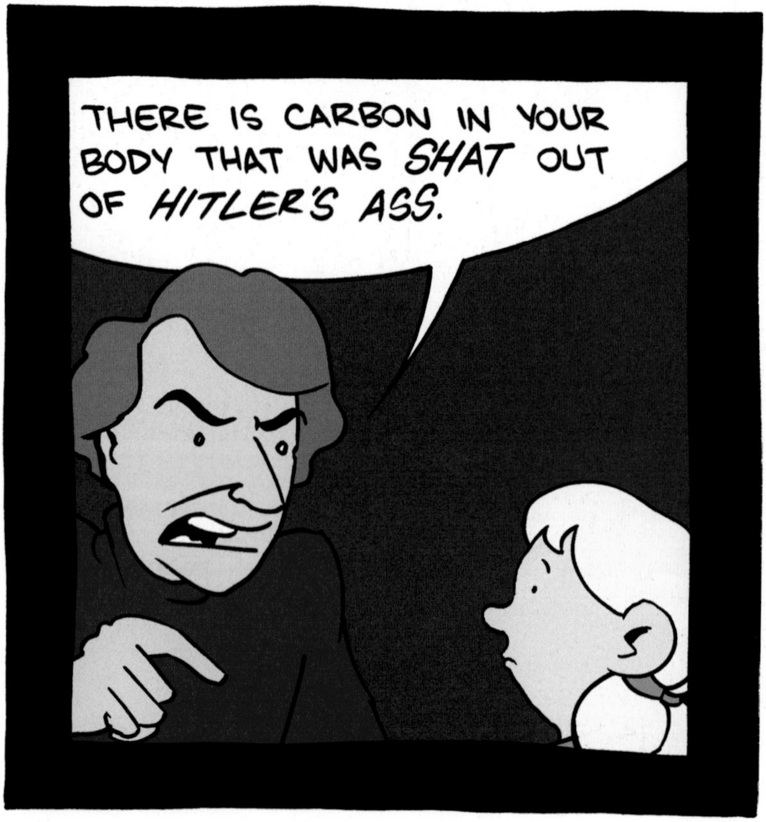
THERE IS CARBON IN YOUR BODY THAT WAS *SHAT* OUT OF *HITLER'S ASS.*

Nobody liked Evil Carl Sagan.

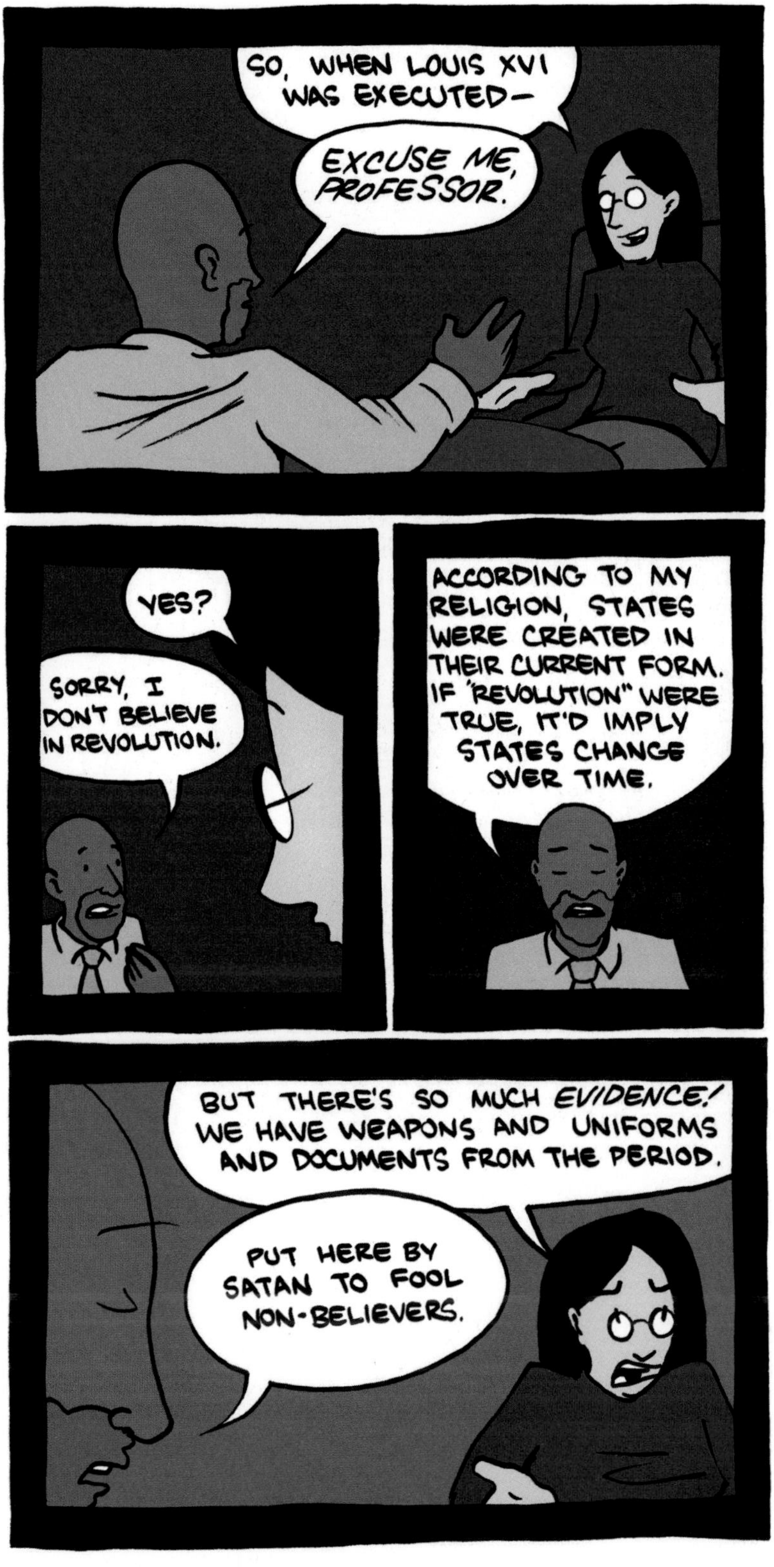
SO, WHEN LOUIS XVI WAS EXECUTED—
EXCUSE ME, PROFESSOR.
YES?
SORRY, I DON'T BELIEVE IN REVOLUTION.
ACCORDING TO MY RELIGION, STATES WERE CREATED IN THEIR CURRENT FORM. IF "REVOLUTION" WERE TRUE, IT'D IMPLY STATES CHANGE OVER TIME.
BUT THERE'S SO MUCH EVIDENCE! WE HAVE WEAPONS AND UNIFORMS AND DOCUMENTS FROM THE PERIOD.
PUT HERE BY SATAN TO FOOL NON-BELIEVERS.

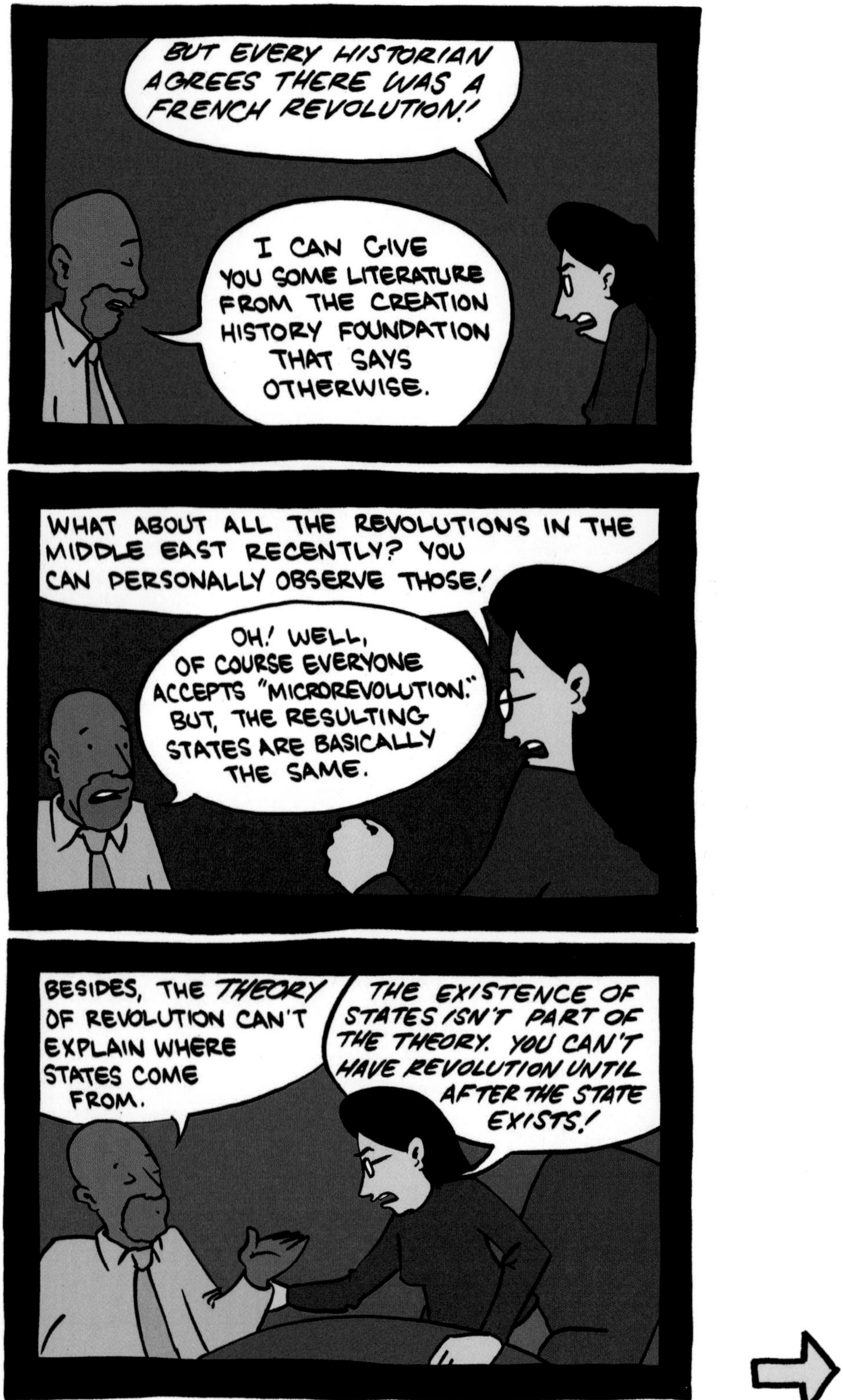
BUT EVERY HISTORIAN AGREES THERE WAS A FRENCH REVOLUTION!
I CAN GIVE YOU SOME LITERATURE FROM THE CREATION HISTORY FOUNDATION THAT SAYS OTHERWISE.
WHAT ABOUT ALL THE REVOLUTIONS IN THE MIDDLE EAST RECENTLY? YOU CAN PERSONALLY OBSERVE THOSE!
OH! WELL, OF COURSE EVERYONE ACCEPTS "MICROREVOLUTION." BUT, THE RESULTING STATES ARE BASICALLY THE SAME.
BESIDES, THE *THEORY* OF REVOLUTION CAN'T EXPLAIN WHERE STATES COME FROM.
THE EXISTENCE OF STATES ISN'T PART OF THE THEORY. YOU CAN'T HAVE REVOLUTION UNTIL AFTER THE STATE EXISTS!

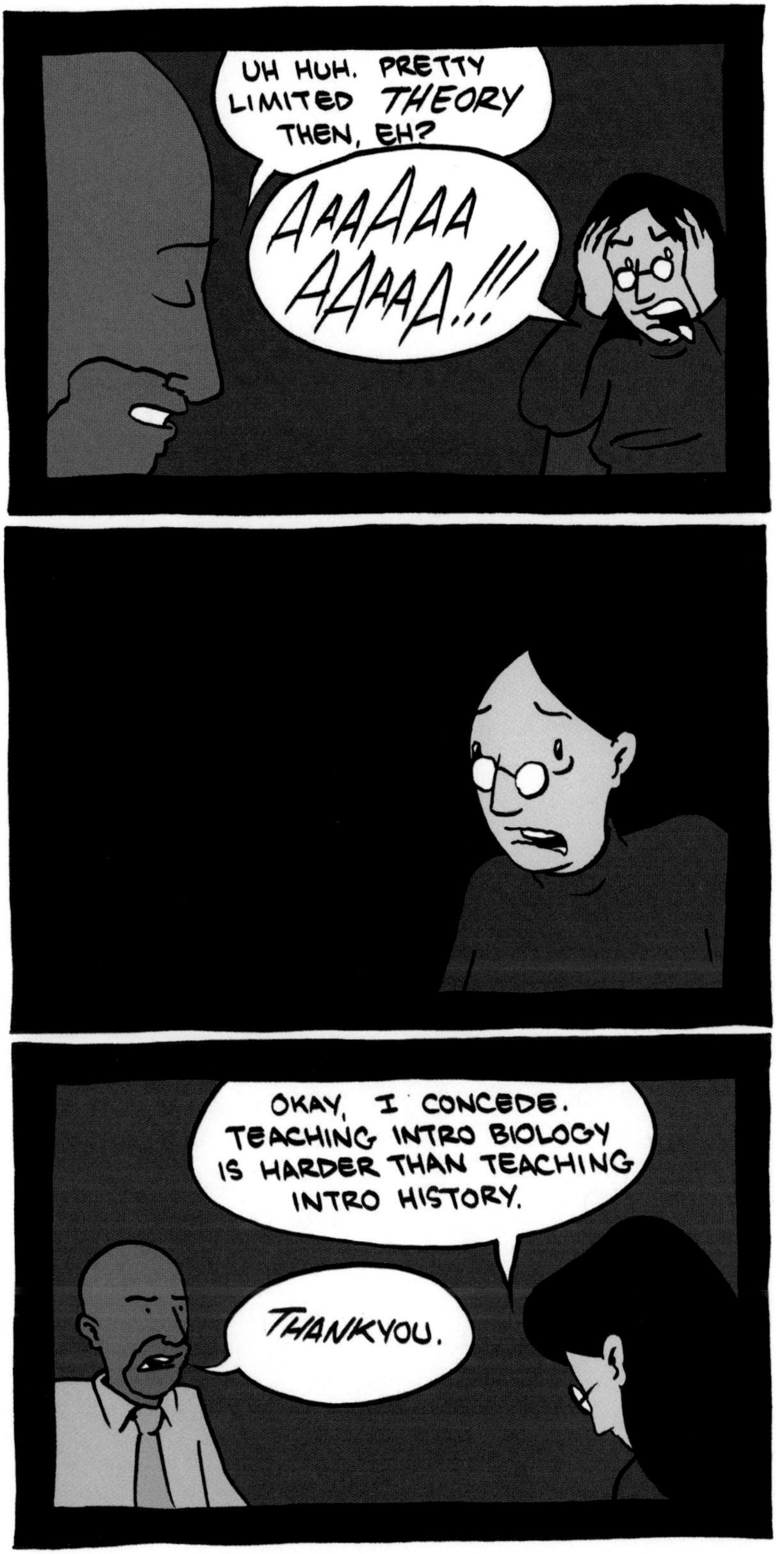
UH HUH. PRETTY LIMITED THEORY THEN, EH?
AAAAAA AAAAA..!!!
OKAY, I CONCEDE. TEACHING INTRO BIOLOGY IS HARDER THAN TEACHING INTRO HISTORY.
THANKYOU.

END!

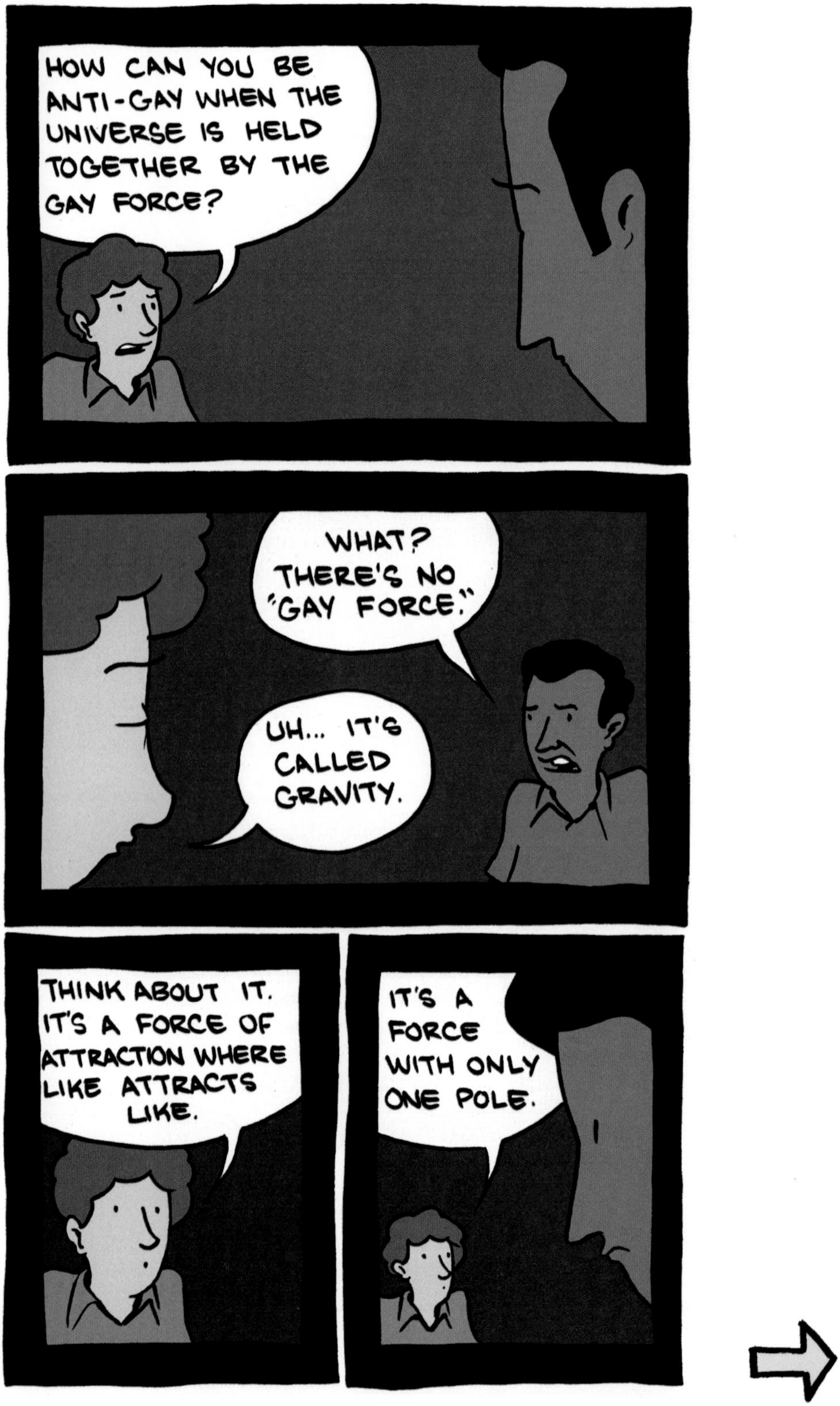
HOW CAN YOU BE ANTI-GAY WHEN THE UNIVERSE IS HELD TOGETHER BY THE GAY FORCE?
WHAT? THERE'S NO "GAY FORCE."
UH... IT'S CALLED GRAVITY.
THINK ABOUT IT. IT'S A FORCE OF ATTRACTION WHERE LIKE ATTRACTS LIKE.
IT'S A FORCE WITH ONLY ONE POLE.

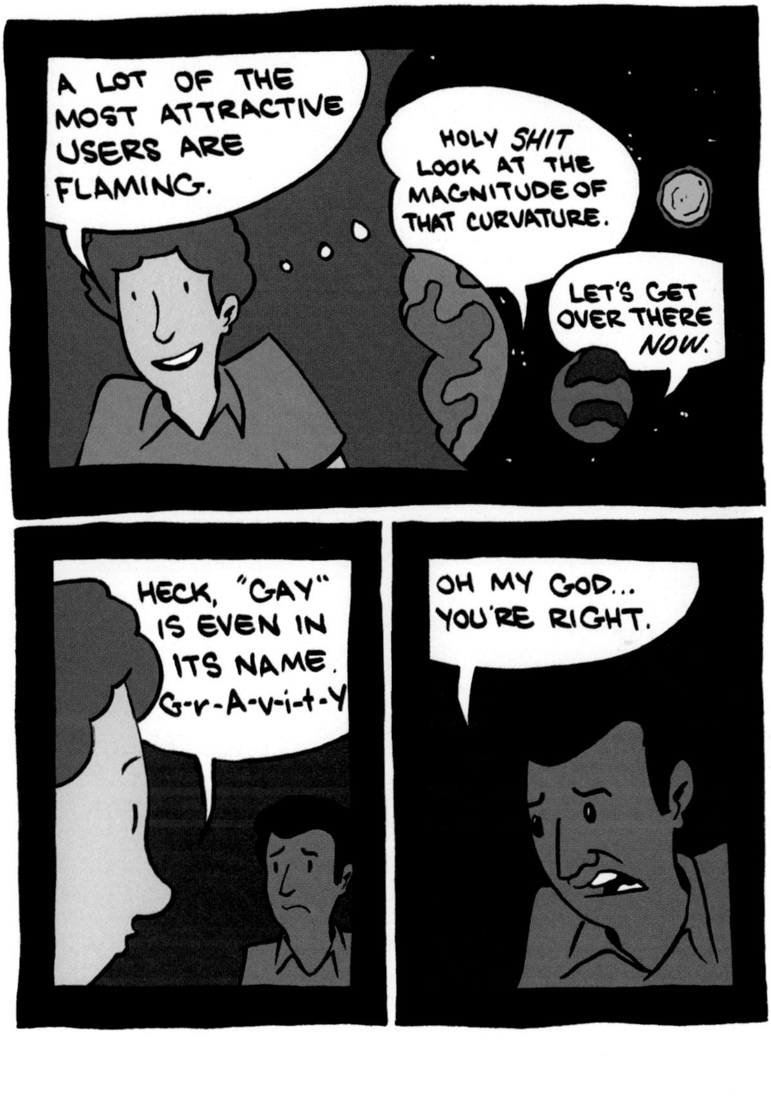
A LOT OF THE MOST ATTRACTIVE USERS ARE FLAMING.
HOLY SHIT LOOK AT THE MAGNITUDE OF THAT CURVATURE.
LET'S GET OVER THERE NOW.
HECK, "GAY" IS EVEN IN ITS NAME. G-r-A-v-i-t-Y
OH MY GOD... YOU'RE RIGHT.

LATER...
HOW'D IT GO?
CHECK THE NEWS.
Newsness.com
ANTI-GAY FACTIONS ALL GO TO SPACE
"UP HERE WE ONLY ALLOW ELECTRO-MAGNETISM!"

END!

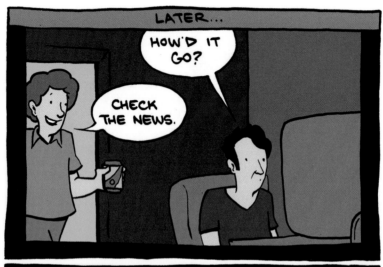

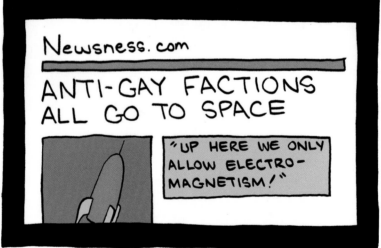

Cable does not enter slot.

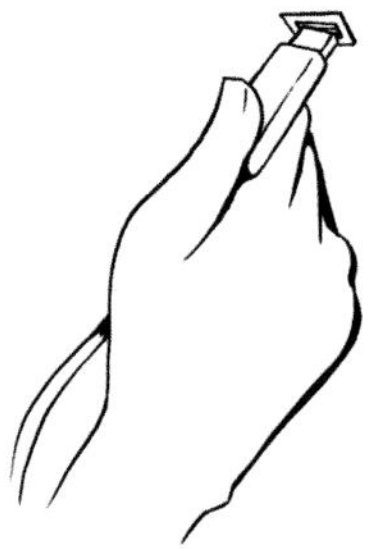

Rotate 180°.

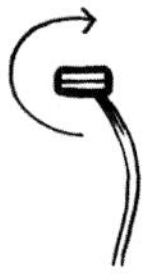

Cable does not enter slot.

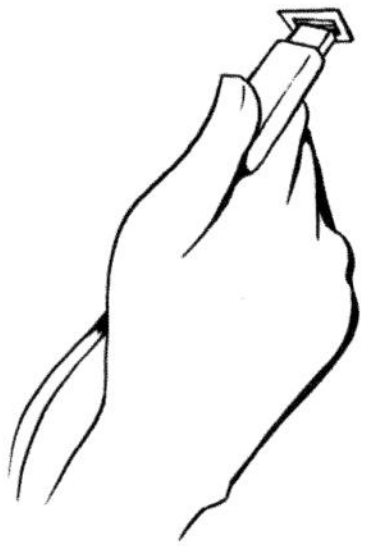

Rotate 180°.

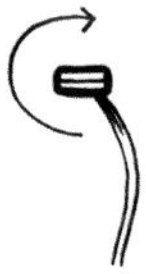

Cable enters slot.

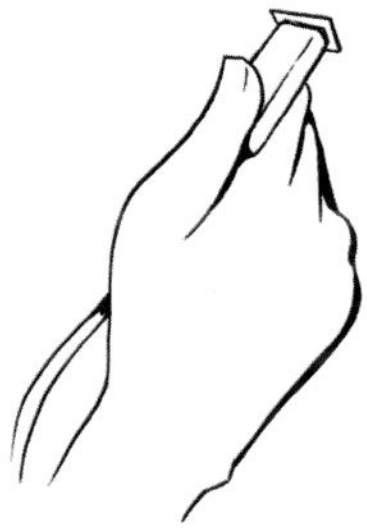

PROVED:
Cables exist in 4-dimensional space.

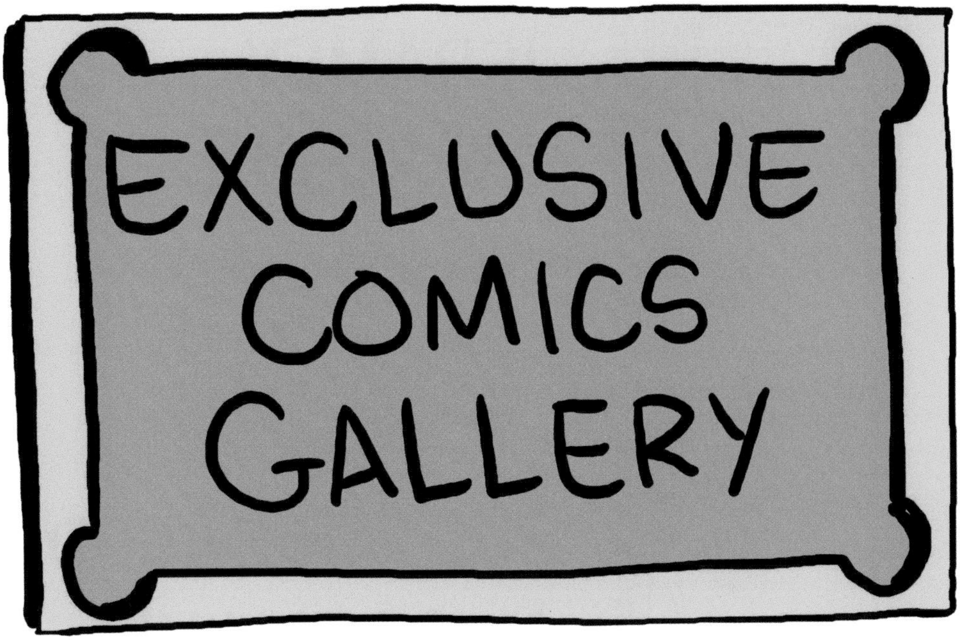
EXCLUSIVE
COMICS
GALLERY

SPECIAL THANKS TO

JERAMEY CRAWFORD

SULTAN SAEED AL DARMAKI

ADAM TIBBALDS

FOR MAKING POSSIBLE THREE EXCLUSIVE COMICS!

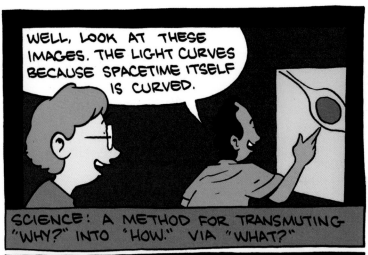

WELL, LOOK AT THESE IMAGES. THE LIGHT CURVES BECAUSE SPACETIME ITSELF IS CURVED.
SCIENCE: A METHOD FOR TRANSMUTING "WHY?" INTO "HOW." VIA "WHAT?"
THIS NANOFIBER STRUCTURE ALLOWS INCREDIBLE TENSILE STRENGTH.
SO YOU CAN THROW PUMPKINS REALLY HARD WITH IT?
BINGO.
ENGINEERING: A METHOD FOR TRANSMUTING "HOW." INTO "TREBUCHETS."

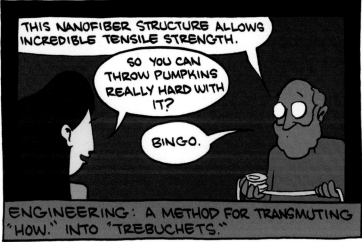

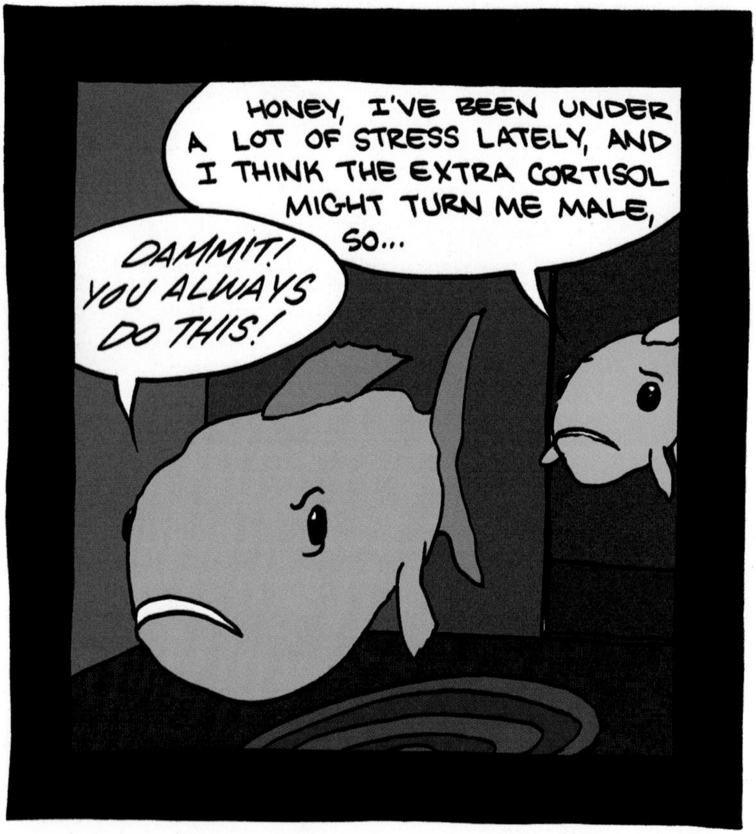
HONEY, I'VE BEEN UNDER A LOT OF STRESS LATELY, AND I THINK THE EXTRA CORTISOL MIGHT TURN ME MALE, SO...
DAMMIT! YOU ALWAYS DO THIS!

Sally angles for a massage.

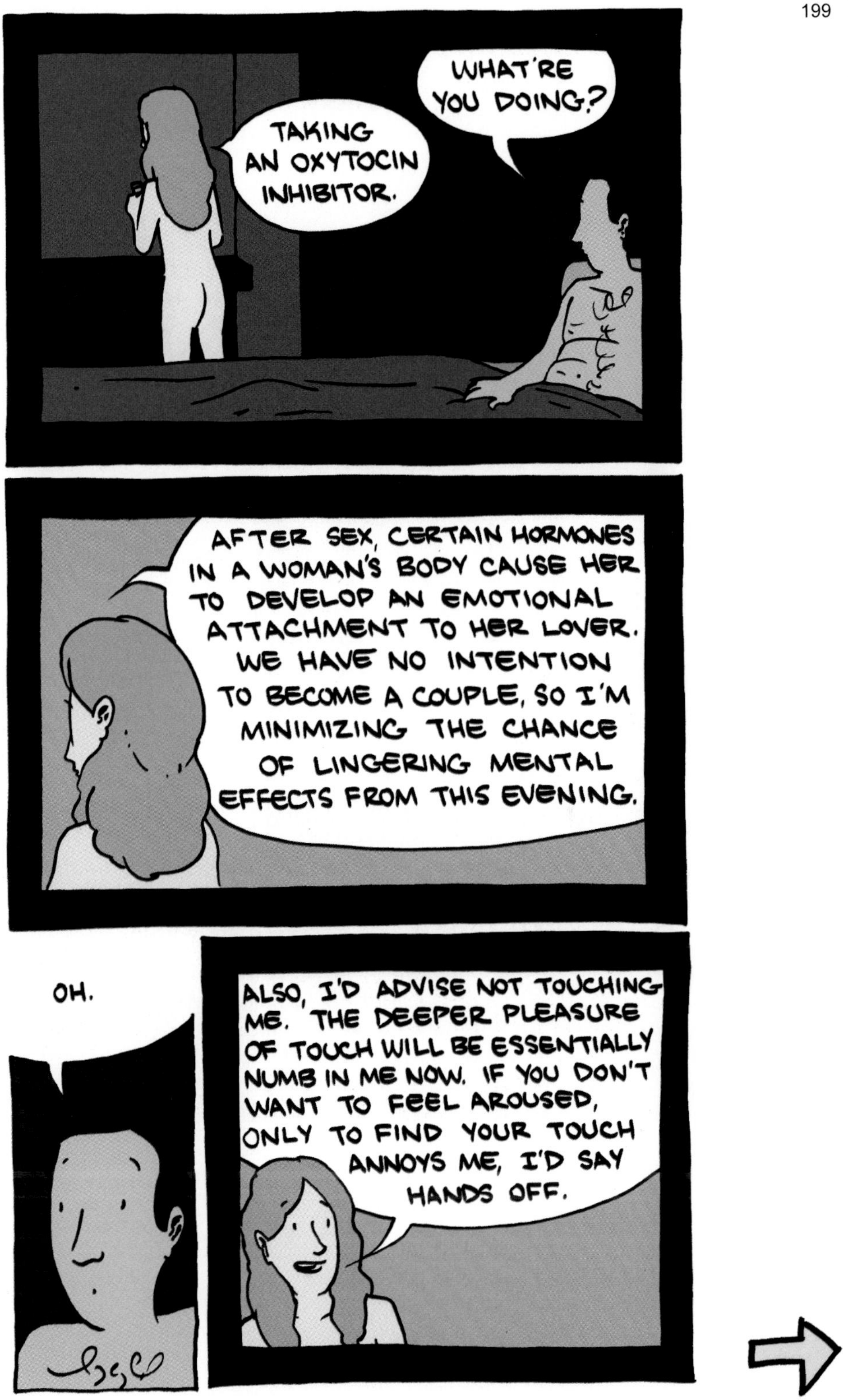
WHAT'RE YOU DOING?
TAKING AN OXYTOCIN INHIBITOR.
AFTER SEX, CERTAIN HORMONES IN A WOMAN'S BODY CAUSE HER TO DEVELOP AN EMOTIONAL ATTACHMENT TO HER LOVER. WE HAVE NO INTENTION TO BECOME A COUPLE, SO I'M MINIMIZING THE CHANCE OF LINGERING MENTAL EFFECTS FROM THIS EVENING.
OH.
ALSO, I'D ADVISE NOT TOUCHING ME. THE DEEPER PLEASURE OF TOUCH WILL BE ESSENTIALLY NUMB IN ME NOW. IF YOU DON'T WANT TO FEEL AROUSED, ONLY TO FIND YOUR TOUCH ANNOYS ME, I'D SAY HANDS OFF.

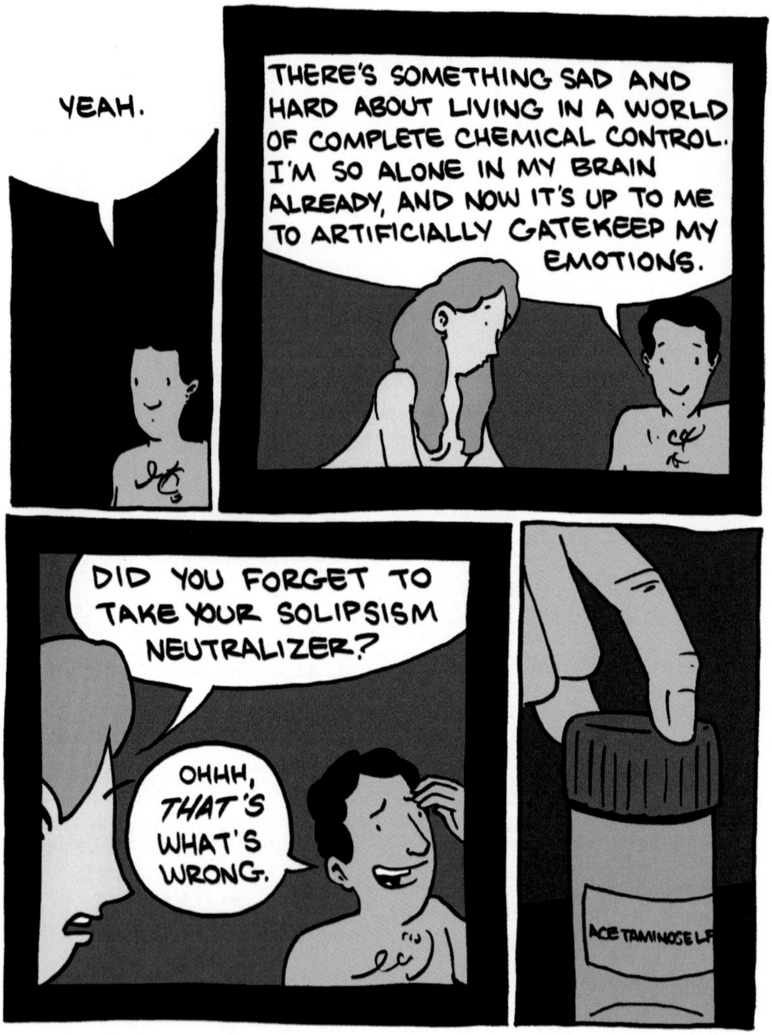
YEAH.
THERE'S SOMETHING SAD AND HARD ABOUT LIVING IN A WORLD OF COMPLETE CHEMICAL CONTROL. I'M SO ALONE IN MY BRAIN ALREADY, AND NOW IT'S UP TO ME TO ARTIFICIALLY GATEKEEP MY EMOTIONS.
DID YOU FORGET TO TAKE YOUR SOLIPSISM NEUTRALIZER?
OHHH, *THAT'S* WHAT'S WRONG.
ACETAMINOSELF

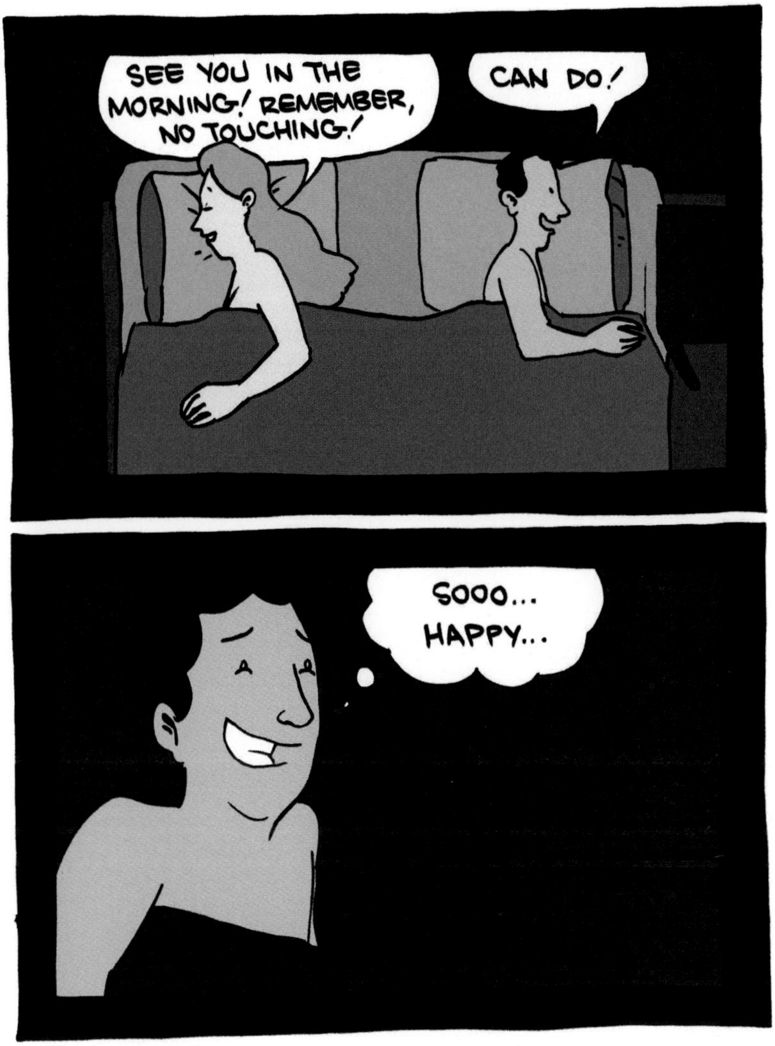
SEE YOU IN THE MORNING! REMEMBER, NO TOUCHING!
CAN DO!
SOOO... HAPPY...

END!

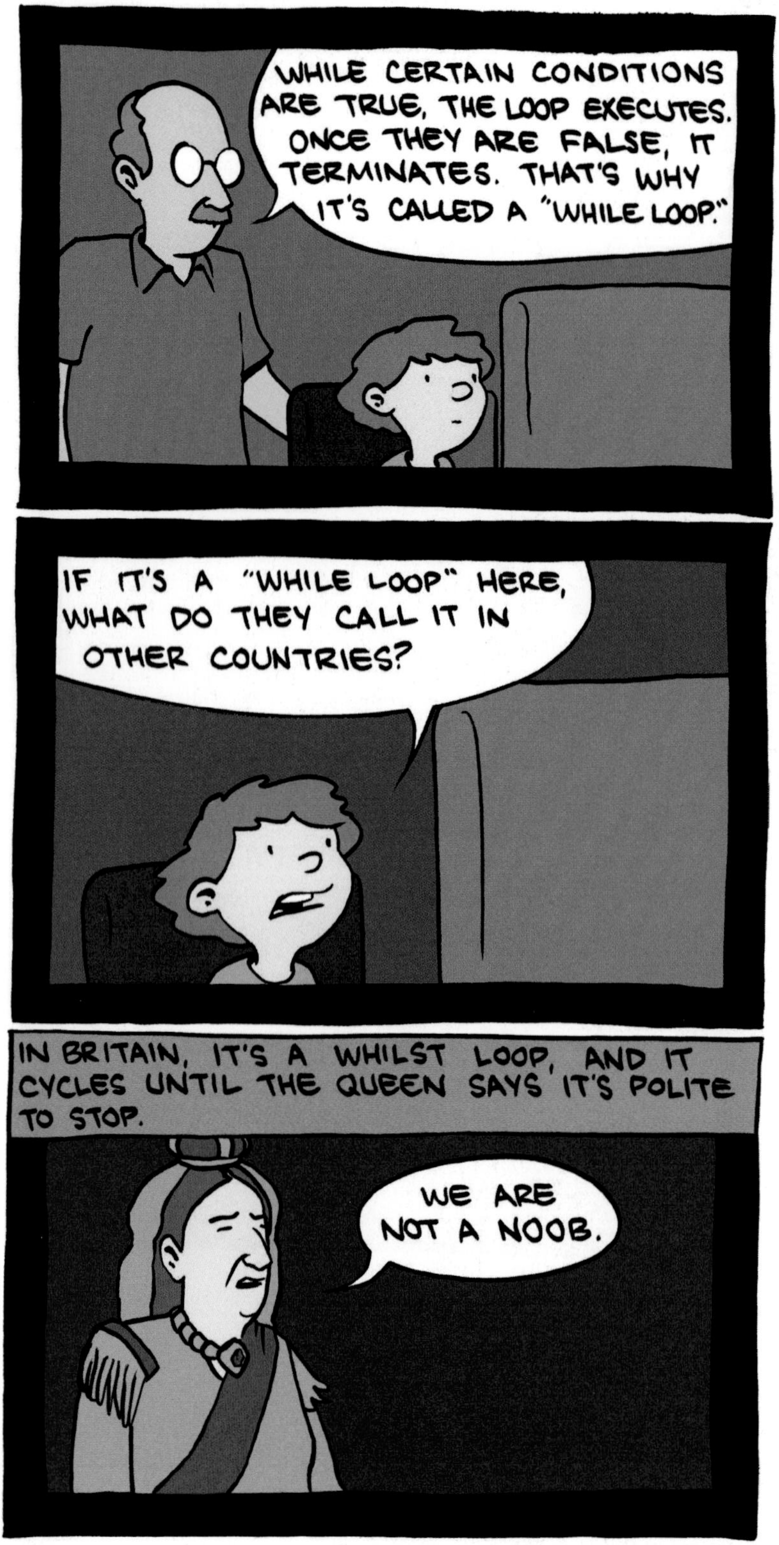
WHILE CERTAIN CONDITIONS ARE TRUE, THE LOOP EXECUTES. ONCE THEY ARE FALSE, IT TERMINATES. THAT'S WHY IT'S CALLED A "WHILE LOOP."
IF IT'S A "WHILE LOOP" HERE, WHAT DO THEY CALL IT IN OTHER COUNTRIES?
IN BRITAIN, IT'S A WHILST LOOP, AND IT CYCLES UNTIL THE QUEEN SAYS IT'S POLITE TO STOP.
WE ARE NOT A NOOB.

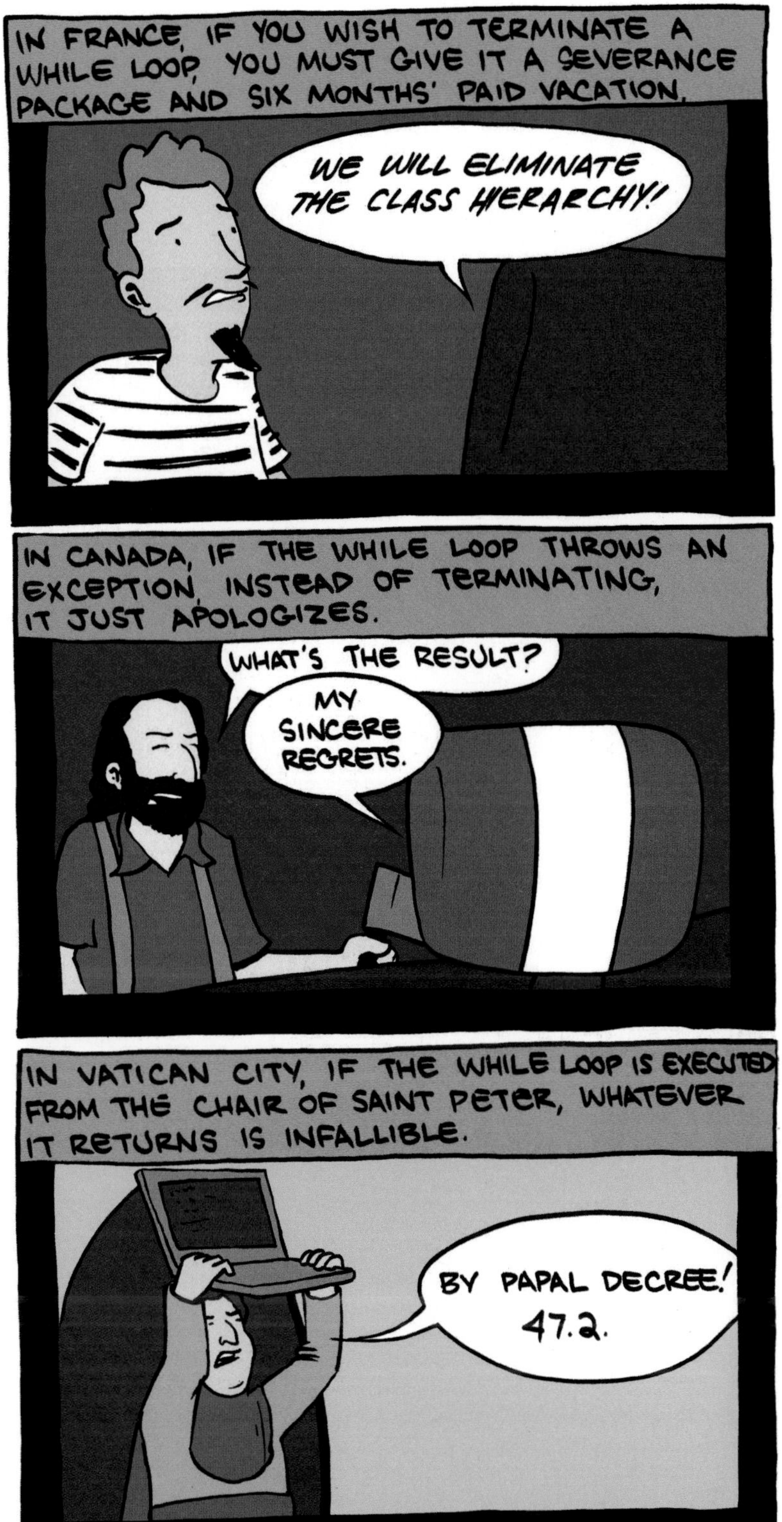
IN FRANCE, IF YOU WISH TO TERMINATE A WHILE LOOP, YOU MUST GIVE IT A SEVERANCE PACKAGE AND SIX MONTHS' PAID VACATION.
WE WILL ELIMINATE THE CLASS HIERARCHY!
IN CANADA, IF THE WHILE LOOP THROWS AN EXCEPTION, INSTEAD OF TERMINATING, IT JUST APOLOGIZES.
WHAT'S THE RESULT?
MY SINCERE REGRETS.
IN VATICAN CITY, IF THE WHILE LOOP IS EXECUTED FROM THE CHAIR OF SAINT PETER, WHATEVER IT RETURNS IS INFALLIBLE.
BY PAPAL DECREE! 47.2.

ARE YOU SURE ABOUT ALL THAT?
OF COURSE I'M SURE. I'M A DAD.
10 YEARS LATER...
HEY, YOU FORGOT TO PUT IN A LINE ABOUT THE QUEEN'S APPROVAL.
WHAT?
I... *NOTHING*. I JUST NEED TO GO KILL MY PARENTS.

END!

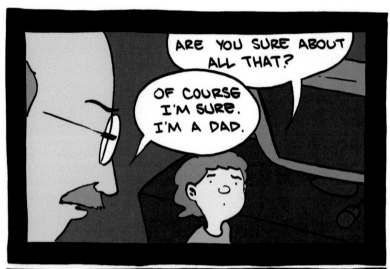

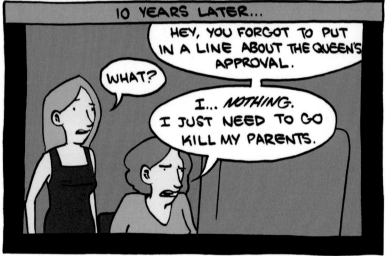

FOR MILLENIA, WE STRUGGLED FOR TRUTH, EXPERIMENTING, ARGUING, UNIFYING.

WE WERE DRIVEN BY THE HOPE THAT ONE DAY WE WOULD DISCOVER THE ROOT OF EVERYTHING. WE BELIEVED THE FINAL TRUTH WOULD BE SO SIMPLE AND BEAUTIFUL IT WOULD MAKE THE END OF DISCOVERY PALATABLE.

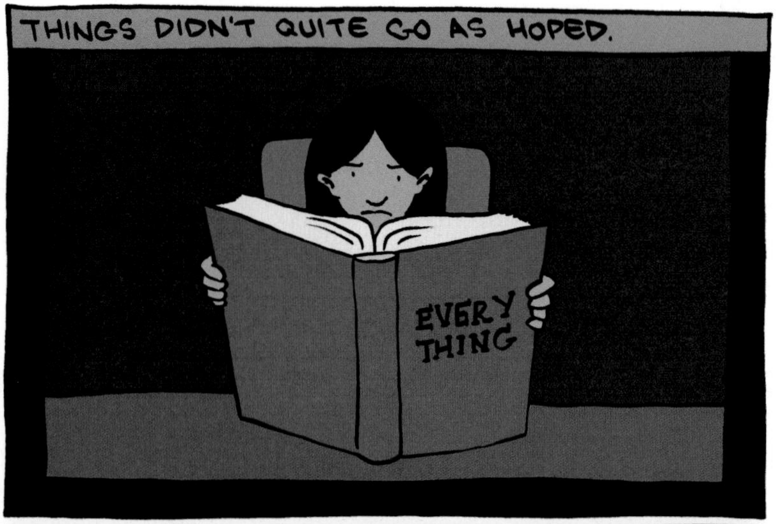
THINGS DIDN'T QUITE GO AS HOPED.
EVERY THING

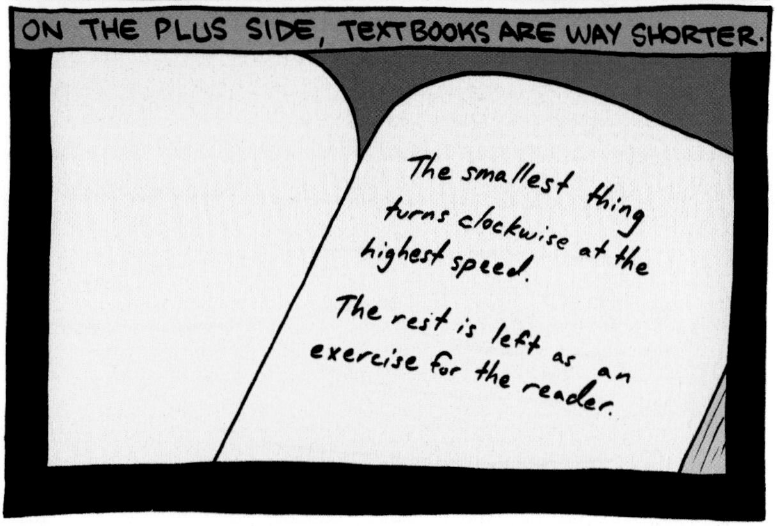
ON THE PLUS SIDE, TEXTBOOKS ARE WAY SHORTER.
The smallest thing turns clockwise at the highest speed.
The rest is left as an exercise for the reader.

END!

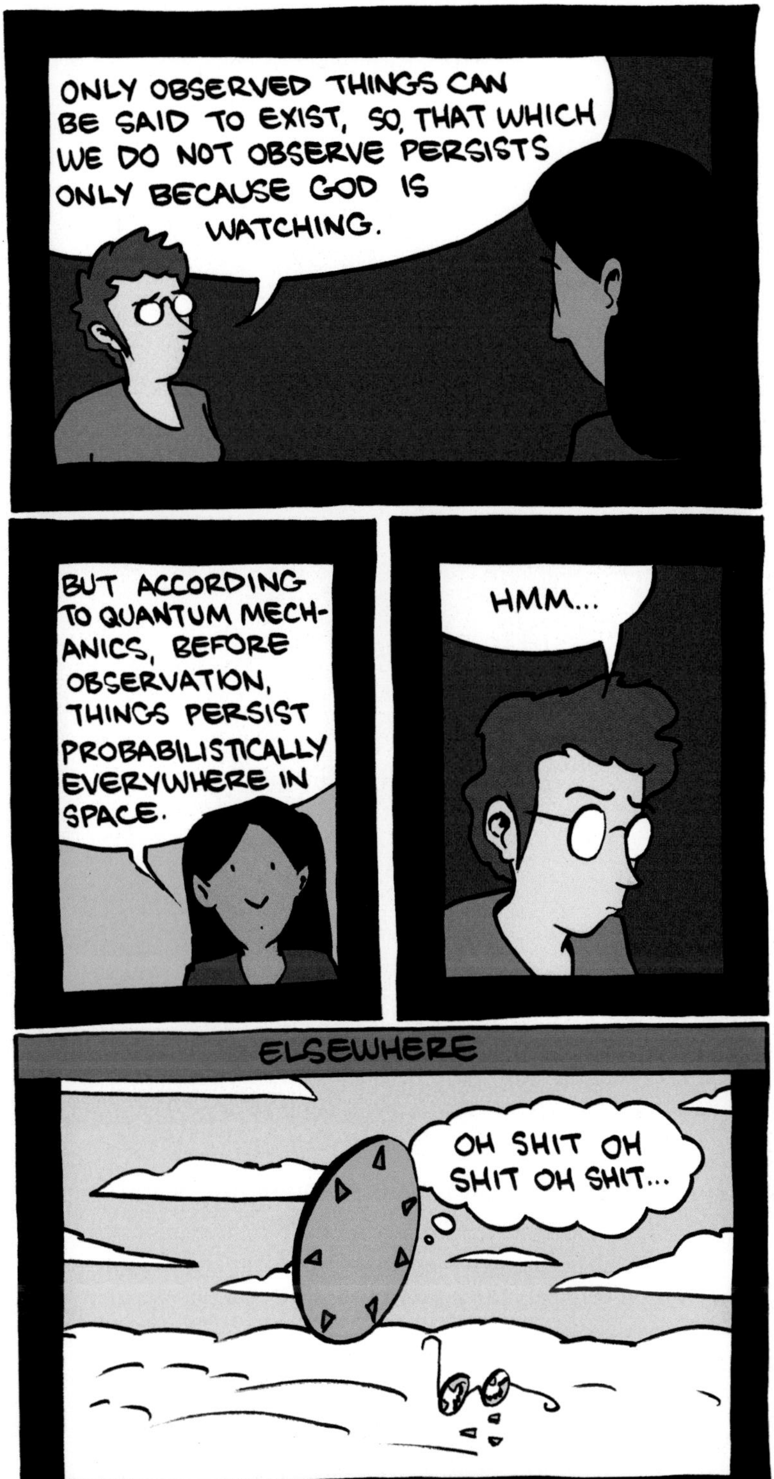
ONLY OBSERVED THINGS CAN BE SAID TO EXIST, SO, THAT WHICH WE DO NOT OBSERVE PERSISTS ONLY BECAUSE GOD IS WATCHING.
BUT ACCORDING TO QUANTUM MECH-ANICS, BEFORE OBSERVATION, THINGS PERSIST PROBABILISTICALLY EVERYWHERE IN SPACE.
HMM...
ELSEWHERE
OH SHIT OH SHIT OH SHIT...

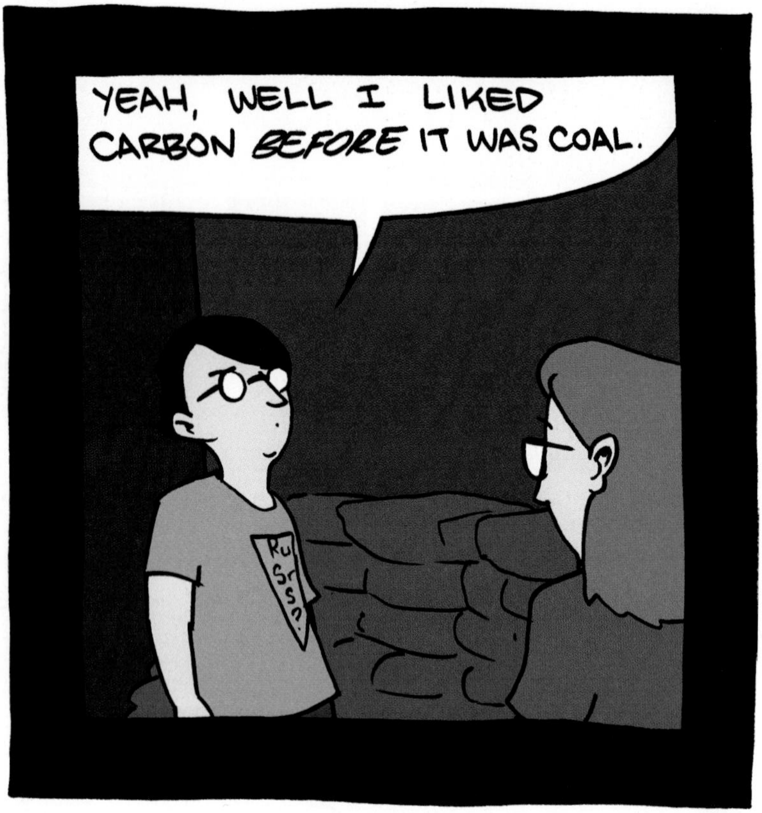
YEAH, WELL I LIKED CARBON BEFORE IT WAS COAL.
Ru Sr S ?

Nobody likes chemistry hipsters.

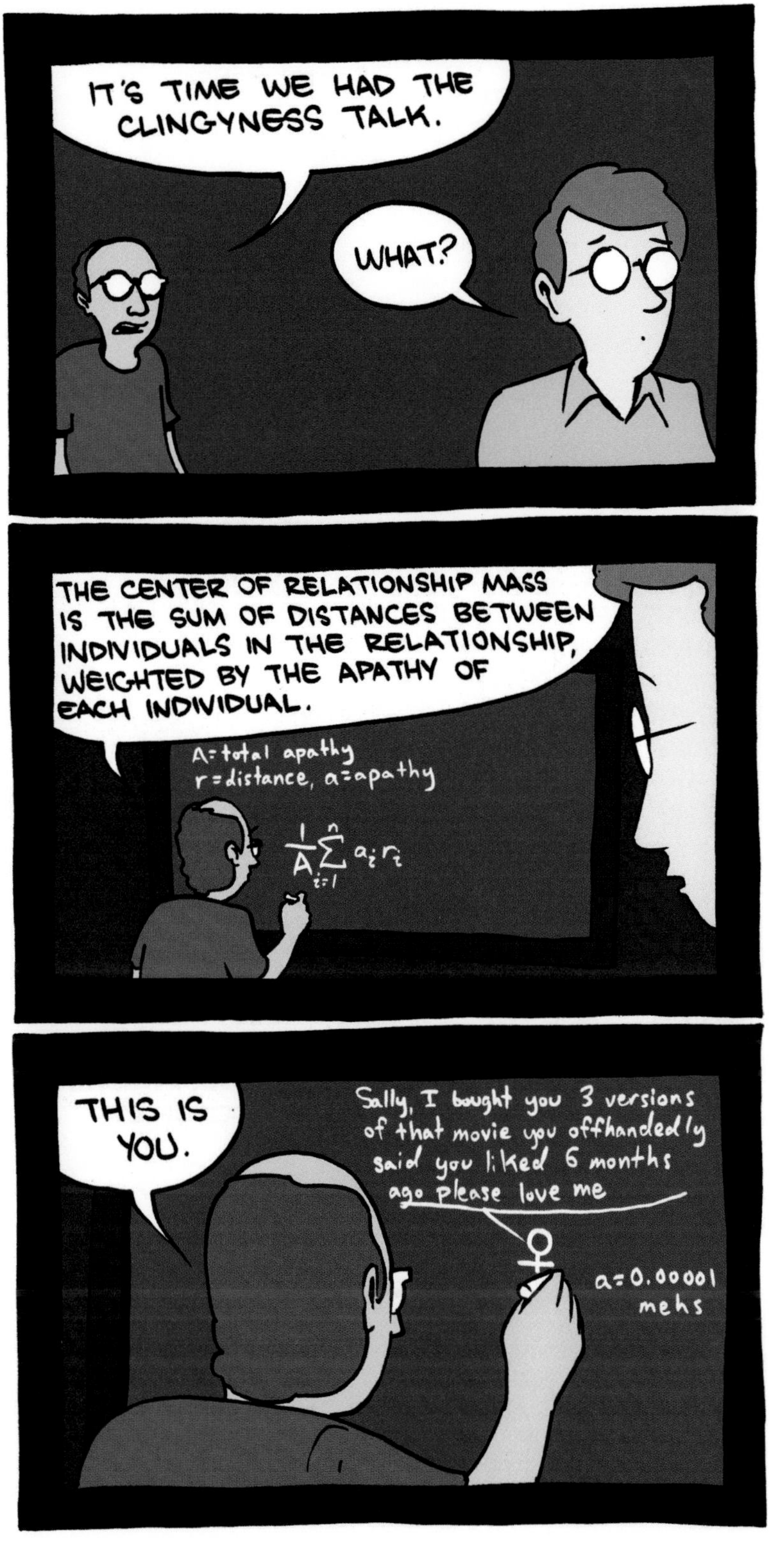
IT'S TIME WE HAD THE CLINGYNESS TALK.
WHAT?
THE CENTER OF RELATIONSHIP MASS IS THE SUM OF DISTANCES BETWEEN INDIVIDUALS IN THE RELATIONSHIP, WEIGHTED BY THE APATHY OF EACH INDIVIDUAL.
A = total apathy
r = distance, a = apathy
$\frac{1}{A}\sum_{i=1}^{n} a_i r_i$
THIS IS YOU.
Sally, I bought you 3 versions of that movie you offhandedly said you liked 6 months ago please love me
♀
a = 0.00001 mehs

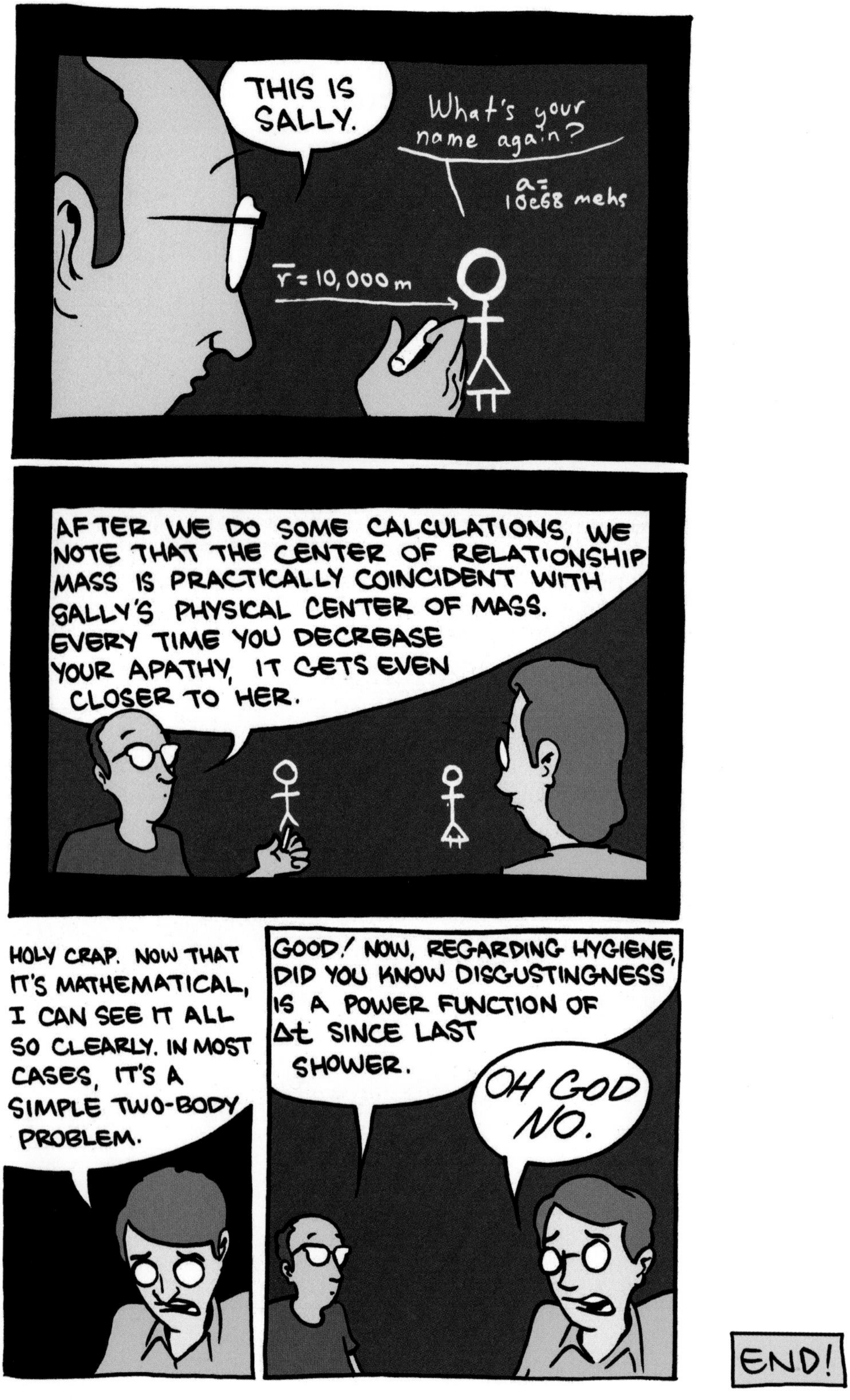
THIS IS SALLY.
What's your name again?
a= 10e68 mehs
r = 10,000 m
AFTER WE DO SOME CALCULATIONS, WE NOTE THAT THE CENTER OF RELATIONSHIP MASS IS PRACTICALLY COINCIDENT WITH SALLY'S PHYSICAL CENTER OF MASS. EVERY TIME YOU DECREASE YOUR APATHY, IT GETS EVEN CLOSER TO HER.
HOLY CRAP. NOW THAT IT'S MATHEMATICAL, I CAN SEE IT ALL SO CLEARLY. IN MOST CASES, IT'S A SIMPLE TWO-BODY PROBLEM.
GOOD! NOW, REGARDING HYGIENE, DID YOU KNOW DISGUSTINGNESS IS A POWER FUNCTION OF Δt SINCE LAST SHOWER.
OH GOD NO.
END!

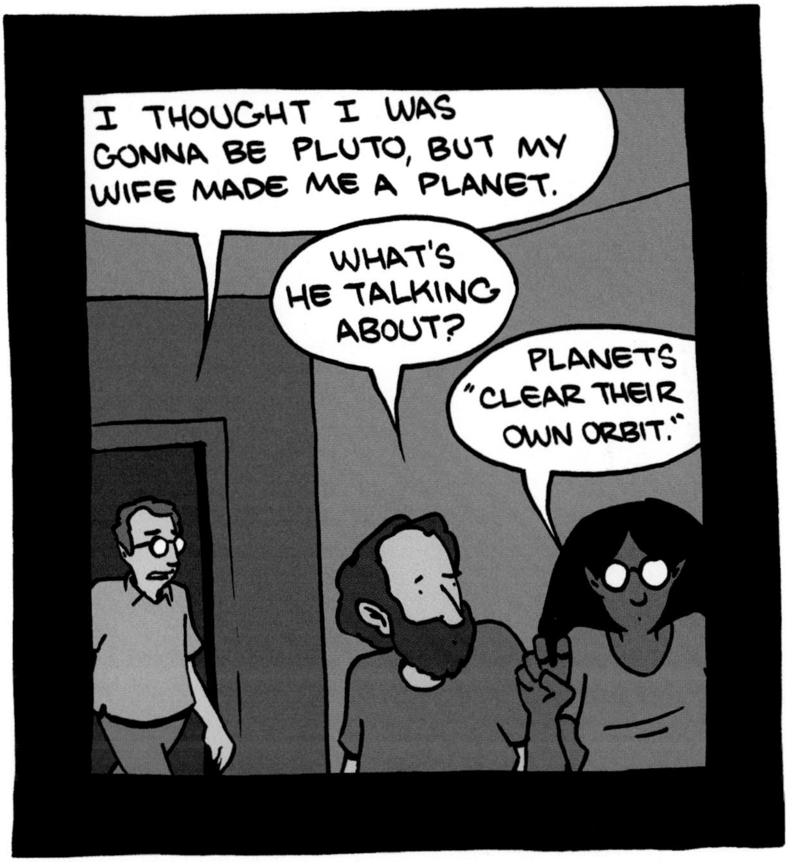
I THOUGHT I WAS GONNA BE PLUTO, BUT MY WIFE MADE ME A PLANET.
WHAT'S HE TALKING ABOUT?
PLANETS "CLEAR THEIR OWN ORBIT."

Astronomers have weird masturbation euphemisms.

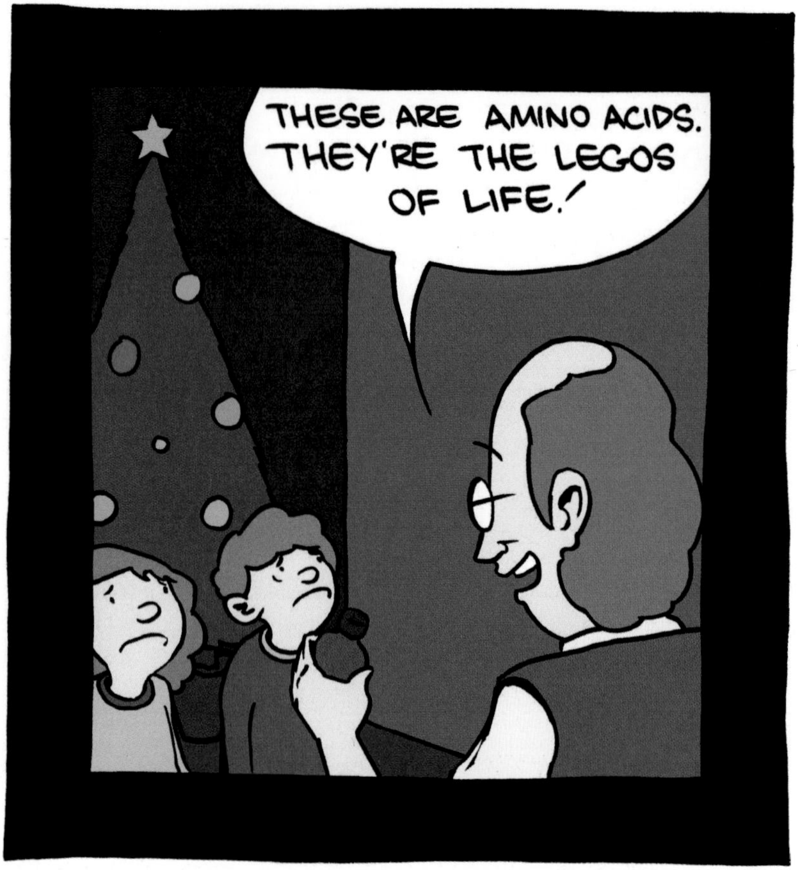
THESE ARE AMINO ACIDS.
THEY'RE THE LEGOS
OF LIFE!

It's hard being the child of a biochemist

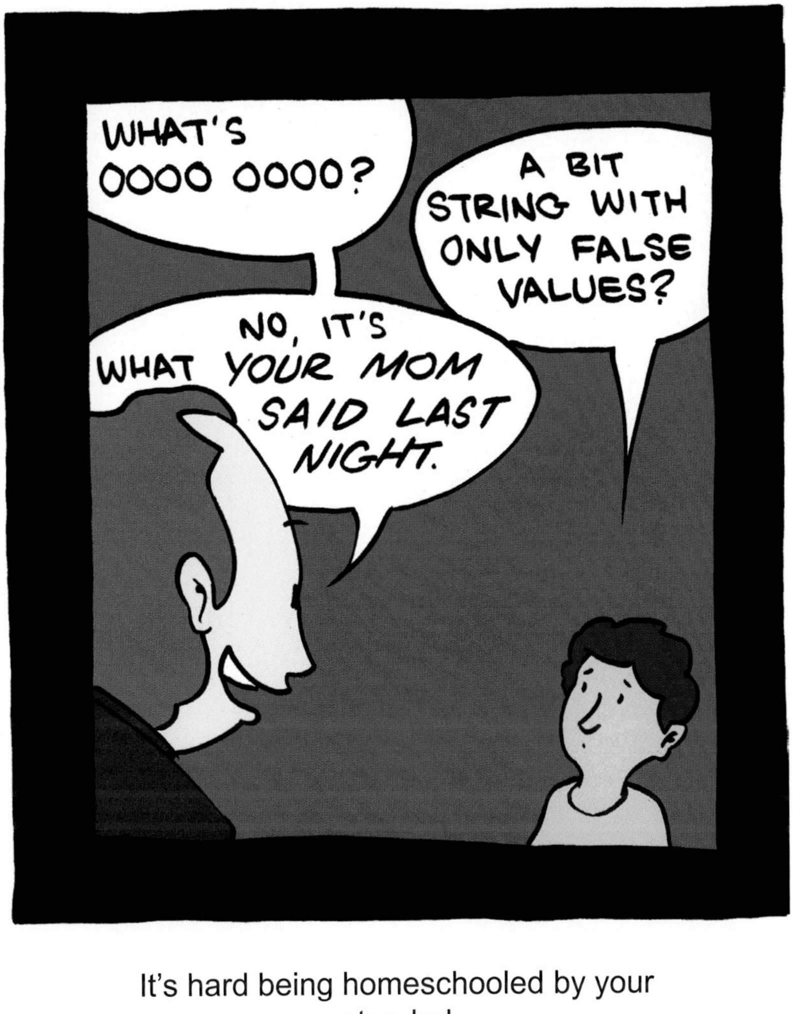
WHAT'S
OOOO OOOO?
A BIT STRING WITH ONLY FALSE VALUES?
NO, IT'S WHAT YOUR MOM SAID LAST NIGHT.

It's hard being homeschooled by your stepdad

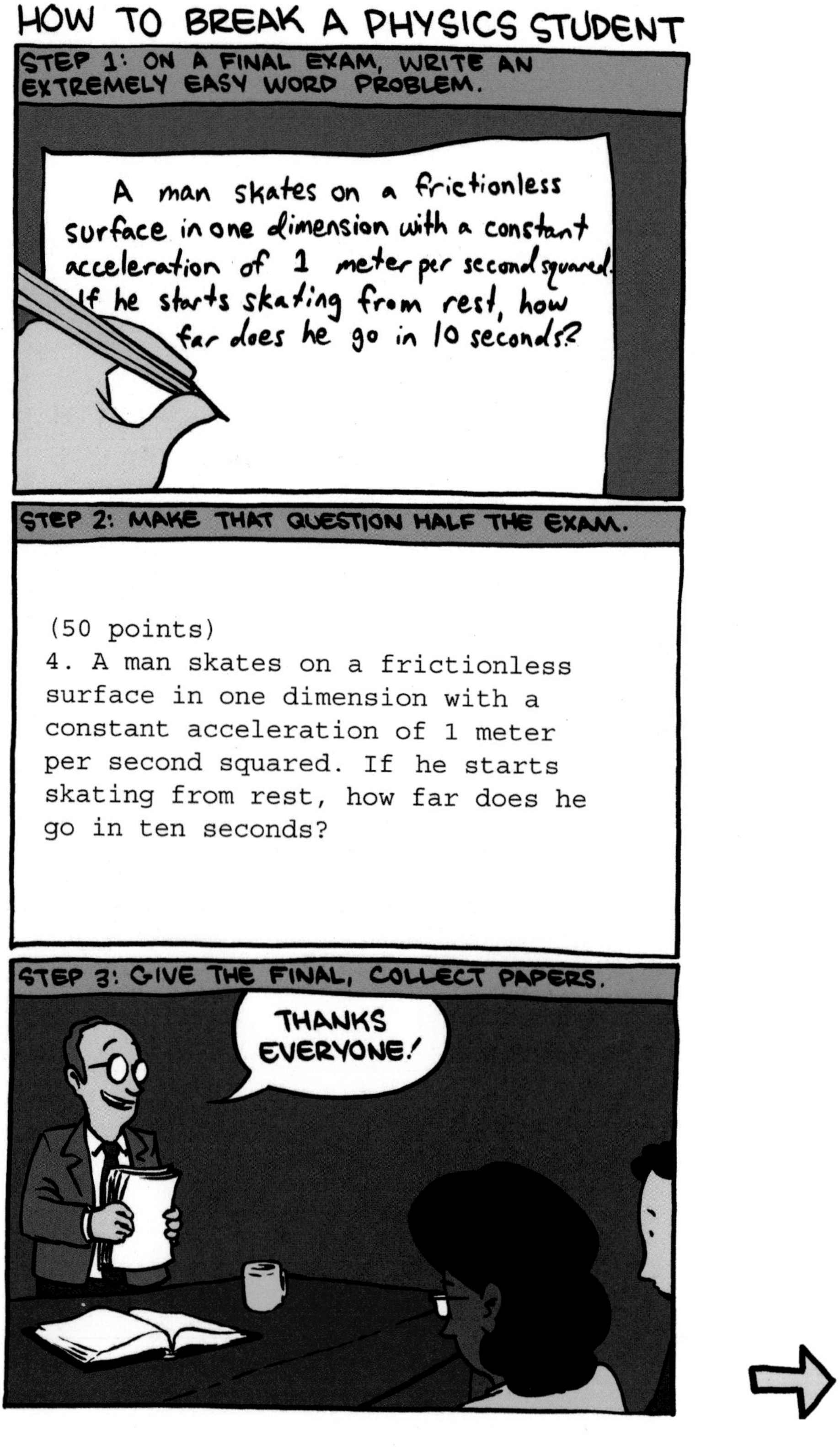
HOW TO BREAK A PHYSICS STUDENT
STEP 1: ON A FINAL EXAM, WRITE AN EXTREMELY EASY WORD PROBLEM.
A man skates on a frictionless surface in one dimension with a constant acceleration of 1 meter per second squared. If he starts skating from rest, how far does he go in 10 seconds?
STEP 2: MAKE THAT QUESTION HALF THE EXAM.
(50 points)
4. A man skates on a frictionless surface in one dimension with a constant acceleration of 1 meter per second squared. If he starts skating from rest, how far does he go in ten seconds?
STEP 3: GIVE THE FINAL, COLLECT PAPERS.
THANKS EVERYONE!

STEP 4: BEFORE EVERYONE LEAVES, SAY
HOPE YOU ALL FIGURED OUT THE 50 POINT CHALLENGE PROBLEM!
STEP 5: RUN OUT THE DOOR.
ENJOY SPRING BREAK! HAHAHAHAHA!

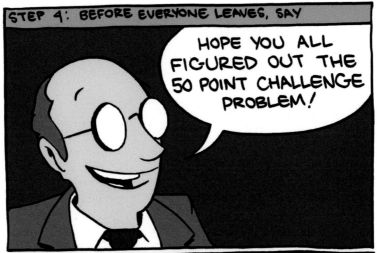

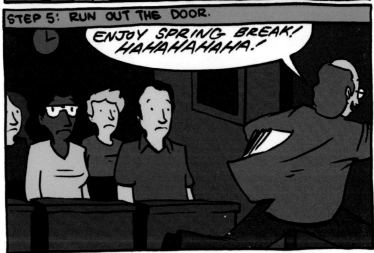

END!

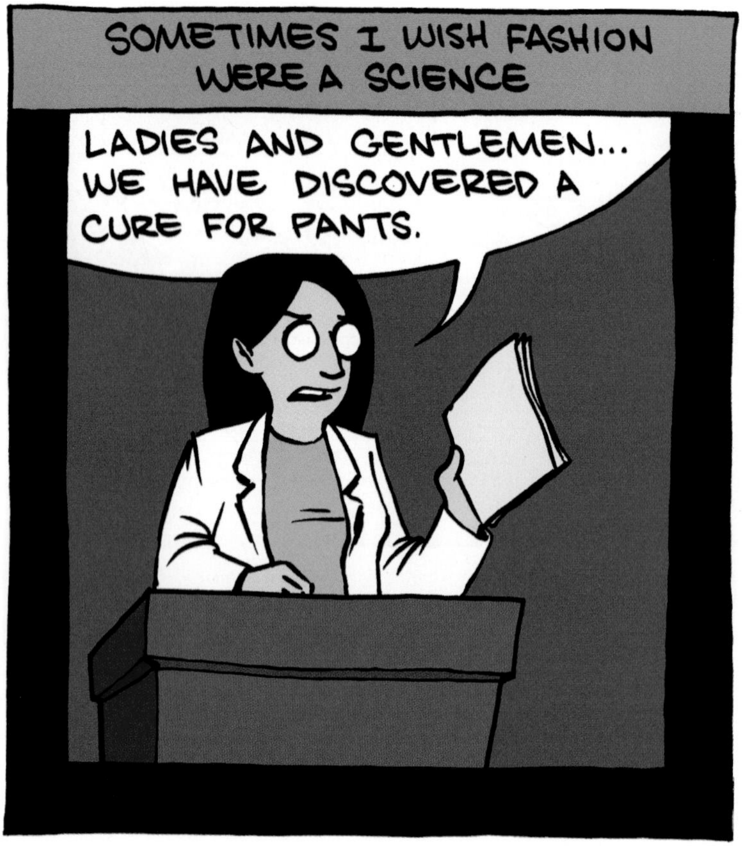
SOMETIMES I WISH FASHION WERE A SCIENCE
LADIES AND GENTLEMEN... WE HAVE DISCOVERED A CURE FOR PANTS.

LIFE TIP:
ALL SOCIAL HIERARCHY RULES LOOK STUPID OVER EVOLUTIONARY TIME.
WHEN YOU LIKED THAT BAND
WHEN I LIKED THAT BAND
DAWN OF HUMANITY
NOW

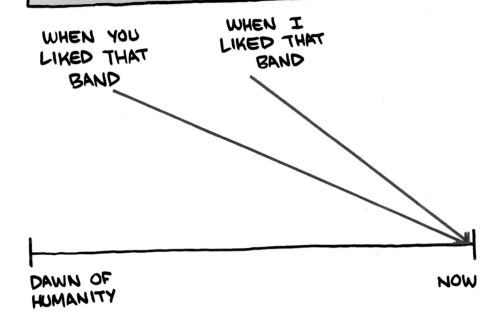

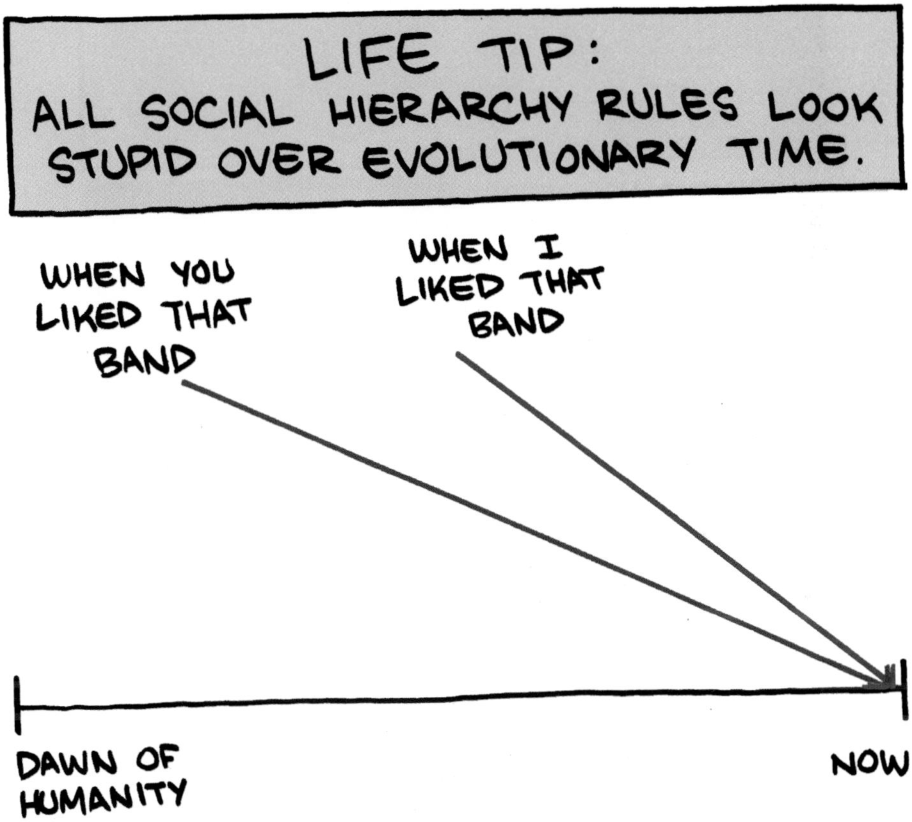

YOU HAVE 3 WISHES! YOU MAY WISH FOR ANYTHING BUT MORE WISHES.

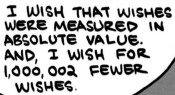

I WISH THAT WISHES WERE MEASURED IN ABSOLUTE VALUE. AND, I WISH FOR 1,000,002 FEWER WISHES.

I'M PRETTY SURE THIS IS WHY NOBODY LIKES MATHEMATICIANS.

I'M PRETTY SURE THIS IS HOW GOD GOT STARTED.

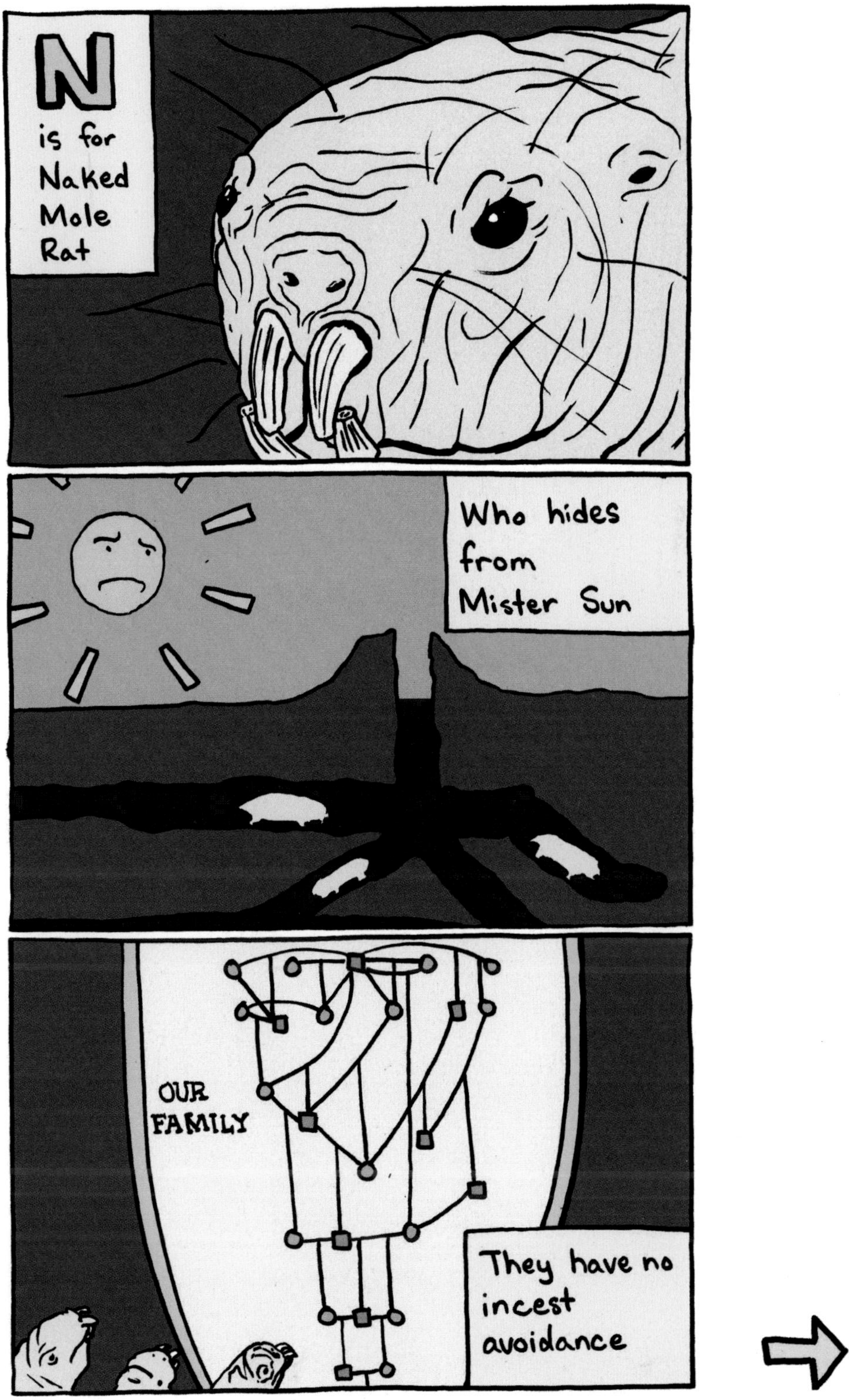
N
is for
Naked
Mole
Rat
Who hides
from
Mister Sun
OUR
FAMILY
They have no
incest
avoidance

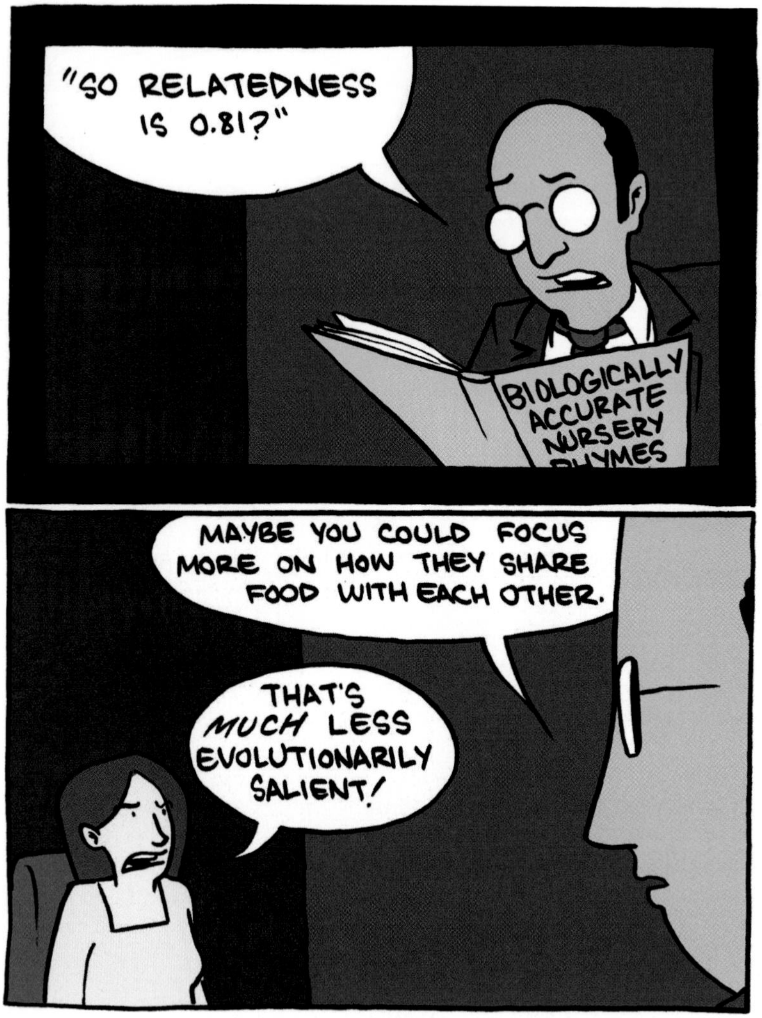
"SO RELATEDNESS IS 0.81?"
BIOLOGICALLY ACCURATE NURSERY RHYMES
MAYBE YOU COULD FOCUS MORE ON HOW THEY SHARE FOOD WITH EACH OTHER.
THAT'S *MUCH* LESS EVOLUTIONARILY SALIENT!

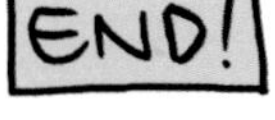
END!

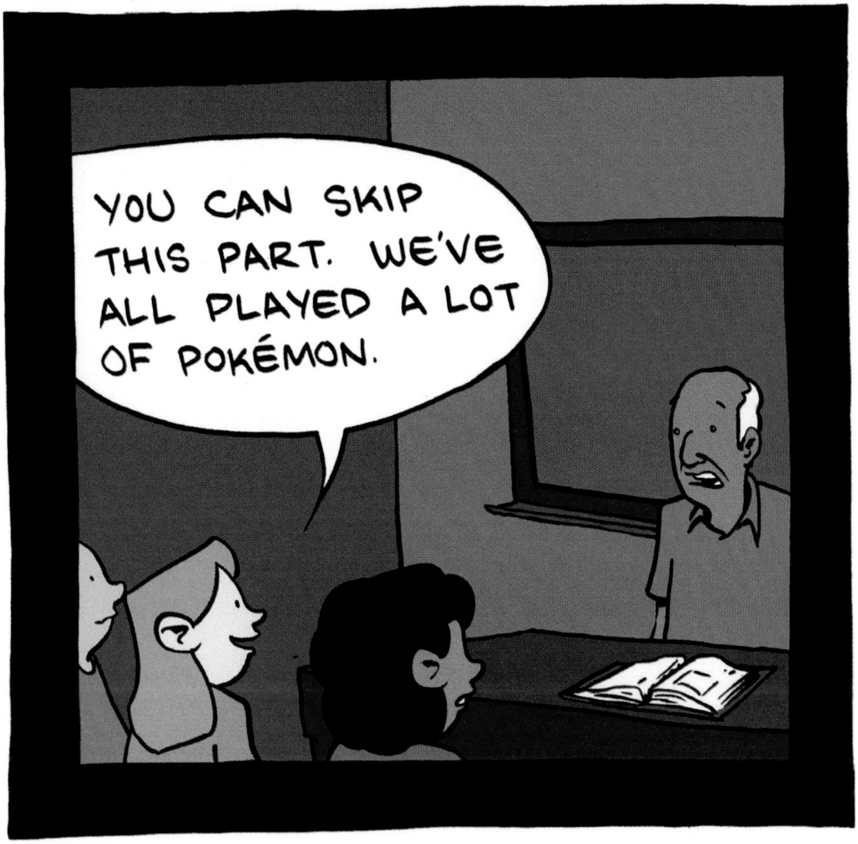
YOU CAN SKIP THIS PART. WE'VE ALL PLAYED A LOT OF POKÉMON.

Causing our evolution teacher to explode was remarkably easy.

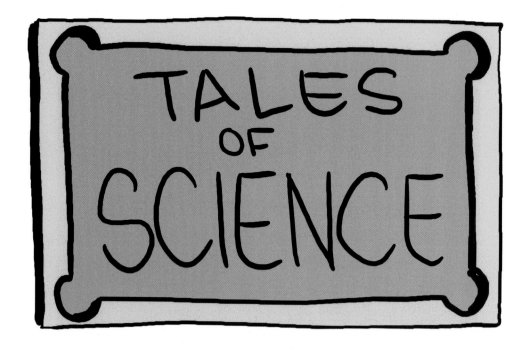

BEHOLD OUR TALES OF SCIENCE!

When we decided to make a science-themed book, we wanted to
make some exclusive, special content to supplement it. Since so
many of the jokes in this book are inspired by the friendships (and
marriages!) we're lucky enough to have with amazing scientists, we
thought we'd share some of their stories about science with you.
Some of them are funny, some are sweet, some are disgusting. Really
disgusting. Christina Agapakis's story is really disgusting.

We hope you enjoy these Tales of Science, and we encourage you
to follow these geeks online in their present and future endeavors
instead of pissing away your time on comics.

EMILY LAKDAWALLA

SENIOR EDITOR AND PLANETARY EVANGELIST
THE PLANETARY SOCIETY

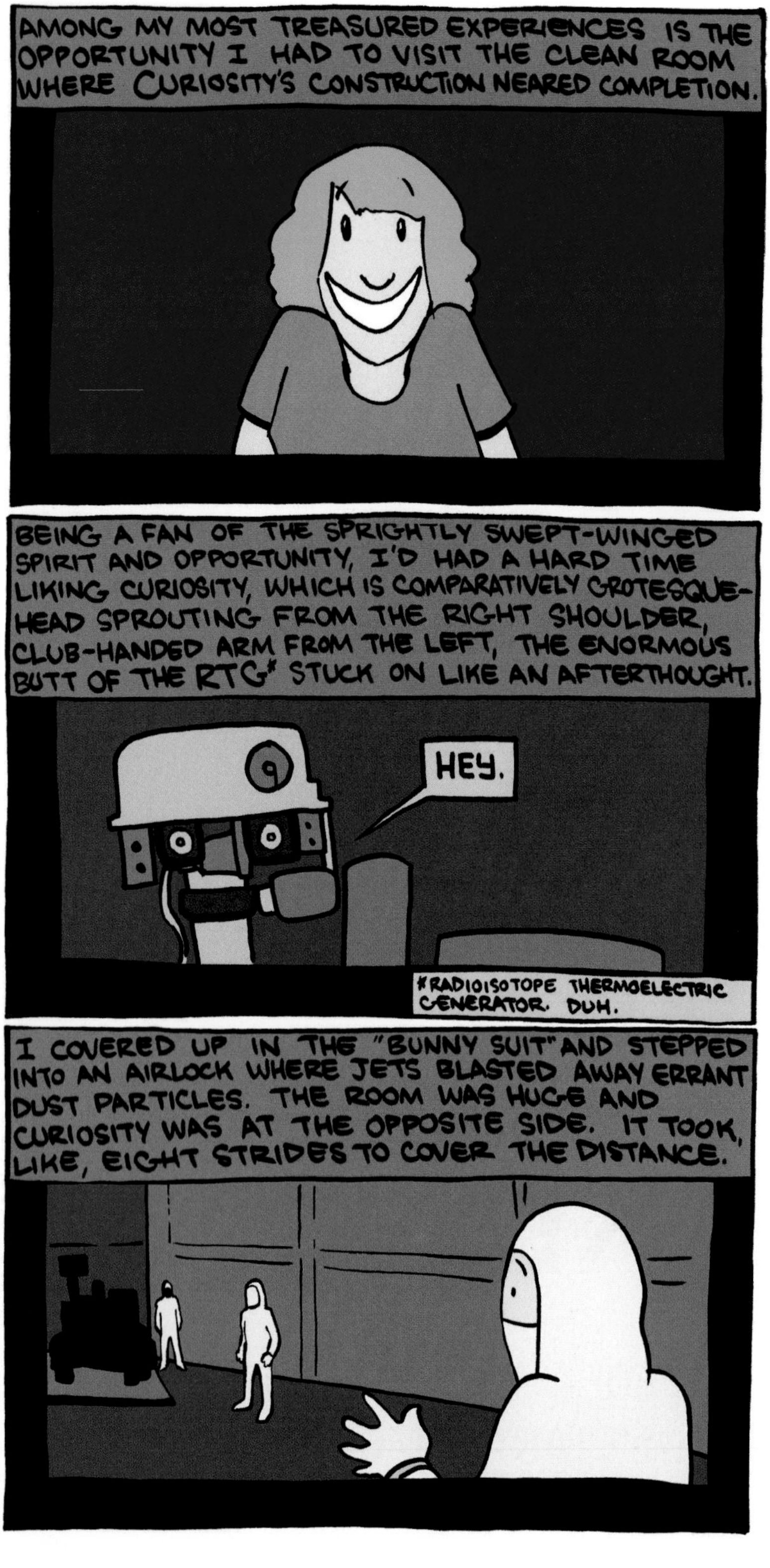
AMONG MY MOST TREASURED EXPERIENCES IS THE OPPORTUNITY I HAD TO VISIT THE CLEAN ROOM WHERE CURIOSITY'S CONSTRUCTION NEARED COMPLETION.
BEING A FAN OF THE SPRIGHTLY SWEPT-WINGED SPIRIT AND OPPORTUNITY, I'D HAD A HARD TIME LIKING CURIOSITY, WHICH IS COMPARATIVELY GROTESQUE- HEAD SPROUTING FROM THE RIGHT SHOULDER, CLUB-HANDED ARM FROM THE LEFT, THE ENORMOUS BUTT OF THE RTG* STUCK ON LIKE AN AFTERTHOUGHT.
HEY.
*RADIOISOTOPE THERMOELECTRIC GENERATOR. DUH.
I COVERED UP IN THE "BUNNY SUIT" AND STEPPED INTO AN AIRLOCK WHERE JETS BLASTED AWAY ERRANT DUST PARTICLES. THE ROOM WAS HUGE AND CURIOSITY WAS AT THE OPPOSITE SIDE. IT TOOK, LIKE, EIGHT STRIDES TO COVER THE DISTANCE.

IN THE FIRST COUPLE STRIDES, I WAS THINKING "IT IS SO AWESOME THAT I GET TO BE INSIDE THIS PLACE!"

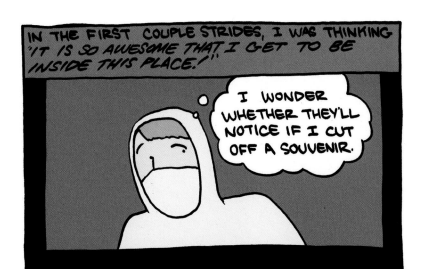

I WONDER WHETHER THEY'LL NOTICE IF I CUT OFF A SOUVENIR.

NEXT COUPLE STRIDES, AND I WAS LIKE "LOOK AT ALL THOSE WIRES — THIS MACHINE IS INCREDIBLY COMPLICATED."

SO MANY WIRES... THEY WON'T MISS JUST A FEW.

ANOTHER COUPLE OF STRIDES, AND IT HIT ME LIKE A BOARD UPSIDE THE HEAD — THIS MACHINE WILL SOON BE LEAVING THIS PLANET FOREVER. IT WILL LEAVE US BEHIND AND TRAVEL TO MARS. IT'S A MARTIAN.

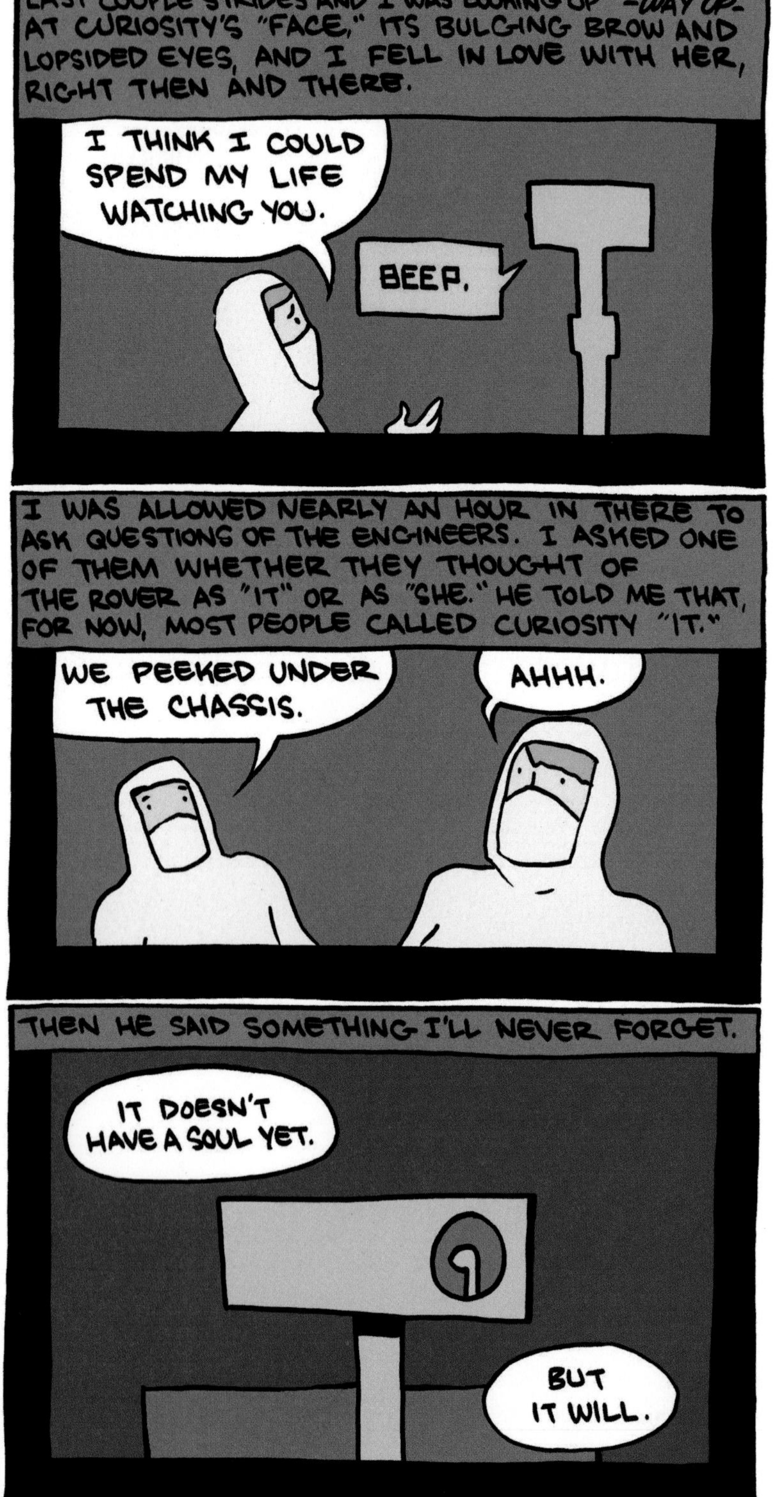
LAST COUPLE STRIDES AND I WAS LOOKING UP —WAY UP— AT CURIOSITY'S "FACE," ITS BULGING BROW AND LOPSIDED EYES, AND I FELL IN LOVE WITH HER, RIGHT THEN AND THERE.
I THINK I COULD SPEND MY LIFE WATCHING YOU.
BEEP.
I WAS ALLOWED NEARLY AN HOUR IN THERE TO ASK QUESTIONS OF THE ENGINEERS. I ASKED ONE OF THEM WHETHER THEY THOUGHT OF THE ROVER AS "IT" OR AS "SHE." HE TOLD ME THAT, FOR NOW, MOST PEOPLE CALLED CURIOSITY "IT."
WE PEEKED UNDER THE CHASSIS.
AHHH.
THEN HE SAID SOMETHING I'LL NEVER FORGET.
IT DOESN'T HAVE A SOUL YET.
BUT IT WILL.

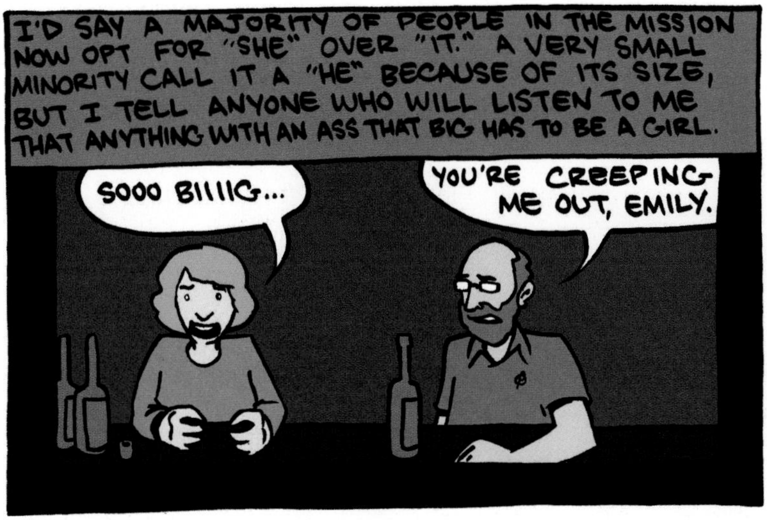
I'D SAY A MAJORITY OF PEOPLE IN THE MISSION NOW OPT FOR "SHE" OVER "IT." A VERY SMALL MINORITY CALL IT A "HE" BECAUSE OF ITS SIZE, BUT I TELL ANYONE WHO WILL LISTEN TO ME THAT ANYTHING WITH AN ASS THAT BIG HAS TO BE A GIRL.
SOOO BIIIIG...
YOU'RE CREEPING ME OUT, EMILY.

END!

HENRY REICH

CREATOR OF *MINUTEPHYSICS* AND *MINUTEEARTH*

WHEN I VISITED MY FRIEND DESTIN IN ALABAMA, WE WENT TO THE U.S. SPACE AND ROCKET CENTER. IT'S LIKE THE SMITHSONIAN AIR AND SPACE MUSEUM, EXCEPT THERE'S NO ONE ELSE AROUND AND YOU CAN CLIMB ON STUFF.

YEEHA! I'M AN ASTRONAUT!

DON'T MIND HIM. HE'S FROM THE INTERNET.

AND WHILE WE WERE GAWKING AT THE *TWO* FULL-SIZE SATURN V ROCKETS, SOMETHING CAUGHT OUR INTEREST.

WHOAAA...

APOLLO WASTE MANAGEMENT SYSTEM

AS A KID, YOU LEARN ALL ABOUT THE AWESOME PARTS OF SPACE EXPLORATION: ABOUT MOONWALKS AND DOCKING WITH SOVIETS AND THE HARROWING TALE OF APOLLO 13.

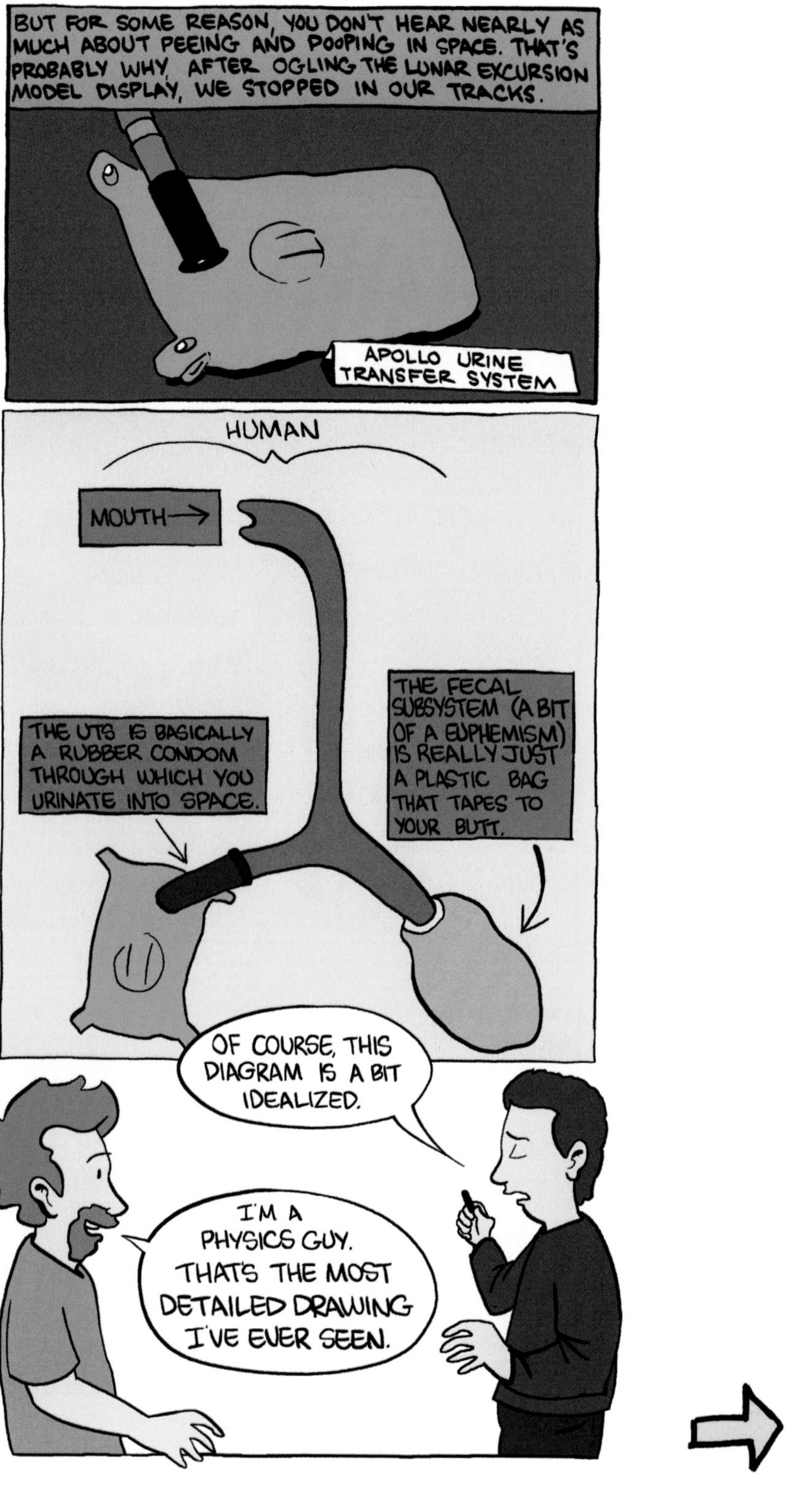
BUT FOR SOME REASON, YOU DON'T HEAR NEARLY AS MUCH ABOUT PEEING AND POOPING IN SPACE. THAT'S PROBABLY WHY, AFTER OGLING THE LUNAR EXCURSION MODEL DISPLAY, WE STOPPED IN OUR TRACKS.
APOLLO URINE TRANSFER SYSTEM
HUMAN
MOUTH
THE UTS IS BASICALLY A RUBBER CONDOM THROUGH WHICH YOU URINATE INTO SPACE.
THE FECAL SUBSYSTEM (A BIT OF A EUPHEMISM) IS REALLY JUST A PLASTIC BAG THAT TAPES TO YOUR BUTT.
OF COURSE, THIS DIAGRAM IS A BIT IDEALIZED.
I'M A PHYSICS GUY. THAT'S THE MOST DETAILED DRAWING I'VE EVER SEEN.

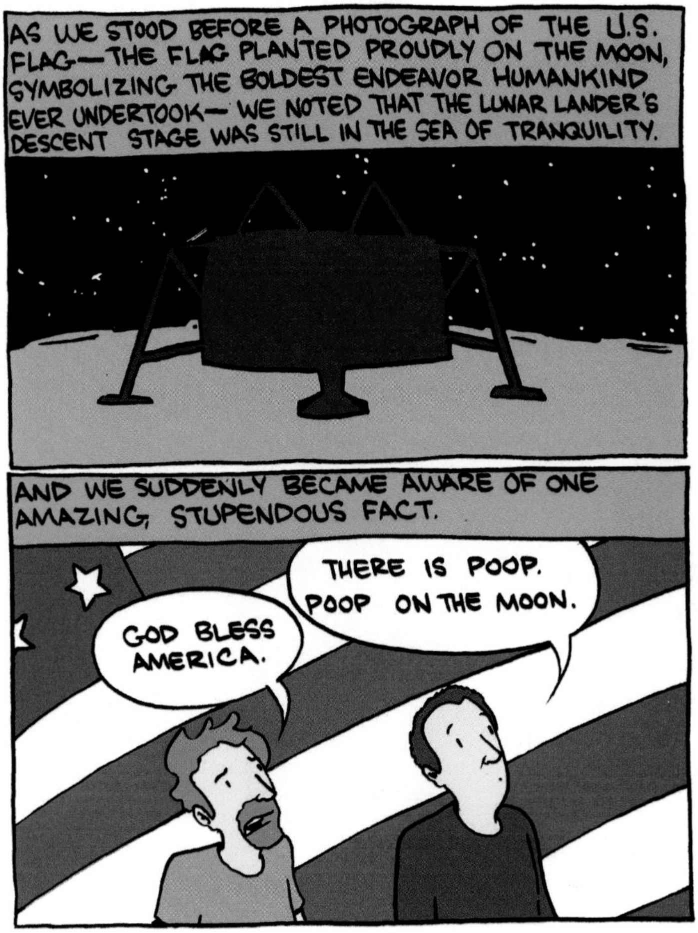
AS WE STOOD BEFORE A PHOTOGRAPH OF THE U.S. FLAG—THE FLAG PLANTED PROUDLY ON THE MOON, SYMBOLIZING THE BOLDEST ENDEAVOR HUMANKIND EVER UNDERTOOK—WE NOTED THAT THE LUNAR LANDER'S DESCENT STAGE WAS STILL IN THE SEA OF TRANQUILITY.
AND WE SUDDENLY BECAME AWARE OF ONE AMAZING, STUPENDOUS FACT.
GOD BLESS AMERICA.
THERE IS POOP. POOP ON THE MOON.

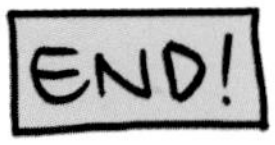
END!

SEAN
CARROLL

THEORETICAL PHYSICIST
CALIFORNIA INSTITUTE OF TECHNOLOGY

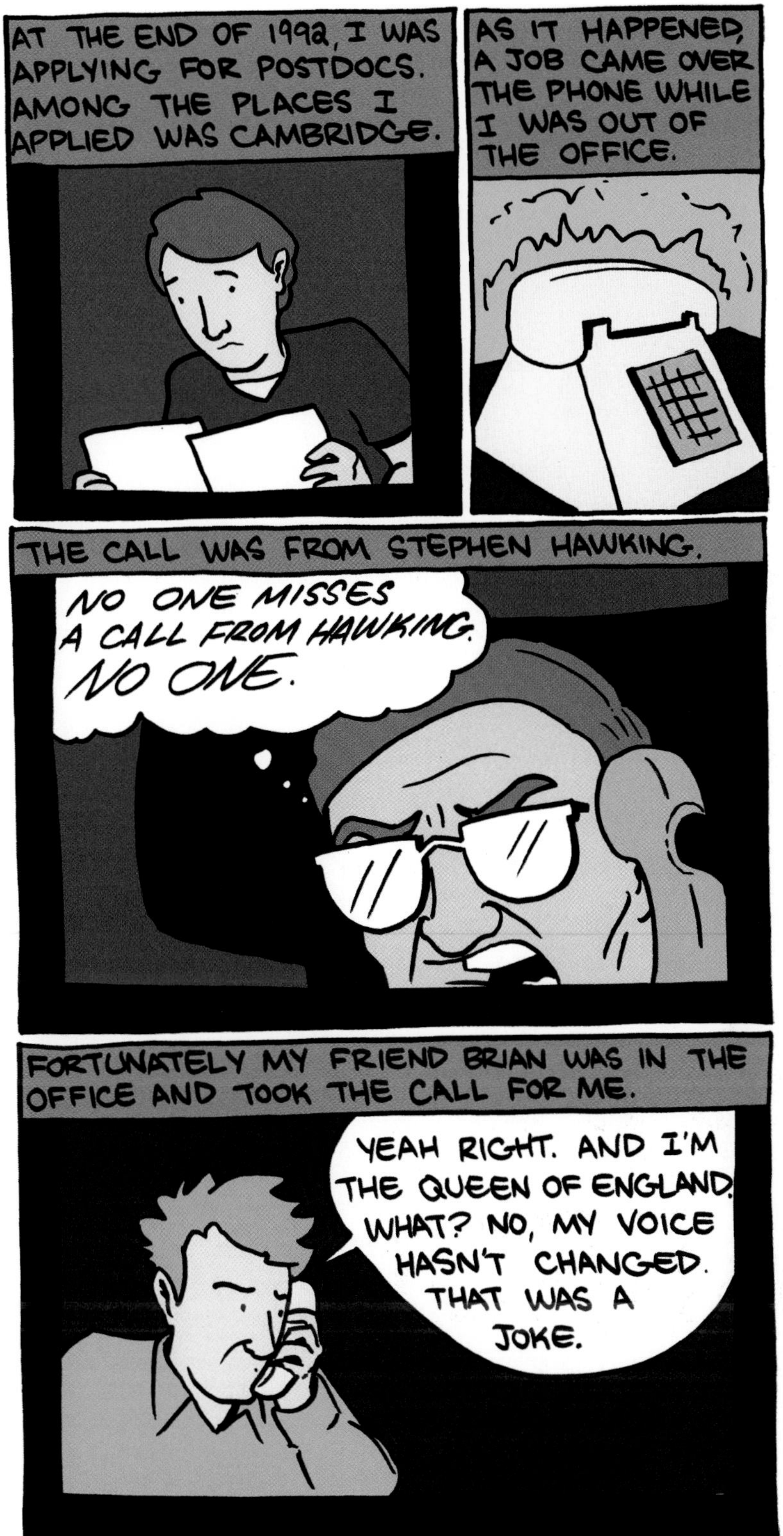
AT THE END OF 1992, I WAS APPLYING FOR POSTDOCS. AMONG THE PLACES I APPLIED WAS CAMBRIDGE.
AS IT HAPPENED, A JOB CAME OVER THE PHONE WHILE I WAS OUT OF THE OFFICE.
THE CALL WAS FROM STEPHEN HAWKING.
NO ONE MISSES A CALL FROM HAWKING. NO ONE.
FORTUNATELY MY FRIEND BRIAN WAS IN THE OFFICE AND TOOK THE CALL FOR ME.
YEAH RIGHT. AND I'M THE QUEEN OF ENGLAND. WHAT? NO, MY VOICE HASN'T CHANGED. THAT WAS A JOKE.

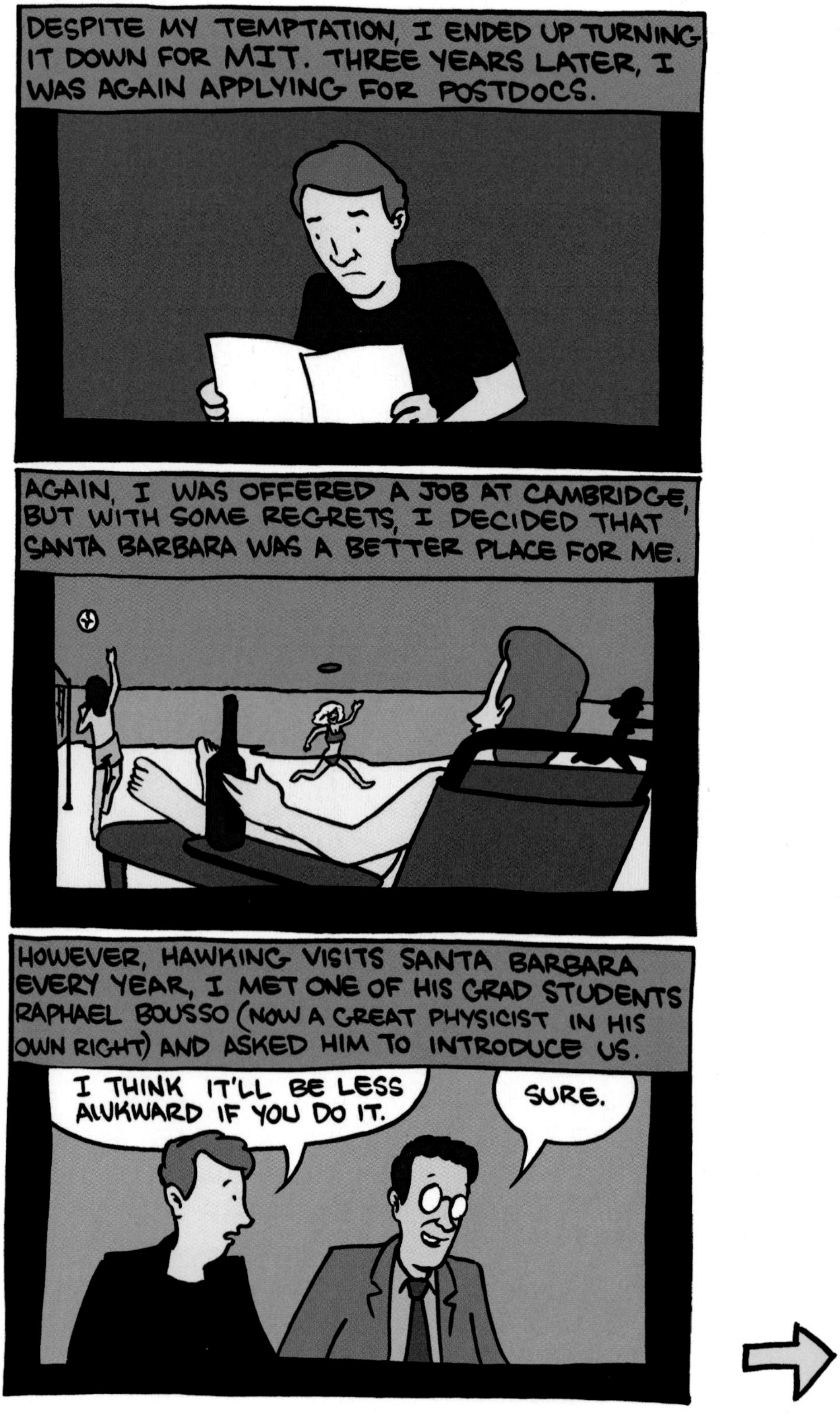
DESPITE MY TEMPTATION, I ENDED UP TURNING IT DOWN FOR MIT. THREE YEARS LATER, I WAS AGAIN APPLYING FOR POSTDOCS.
AGAIN, I WAS OFFERED A JOB AT CAMBRIDGE, BUT WITH SOME REGRETS, I DECIDED THAT SANTA BARBARA WAS A BETTER PLACE FOR ME.
HOWEVER, HAWKING VISITS SANTA BARBARA EVERY YEAR, I MET ONE OF HIS GRAD STUDENTS RAPHAEL BOUSSO (NOW A GREAT PHYSICIST IN HIS OWN RIGHT) AND ASKED HIM TO INTRODUCE US.
I THINK IT'LL BE LESS AWKWARD IF YOU DO IT.
SURE.

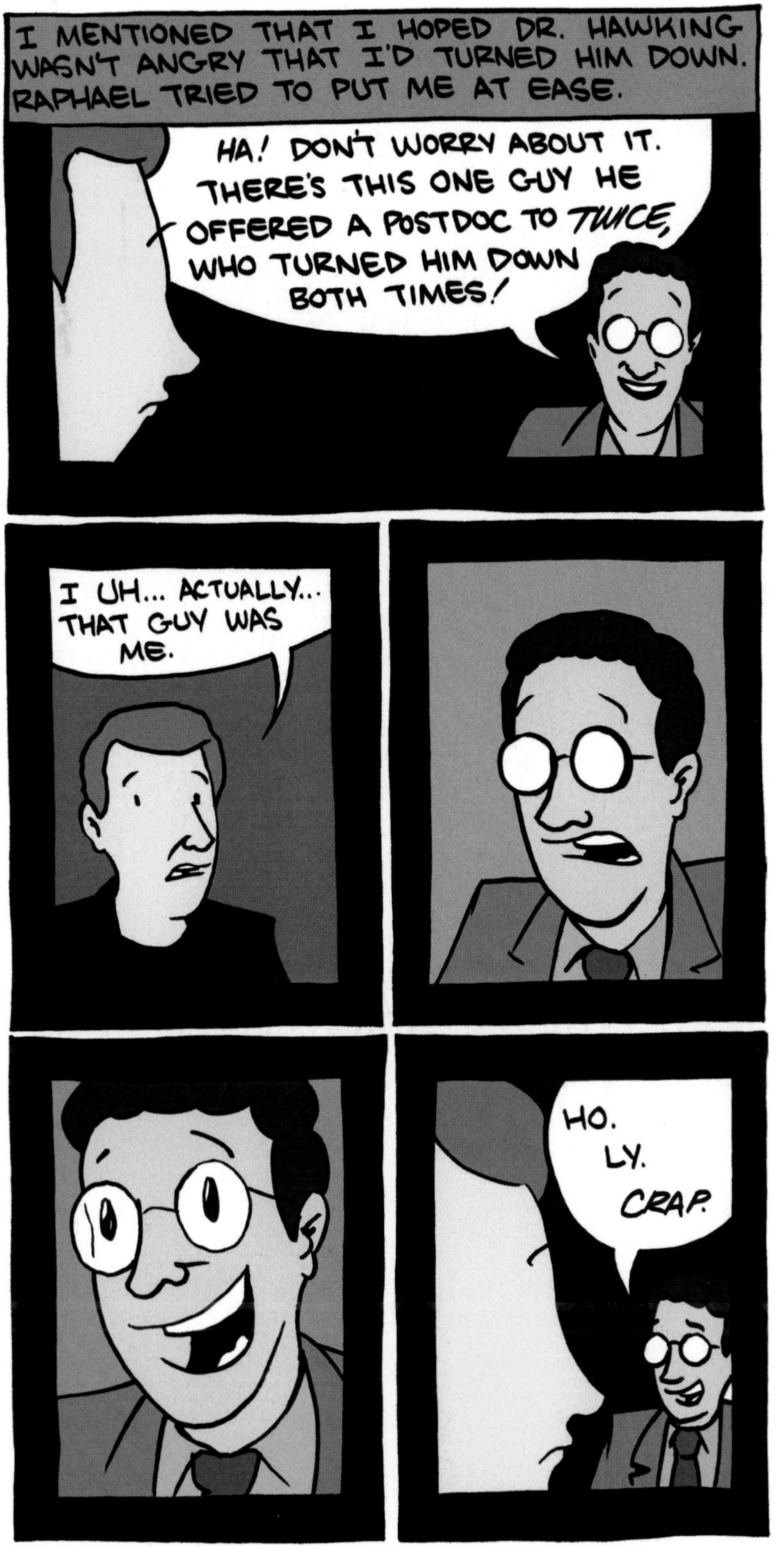
I MENTIONED THAT I HOPED DR. HAWKING WASN'T ANGRY THAT I'D TURNED HIM DOWN. RAPHAEL TRIED TO PUT ME AT EASE.
HA! DON'T WORRY ABOUT IT. THERE'S THIS ONE GUY HE OFFERED A POSTDOC TO TWICE, WHO TURNED HIM DOWN BOTH TIMES!
I UH... ACTUALLY... THAT GUY WAS ME.
HO. LY. CRAP.

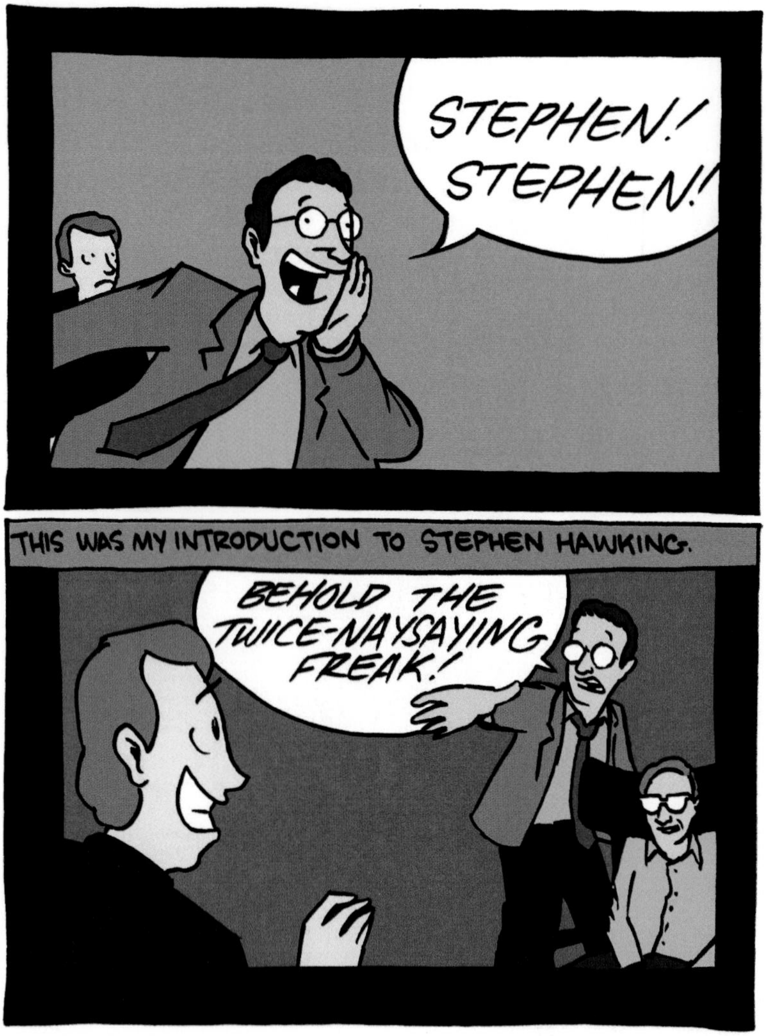
STEPHEN! STEPHEN!
THIS WAS MY INTRODUCTION TO STEPHEN HAWKING.
BEHOLD THE TWICE-NAYSAYING FREAK!

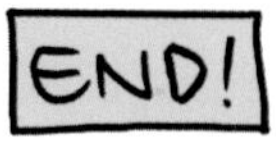
END!

ADAM SAVAGE

MASTER MAKER, TELEVISION PRODUCER, AND HOST OF *MYTHBUSTERS*

WE'D BEEN DOING MYTHBUSTERS FOR 1.5 YEARS. IT WAS AROUND 2004.

IF YOU FIRE A BULLET STRAIGHT UP, WHEN IT COMES BACK DOWN, WILL IT KILL YOU?

HOLD STILL. I'LL GET YOU MY RIFLE.

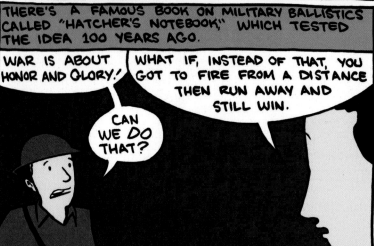

THERE'S A FAMOUS BOOK ON MILITARY BALLISTICS CALLED "HATCHER'S NOTEBOOK," WHICH TESTED THE IDEA 100 YEARS AGO.

WAR IS ABOUT HONOR AND GLORY!

WHAT IF, INSTEAD OF THAT, YOU GOT TO FIRE FROM A DISTANCE THEN RUN AWAY AND STILL WIN.

CAN WE DO THAT?

THEY SET UP A PROCEDURE WHERE THEY WENT TO A LAKE, ASSUMING THEY COULD HEAR BULLETS LAND, THEN FIRED ABOUT 500 ROUNDS INTO THE AIR. THE END RESULTS WERE NOT PROMISING.

beach. Here it proved impossible to locate any of the returning shots, until a system of sounding balloons was used to plot the winds aloft, which were usually found to be reversed in direction from what they were at the ground level.

The firing platform at Miami was about ten feet square. There was a shield of thin armor plate over the heads of the men at the gun.

Out of more than 500 shots fired after adjusting the gun so as to bring the shots as nearly as possible onto the platform, only 4 shots hit it, and one more fell into the boat.

One of the shots that hit the platform was a Service .30-'06, 150-grain flat based bullet, which came down base first, (as that bullet usually does), and bounced into the water after striking the edge of the lower platform. It left a mark about 1/16 inch deep in the soft pine board.

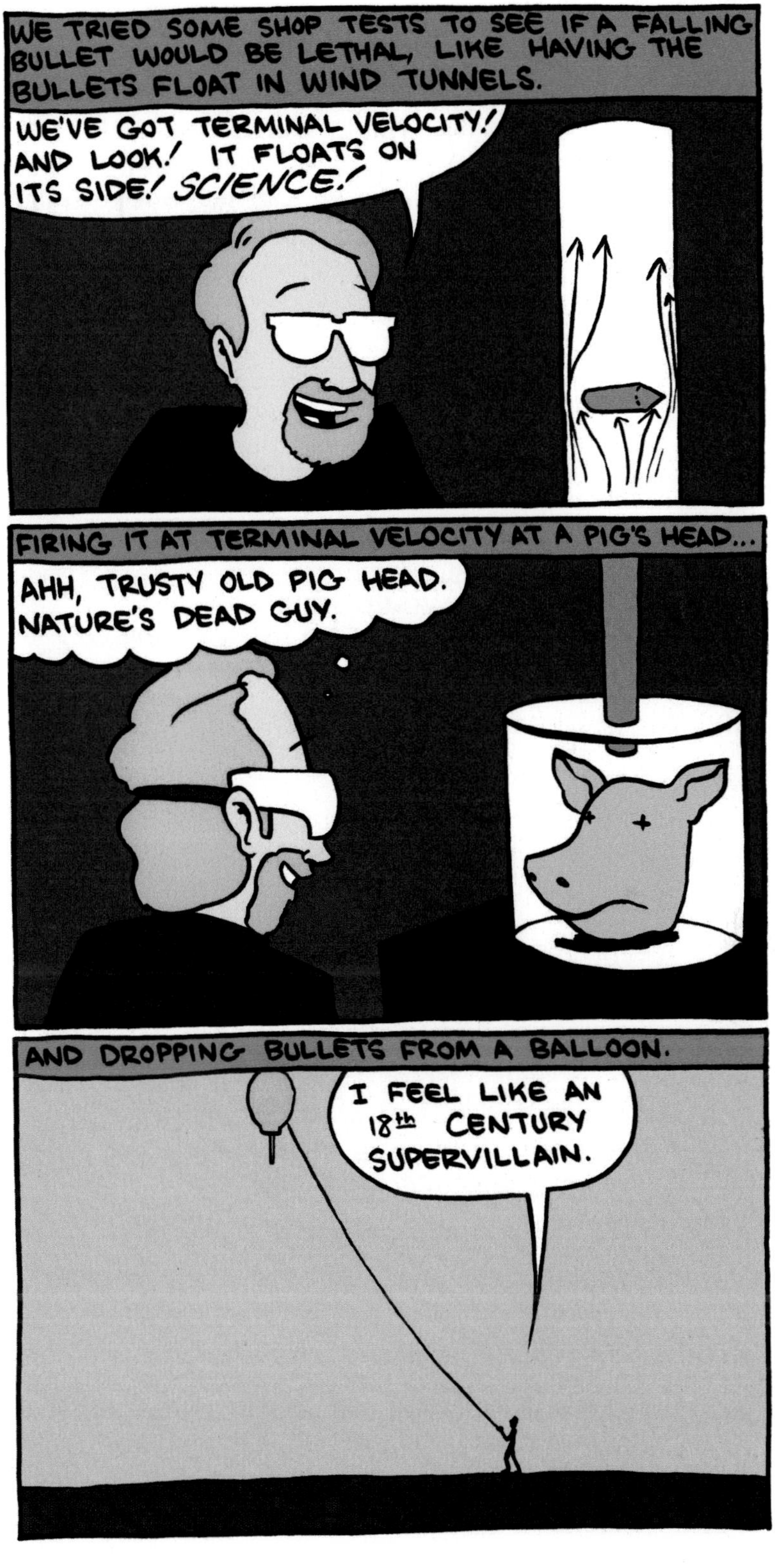
WE TRIED SOME SHOP TESTS TO SEE IF A FALLING BULLET WOULD BE LETHAL, LIKE HAVING THE BULLETS FLOAT IN WIND TUNNELS.
WE'VE GOT TERMINAL VELOCITY! AND LOOK! IT FLOATS ON ITS SIDE! SCIENCE!
FIRING IT AT TERMINAL VELOCITY AT A PIG'S HEAD...
AHH, TRUSTY OLD PIG HEAD. NATURE'S DEAD GUY.
AND DROPPING BULLETS FROM A BALLOON.
I FEEL LIKE AN 18th CENTURY SUPERVILLAIN.

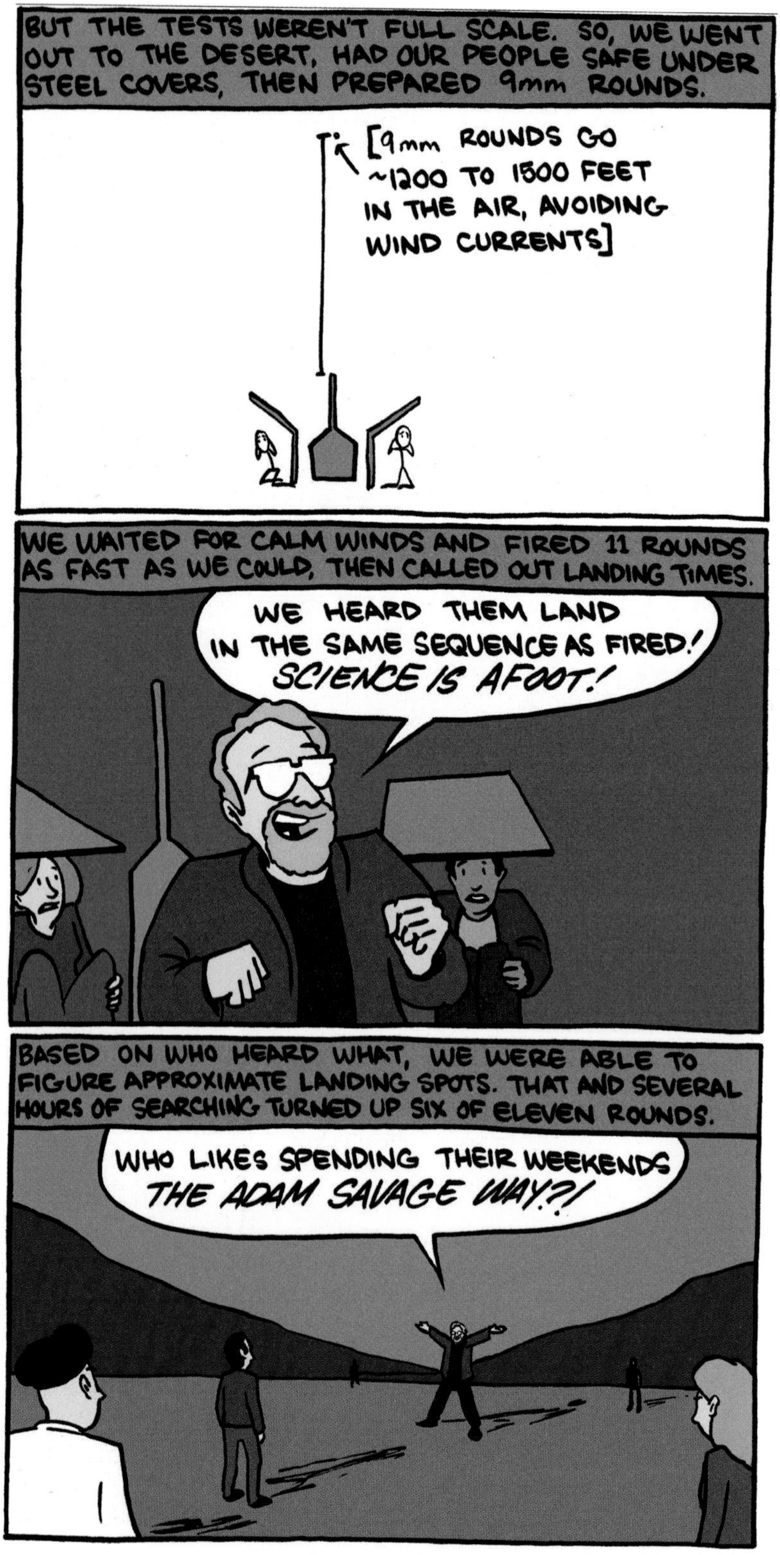
BUT THE TESTS WEREN'T FULL SCALE. SO, WE WENT OUT TO THE DESERT, HAD OUR PEOPLE SAFE UNDER STEEL COVERS, THEN PREPARED 9mm ROUNDS.
[9mm ROUNDS GO ~1200 TO 1500 FEET IN THE AIR, AVOIDING WIND CURRENTS]
WE WAITED FOR CALM WINDS AND FIRED 11 ROUNDS AS FAST AS WE COULD, THEN CALLED OUT LANDING TIMES.
WE HEARD THEM LAND IN THE SAME SEQUENCE AS FIRED! SCIENCE IS AFOOT!
BASED ON WHO HEARD WHAT, WE WERE ABLE TO FIGURE APPROXIMATE LANDING SPOTS. THAT AND SEVERAL HOURS OF SEARCHING TURNED UP SIX OF ELEVEN ROUNDS.
WHO LIKES SPENDING THEIR WEEKENDS THE ADAM SAVAGE WAY?!

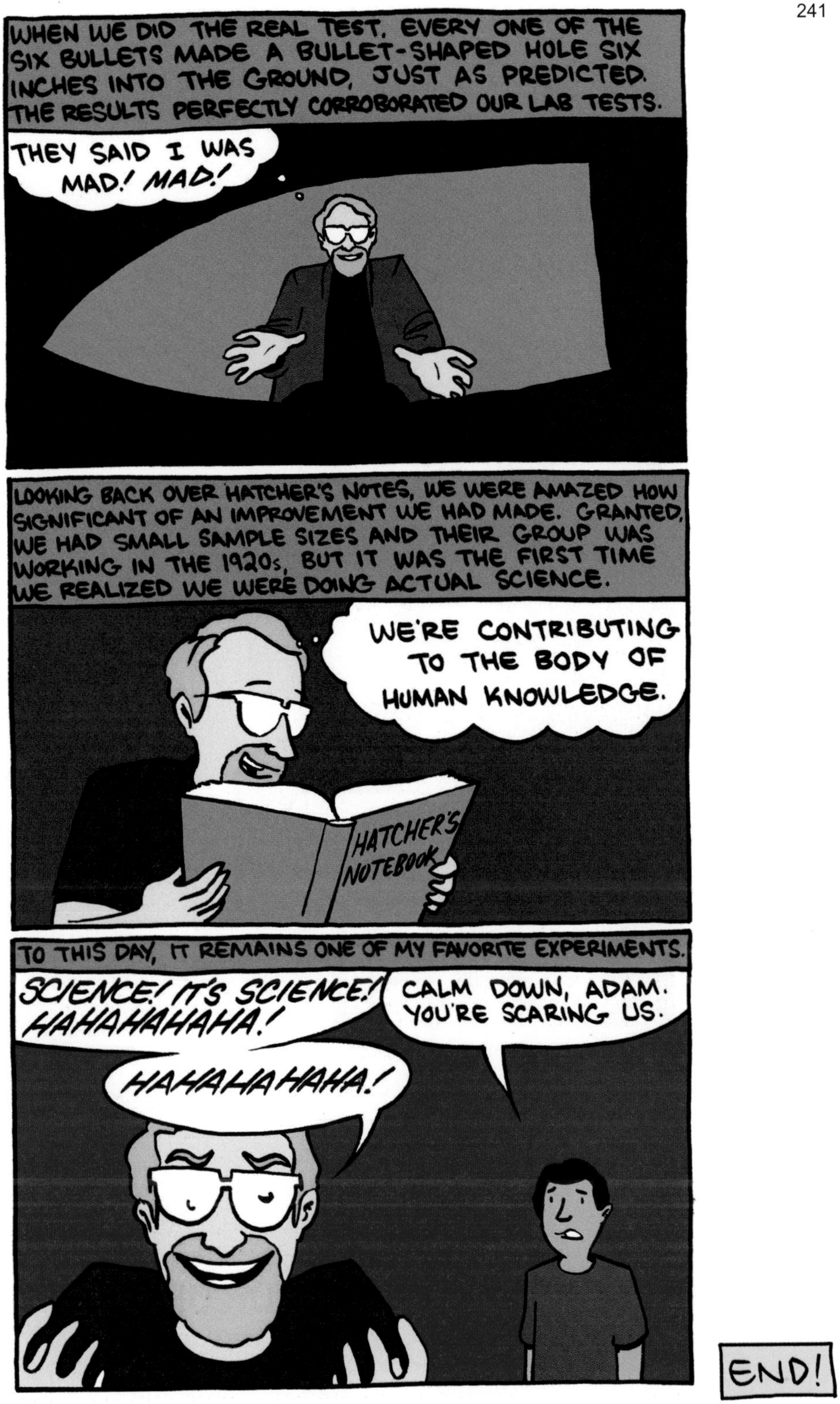
WHEN WE DID THE REAL TEST, EVERY ONE OF THE SIX BULLETS MADE A BULLET-SHAPED HOLE SIX INCHES INTO THE GROUND, JUST AS PREDICTED. THE RESULTS PERFECTLY CORROBORATED OUR LAB TESTS.
THEY SAID I WAS MAD! MAD!
LOOKING BACK OVER HATCHER'S NOTES, WE WERE AMAZED HOW SIGNIFICANT OF AN IMPROVEMENT WE HAD MADE. GRANTED, WE HAD SMALL SAMPLE SIZES AND THEIR GROUP WAS WORKING IN THE 1920s, BUT IT WAS THE FIRST TIME WE REALIZED WE WERE DOING ACTUAL SCIENCE.
WE'RE CONTRIBUTING TO THE BODY OF HUMAN KNOWLEDGE.
HATCHER'S NOTEBOOK
TO THIS DAY, IT REMAINS ONE OF MY FAVORITE EXPERIMENTS.
SCIENCE! IT'S SCIENCE! HAHAHAHAHA!
CALM DOWN, ADAM. YOU'RE SCARING US.
HAHAHAHAHA!
END!

DR. PHIL PLAIT

ASTRONOMER AND CREATOR OF
THE BAD ASTRONOMY BLOG

I HAVE A DIFFERENT KIND OF TRADITION FOR HALLOWEEN. EVERY OCTOBER 31, I TAKE A BUCKET OF CANDY TO THE END OF MY DRIVEWAY.

AHH, THE ONE NIGHT A YEAR WHEN THIS ISN'T CREEPY.

NEXT TO IT — IF IT'S CLEAR OUTSIDE — I SET UP MY TELESCOPE. WHEN KIDS COME AROUND, I TELL THEM THEY HAVE TO LOOK THROUGH THE TELESCOPE FIRST TO GET A PIECE OF CANDY.

FIRST SCIENCE. THEN CANDY.

WELL, A FEW YEARS BACK I LIVED ON THE EDGE OF A TOUGH NEIGHBORHOOD, AND HALLOWEEN WOULD BRING THE SOMEWHAT MORE SUSPECT TEENAGERS TRICK-OR-TREATING.

GIMME ALL YER CANDY KID! THIS KNIFE AIN'T FUN-SIZE!

TRUE STORY!

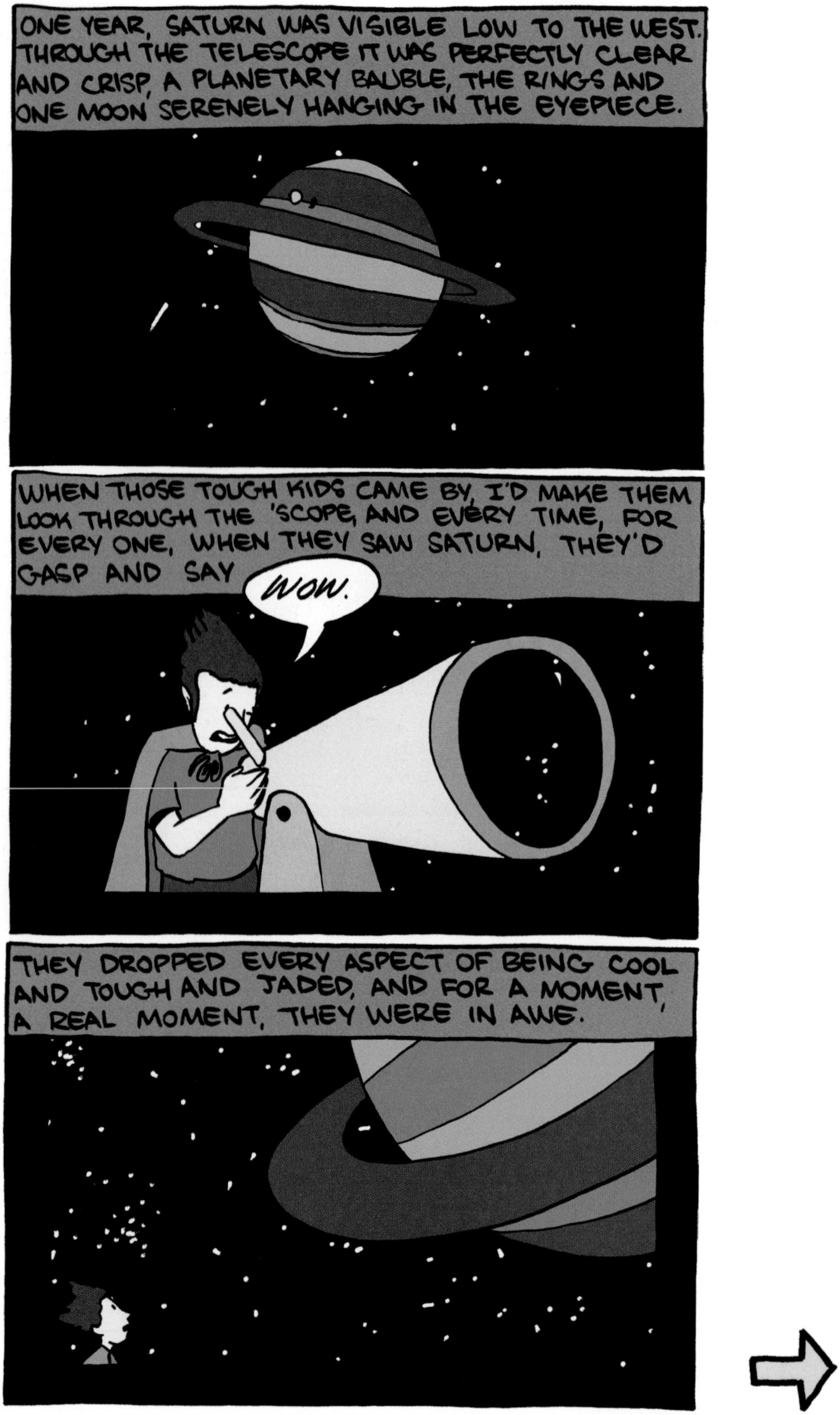
ONE YEAR, SATURN WAS VISIBLE LOW TO THE WEST. THROUGH THE TELESCOPE IT WAS PERFECTLY CLEAR AND CRISP, A PLANETARY BAUBLE, THE RINGS AND ONE MOON SERENELY HANGING IN THE EYEPIECE.
WHEN THOSE TOUGH KIDS CAME BY, I'D MAKE THEM LOOK THROUGH THE 'SCOPE, AND EVERY TIME, FOR EVERY ONE, WHEN THEY SAW SATURN, THEY'D GASP AND SAY
WOW.
THEY DROPPED EVERY ASPECT OF BEING COOL AND TOUGH AND JADED, AND FOR A MOMENT, A REAL MOMENT, THEY WERE IN AWE.

I'VE BEEN AN ASTRONOMER SINCE I WAS A KID, AND I'VE DEVOTED MY LIFE TO SPREADING MY OWN LOVE FOR SCIENCE TO EVERYONE WHO WILL LISTEN.
EVERYONE! THE ASTEROID IS COMING! IN 2029! IT'LL MISS US BY 29,000 Km. CHECK MY BLOG FOR ADDITIONAL FUN FACTS.
IT'S COMING
AND FOR AS LONG AS I LIVE, THAT DAY WILL ALWAYS BE MY FAVORITE.

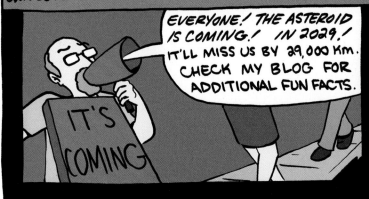

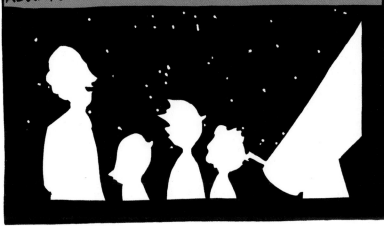

END!

ED
YONG

SCIENCE WRITER,
NOT EXACTLY ROCKET SCIENCE

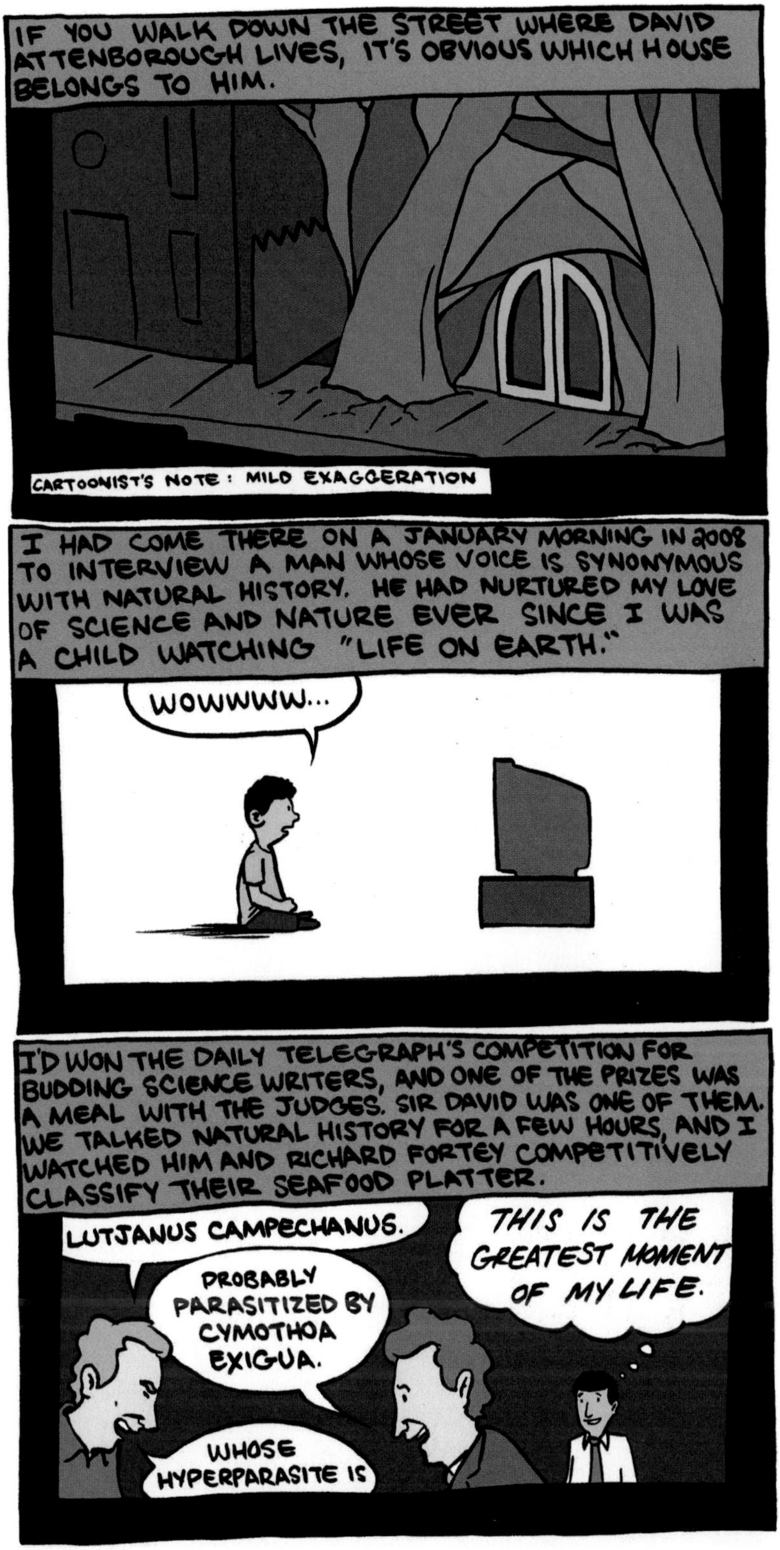
IF YOU WALK DOWN THE STREET WHERE DAVID ATTENBOROUGH LIVES, IT'S OBVIOUS WHICH HOUSE BELONGS TO HIM.
CARTOONIST'S NOTE: MILD EXAGGERATION
I HAD COME THERE ON A JANUARY MORNING IN 2008 TO INTERVIEW A MAN WHOSE VOICE IS SYNONYMOUS WITH NATURAL HISTORY. HE HAD NURTURED MY LOVE OF SCIENCE AND NATURE EVER SINCE I WAS A CHILD WATCHING "LIFE ON EARTH."
WOWWWW...
I'D WON THE DAILY TELEGRAPH'S COMPETITION FOR BUDDING SCIENCE WRITERS, AND ONE OF THE PRIZES WAS A MEAL WITH THE JUDGES. SIR DAVID WAS ONE OF THEM. WE TALKED NATURAL HISTORY FOR A FEW HOURS, AND I WATCHED HIM AND RICHARD FORTEY COMPETITIVELY CLASSIFY THEIR SEAFOOD PLATTER.
LUTJANUS CAMPECHANUS.
PROBABLY PARASITIZED BY CYMOTHOA EXIGUA.
WHOSE HYPERPARASITE IS
THIS IS THE GREATEST MOMENT OF MY LIFE.

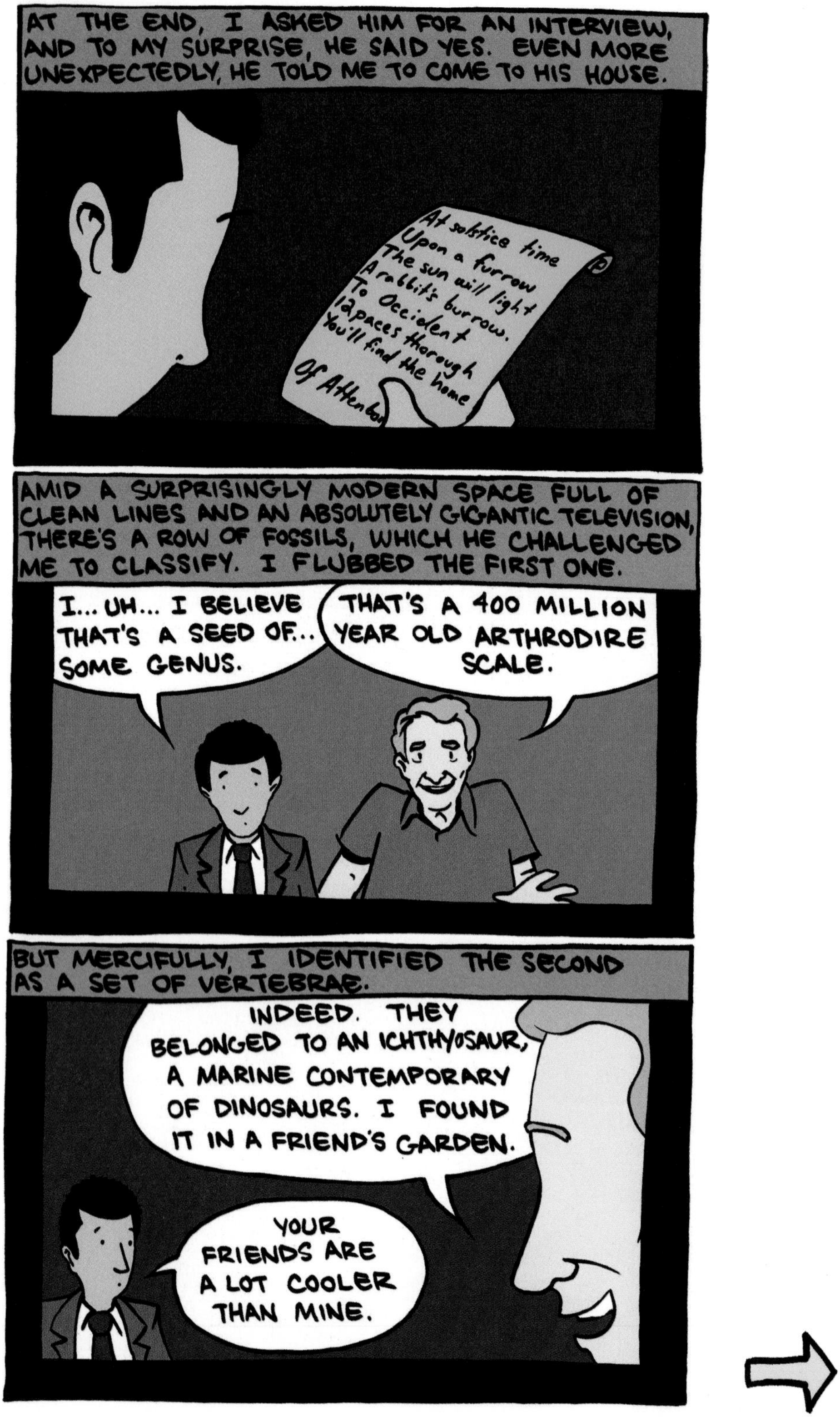
AT THE END, I ASKED HIM FOR AN INTERVIEW, AND TO MY SURPRISE, HE SAID YES. EVEN MORE UNEXPECTEDLY, HE TOLD ME TO COME TO HIS HOUSE.
At solstice time
Upon a furrow
The sun will light
A rabbit's burrow.
To Occident
12 paces thorough
You'll find the home
Of Attenbo
AMID A SURPRISINGLY MODERN SPACE FULL OF CLEAN LINES AND AN ABSOLUTELY GIGANTIC TELEVISION, THERE'S A ROW OF FOSSILS, WHICH HE CHALLENGED ME TO CLASSIFY. I FLUBBED THE FIRST ONE.
I... UH... I BELIEVE THAT'S A SEED OF... SOME GENUS.
THAT'S A 400 MILLION YEAR OLD ARTHRODIRE SCALE.
BUT MERCIFULLY, I IDENTIFIED THE SECOND AS A SET OF VERTEBRAE.
INDEED. THEY BELONGED TO AN ICHTHYOSAUR, A MARINE CONTEMPORARY OF DINOSAURS. I FOUND IT IN A FRIEND'S GARDEN.
YOUR FRIENDS ARE A LOT COOLER THAN MINE.

EARLIER, I HAD CHALLENGED MYSELF TO ASK HIM A QUESTION NO ONE HAD ASKED HIM BEFORE.

DID YOU HAVE ANY SHOOTS THAT WENT BADLY WRONG OR ANY SUBJECTS THAT WERE UNCOOPERATIVE?

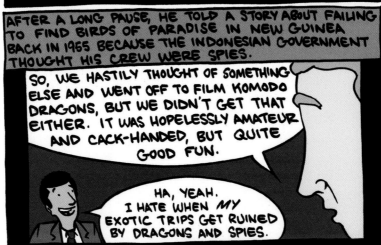

AFTER A LONG PAUSE, HE TOLD A STORY ABOUT FAILING TO FIND BIRDS OF PARADISE IN NEW GUINEA BACK IN 1955 BECAUSE THE INDONESIAN GOVERNMENT THOUGHT HIS CREW WERE SPIES.

SO, WE HASTILY THOUGHT OF SOMETHING ELSE AND WENT OFF TO FILM KOMODO DRAGONS, BUT WE DIDN'T GET THAT EITHER. IT WAS HOPELESSLY AMATEUR AND CACK-HANDED, BUT QUITE GOOD FUN.

HA, YEAH. I HATE WHEN *MY* EXOTIC TRIPS GET RUINED BY DRAGONS AND SPIES.

THIS WAS MY FIRST BIG INTERVIEW, AND I HADN'T QUITE MASTERED THE ART OF LISTENING TO ANSWERS, THINKING ABOUT NEW QUESTIONS ON THE FLY, AND SUPPRESSING THE MAJORITY OF YOUR BRAIN.

YOU ARE SITTING IN DAVID ATTENBOROUGH'S LIVING ROOM AND HE'S MAKING YOU COFFEE AAH! AAAAH! AAAH!

NO CREAM, THANKS.

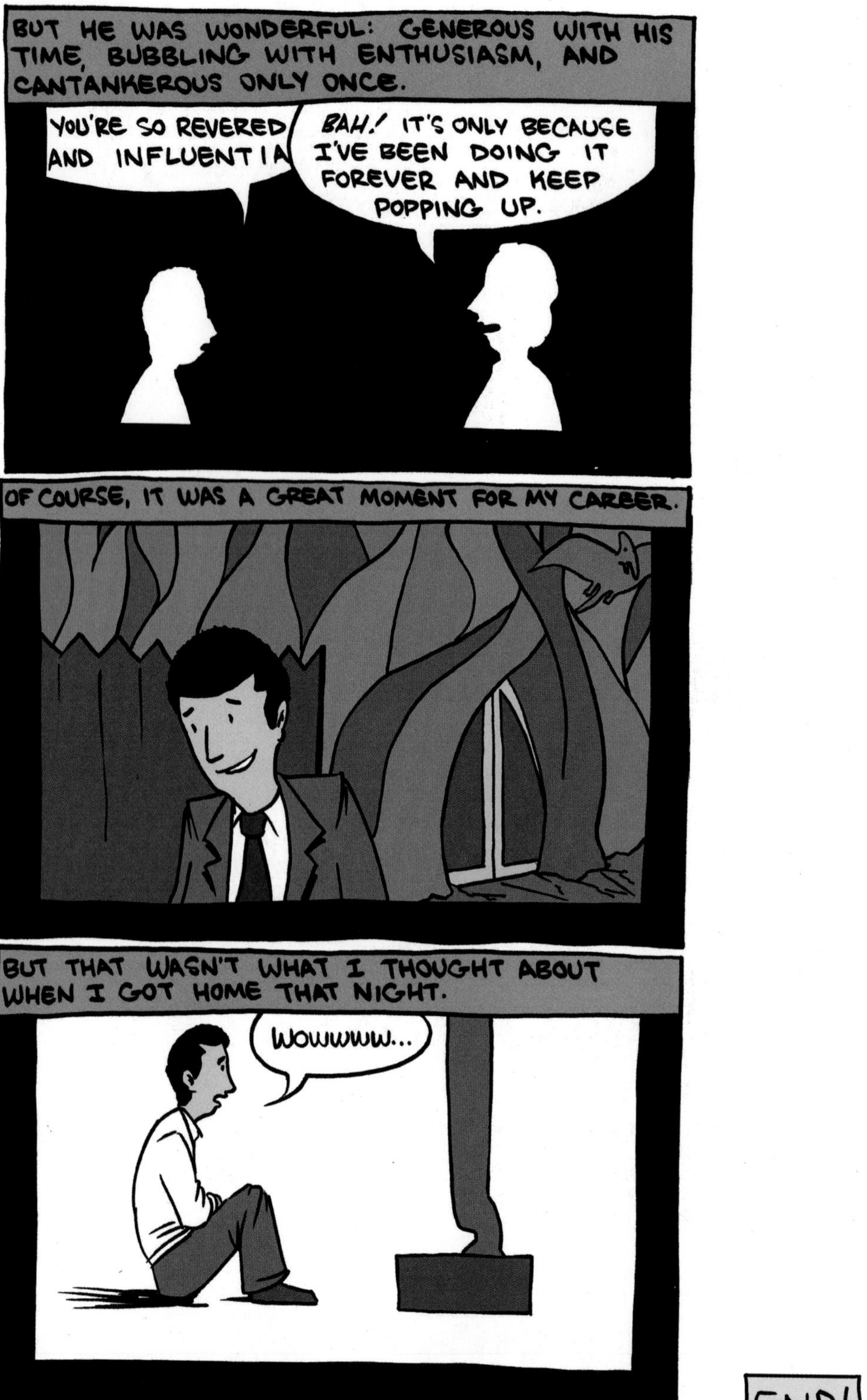
BUT HE WAS WONDERFUL: GENEROUS WITH HIS TIME, BUBBLING WITH ENTHUSIASM, AND CANTANKEROUS ONLY ONCE.
YOU'RE SO REVERED AND INFLUENTIA
BAH! IT'S ONLY BECAUSE I'VE BEEN DOING IT FOREVER AND KEEP POPPING UP.
OF COURSE, IT WAS A GREAT MOMENT FOR MY CAREER.
BUT THAT WASN'T WHAT I THOUGHT ABOUT WHEN I GOT HOME THAT NIGHT.
WOWWWW...
END!

ELIZABETH IORNS, PH. D.

CO-FOUNDER,
THE SCIENCE EXCHANGE

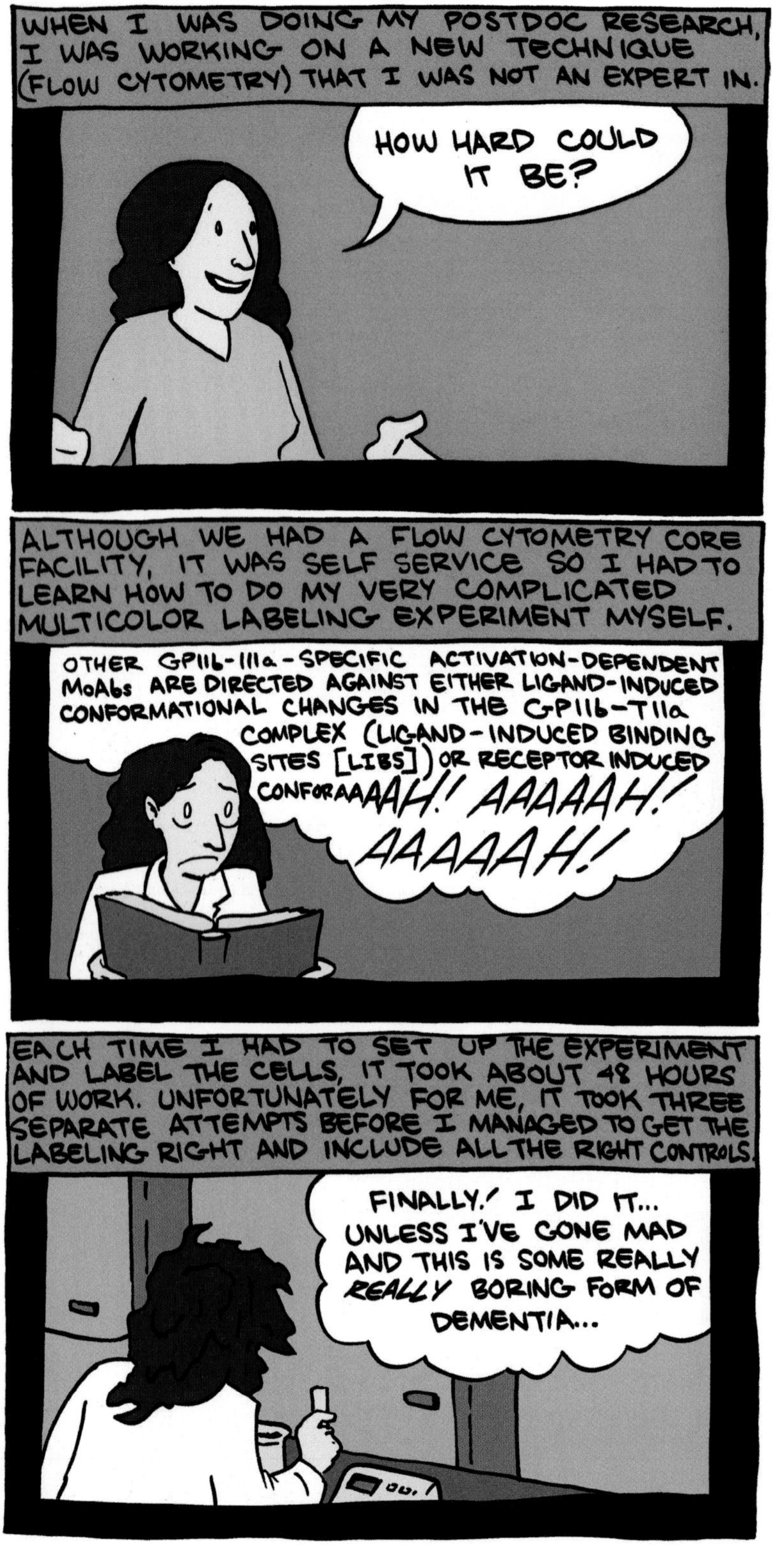
WHEN I WAS DOING MY POSTDOC RESEARCH, I WAS WORKING ON A NEW TECHNIQUE (FLOW CYTOMETRY) THAT I WAS NOT AN EXPERT IN.
HOW HARD COULD IT BE?
ALTHOUGH WE HAD A FLOW CYTOMETRY CORE FACILITY, IT WAS SELF SERVICE SO I HAD TO LEARN HOW TO DO MY VERY COMPLICATED MULTICOLOR LABELING EXPERIMENT MYSELF.
OTHER GPIIb-IIIa-SPECIFIC ACTIVATION-DEPENDENT MoAbs ARE DIRECTED AGAINST EITHER LIGAND-INDUCED CONFORMATIONAL CHANGES IN THE GPIIb-TIIa COMPLEX (LIGAND-INDUCED BINDING SITES [LIBS]) OR RECEPTOR INDUCED CONFORAAAAH! AAAAAH! AAAAAH!
EACH TIME I HAD TO SET UP THE EXPERIMENT AND LABEL THE CELLS, IT TOOK ABOUT 48 HOURS OF WORK. UNFORTUNATELY FOR ME, IT TOOK THREE SEPARATE ATTEMPTS BEFORE I MANAGED TO GET THE LABELING RIGHT AND INCLUDE ALL THE RIGHT CONTROLS.
FINALLY! I DID IT... UNLESS I'VE GONE MAD AND THIS IS SOME REALLY *REALLY* BORING FORM OF DEMENTIA...

THIS WAS OBVIOUSLY NOT A GREAT USE OF TIME OR RESOURCES: IF THERE HAD BEEN AN EXPERT WHO WAS WILLING TO DO MY EXPERIMENT FOR ME ON A FEE FOR SERVICE BASIS, EVERYONE WOULD HAVE BEEN MUCH BETTER OFF.

I HAVE THIS CRAZY IDEA. WHAT IF YOU COULD PAY MONEY IN EXCHANGE FOR SERVICES?

YOU OBVIOUSLY HAVEN'T BEEN IN ACADEMIA LONG.

IN THE ACADEMIC SYSTEM, I WOULD HAVE HAD TO BARTER CO-AUTHORSHIP OR SOME OTHER FAVOR TO GET SOMEONE TO DO MY EXPERIMENT FOR ME. SINCE EVERYONE HATES FLOW CYTOMETRY, THAT WOULD BE A PRETTY BIG FAVOR.

THIS PAPER TOOK ME SIX MONTHS TO WRITE. I'LL GIVE YOU SECOND AUTHORSHIP IF YOU DO HALF A DAY OF TECH WORK FOR ME.

MEH.

THIS EXPERIENCE LED ME TO CREATE SCIENCE EXCHANGE: A MARKETPLACE TO SELL YOUR EXPERTISE AND SERVICES. SCIENTISTS GET SERVICES CHEAPER AND MORE EASILY, AND CORE FACILITIES GET USED MORE EFFICIENTLY.

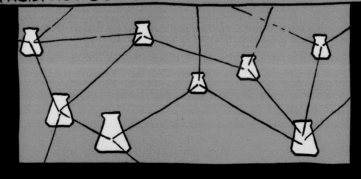

WE'VE HAD SOME RESISTANCE.
WHAT IF ANIMAL HUSBANDRY COULD BE DONE BY ANIMAL EXPERTS, AND GENE SEQUENCING COULD BE DONE BY GENETICISTS, AND STATS COULD BE DONE BY STATISTICIANS.
YOU SPEAK OF UTOPIA!
IT JUST DOESN'T FEEL RIGHT.
BUT WE NOW HAVE OVER A THOUSAND PROVIDERS INCLUDING SOME AT THE MOST TRUSTED INSTITUTIONS IN RESEARCH. WITH SOME LUCK, WE MAY JUST CHANGE THE WAY EXPERIMENTS GET DONE.
I NEED YOUR IMMUNOHISTOCHEMIST.
YOU'LL HAVE TO BE MORE SPECIFIC, SIR.

END!

CHRISTINA AGAPAKIS

POSTDOCTORAL RESEARCHER AT
UNIVERSITY OF CALIFORNIA, LOS ANGELES

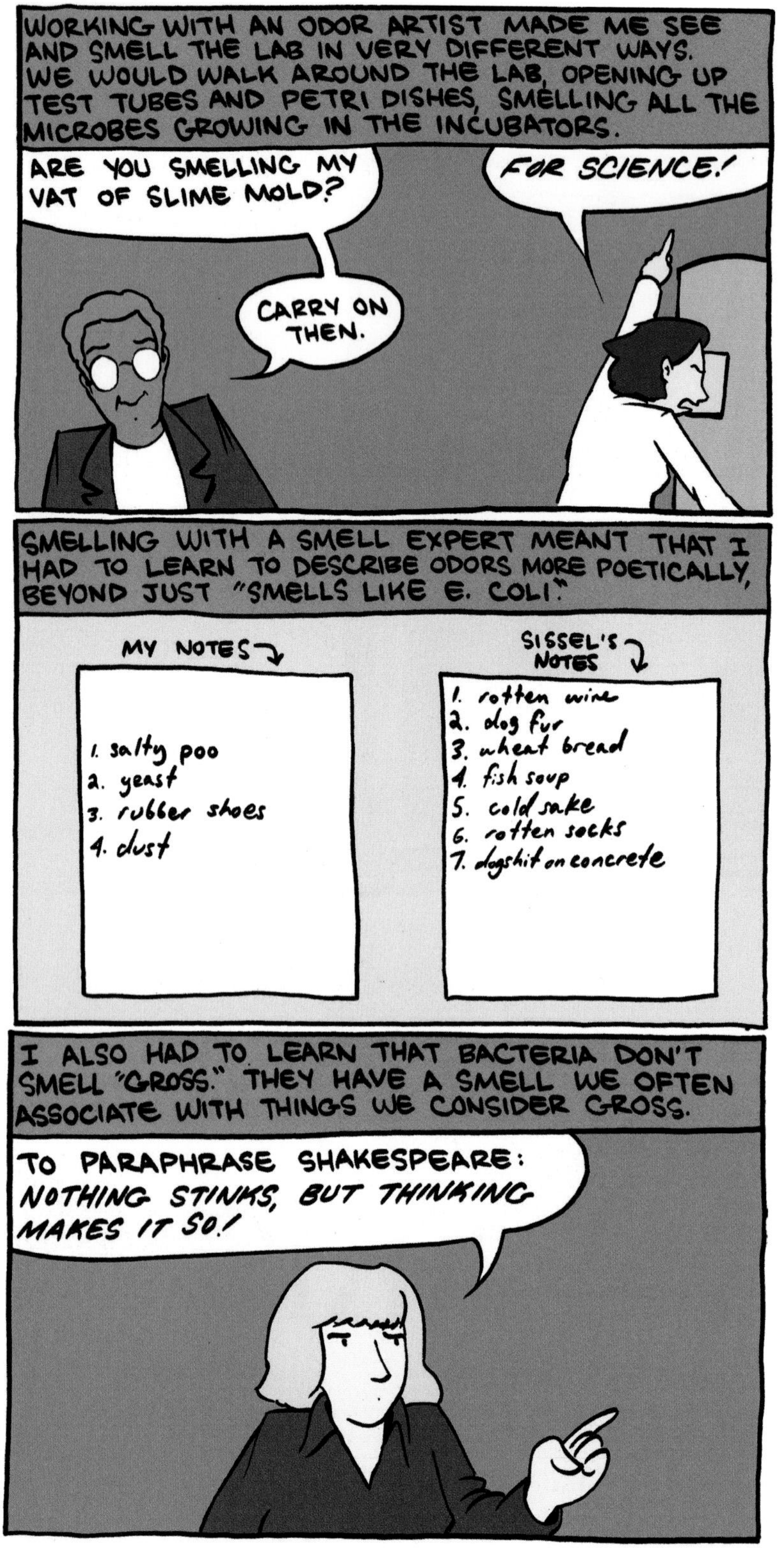
WORKING WITH AN ODOR ARTIST MADE ME SEE AND SMELL THE LAB IN VERY DIFFERENT WAYS. WE WOULD WALK AROUND THE LAB, OPENING UP TEST TUBES AND PETRI DISHES, SMELLING ALL THE MICROBES GROWING IN THE INCUBATORS.
ARE YOU SMELLING MY VAT OF SLIME MOLD?
FOR SCIENCE!
CARRY ON THEN.
SMELLING WITH A SMELL EXPERT MEANT THAT I HAD TO LEARN TO DESCRIBE ODORS MORE POETICALLY, BEYOND JUST "SMELLS LIKE E. COLI."
MY NOTES
1. salty poo
2. yeast
3. rubber shoes
4. dust
SISSEL'S NOTES
1. rotten wine
2. dog fur
3. wheat bread
4. fish soup
5. cold sake
6. rotten socks
7. dogshit on concrete
I ALSO HAD TO LEARN THAT BACTERIA DON'T SMELL "GROSS." THEY HAVE A SMELL WE OFTEN ASSOCIATE WITH THINGS WE CONSIDER GROSS.
TO PARAPHRASE SHAKESPEARE: NOTHING STINKS, BUT THINKING MAKES IT SO!

THE MORE WE RESEARCHED THE SMELLS OF BACTERIA, THE MORE I SAW HOW TRUE THIS IS. THE BACTERIA RESPONSIBLE FOR BODY ODOR AND THE SMELL OF FEET ARE VERY SIMILAR TO THE BACTERIA THAT FLAVOR CHEESE.

SO... CAMEMBERT ACTUALLY SMELLS LIKE THE UNWASHED KID FROM HIGH SCHOOL.

YES, BUT DON'T TELL FRANCE.

EVEN THOUGH THE BACTERIA AND SMELL MOLECULES ARE ALMOST IDENTICAL, IT IS VERY GROSS TO SMELL LIKE CHEESE BETWEEN YOUR TOES, BUT VERY CIVILIZED TO APPRECIATE A CHEESE THAT SMELLS LIKE FEET.

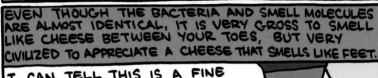

I CAN TELL THIS IS A FINE *FROMAGERIE* FROM THE PROFOUND AROMA OF CANINE EXCRETION!

TO EXPLORE THE ART AND SCIENCE OF CHEESE AND SKIN BACTERIA, WE MADE CHEESE WITH OUR OWN MICROBES, SAMPLED FROM BETWEEN TOES AND UNDER ARMS.

WHAT ARE YOU DOING?

MAKING FOOD.

STAY AWAY FROM OUR FRIDGE.

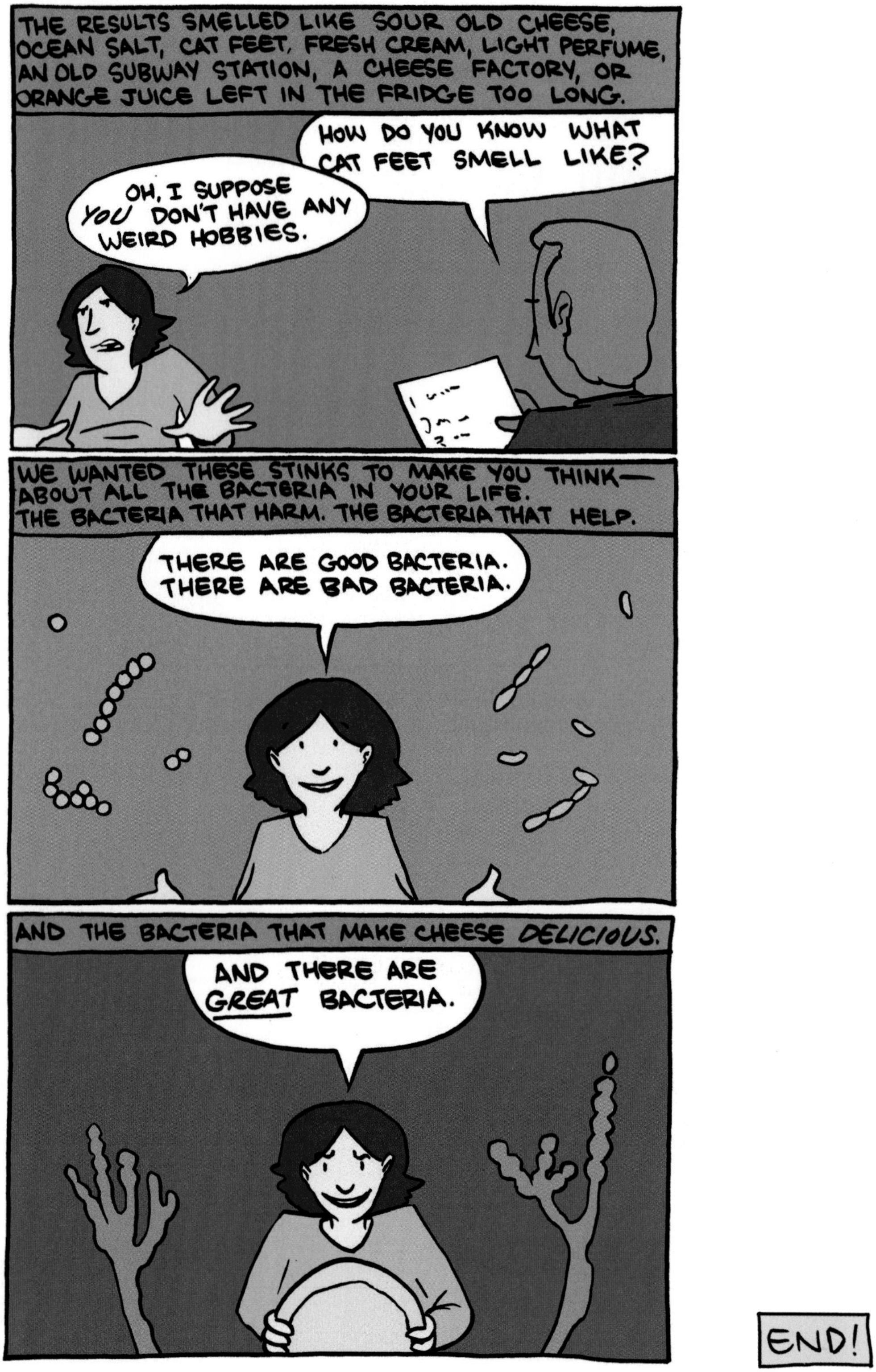
THE RESULTS SMELLED LIKE SOUR OLD CHEESE, OCEAN SALT, CAT FEET, FRESH CREAM, LIGHT PERFUME, AN OLD SUBWAY STATION, A CHEESE FACTORY, OR ORANGE JUICE LEFT IN THE FRIDGE TOO LONG.
HOW DO YOU KNOW WHAT CAT FEET SMELL LIKE?
OH, I SUPPOSE *YOU* DON'T HAVE ANY WEIRD HOBBIES.
WE WANTED THESE STINKS TO MAKE YOU THINK— ABOUT ALL THE BACTERIA IN YOUR LIFE. THE BACTERIA THAT HARM. THE BACTERIA THAT HELP.
THERE ARE GOOD BACTERIA. THERE ARE BAD BACTERIA.
AND THE BACTERIA THAT MAKE CHEESE *DELICIOUS*.
AND THERE ARE GREAT BACTERIA.
END!

DR. PAUL BARRETT

DINOSAUR RESEARCHER
THE NATURAL HISTORY MUSEUM, LONDON

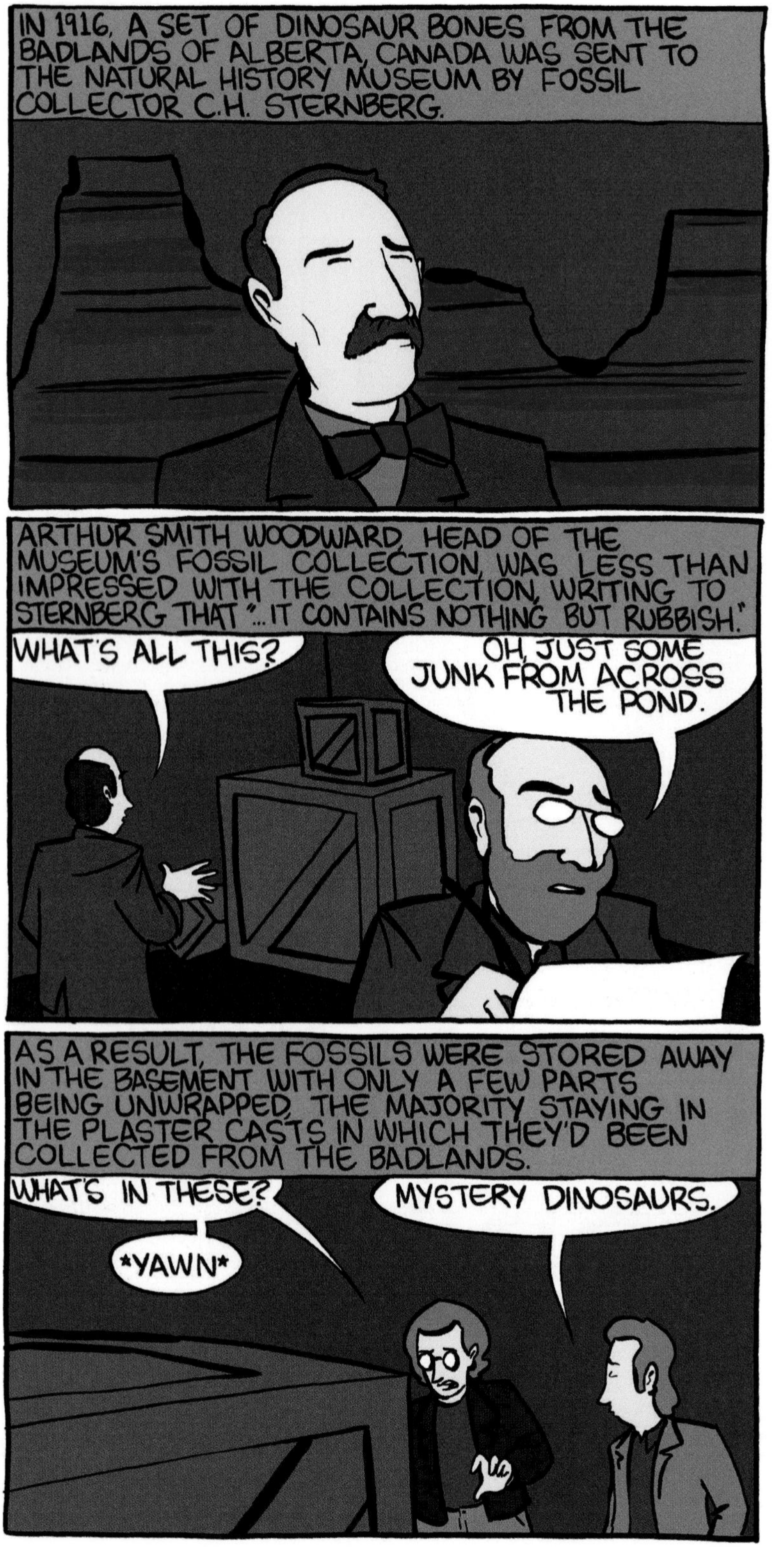
IN 1916, A SET OF DINOSAUR BONES FROM THE BADLANDS OF ALBERTA, CANADA WAS SENT TO THE NATURAL HISTORY MUSEUM BY FOSSIL COLLECTOR C.H. STERNBERG.
ARTHUR SMITH WOODWARD, HEAD OF THE MUSEUM'S FOSSIL COLLECTION, WAS LESS THAN IMPRESSED WITH THE COLLECTION, WRITING TO STERNBERG THAT "...IT CONTAINS NOTHING BUT RUBBISH."
WHAT'S ALL THIS?
OH, JUST SOME JUNK FROM ACROSS THE POND.
AS A RESULT, THE FOSSILS WERE STORED AWAY IN THE BASEMENT WITH ONLY A FEW PARTS BEING UNWRAPPED, THE MAJORITY STAYING IN THE PLASTER CASTS IN WHICH THEY'D BEEN COLLECTED FROM THE BADLANDS.
WHAT'S IN THESE?
YAWN
MYSTERY DINOSAURS.

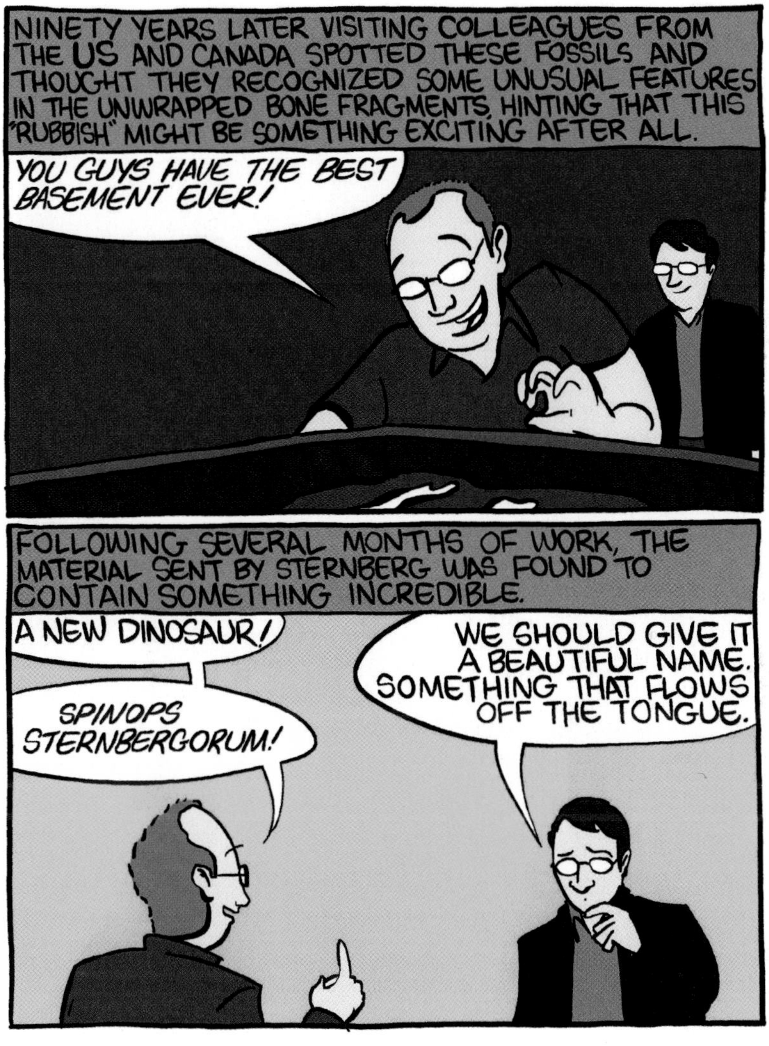
NINETY YEARS LATER VISITING COLLEAGUES FROM THE US AND CANADA SPOTTED THESE FOSSILS AND THOUGHT THEY RECOGNIZED SOME UNUSUAL FEATURES IN THE UNWRAPPED BONE FRAGMENTS, HINTING THAT THIS "RUBBISH" MIGHT BE SOMETHING EXCITING AFTER ALL.
YOU GUYS HAVE THE BEST BASEMENT EVER!
FOLLOWING SEVERAL MONTHS OF WORK, THE MATERIAL SENT BY STERNBERG WAS FOUND TO CONTAIN SOMETHING INCREDIBLE.
A NEW DINOSAUR!
SPINOPS STERNBERGORUM!
WE SHOULD GIVE IT A BEAUTIFUL NAME. SOMETHING THAT FLOWS OFF THE TONGUE.

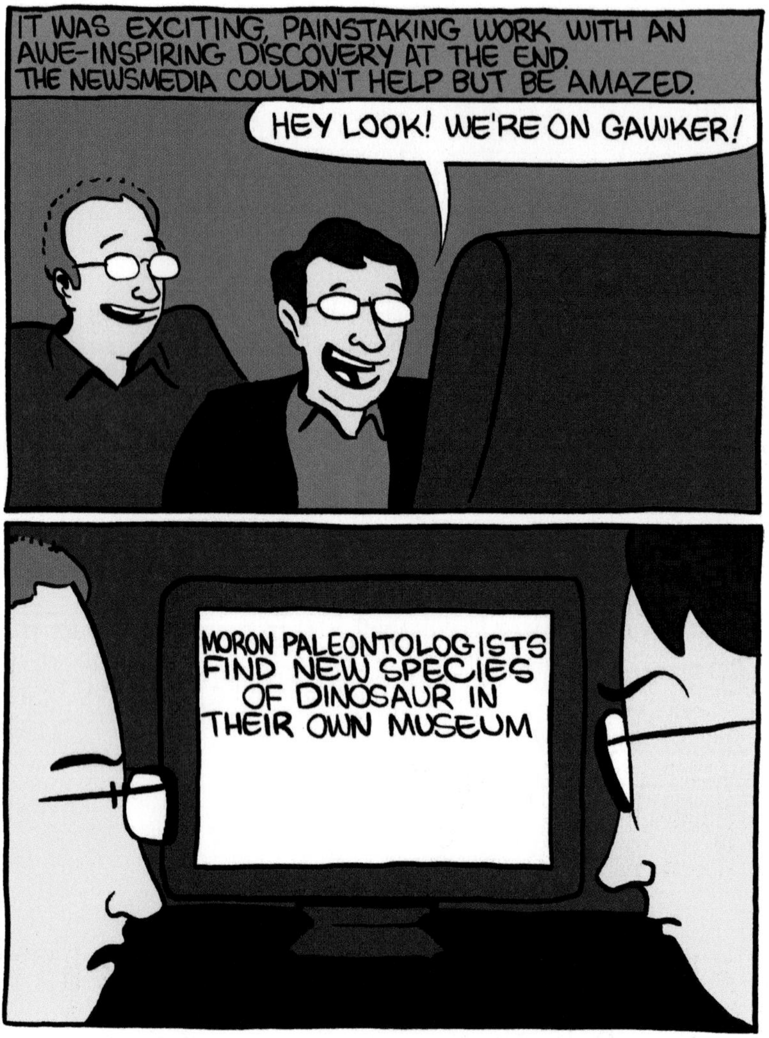
IT WAS EXCITING, PAINSTAKING WORK WITH AN AWE-INSPIRING DISCOVERY AT THE END. THE NEWSMEDIA COULDN'T HELP BUT BE AMAZED.
HEY LOOK! WE'RE ON GAWKER!
MORON PALEONTOLOGISTS FIND NEW SPECIES OF DINOSAUR IN THEIR OWN MUSEUM

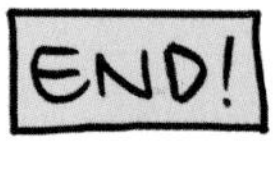
END!

KELLY WEINERSMITH

PH. D. STUDENT
UNIVERSITY OF CALIFORNIA, DAVIS

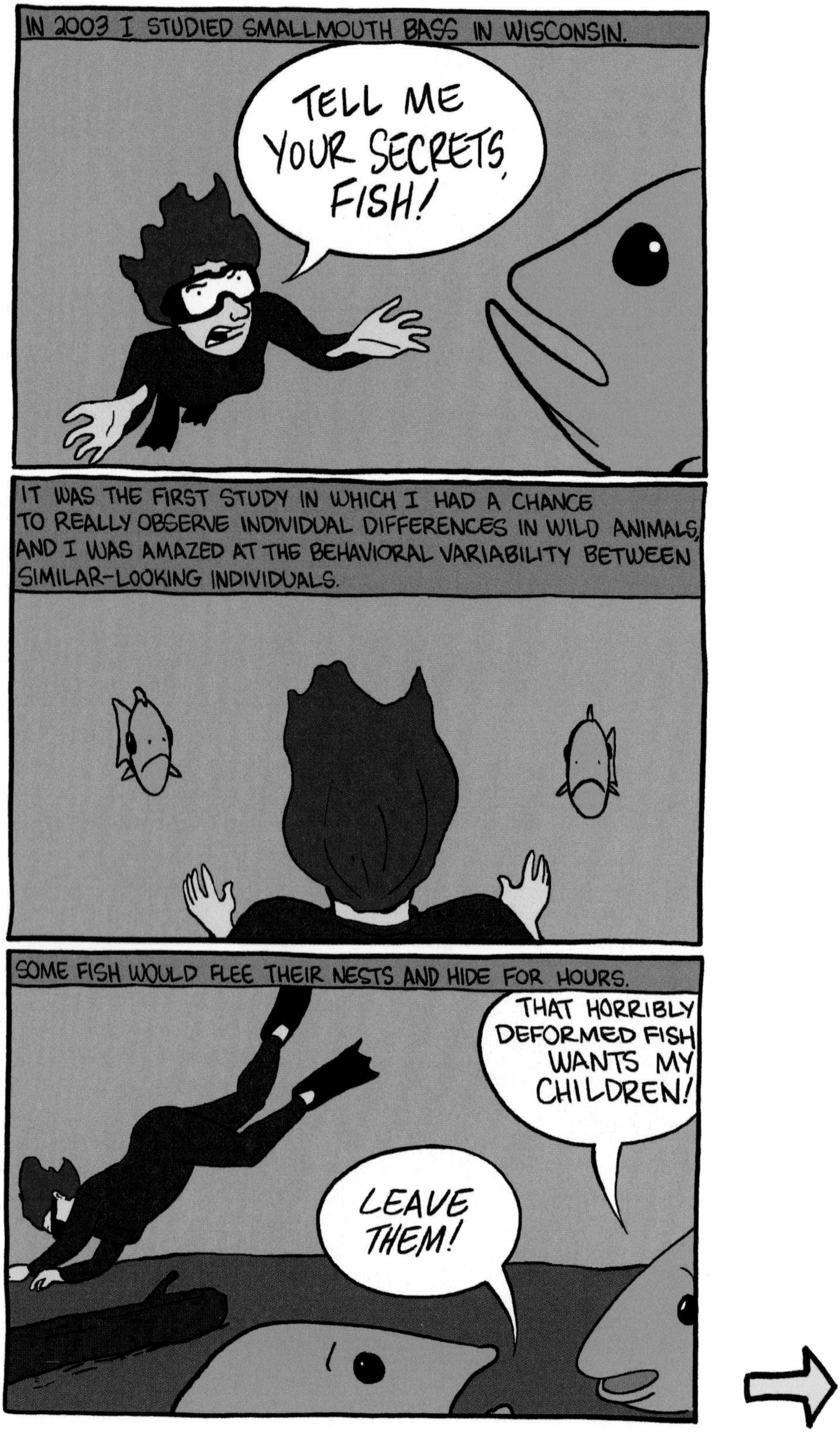
IN 2003 I STUDIED SMALLMOUTH BASS IN WISCONSIN.
TELL ME YOUR SECRETS, FISH!
IT WAS THE FIRST STUDY IN WHICH I HAD A CHANCE TO REALLY OBSERVE INDIVIDUAL DIFFERENCES IN WILD ANIMALS, AND I WAS AMAZED AT THE BEHAVIORAL VARIABILITY BETWEEN SIMILAR-LOOKING INDIVIDUALS.
SOME FISH WOULD FLEE THEIR NESTS AND HIDE FOR HOURS.
THAT HORRIBLY DEFORMED FISH WANTS MY CHILDREN!
LEAVE THEM!

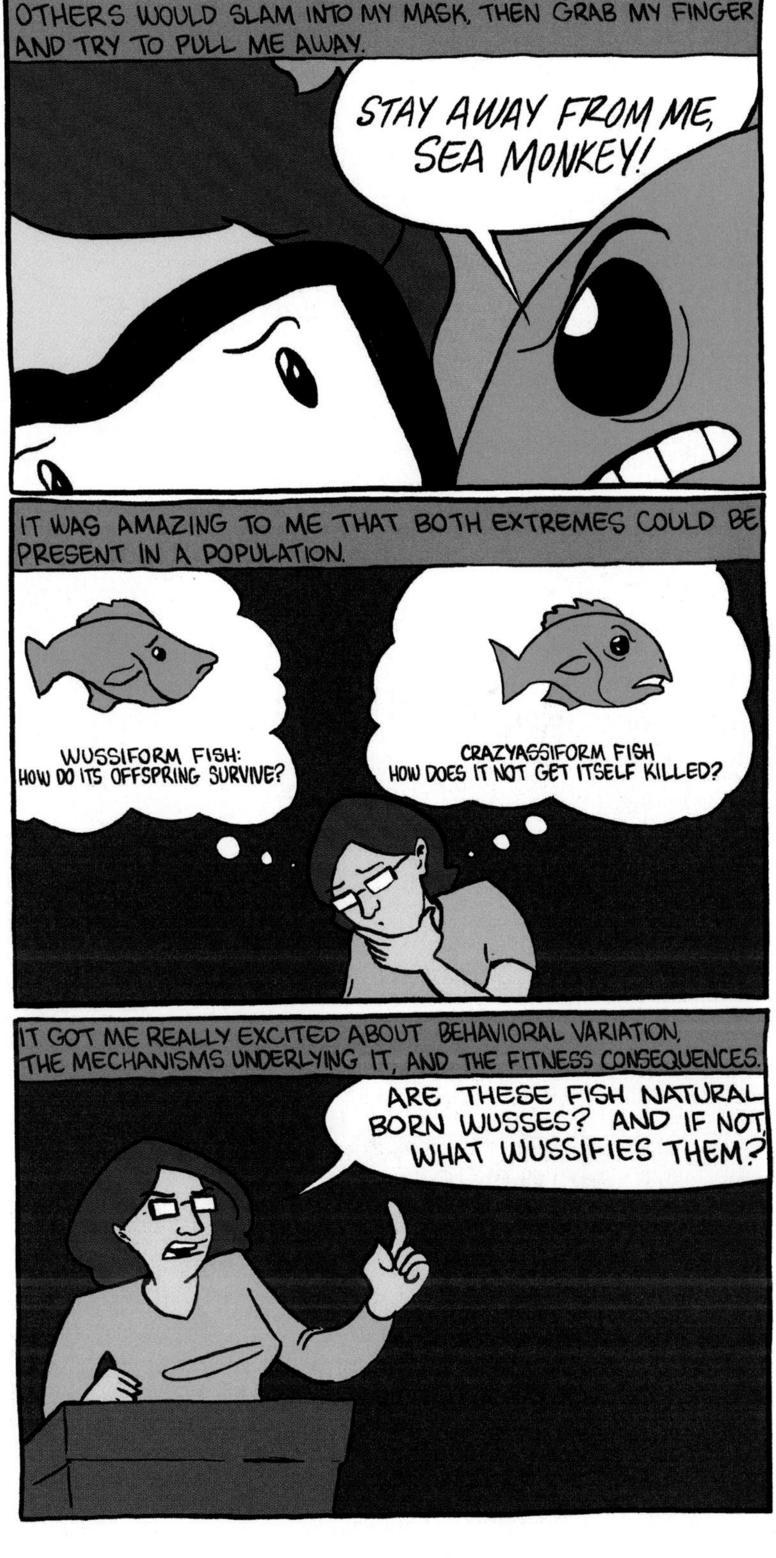
OTHERS WOULD SLAM INTO MY MASK, THEN GRAB MY FINGER AND TRY TO PULL ME AWAY.
STAY AWAY FROM ME, SEA MONKEY!
IT WAS AMAZING TO ME THAT BOTH EXTREMES COULD BE PRESENT IN A POPULATION.
WUSSIFORM FISH: HOW DO ITS OFFSPRING SURVIVE?
CRAZYASSIFORM FISH HOW DOES IT NOT GET ITSELF KILLED?
IT GOT ME REALLY EXCITED ABOUT BEHAVIORAL VARIATION, THE MECHANISMS UNDERLYING IT, AND THE FITNESS CONSEQUENCES.
ARE THESE FISH NATURAL BORN WUSSES? AND IF NOT, WHAT WUSSIFIES THEM?

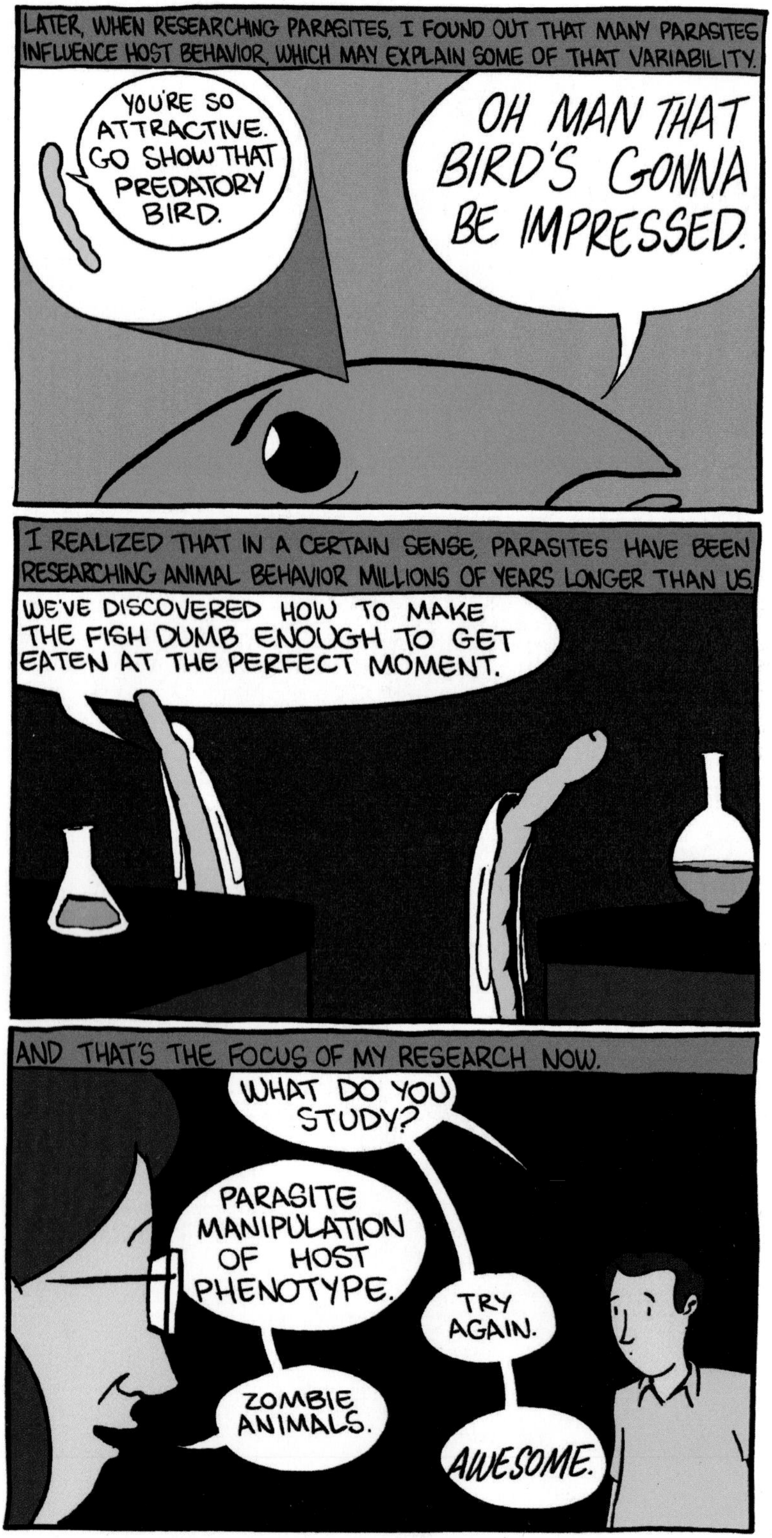
LATER, WHEN RESEARCHING PARASITES, I FOUND OUT THAT MANY PARASITES INFLUENCE HOST BEHAVIOR, WHICH MAY EXPLAIN SOME OF THAT VARIABILITY.
YOU'RE SO ATTRACTIVE. GO SHOW THAT PREDATORY BIRD.
OH MAN THAT BIRD'S GONNA BE IMPRESSED.
I REALIZED THAT IN A CERTAIN SENSE, PARASITES HAVE BEEN RESEARCHING ANIMAL BEHAVIOR MILLIONS OF YEARS LONGER THAN US.
WE'VE DISCOVERED HOW TO MAKE THE FISH DUMB ENOUGH TO GET EATEN AT THE PERFECT MOMENT.
AND THAT'S THE FOCUS OF MY RESEARCH NOW.
WHAT DO YOU STUDY?
PARASITE MANIPULATION OF HOST PHENOTYPE.
TRY AGAIN.
ZOMBIE ANIMALS.
AWESOME.

END!